Disruptive Christian Ethics

Disruptive Christian Ethics

When Racism and Women's Lives Matter

Traci C. West

Westminster John Knox Press
LOUISVILLE • LONDON

Book design by Sharon Adams
Cover design by Lisa Buckley

First edition
Published by Westminster John Knox Press
Louisville, Kentucky

This book is printed on acid-free paper that meets the American National Standards Institute Z39.48 standard. ♾

PRINTED IN THE UNITED STATES OF AMERICA

08 09 10 11 12 13 14 15—10 9 8 7 6 5 4 3 2

Library of Congress Cataloging-in-Publication Data is on file at the Library of Congress, Washington, D.C.

ISBN-13: 978-0-664-22959-7

ISBN-10: 0-664-22959-X

For the justice-seeking activist/intellectuals who routinely confront racist insults and paternalistic dismissals by politicians and religious leaders but refuse to let them have the last word on morality and women's worth

Contents

Acknowledgments

I would like to thank Irene Monroe, Sylvia Rhue, Mandy Carter, Youtha Hardman-Cromwell, Leontyne Kelly, Lynice Pinkard, Wanda Floyd, Ruby Wilson, Lisa Robinson, Alma Crawford, and Janyce Jackson for their generosity with their time and their stories and for being such amazing leaders. I owe a tremendous debt of gratitude to Karen King, Virginia Burrus, Elizabeth Bounds, Ruth Smith, and Jerry Watts for reading sections of the manuscript and offering comments, and to Suzanne Sellinger for reading all of it, and thanks to Mark Miller and Heather Elkins for contributing ideas incorporated in my liturgy chapter. I am especially indebted to Jane Ellen Nickell and thankful to Monica Miller, Tessa Russell, and Lynn Darden for their great research assistance. I am extremely grateful for the funding from Harvard Divinity School's Women's Studies in Religion Program and from the ATS small-grant program that allowed me to launch this project. I thank my wonderful colleagues at the WSRP who offered comments on my early drafts and support on ideas: Anne Braude, Sue Houchins, Sydney Crawford, Oyeronke Olajubu, Tracy Pintchman, my HDS Christian Ethics class, and HDS reference librarian Renata Kalnins. I offer my humblest thanks to my Drew Theological School Christian ethics students for teaching me so much about this topic and inspiring me to do this project. I am also grateful to the hard-working staff at WJK for all their help with publishing this project.

Those who had to listen to me complain about the process of completing this book are too numerous to list, but I am especially thankful for the caring, loving responses to my longest diatribes by Nina Schwarzschild, Amy Ballin, Jennifer Wriggins, Robert Watts, Stephanie Theodorou, Bil

Wright, and HH: Liz Bounds, Toddie Peters, Pam Brubaker, Marilyn Legge, Jane Hicks, and Bev Harrison.

I do not know how to adequately express my gratitude to my life partner, Jerry G. Watts, for being there for me intellectually and emotionally every step of the difficult journey of writing and publishing this book, giving me an enormous amount of help on it, and offering just the right mixture of patience and impatience with my self-pity and frustration. Jerry: I'm glad that I waited when you were late for our dinner in 1978. I can't imagine getting through this book project, or my life, without you.

Preface

This book focuses on topics that a lot of people don't like to discuss, like racism and the sexual violation of women. Too often I hear comments about these topics along the lines of, "You people really need to get over it already!" Or in academia, this sentiment might be expressed more subtly as, "In postmodernity haven't we actually moved beyond such simplistic discursive frameworks?" I refuse to "get over it" because the idea that we've "moved beyond" our society's need for concretely identifying these concerns is a costly lie.

I do want to get beyond merely naming specific social problems. I want authentic engagement of them, utilizing all of the relevant analytical and activist resources that can be called upon, with a particular expectation of some help from my own religious tradition of Christianity. I started this project because I felt it was imperative to work on a Christian ethics project that explores a range of dissimilar sources, perspectives, and methods for addressing moral problems in our society and creating strategies that can help bring about radical social change.

In this project, attention to multiple sites of social conflict is continuous and unavoidable. I believe that there has to be a way to embrace conflicts over morality and learn from them while maintaining a commitment to undermine dehumanizing behavior. The inevitability of conflict over moral issues seems to grant permission to wound those one opposes by targeting and trampling the most vulnerable, manipulating those who are least informed and most fearful, and doing whatever else seems necessary to claim moral superiority and power over others.

One of my major goals here is to discover less brutalizing and demeaning ways of building just and compassionate relationships within and across our differing communities. I want a method for doing this that precludes any form of monologue, and which also deliberately violates elitist assumptions about how important ideas for this work are generated. A dialogue partner helps to hold one accountable by asking: so what? So, what does this specific public policy regulating the poor that is discussed in the newspaper mean for the Christian interpreting God's mandates in scripture about the treatment of the poor and the rich? Or, so what does this theoretical idea in feminist/womanist liberative ethics mean for a woman who is in prison?

My obsession with this kind of concretely rooted, dialogical engagement can be blamed first and foremost on my students, but also on worship service attendees, workshop participants, and audience members, who have raised such difficult questions after I have offered some form of leadership to their groups. They have been my most recent, formative teachers on the subject of practicing ethics. Sometimes they have tormented me with their implacability; many more times they have reversed my despair about academia, church, or society. They have taught me by requiring me to engage them no matter what their politics, their theology, their perspectives on race/ethnicity and homosexuality, or their socioeconomic background might be. Every time, they have left me hungering for more, questing after strategies for more meaningful, substantive, and possibly even radically social-order-changing engagement among strangers and friends.

Introduction

Maria Gonzalez applied for welfare benefits in New York City.[1] In response to her request for assistance, she was assigned to a workfare program. While in the program, she objected to being sexually harassed by her supervisor. She complained that her supervisor would "go behind me and blow on my neck,"[2] and that "he would tell other workers I was a lesbian because I did not want to have sex with him."[3] Ms. Gonzalez complained about this problem to her supervisor's boss, who told her to go back and work it out with the supervisor. When a complaint was lodged on her behalf with officials in Mayor Rudolph Giuliani's administration, the city's response was to assert that welfare recipients in the city's workfare program were not city employees and therefore had no legal right to protection from sexual discrimination or sexual harassment.[4]

A lawsuit was filed against the city by the U.S. Justice Department on behalf of Ms. Gonzalez and others in the workfare program who had similar complaints about discriminatory, harassing treatment.[5] In the joint complaint one woman reported that her supervisor had turned off the lights and told her to pull down her pants for a sexual encounter. Another black woman worker charged that officials in the program told her that it "didn't mean anything" that she found a noose hanging up inside a building she was painting with racial caricatures drawn beside it that were placed there by other workers for her to find. Norma Colon, a mother of two young children and living in a homeless shelter, complained that the supervisor at her workfare job suggested they go to a motel, offering to bend some of the rules for her in exchange for sexual favors.[6]

From the perspective of Christian social ethics, how should the complaints filed by Maria Gonzalez and the other welfare recipients be understood? As she sought public financial assistance, Maria Gonzalez, already confronting emergency conditions of poverty, now also faced a debasing use of (state) governmental power and sexual harassment that included comments stigmatizing lesbian sexual identity. Surely Christian social ethics offers some terminology or method for analyzing this range of problems, but how do we know what that would be? Many Christians would agree that their faith compels them to be responsive to the concerns of poor women such as Maria Gonzalez and the others mentioned above. Yet, there is a need for more clarity about exactly how to formulate a moral critique of the circumstances of these women.

A Focus on Method

It should be possible to identify the distinctive method—the starting point and process—for understanding social problems that a Christian social ethic offers. Method matters because it represents the pathway that we follow when reflecting on societal concerns and making decisions about "what's wrong here?" It allows us to assess how that wrong can be addressed constructively. A basic yet crucial factor to remember is that whatever approach is chosen to interpret social problems, it determines the entire focus and definition attached to those problems. Unfortunately, a common practice, for most of us, is to uncritically accept the moral focus and definitions that have already been chosen by the author of the newspaper headlines, politician's speechwriter, or producers of an episode of a popular television drama about law and government. This habitual, uncritical acceptance deadens the mental and spiritual capacities needed to do ethics. Therefore, a foundational part of faithfulness for Christians involves seeking out a deliberate, thoughtful process for crafting ethics that is responsive to social problems. Such a process increases the possibility that Christians will be able to recognize the issues of injustice in situations like that of Maria Gonzalez.

I am not encouraging a focus on our shared (public) moral life for the development of Christian social ethics so that the social order might be Christianized. Christians need clarity about their own Christian religious approach to social justice in order to figure out how to make responsible contributions to the shared values of our pluralistic world. Besides Christian ones, there are, of course, varied, long-standing, and deeply held approaches to creating ethical social relations embraced by the diverse members of our communities. These approaches include the moral values of Muslim, Jewish, Buddhist, Hindu, and Sikh believers and those belonging to many other religious traditions, as well as numerous secular systematic ideas about morality that are shared by people in our communities.

Thus, for Christians, especially in the United States where they are accustomed to monopolizing the discussion of public values, it becomes even more important to clarify how Christian social ethics constructively contributes to and equitably shares in the communal process of building more ethical communal relations. By working together across boundaries, we might be able to create public practices that respond in a more supportive manner than the way that Maria Gonzalez was treated as she turned to the community for urgent economic assistance. I want to identify the kind of Christian ethics method that most constructively contributes to such shared communal responsibilities. It might even be possible to develop a Christian ethical approach to society that fosters cooperative negotiation of these shared values and respects the maintenance of culturally and religiously diverse traditions in our communities.

Community cooperation across cultural and religious boundaries depends upon our ability to dialogue with one another, and dialogue is precisely the core element of a socially liberative method for Christian ethics that I stress in this book. A method for Christian social ethics that trains us in how to have "conversations" across boundaries prepares us for the task of building shared ethics in a pluralistic world. To develop liberative Christian social ethics, some process of dialogue has to occur between the type of specific struggles represented in the experience of Maria Gonzalez and core Christian understandings of what constitutes justice in our society.

There are many established approaches to Christian social ethics, but I want to contribute to the liberationist traditions that make it a priority to pay attention to the conditions that entrap socially marginalized people. Those Christians who mainly reflect upon and practice their ethics in relation to experiences within daily life have to be equipped to develop an ethical response to social problems that extends beyond charity. That is, beyond the need "to help Maria Gonzalez with her problems," they must also recognize the necessity to shift all of the moral norms that generate those problems. Other Christians, and I would include myself in this group, also reflect upon and practice Christian ethics in our daily experiences, but additionally commit considerable effort to learning and teaching Christian ethics in academic or church classrooms. We often need to alter our assumptions as well. Christians, like myself, must recognize the conditions Maria Gonzalez faced as more than an illustration of particular social problems but additionally find universal significance in those conditions for defining overarching moral norms relevant to our entire society. Christian social ethics will remain inadequately formed without a primary concern for socially and economically marginalized people that shapes both core notions for conceiving ethics as well as overarching goals for practicing it.

We must resist the temptation to craft an approach to ethical public practices by concentrating exclusively upon generic concepts, e.g., what constitutes an honoring of human dignity and worth, or how state power influences the social ordering of communities. Formulating a Christian ethical method that comprehensively addresses the kinds of injustices that Ms. Gonzalez encountered also requires attention to concrete social practices. How does Christianity guide one to ethically respond to the details in the story of someone like Maria Gonzalez?

As I explain more fully in the following chapters, a liberative method allows for the consideration of multiple layers of subjugating assumptions related to gender, race/ethnicity, socioeconomic class, and sexuality, like those present in Maria Gonzalez's situation. It also prompts a critique of the web of public moral assumptions, such as the indifference in workfare policy to her individual circumstances and emergency needs, that prejudges her as lazy and makes the degrading demand that she accept any kind of work in order to receive emergency financial assistance. My method insists that we appreciate the lessons her situation offers about victimization as well as courageous resistance. Evidence of resistance includes the historical legacy of certain church-based activists who struggled for the creation of the laws from which she benefits when filing her complaint that sought civil rights protection through the U.S. Justice Department. There are also lessons about how personal "public" ethics can be. Public issues of state power could not be more personal than when the use of that power is linked to her survival needs, refusal of sexual intercourse, and sexual identity. The opportunistic use of the label "lesbian" by her supervisor demonstrates moral costs to our society's communal relations that the stigmatizing of lesbian (and gay) sexual identities exacts. Her story reveals some of the far-reaching destructive implications of heterosexist practices in church and society that give this labeling its currency as an acceptable form of human devaluation. In the many details of her story and of others like her, crucial resources are found for sorting out what is wrong within certain accepted practices of our society that breeds such devaluation and what is required to address those wrongs.

In the field of Christian ethics (as in most academic work), conceptualization is too often divorced from the practical realities of situations like that of Ms. Gonzalez. It is assumed that practical realities are most helpfully examined as case studies, while conceptualization of what should be considered virtuous and nonvirtuous social behavior is seen as a distinctly different, more theoretical task. Some social ethicists emphasize concrete practices because theory seems tedious and irrelevant. Others emphasize theory because concrete practices seem too idiosyncratic and transitory. I contend, however, that both theory and practice, and a fluid conversation between them, are most fruitful for conceiving Christian social ethics. Theory needs practice in order to be authentic, relevant, and truthful. Practice needs theory so that practices might be fully comprehended. For the kind of liberative Christian ethics that I develop in this book, theory provides critical analysis that reveals subjugating assumptions in social and religious practices. At the same time, attention to concrete practices is necessary to reveal the rehearsal of those subjugating assumptions within the patterns of our everyday lives. Creative strategies promoting human well-being can be discovered in concrete practices as well.

Perhaps the hardest challenge for doing this work is overcoming apathy and cynicism about participation in social justice that infects too many of us. Many ongoing cultural dynamics nurture apathy about accomplishing just social change, like the sense of futility generated by how bureaucratic social service organizations function. Their stated purpose is to address social problems, and knowledge of their very existence convinces us that some effort is being made, even though these agencies are usually perpetually ineffective in reversing the social problems they try to address. These unsatisfactory social service bureaucracies actually mask the absence of any real commitment to change by the political and economic leaders of our society. Cynicism is bred by a steady diet of duplicitous rhetoric fed to the public through the mass media by those same leaders and others with elite status, wealth, and privilege. Their public rhetoric is designed to sound caring and make one feel good about how things are going in America, while it simultaneously persuades individuals to willingly remain indifferent to massive socioeconomic human exploitation that could be stopped. Moreover, the mass media news industry refuses to engage in critical reflection on issues of social injustice, treating the problems that result from unethical government policies as if they are unintended consequences of morally minded political leaders.

When trying to wade through this stupefying moral environment, we are confronted by further unique obstacles for discernment of what is authentic Christian morality in U.S. society. Christian morality is already welded with official public acts. The language in presidential speeches, the

Christian religious faith pronouncements of the majority of political candidates for national election, or the naming of U.S. warships, e.g., the *Corpus Christi*, Latin for the body of Christ, all indicate a Christianity that is serviceable to the powers that be.[7] Even a cultural icon that captured the imagination of masses of children and adults alike, Harry Potter, and his entire Wizard community celebrated Christmas! This ubiquitous presence of Christianity saturates conventional sensibilities and stifles an ability to even imagine how Christianity could be truly oppositional to public culture.

A liberative Christian social ethic is desperately needed by most U.S. Christians in order for them to equitably participate in building a shared communal (public) ethic with non-Christians and to find a way to force a rupture between prevailing cultural arrangements of power that reproduce oppressive conditions, like poverty, and communal tolerance for permanently maintaining such conditions.

Gathering Tools

A methodological tool kit with wide-ranging resources is essential to create the rupture that we need. I focus on locating an assortment of such tools for Christian social ethics and practicing what it means to put them to use. For instance, basic concepts such as notions of power or autonomy in society, and foundational elements for Christian ethics such as the use of Christian scripture can be understood through a method that places at its center the social problems of and struggles for change by African American women and poor U.S. women from diverse racial backgrounds. I explore how women's stories of sexual violation, economic exploitation, as well as their activism, might shape the construction of Christian social ethics.

I also emphasize the value of interdisciplinary resources for Christian social ethics, borrowing from African American studies, women's studies, theories of whiteness in sociology, and from subfields within religious studies such as liturgy and biblical studies. How can interdisciplinary conceptual frameworks be utilized by Christian social ethics to describe liberative public practices? Material from African American religious studies research on the Harlem YWCA or on the Father Divine movement can contribute to the formulation of Christian public ethics. When crossing boundaries within the area of religious studies I experiment with what it means to employ liberationist ideas in feminist biblical studies in the task of prescribing ethical public policy addressing poverty. Even within the established boundaries of Christian social ethics, I nurture an analytical link between the Christian realism of Reinhold Niebuhr and a feminist/

womanist approach through my method of engaging both of them with stories and ideas from women's lives.

A good tool kit has to include familiar, everyday equipment as well. Ethical tools for just social change are available in the core elements of Christianity, such as scripture, worship, and church ministerial leadership. Steeped in the liberative foundation of the mission and ministry of Jesus, a Christian tradition–based method for scrutinizing specific social problems emerges as a way of doing ethics. Close consideration must be given, for example, to the forms that denial of white privilege can take when residing in everyday interactions and how Christian congregational prayer might foster that denial. I describe Christian recognition of God as centered in liberative struggle, and as a way of bridging seemingly disparate, unrelated sites of struggle. This recognition may come in the form of theo-ethical insight connecting the attack on Jesus by the Roman state to women's stories of their sexually violated bodies, or in clarifying how the church should manifest the body of Christ based upon women's leadership of black, predominantly lesbian and gay congregational outreach ministries. The liberative dimensions of fundamental Christian ideas and practices serve as guideposts for crafting a transformative ethic.

How the Conversations Unfold

The ability to recognize and oppose racist subjugation is a tool that is honed throughout all of the chapters. The first section brings to the surface some of the ways that racism can impact the conceptualization of key ideas in Christian ethics (chapters 1 and 2). The second section explores concerns about how racist assumptions in government policies and church liturgies can infect public practices (chapters 3 and 4). In chapter 5 there are examples of a thoroughly antiracist method for ministry and activism.

Each chapter explores what it would mean to practice this liberative method of Christian social ethics and offers a conversation between text and social context. In chapter 1, I establish the necessity and benefits of Christian ethical engagement with a broad range of social realities by presenting a conversation between texts by a foundational author of Christian social ethics, Reinhold Niebuhr, and the lives and activist work of African American women who were his contemporaries in 1930s and 1940s Harlem. My consideration of these coexisting sources provides some criteria for analyzing power and privilege in a progressive approach to public ethics.

In chapter 2, I define what is particularly Christian about the justice-oriented vision that this liberative Christian social ethic brings. Ideas from feminist and womanist texts about the fundamentals of liberative Christian social ethics are explored in conversation with testimony about public practices related to sexual violation. Utilizing the stories of contemporary African American women and poor women from diverse racial backgrounds, this discussion underscores the inseparably public and private factors when reflecting on social practices in liberative ethics.

Chapter 3 launches a slight shift in focus from defining method to a more sustained discussion of concrete practices in the broader society and in the church. In this chapter on public policy, I contrast one of the most indicting Christian gospel texts that addresses poverty—the speech often called the Magnificat, by Mary of Nazareth (the mother of Jesus)—with public pronouncements about the poor by contemporary public officials, such as Presidents Bill Clinton and George W. Bush, and comments by media pundits. These are two vastly differing collections of sources with clashing approaches to public practices and moral assumptions about the poor. Studying them interactively allows us to examine the manipulative use of state power through public rhetoric and the prospects for interrupting that manipulation with ideas from Christian scripture.

Chapter 4 considers public practices that order church life—Sunday morning worship rituals. I begin with a few personal stories describing my own experiences with racism in predominantly white worship settings. Critical social theories of white racism and theories of multiculturalism help to analyze moral values related to race that often show up in Christian worship rituals.

Chapter 5 presents the testimonies of living texts, black women ministers and activists who create strategies to confront assumptions about the superiority of heterosexuality in public discussions of morality. The chapter consists of interviews that I conducted with Rev. Irene Monroe, Dr. Sylvia Rhue, Ms. Mandy Carter, Rev. Dr. Youtha Hardman-Cromwell, Bishop Leontyne Kelly, Rev. Lynice Pinkard, Rev. Wanda Floyd, Rev. Ruby Wilson, Rev. Lisa Robinson, Rev. Alma Crawford, and Minister Janyce Jackson. I have compiled their testimonies so that a breadth of strategies are discussed, and I present the interviewees in pairs so that the women's ideas are in conversation with each other. Their stories offer hope-filled accounts about the capacity for church-related leadership to confront powerful public opposition and for Christian ministries to create affirming public space for reviled people.

In this book I insist upon moral inquiry where the categories of theory and practice and text and context take on shared meaning. Usually theory maintains a focus on conceptualizing what is ethical, while practice focuses upon actions that shape concrete moral (social) realities. Texts are most often seen as stable, discrete repositories of information, while contexts are a dynamic collection of circumstances. Here, the theories and practices, texts and contexts that are examined critique each other. They also overlap and merge together as tools of analysis that I invite the reader to creatively engage with me.

My hope is that this dialogical method of developing Christian social ethics will provide practice in how to conceive of what it means to share power rather than hoard it; how to make the transformation of unjust, marginalizing conditions for women key criteria for evaluating society's healthiness; and how to generate such commitments through Christian faith and practice. It is my further hope that expanding our ability to think critically about these Christian ethical goals will inspire actual practices that move our society away from such a high tolerance for social injustice.

Part I

Liberating Concepts

Chapter One

Context

Niebuhr's Ethics and Harlem Activists

Those of us who have been educated in the United States and in many other Western societies have been socialized to depend upon great individual thinkers when seeking moral resources for analyzing social problems in our society. In U.S. history, the majority of those who are designated as great thinkers with important moral ideas tend to be white, male, and Christian. While many ideas from these scholars and leaders can help us to investigate social problems and create change, this socialization teaches us to treat these great thinkers as if they were isolated islands of knowledge, removed from any community context. As a result, ignoring the impact of societal influences on them and their ideas is all too easy. Particular influences such as popular political beliefs or the state of racial/ethnic relations and socioeconomic class conditions that surrounded them are too often seen as having an insignificant relationship to the creation of moral ideas by great thinkers.

These assumptions about isolating great thinkers produce a further misperception. Members of the communities who are most adversely affected by the social problems being investigated are not considered moral agents who also generate ideas about improving society. As black feminist sociologist Patricia Hill Collins asserts, it is not true that only members of elite groups "produce theory while everyone else produces mere thought. Rather, elites possess the power to legitimate the knowledge that they define as theory" as universal and normative.[1] We are trained to accept this understanding of how knowledge is produced. What would it mean to break out of our acceptance of this training and broaden our understanding of what constitutes valuable sources of moral knowledge?

Our tendency to designate certain individuals as great thinkers and then detach them from societal influences allows us to maintain false boundaries between the "great thinkers" and the "everyday people"—especially those who are part of areas commonly identified as problem communities. Attempting to avoid reliance on great individual thinkers by ignoring them is not a helpful correction for this tendency because it could mean ignoring some very good ideas or creating ethical analyses that fail to interrogate problematic assumptions in culturally dominant and influential traditions of thought in our society. A more helpful response is to incorporate ideas from a range of community sources together with those of individual great thinkers to comprehensively analyze the destructive realities in our society. Community sources can hold accountable the ideas of dominant thinkers and traditions, ensuring that those dominant ideas are useful for the common good. One of the major goals of developing social ethics for our society should be to build shared communal values with justice-oriented benefits for people across cultural groupings and with unequal status and power. Sources of knowledge that cross these boundaries of culture, status, and power are the best guarantors for creating public practices that sustain justice-oriented values.

My approach to Christian social ethics is centered on creating a dialogue between individual thinkers and community-based persons who also create valuable moral knowledge. In this chapter I gather insights about how to formulate Christian social ethics by focusing on a particular historical time period, the 1930s and 1940s; one individual ethicist from the dominant religious tradition of Christianity, Reinhold Niebuhr; and a range of coexisting community efforts and experiences by black women in Harlem who shared the same neighborhood with Niebuhr during that time.

In his pioneering work of constructing Christian social ethics Reinhold Niebuhr sought universal moral terms to describe the plight of "man" and the historical conditions of society. When he arrived on the faculty of Union Theological Seminary in New York City in 1928, Niebuhr continued to write about many of the troubling social concerns of his time by offering a moral vision for public life based upon Christian theology and scripture. His essays and books from about 1930 to 1943 provide the focus for exploring the relevance of his moral vision for his immediate social context of Harlem, especially the lives and activism of black women.[2] How might Niebuhr's Christian social ethics be instructive for addressing the socioeconomic injustice that these women confronted?

During the Depression and World War II, Harlem generated a wide spectrum of religious, political, and literary responses to the social disparities confronting black members of the community. There was intense community organizing and an explosion of writing in newspapers, journals, and books concerning their social and economic problems. How do some of these activist efforts and writings, particularly by black women leaders seeking to challenge socioeconomic injustices, overlap and differ with the ethical approach crafted by Niebuhr during this time? How might these community sources broaden Niebuhr's Christian moral vision for society? The vantage point of the Harlem women, who were already negotiating and opposing pervasive, dehumanizing moral assumptions related to race and class, could alter certain academic formulations in Christian ethics about what kind of social change is needed.

Jointly examining these historical sources allows us to investigate how Christian moral claims about society might be meaningful across gender, racial, and cultural boundaries. We can analytically probe and venture across these boundaries by comparing the ideas of a son of German immigrants as he taught and lived in an all-white, predominantly male, seminary community, with the ideas and experiences of daughters and granddaughters of former slaves and free Negroes. These women were the progeny of Africans and worked as leaders of religious community organizations, journalists, fiction writers, and domestics, and lived in predominantly African American and Caribbean American communities.

Finally, analyzing historical sources from this Depression-era urban setting and the theo-ethical vision produced in its midst provides broader training for understanding Christian religion. Skills for understanding history are of central importance to Christian faith and theology. For Christians, routine practices that rely upon an ability to decode history can range from New Testament Bible study, where there is a need to understand how the activities of Jesus were interpreted by first-century writers, to Sunday worship where ancient creeds are regularly recited and there is a need to interpret those theological references. The theological meaning of core tenets of Christian faith, like the Trinity and the divine/human nature of Jesus, expressed in those creeds are bound up with the proceedings of ancient church councils and the power struggles between the communities that were represented there. To practice thoughtful expressions of Christian faith, Christians have to be dedicated and skillful interpreters of history. Deciphering how Christian ethics might be connected to varied historical and cultural realities not only aids in cultivating these skills for Christians, but it can also encourage all of us in the general public to challenge the common tendency to overgeneralize about the role of dominant Christian voices in shaping contemporary societal values.

Niebuhr's Ideas and Their Relevance to Harlem

There are many ways in which an ethical inquiry that is focused upon a certain historical time period and empirically based upon Harlem is especially fitting for a discussion that features Reinhold Niebuhr's work. Concern for history and empirical realities could not be more strongly reflected in his body of writings.[3] Though not precisely concerned with Harlem, nor always consistent, his thoughtful engagement of his social context was explicit.

Niebuhr is a premier example of a public intellectual, that is, an intellectual who embraced the opportunity to study and participate in public affairs and to make academic ideas accessible to a broader public audience. John C. Bennett, social ethicist and his faculty colleague, observed, "To understand Niebuhr's thought we must move back and forth between his books, which provide the theological frame for his thought, and his articles and editorials, which show his response to contemporary events."[4] Besides publishing five books on Christianity, morality, and society during the 1930s, he wrote almost two hundred articles in journals with widely ranging audiences, including the Evangelical and Reform Church denominational publication the *Messenger*, the interdenominational church publication the *Christian Century*, the labor movement journal the *New Leader*, political affairs journals like the *Nation* and the *New Republic*, and *Radical Religion*, the socialist Christian journal that he helped to found. He had been a full-time faculty member at Union Theological Seminary for barely four years when he ran for Congress in 1932 on the Socialist ticket (to resounding defeat), despite the fact that "the seminary board of directors had expressed grave concern" about it.[5]

Reinhold Niebuhr's ideas of the 1930s and early 1940s do not necessarily typify his vast canon of writings, which spanned more than fifty years. As we would expect with anyone's work over a lifetime, there are important shifts and contradictions, as well as some uniformity in his thought. In many ways his identification with socialism during the Depression contrasts considerably with his conservative cold-war perspectives of the 1950s and 1960s.[6] When studying Niebuhr one must closely examine the contradictions and shifts in his work; offer qualified, historicized observations of the consistencies; and refuse to erase certain "extremes" in his thought. Nonetheless, Niebuhr's quest to address questions about the public role of Christians in society remained constant throughout his life. Some of his responses to those questions were modified and varied with transitions in world affairs and U.S. social conditions. Locating his thought in a particular time period and social context invites us to be attentive to details that can get lost when his ideas are evaluated for the sake of a "master narrative" about his contributions to Christian ethics or to the tradition of twentieth-century public intellectuals.

Moreover, a contextualized approach to Niebuhr provides an arena for constructing Christian ethics in which universal moral concerns are tethered to particular ones. (I explore this connection between the universal and the particular in chapter 2.) Ethical principles that Niebuhr posits as universal for Christians, because, supposedly, they are not culturally bound, can be usefully engaged with and sometimes contested by particular historical and cultural realities in Harlem.

It is impossible to address the realities of socioeconomic injustice and exploitation without understanding power relations in society. Niebuhr interpreted certain historical and political problems by focusing on how the need for power is part of human nature and sinfulness. As Christian social ethicist Robin Lovin formulates it, Niebuhr gave such interpretations "a more nuanced, universal form, so that motives and actions were never pure manifestations of good or evil, and every fault of the evil or the enemy could be related to some more basic form of pride or will to power that all people share."[7] Would Harlem activists and exploited workers agree with this approach to the "enemies" that they confronted? Would they share his assumptions about human nature and the use of power?

The treatment of Harlem sources that I am proposing differs from Niebuhr's treatment of the sources he selected. Niebuhr articulated universal moral principles to "cast light upon particulars" of unjust social conditions that he observed.[8] For him, particular historical and empirical circumstances served as examples for ethical principles, exemplifying, for instance, a universal human proclivity toward pride and a "will to power." In contrast to Niebuhr, my own liberationist approach does not assume that the experiences of oppression by Harlem women and their activist responses to that oppression merely present us with examples for predetermined moral theories about natural human proclivities.[9] Harlem is not just a place to find illustrations for ideas about social morality as preconceived by theologians and other great thinkers. Certainly, the moral knowledge of and actions by these Harlem women sometimes exemplify and give deeper insight into ethical principles that are already known or convictions already held before encountering their stories. However, one must also take note of the ways that their voices and ethical actions offer alternatives and challenges to what is assumed by Niebuhr (and us?) to be the essential terms for describing human moral behavior.

Certain generalizations may be tempting when constructing ethical analysis based upon Niebuhr's work but are actually pitfalls that could be avoided by connecting Niebuhr's thought with his Harlem context. For instance, Niebuhr described how dominant groups can make use of non-violent force to maintain their power. He also appreciated the ways that oppressed groups might use nonviolent force to resist dominant groups. Christian social ethicist Larry Rasmussen explains Niebuhr's understanding of nonviolent resistance as a coercive use of power, but one that is "likely to do good . . . Niebuhr's 1932 volume, *Moral Man and Immoral Society*, practically laid out the full strategy later used in the Civil Rights Movement."[10] And if we look up this intriguing reference we find an extensive list in *Moral Man and Immoral Society* of tactical suggestions that he says we are waiting for Negroes to carry out, including boycotts against banks that discriminate by refusing Negroes credit, stores that refuse to employ Negroes "while serving Negro trade," and public service organizations that practice racial discrimination.[11] After reviewing this statement by Niebuhr, we might return to Rasmussen's comment linking such suggestions to 1960s civil rights tactics, and conclude that Niebuhr was indeed an extraordinary visionary. He appears to be uncannily prophetic in devising a tactical strategy for resistance that black leaders would not think of implementing until twenty-five years later in the civil rights movement.[12]

Except . . . in Harlem, throughout the 1920s, organizations like the NAACP and the New York Urban League had been steadily working to change discriminatory practices by white employers against blacks. In 1930, one of the groups at the forefront of these efforts was the Harlem Housewives League.[13] By 1931 it claimed over a thousand members and met every Monday night at the Urban League building. In their campaign, these black women visited department stores like Woolworth's and the Atlantic and Pacific Tea Company (A&P), urging them to hire blacks and pointing out how much money blacks spent in those stores. This group "encouraged all Harlem wives to shop only at stores that belonged to the Colored Merchants Association or that hired blacks."[14] This was only the beginning of a massive "Don't Buy Where You Can't Work" campaign of boycotts in the 1930s that relied upon leadership from many groups, including some of the largest black churches in Harlem.

I do not know if Niebuhr was influenced by social movements such as these boycotts when he suggested the nonviolent strategies in *Moral Man and Immoral Society*, and I am not trying to prove that he might have been.[15] This example illustrates the influence that assumptions about historical context can have upon ethical inquiry. It shows how easy it is to place only important white thinkers at the center of our narratives of history and moral innovation. When we do so, it conceals the multiple actors and innovators in the moral dramas of history, and reinforces the supremacy of whites in our understanding of how important moral knowledge is generated.

I am suggesting that Christians resist this tendency and instead foster an ethical vision that recognizes multiple, dissimilar sources of valuable moral knowledge, especially from those unequal in social power and status, such as Reinhold Niebuhr's ideas and the ideas and actions of the Harlem Housewives League. To allow the experiences and activist ideas of the black Harlem women to broaden and occasionally critique Niebuhr's ideas about public ethics opens up possibilities for developing liberative Christian social ethics.

Harlem Context and Individual Women's Ideas

According to categories specified by the U.S. Census in the 1930s and 1940s "native whites" of foreign or mixed parentage referred to those with parentage from Germany, like Niebuhr's parents, and from dozens of other countries in Europe. The list for "native whites" with foreign parentage also included parentage from Palestine, Turkey, Mexico, Cuba, and other places in the world.[16] In a separate list of nonwhites, Negroes were the largest category included in this census data. Besides Negroes, nonwhites were recorded under the following categories: Indians, Chinese, Japanese, Filipinos, Hindus, and "all others." In the 1930s and 1940s, Negroes were over 95 percent of the nonwhite population in Manhattan, and most lived in Harlem.[17]

It is difficult to overstate the devastating impact of the Depression on blacks in Harlem during this period. The Depression brought terrible shortages of food, clothing, jobs, and health care in a community already overburdened with impoverished conditions. Furniture and other personal belongings of evicted families on the sidewalk, daily, long lines at the relief office, and people searching garbage cans scrounging for food were all common sights in Harlem neighborhoods.[18] Among other consequences of the Depression, "one in four Harlem families broke up, a result, many blacks charged, of the ban on relief to any family with a male wage earner."[19] Daily insults of racial discrimination played a compounding role in the midst of these socioeconomic challenges for black Harlemites. A black woman shopping at Blumstein's or Koch's on 125th Street was not permitted to try on a dress or a hat within the store, and no black patron was allowed to use the toilet facilities reserved for customers (most of whom were black).[20] Most hospitals in New York, with the exception of Harlem Hospital, refused to care for black patients.

Bessie Delany, who earned a doctorate of dental surgery degree from Columbia University in the 1920s and became the second black woman to practice dentistry in New York, explained: "There were many dentists in my day who would not take colored patients. That was why it was so important that there were colored dentists!"[21] (She and her sister had moved from North Carolina to New York City to attend college and graduate school.) Dr. Delany's professional life was thoroughly imbued with a sense of responsibility to her community. She willingly examined patients who were unable to pay her, especially the children of poor black parents.[22] Her office was a gathering place for the planning of protest demonstrations against various forms of racist discrimination practiced by whites during the 1920s, including planning for protests at lunch counters of white restaurants that "wouldn't serve colored people."[23] But, for Delany, those sit-ins at lunch counters were "not my style of activism at all. I was afraid some nasty white person would spit in my food in the back, then serve it to me. I didn't want their germs, no sir."[24]

As Dr. Delany describes, in the 1930s, even "prominent, educated" professional African Americans, such as herself, suffered under the devastating effects of the Depression; she was able to keep her "practice going during the Depression, although now I wonder how I did."[25] Even when many more patients were unable to pay her, she felt compelled to try to also respond to the nondental crises of her patients, for instance, offering bread "or whatever I had for myself" to those who were hungry.[26] Delany was a dedicated professional who generously incorporated charity and concern for her society into her practice of that profession. She took pride in being a dignified, highly educated, hard-working professional who was "the kind of Negro that most white people don't know about."[27] She interpreted her achievements, privileges of education, "good family" background, and never having had to take "a handout from the government" or scrub floors, as defiance of white racist expectations. Unlike Niebuhr's view of pridefulness as a quintessentially sinful human need that fuels the drive to dominate others, for Delany, taking pride in her achievements represented an empowering reassurance of her own human dignity. For blacks, the ability to take pride in one's self (and group) is a source of power that white racism tries to rob.

In contrast to Delany, Ann Petry's professional life addressed the suffering of blacks in Harlem with a different kind of community concern.

She became a fiction writer who published her second short story in 1943 in *Crisis* magazine (the NAACP journal founded by W. E. B. Du Bois). That short story, like her subsequent first novel *The Street*, depicted hopelessness, despair, and tragedy in the grinding poverty of ghetto life for black Harlem families. Such realities did not reflect her own background. She had grown up comfortably in Old Saybrook, Connecticut, and only moved to New York City with her husband in 1938. From 1938 to 1941 Petry worked as a journalist in Harlem for the *Amsterdam News*, then as editor of the woman's page for the *People's Voice*, and as an activist who helped to found a consumer protection group called Negro Women Inc.[28] In her fiction, Petry "identified with the people of her own race and wanted to put their struggle into words."[29]

At the conclusion of Petry's 1946 novel *The Street*, Lutie, the main character, repels an attempted rape and bludgeons her attacker to death while thinking about the everyday conditions she faced in Harlem. As she strikes him with repeated blows, Lutie vents

> her rage against the dirty, crowded street. She saw the rows of dilapidated old houses; the small dark rooms; the long steep flights of stairs; the narrow dingy hallways . . . the smashed homes where the women did the drudgery because their men had deserted them. . . . The limp figure on the sofa became, in turns . . . the insult in the moist eyed glances of white men on the subway; became the hostility in the eyes of white women; became the greasy lecherous man at the Cross School. . . ."[30]

Lutie's homicidal rage seems to be a desperate quest to recover pride and dignity that is constantly under attack. Petry's writing ensures that her readers will not make the mistake of treating sexist racism and socioeconomic oppression dismissively or with matter-of-fact acknowledgment. She sought to expose the destructive consequences of poverty, racism, and sexism that result in assaults on the individual's mind, body, and spirit, as well as the breakdown of family and community relationships. The horrific elements and consuming power of these assaults on black life must be understood in order to find a remedy. Rather than Niebuhr's starting point of how "man's" will to power is a distorting impulse, Petry's realism encourages one to start with the distorting consequences for the people who are systematically disempowered, that is, with an examination of the distorting consequences to one's pride in one's self, community, and womanhood.

While Delany was adamant about the need to recognize how some blacks, such as herself, avoided being fully ensnared by the assaults of poverty, racism, and sexism, Petry was relentless in her insistence upon public immersion (through her writing) into the despair that these realities spread. Both women offer insights about basic human needs for pride and power as Niebuhr did. And, although Petry and Delany contribute alternative perspectives from his, they similarly compel us to investigate the potential and dangers in human pride and use of power.

Claudia Jones, who also lived and worked in Harlem, was dedicated to radical, direct action to alter unjust power relations. Claudia Jones was born in Trinidad in 1915 and moved with her parents to Harlem in 1922. Her family was very poor, and her mother died only a few years after they moved from Trinidad. Her father's janitor's apartment was so damp that she contracted tuberculosis when she was in high school, the effects of which stayed with her throughout her life.[31] Claudia Jones found employment in laundry, factory, and sales clerk jobs. In the mid-1930s she became an organizer in the Young Communist League and the National Negro Congress (a communist-led organization also), and campaigned against lynching, and in support of improving schools in Harlem and increasing job opportunities for black youth. Throughout the 1940s Jones increasingly gained leadership responsibilities in communist organizations, especially focusing on writing and editing for their publications. In her writings, she was one of the strongest proponents of the Communist Party's (CPUSA's) idea of complete self-determination for African Americans in the South, arguing for their right to land, equality, and freedom.[32] As a result of the public expression of her political views the U.S. government imprisoned and then eventually deported Jones in the 1950s.[33]

The ethical work of these three women varied in method but each contributed some form of resistance to the suffocating combination of racism and socioeconomic poverty. They created initiatives that refused to allow silent acceptance of that suffocation, whether providing private space for activist organizing in the 1920s as well as ongoing charitable sharing with strangers, engaging in communist organizing in the 1930s and 1940s, or writing gritty, realist fiction about a poor African American mother in the 1940s. These are merely snapshots of ideas about shifting power relations that were generated by individuals. There were also much more broadly based communal efforts offered by women during this period, such as the Harlem YWCA, and these coordinated communal efforts were probably more effective inhibitors of entrenched social problems confronting the black Harlem community than individual efforts.

Niebuhr and the Negro Cause

Niebuhr's Christian social ethics also addressed the issue of activist organizing among Negroes. His depiction of their efforts is significantly different from my depiction above, illustrated by Petry, Delany, and Jones. In his 1932 *Moral Man and Immoral Society*, Niebuhr urged the black community to arise from its lethargy and try to take action against the oppressive conditions it faced. At the end of his list of suggested nonviolent strategies for challenging racial discrimination, Niebuhr wrote:

> One waits for such a campaign with all the more reason and hope because the peculiar spiritual gifts of the Negro endow him with the capacity to conduct it successfully. He would need only to fuse the aggressiveness of the new and young Negro with the patience and forbearance of the old Negro, to rob the former of its vindictiveness and the latter of its lethargy.[34]

This kind of paternalism toward blacks flavored much of his analysis of racial problems. This passage demonstrates his detached, somewhat arrogant posture of waiting for blacks to take up his suggestions. Unfortunately Niebuhr did not similarly propose that whites like himself should also engage in these tactics in order to challenge racial discrimination at the stores and banks that *they* used.

Nonetheless, Niebuhr, especially in journal articles, devoted substantial attention to African Americans in his ethical writings about society.[35] For many, perhaps the most obvious resource in his writings for formulating ethics that connects Niebuhr's ideas to the experiences and activism of black women in Harlem would be these references to blacks. But I would strongly argue that they are not the only or even necessarily the most instructive point of connection. It would be a serious misreading of Niebuhr's construction of Christian social ethics to assume that blacks are only to be considered part of his moral vision for "man," society, or Christianity based upon his direct references to them in his writings. He was deeply committed to identifying principles of Christian social ethics that were universally applicable. However, since he did mention blacks so often when articulating his moral vision for society, what were some of his views? Besides his criticism about certain flaws in black leadership, what are other examples of his ideas about strategies to oppose racial oppression?

Niebuhr was genuinely concerned about the persistence of racial and economic inequalities plaguing African Americans, asserting that "however large the number of individual white men who do and who will identify themselves completely with the Negro cause, the white race in America will not admit the Negro to equal rights if it is not forced to do so."[36] In fact, he based his call for nonviolent campaigns by Negroes against discrimination upon this assertion about the resilience of white racism. He also argued against Christian complacency regarding race relations and endorsed the social struggle of blacks for their citizenship rights. Niebuhr contended that "only a religion full of romantic illusions could seek to persuade the Negro to gain justice from the white man merely by forgiving him. . . . [All] must seek according to the best available moral insights to contend for what they believe to be right."[37]

When concerned with particular practices in church and society, Niebuhr's approach to race relations appears to have sometimes been one of gradualism.[38] Adelbert Helm, his successor as pastor of the Detroit (Michigan) Bethel Evangelical Church (1929–1930) tried unsuccessfully to encourage this all-white church to admit African Americans into their membership. Niebuhr recommended a less insistent approach. Niebuhr's intervention probably undermined Helm's attempts to create change.[39] Because Helm refused to stop preaching about racism and calling for integration of the church, he was forced out.[40] The church council subsequently voted at their annual meeting in 1930 to bar blacks from the church. From New York Niebuhr wrote to the church council about his distress over their decision: "I never envisaged a fully developed interracial church at Bethel. . . . I do not think we are ready for that. But I do not see how any church can be so completely disloyal to the Gospel of love as to put up bars against members of another racial group."[41] In advocating for integration, Helm, perhaps mistakenly, thought that he was fulfilling the legacy of Niebuhr's ministry. (Niebuhr had been openly sympathetic to issues of discrimination against blacks when he was a pastor in Detroit.)[42] Niebuhr believed that full integration was something that "no congregation" would be able to face at that time,[43] though he also believed that Bethel could have taken some steps to be open to the few blacks who might have applied for membership.

This message of gradualism is similar to positions that Niebuhr took much later in his career in response to the civil rights movement. Sometimes he gave a qualified endorsement, arguing in 1956 that it "may be politically unwise to advocate 'gradualism;' but it is morally wise to practice it as long as the gradualism is genuine," that is, as long as there is some degree of progress "to give the Negro minority hope for a better future."[44]

In the 1950s he did call for recognition of the evils of racial prejudice, and supportively recognized the Negro movement against segregation as an assertion of human dignity.[45] In the same discussion, he also expressed sympathy for (white?) "anxious parents" who opposed school desegregation and were concerned about the immediate educational effects, especially in light of "the cultural differences" between the two races. In the midst of this expression of sympathy for the parents, he explained, "One may hope that ultimately the Negro people will have the same advantages as our children."[46] I do not know if he consciously meant to equate "the Negro people" with "our children" (white children), but this statement again communicates his paternalism toward blacks. In addition, why would attending school with "culturally different" students be a concern for white parents and why is it a concern that deserves sympathy? It would be a reasonable matter of concern only if it meant subjecting their children to some inferior or negative influence manifested in these supposedly culturally different (black) children. Niebuhr seems, therefore, to have sometimes been an apologist for racial assumptions based upon prejudice.

In both of these instances, that of the 1930 Detroit church and the 1950s school desegregation movement, he maintains a stance that identifies moral wrong from a distant, objective stance. He demonstrates a kind of objectivity that on the one hand articulates consistent support for racial justice, but on the other hand notes the untimeliness of church integration (in one case) and empathizes with white parents who resist school integration (in the other case). This stance seems to endorse actual practices that make compromises with his convictions about the moral wrong of racial oppression. At best, it sends a contradictory moral message about the role of whites in furthering racial justice. Instead of offering more examples exploring his writings about race and blacks in the 1950s and 1960s, my focus will remain on his thought during the 1930s and 1940s because it is where he first developed this fundamental element in his ethical approach to public practices of engaging them by trying to "remain above the fray."[47]

Niebuhr highly valued the quality of disinterestedness as a moral ideal.[48] A commitment to disinterestedness or rational objectivity, he argued, counters the corrupting, sinful human tendency to pursue one's own self-interest at the expense of others' interests. This quality is difficult if not impossible to fully achieve. According to Niebuhr, African Americans have practiced a form of moral disinterestedness, but unfortunately for them it has failed to deliver moral changes that would liberate them from oppression.[49] He supports this claim about blacks by explaining that their failure to rise up against their masters during the Civil War was evidence of their failure to pursue their own self-interest. Although noting exceptions in the 1930s to this failure to act, he believed that, for the most part, since the Civil War, Negroes "have been compounded of genuine religious virtues of forgiveness and forbearance, and a certain social inertia which was derived not from religious virtue but from racial weakness."[50] Thus not only does its effectiveness elude them when they live out this ideal of disinterestedness, but their own inadequacy also dooms their struggle for freedom, an inadequacy that stems from the character of the Negro race.

Niebuhr does offer hope about how some people are able to achieve a degree of disinterestedness that has efficacy. As he explains, "The influence of the relatively disinterested, who view the struggle in rational and moral terms, is always considerable. . . . The Negroes did not achieve their emancipation nor will they be able to gain further extension of rights in our society without the aid of white men of sensitive conscience."[51] For Niebuhr, the most successful form of black emancipation requires the assistance of rational, moral, and sensitive individual whites. They step in to fill the gap created by black inferiority and inadequate leadership, as well as the intransigent racism of whites as a group. Again, he did not think that this assistance would be sufficient; he believed that "the white race" would have to be forced to give the Negro equal rights.

A Space to Be Free of Whites

Christian activist contemporaries and Harlem neighbors of Niebuhr offer an alternative ethical perspective on the black struggle for freedom from social and economic oppression. For example, Anna Arnold Hedgeman was the membership secretary at the Harlem Young Women's Christian Association in the 1930s.[52] The Harlem YWCA had opened its own newly constructed building in 1920 and was among the earliest African American YWCA branches in the country. After working at other black branches in Ohio and New Jersey, Hedgeman commented about the great sense of relief that she experienced at the more financially well-off Harlem branch: "I would have equipment with which to work and the challenge of the largest Negro community in the nation. The wall of separation had done its work. I was completely free of and done with white people."[53]

However, considering the existence of some of the most brutal conditions of racist violence, such as lynching in the South, and the economic hardships brought by the Depression, it was very difficult for blacks to be truly free of whites anywhere in the United States. And in Harlem, a white man, John D. Rockefeller Jr., had helped to fund a new residence for the

Harlem YWCA during the 1920s. Such individual white actions represented the kind of impetus for change about which Niebuhr was so optimistic. He correctly pointed out that blacks could not be emancipated from their subjugated position without some realignment and redistribution of the power and privilege of whites. But the perspectives of Harlem YWCA leaders broaden and contest Niebuhr's ideas about the role of blacks in this kind of social change. Hedgeman and other Harlem YWCA leaders displayed tremendous skill in the ongoing tasks of fund-raising to maintain their buildings and projects;[54] providing food, shelter, education, job training, leisure and fun activities; ensuring that cultural celebration and preservation of black literature and history took place; and giving spiritual nurture to help women and girls cope with the daily insults of racist discrimination.

The nature of their leadership helps us to formulate a critical perspective on Niebuhr's approach to addressing racism. Niebuhr stressed the necessity for confronting both white supremacy and what he believed to be the weakness of black leadership. As he suggested, actions by whites are needed to comprehensively challenge racist realities, but how can Christian social ethics envision change that diminishes the destructive hold of society's commitment to white domination in a manner that is not as white-centered as Niebuhr's view? (This question also represents a challenge for the contemporary critical studies of whiteness that I discuss in chapter 4.)

The activist Christian ethical work by Harlem YWCA leaders offers some possibilities. Studying their Christian ethics opens the way for conceiving ethical proscriptions that appreciate the means and opportunities for change created by blacks, as well as the relentless nature of that struggle. The organizing work of these Christian women leaders demonstrates the efficacy of coordinating efforts to bring about change, by creating a means of simultaneously getting away from and confronting white control. An ideal of disinterestedness could not be more distant from the aims of their justice work. They put together programs that involved both self-criticism and self-interest. Their Christian ethical work furthered broad principles of faithful Christian living through an organization that wholeheartedly sided with poor and oppressed women and girls.

According to religious historian Judith Weisenfeld, membership during the 1930–1944 period was between forty-five hundred and five thousand women.[55] There are many ways in which the Harlem YWCA provided a respite space for black women and girls as well as a wedge against the burdens of social inequality, discrimination, and economic hardship. The Harlem YWCA provided much-needed affordable housing for black girls and women on a permanent basis, as well as for overnight stays, which was especially valuable at this time when blacks could find very few hotel accommodations open to them. In addition, the Harlem YWCA operated a trade school that trained thousands of women during the 1930s so that they could be placed, as its 1931 brochure indicated, "in the major employment fields in which Negro girls are working, or in which trends indicate their possible employment."[56] This training work had to respond to employment trends dictated by the dire economic circumstances of the Depression as well as the level of skill the women brought (many had recently migrated from poor rural communities in the South and the Caribbean). The task of creating an adequate response to both of these factors was exacerbated by rampant racial discrimination by employers and required an array of strategies.

While he failed to account for this kind of creative and persistent black resistance, Niebuhr rightly identified the stubbornness of white racism, asserting that it "is hopeless for the Negro to expect complete emancipation from the menial social and economic position into which the white man has forced him, merely by trusting the moral sense of the white race."[57] Harlem leaders understood quite well that waiting on and trusting in "the moral sense" of whites would be futile and that protest was necessary. For instance, Cecelia Cabaniss Saunders, the long-standing executive director of the Harlem YWCA, raised her voice in protest when she testified before the Mayor's Commission on Conditions in Harlem. The Commission held hearings after the 1935 riot in Harlem, which was sparked by the unresponsiveness of local stores to black protests against their discriminatory hiring practices and by suspected police brutality against a black child.[58] In response to the riot and the black community's concerns it forced into the public spotlight, Mayor Fiorello LaGuardia appointed the interracial commission to investigate discrimination in Harlem.

Saunders had given the Harlem YWCA forceful administrative leadership and was also an articulate spokesperson for women in the broader community. At the hearings, she spoke out about the discriminatory treatment of black women by white employers. In her study of the Harlem YWCA Weisenfeld describes the testimony Saunders gave at a 1935 public hearing of the Mayor's Commission.

> Saunders told panel members that while her YWCA had experienced some successes, the women they worked with had faced discrimination when seeking jobs as domestics, store clerks, secretaries, and civil

> servants. When asked about her experiences with particular companies in the city, Saunders discussed her experience with the telephone company: "We asked for employment of telephone operators at least in the Harlem area. They objected to the voices of colored girls. We said we had someone with a lovely voice. We asked to have her tried out. The telephone company didn't agree to that . . ."[59]

Saunders protested the adamant refusal by most private and public-sector white employers to hire blacks for anything but the most menial jobs, which paid them lower wages than whites and had substandard working conditions. Her outspoken leadership illustrated her awareness of the power of public confrontation. Truth-telling in an open forum directed at community officials served as a crucial means for pursuing the socioeconomic change her community needed.

The work of Saunders, Hedgeman, and the other YWCA leaders teaches us how emancipation can start with alternative space away from oppression—in this case, black woman space for respite, self-nurture, and coordinating resistance. Their Christian ethical work provided a kind of birthing space to foster the ability to confront the realities of subjugation. It teaches us that analysis for addressing antiblack injustice in Christian social ethics that is centered exclusively upon black encounters with whites and attempts to shift the racism of whites is inadequate. Confrontation with whites is certainly integral to the process of bringing change. Yet when narrowly focused only on that confrontational encounter with whites the ethical analysis reflects an arrogance about the centrality of whites, that ignores the particulars of black struggle and black life. Ignoring such particulars will mean a loss of some essential ingredients for altering social practices where power is used by privileged whites to exploit blacks. At the same time, strategies to create change must also include scrutiny of the exploitative behavior of whites.

Using Privilege and Power

Reinhold Niebuhr's Christian social ethics included a sharp critique of the use of power by groups in society. More optimistic about the possibilities for moral behavior by individuals, his critique emphasized the exploitative behavior of groups, especially dominant, privileged groups in society. For Niebuhr, groups are ruled by an unrestrained egoism or will to power that leads them to pridefully consider only their own interests. Dominant groups assert their will over others at all costs in order to achieve what is in their own self-interest. They engage in every form of hypocritical reasoning to justify their advantages, and without any hesitation they use force to maintain those advantages. Dominant groups may use overt means to force others to submit, like the police power of the state, or more covert means of coercion, such as economic power.[60]

A profound expression of self-interest as economic domination could not be more apparent than in the treatment by white employers of black women who walked across Harlem to line up for work as domestics at "The Bronx Slave Market." This "slave market," one of many in New York City, consisted of two or three blocks around 167th Street. Black women came there (mostly from Harlem) and waited for white housewives who wanted to "rent" domestic help. The conditions for the workers at the "slave market" were described in an article by Marvel Cooke, investigative reporter for the black-owned *Amsterdam News,* and Ella Baker, journalist and civil rights organizer with the NAACP in the 1930s and 1940s (and later with SCLC and SNCC in the 1950s and 1960s).[61] These black women activist journalists joined the domestics on the corner in order to get a firsthand understanding of what the workers faced. Their 1935 article appeared in the NAACP's *Crisis.*

Cooke and Baker described how lower-middle-class white housewives benefited from the dire economic conditions of the Depression by being able to secure domestic servants under extremely exploitative conditions. They asserted that such a housewife "who, having dreamed of the luxury of a maid, found opportunity staring her in the face in the form of Negro women pressed to the wall by poverty, starvation and discrimination."[62] The workers would haggle with the housewives over a price that ranged from as little as ten or fifteen cents an hour to, "if luck be with them, thirty cents an hour."[63] The women could be "rented" for an hour of work or more—up to a full day.

Besides the unfair pay rates, there were reports by the women workers of employers exploiting them in other ways, such as by deducting five cents for transporting them to the job site, asking them to work for friends and relatives at no extra pay, or giving them used clothing and leftover food instead of the wages they had been expecting. A common trick of employers was to turn the clock back at the end of the day in order to cheat workers on the amount of time that they had worked and the wages due them.[64] This trick was so common that newcomers were warned by old-timers at the market to bring their own clocks.[65]

At the market, there were many humiliations that occurred for the workers, like when white housewives inspected black women's knees supposedly to determine whether or not they scrubbed floors. According to social activist Audley Moore, "They'd look up their dresses and look at their knees. If they had crusts on their knees, they'd hire them. If they didn't have crust on their knees, they wouldn't hire them. . . . It was just like slavery time."[66] At the employers' homes, black domestics sometimes faced sexual harassment from white husbands and sons.[67] They also had to endure the articulation of specific racial prejudices prevalent at the time, such as the accusation that they brought diseases into white homes. For example, a May 1933 article in *Information for Social Work* indicated that gonorrhea in children was commonly caused by soiled toilet seats infected by members of the household such as "the colored maid."[68] One daughter of a black woman who worked as a domestic in New York City during this time recalled how an employer tried to make her mother eat her lunch out of a pet's dish because she "did not want her 'help' eating out of the same dishes from which she ate."[69]

Niebuhr's depiction of the unrestrained egoism of dominant groups aptly describes this behavior by the white women employers toward black women domestics. It appears that the white women employers used whatever exploitative means they could think of in maintaining their own economic self-interests. However, these encounters between whites and blacks also raise questions for Niebuhr's ethical assessment of dominant groups. To describe the actions by the white women employers as illustrative of dominant-group immoral behavior seems analytically unsatisfactory for several reasons.

First, Niebuhr's moral analysis containing generalizations about dominant-group behavior has a quality of inevitability that conceals the series of choices that produce exploitation by dominant groups. Accountability for the choices made by members of dominant groups seems to be lost in this framework. Beyond generalized assessments of how dominant groups behave, Christian social ethics ought to include specific analysis of historical conditions created by such groups. Revelations about, for instance, the multiple, particular choices that uphold white privilege and power challenge the quality of inevitability in any claim that dominant behavior by whites is reflective of a universal human tendency.

Second, Niebuhr's emphasis upon immoral group behavior as somehow separate from individual behavior can be confusing. In *Moral Man and Immoral Society* Niebuhr stressed this firm distinction between the morality of individuals and that of groups (but offers a less stringent distinction in subsequent texts like *The Nature and Destiny of Man*[70]). Niebuhr maintained a viewpoint that envisioned moral relations between individuals as more sustainable than relations between groups. His formulation of this distinction does not make it clear when group moral behavior is operative within an individual's moral behavior. Were white housewives who exploited black domestics acting out group moral behavior or individual moral behavior?

For Niebuhr, the division between the moral relations of groups and that of individuals was necessary because of the power that groups exercise over individuals. He viewed the moral relations between individuals as part of a private sphere, distinct from relations between groups, which were, for him, a matter of public affairs. According to this perspective, would the street-corner exchanges between the white housewife and the black domestic be considered part of private or public life? What about their exchanges within the home of the white employer: are they private or public moral matters representative of individual or group moral behavior?

In *The Nature and Destiny of Man* Niebuhr presents a substantive theological understanding of how the egoism of individuals as well as the collective egoism of groups is an expression of human sinfulness. The relations between whites and blacks serve as one of the examples of this key idea in Niebuhr's work:

> Gentiles, holding the dominant power in their several nations, sin against Semitic minority groups more than the latter sin against them. White men sin against Negroes in Africa and America more than Negroes sin against white men. Wherever the fortunes of nature, the accidents of history or even the virtues of possessors of power endow an individual or group with power, social prestige, intellectual eminence, or moral approval above their fellows, there an ego is allowed to expand. . . . Its vertical expansion, its pride, involves it in sin against God. Its horizontal expansion involves it in an unjust effort to gain security and prestige at the expense of its fellows.[71]

Again, from his supposed objective standpoint, the behavior of blacks and of whites is gathered together under the umbrella category of sinfulness. Although his theo-ethical position acknowledges the disproportionate commission of sin by Gentiles and whites, it treats historical realities of exploitation and domination as happenstance occurrences rather than deliberate choices by particular historical actors.[72] White Gentiles just happen to have had nature, history, and personal virtues on their side, which have allowed them to sinfully express their pride so unjustly.

Much of the feminist criticism of Niebuhr has been focused precisely on the subject of his generalizations about sin.[73] Niebuhr is accused by some feminist ethicists and theologians of having a one-sided understanding of sin as pridefulness that neglects "women's experience." British theologian Daphne Hampson quips that when Niebuhr described "'man's' pride and will to power he may have meant 'man' more literally than he knew."[74] Several feminist religious scholars point out that instead of pridefulness, sin for "women" has much more often meant a lack of self-assertion through self-censoring or hiding behind passivity.[75] In one of the earliest and most detailed feminist treatments of Niebuhr's theology of sin, Jewish feminist theologian Judith Plaskow describes women's sin as primarily a failure to take responsibility for self-actualization.[76] She explains that "defining sin's religious dimension as rebellion against God and its moral dimension as pride, Niebuhr not only fails to convey the nature of women's sin. . . . He actually turns it into a virtue."[77] Hence for Plaskow and other feminists, Niebuhr not only fails to consider the sinfulness of an overemphasis on self-sacrificing and self-effacing behavior that many women practice, but he also celebrates this self-destructive practice as virtuous behavior.

I find these critiques to be only a partial corrective of Niebuhr. Even though these feminist ethicists and theologians do not assert that women are incapable of pridefulness, they assume it to be a minor aspect of women's expression of their sinfulness. The behavior of the white housewives at the "slave market" and their treatment of black domestics in their homes help us to understand otherwise. These white women who came to hire black domestics may have occupied an immoral or sinful position characterized by passivity or a self-destructive failure to assert themselves within their world of whites. But in relation to blacks, these women certainly did not seem to have had any trouble asserting their self-interest at the cost of others. Self-assertive expressions of domination were a primary part of these white women's everyday domestic relations, and their behavior as employers contradicts much of the white feminist ethical analysis of "women's experience" of sin.

When insisting upon taking "women's experience" into account, some white feminist ethicists and theologians seem to have made the mistake of overgeneralizing based upon the privileges of whiteness in much the same way that they accuse Niebuhr of overgeneralizing from the privileged experience of maleness.[78] More recently, scholars such as Rebekah Miles have offered pointed criticism of feminist analyses of Niebuhr's view of sin. She includes an acknowledgement of the problem of racial parochialism in such claims by white middle-class feminists, asserting that they have been "blind" their sin.[79] However, this acknowledgment of how white feminists inserted their self-interests into theology does not alter Miles's work on Niebuhr. She seeks a thorough revision of feminist readings of Niebuhr, excising what she labels as errors and misunderstandings of him. Yet she fails to make any adjustments that include racial/cultural distinctions and realities of subjugation in her feminist Christian realism, such as her descriptions of "women's experience" of family life or of women's maternal experiences.[80] Therefore even when the error of assuming whites are representative of all others is acknowledged, this acknowledgment does not necessarily lead to an overhaul of white feminist analytical categories or presuppositions.

Assertions about certain essential qualities of "women's experience" which reflect white women's experiences of white privilege have frequently been challenged in feminist and womanist scholarship, and more such analysis is needed. Specifically, postcolonial feminist theories have contested and shifted feminist analysis of "women's experience," contributing a wide range of views that cannot be adequately captured here.[81] But their antiessentialist rejection of a fixed category for describing "the" experience of women is crucial for my development of a method in Christian social ethics that embraces plurality when describing gendered experiences of social identity.

Christian social ethics should include a complex integration of the multiple roles that are part of one's experience and the multiple group identities that inform one's moral behavior, e.g., white, woman, white woman. As feminist ethicists and theologians who critique Niebuhr helpfully assert, there has to be movement away from a Christian social ethic that maintains the polarities of self-negating moral behavior as virtuous and self-assertive moral behavior as sinful. As many feminists have also argued, social ethics should repudiate the dangerous erasure of the abuses of power within private, domestic relations that are mistakenly seen as completely separate from public moral relations. In contrast to many feminist reflections on Niebuhr, it is also imperative to understand how persons (even white women) can simultaneously occupy the position of sinfully negating and sacrificing themselves for others as well as sinfully asserting their own interests in a way that sacrifices the well-being, dignity, and fairness others deserve. It is incumbent upon us to recognize how the particular interests of individuals, groups, and the broader society are woven together in the social process of valuing the worth of human beings and the resources of the natural environment. Choices are made within this interwoven process that reproduce particular power abuses, exploitation, and forms of social intolerance that Christians should identify as sinful. Also, an overly generalized notion of sin may obscure rather than illumine an understanding of this unjust, harmful behavior.

Paying attention to the working conditions of the black women domestics permits us to glimpse some of the complex distortions in moral relations that can occur. For instance, within the black community in New York City, some African American critics blamed Caribbean American immigrants for the city's "slave markets." One 1939 article in the Urban League's *Opportunity: Journal of Negro Life* claimed that the large number of West Indian immigrants in the city brought the idea with them from the West Indian Islands.[82] Of course a similar claim could have been made about southern blacks bringing this idea as they migrated in large numbers during this same period. Rather than offering a plausible explanation for why the "slave markets" existed, this example of publicly blaming West Indians more likely reflects antagonism against this group.

With a binary analysis of power that focuses on contact between whites as dominant groups and blacks as oppressed groups we could fail to develop an understanding of further destructive relations that existed *among* groupings of blacks. Such warped dynamics of power between groups may not be solely related to an egotistical will to power (by whites), but may reveal how blame and resentment can arise from independent cultural clashes between groups of similar status in the society (e.g., Caribbean Americans and African Americans).[83] Of course, those conflicts are usually encouraged by the hostile conditions created by the white subjugation these groups faced, but should not be simplistically reduced to merely a consequence of white subjugation.

Another instructive example of complex distortions in moral relations is found in the black-Jewish issues raised by the relationship between domestics and their employers. Since many of the white housewives who went to the "slave markets" were Jewish (several of the "slave markets" were in or near Jewish neighborhoods), the exploitative conditions of the markets and the mistreatment of black domestics exacerbated tensions between Negroes and Jews. In Harlem during the Depression, relations between Negroes and Jews were quite strained anyway.[84] Drawing a clear distinction between the immorality of black anti-Semitism toward Jews and the legitimate anger of blacks against the perpetrators of the oppressive conditions they faced is a complicated task.

When Baker and Cooke describe "a squatty Jewish housewife" who examines them and then questions them about work, their reference to the Jewishness of the housewife seems unnecessary except as a way of invoking a derogatory stereotype. On the other hand, another reference in the article to the Jewishness of the employer seems to be an appropriate one. In this case, a domestic worker uses it within the context of her complaints about the conditions on the job she held before coming to the "slave market." She was fired for asking for a day off. She explained:

> I would have at least twenty-one shirts to do every week. Yeah and ten sheets, and at least two blankets, besides. They all had to be done just so, too. . . . There wasn't a week that I didn't have to wash up every floor in the place and wax it on my hands and knees. And two or three times a week I'd have to beat the mattresses and take all of the furniture covers off and shake 'em out. Why, when I finally went home nights, I could hardly move. One of the sons had "hand trouble" too, and I was just as tired fighting him off, I guess as I was with the work. . . . Did you ever wash dishes for an Orthodox Jewish family? Well you've never washed dishes then. You know they use a different dish cloth for everything they cook. . . . I was always getting the darned things mixed up. . . . She would get other cloths and make me do the dishes all over again.[85]

This woman's reference to the Jewishness of her employer is descriptive of specific religious practices that impacted her duties. She is justifiably resentful about the exploitative demands this employer made that were related to those religious practices, and about being sexually harassed.

There were conjoined individual, group, and societal dynamics at work in the encounters between black women domestic workers and the white housewives who were also Jewish. Niebuhr's depiction of the egoism of dominant groups and individuals cannot fully capture these interlinked, simultaneously public and private dynamics. In her individual interactions with her employee, the white employer exploited her power and privilege by relying upon her white group membership and her economically advantaged group membership (though in some instances, Jewish housewives were only slightly more economically advantaged than the domestics).[86] Their power and privilege was accrued in part from the subjugated status of blacks and of all poorer people within the larger society.

At the same time, the employer's social status was decreased because of her ethnic identity as Jewish and gender identity as a woman, both of which the larger society devalued and could use as a basis for discrimination against her.[87] The exploitative use of power and privilege by a white Jewish employer against a black domestic worker may have been fueled by her privileged status over the domestic, as well as her own angst about her diminished status within the broader society. In keeping with Niebuhr's ideas, the women employers used any form of dominant-group power available to them to exploit others. This context also highlights the need to expand Niebuhr's ideas. The analysis of dominant-group power must account for the membership of some, like those housewives who were Jewish, within disadvantaged and marginalized groups as well as dominant ones.

On the other side of the interaction black women domestics and their defenders were angry and resentful because of the unfair treatment by employers. The devalued status of Jews also produced another kind of resentment by some blacks against the Jewish women employers. As African American Christian leader Anna Hedgeman said when she investigated these "slave markets," "Jews should know better" based upon their own experiences of prejudice in the society.[88] African American anger and resentment was exacerbated by their knowledge that Jews faced prejudice and discrimination also, especially during this time of the buildup of Hitler's powerful regime. The anti-Jewish prejudice expressed by blacks was obviously not based upon their own membership in a dominant group, but more likely upon their daily confrontations with certain Jewish individuals who treated them in an exploitative manner. The black resentment against Jews that arose in response to those negative experiences was reinforced by those prejudices against all Jews present in the broader culture. Resentment and even articulations of anti-Jewish prejudice must not be morally equated with the concrete practices of socioeconomic exploitation by Jewish employers. Christians sometimes promote this travesty of morally equating oppressor and oppressed precisely by encouraging acontextual, universalizing definitions of sin. Christian claims that sinfulness fundamentally necessitates recognizing that "we're all" egotistical and pridefully pursue our self-interest levels those differences in social status, power, and privilege that exist among us. This equivocation problematically hides the benefits to some and harmful consequences for others of practices of domination.

Finally, this particular case of moral relations raises another concern about generalizations about sin. Is it appropriate for me to subsume Jewish behavior under the Christian category of sin when referring to this instance of exploitation by certain Jewish employers of blacks within my construction of Christian social ethics? The history of Christians labeling Jews as sinful has been so costly to the dignity, physical safety, and very lives of Jews. Since derogatory stereotypes about Jews continue to abound, my criticism of these Jewish employers under the rubric of Christian ethics could elicit, in the minds of many, a comfortable, Christian-rooted, anti-Jewish prejudice. If, however, I restrict my moral judgments only to behavior by Christians, I would have to be silent about much of the exploitation of Harlem black women domestics that took place at the "slave markets" and in employers' homes. Some clarifications of these interreligious ethical concerns are in order.

My Christian theology and faith commitment are the primary sources motivating me in a struggle for justice that demands recognition of oppressive conditions like the 1930s "slave markets" in New York City. For Christians, our own immoral behavior is a sinful defiance of our God. This language about sinful Christian behavior helps Christians to make sense of injustices experienced in the world. It helps to identify the tools of discernment Christians should bring to the task of making moral judgments as we take part in a larger struggle to create justice and fairness in our religiously pluralistic society. Therefore, Christian social ethics must make judgments that cross cultural boundaries about moral behavior in our shared communal life.

From my Christian perspective, sin is indeed represented in the very existence of the "slave market" and the host of unjust practices that it generated. However, when I use the term "sinfulness" to judge the actions of Jewish employers at the "slave market," I must simultaneously acknowledge the historical use of this term by Christians to theologically label Jews and other non-Christians in a manner that justified brutal acts by Christians including crusades, pogroms, and enslavement of "heathen" Africans. Acknowledgment of this historical pattern of brutality within Christian tradition does not deny the validity of condemning the "slave market" practices in Christian ethics. It adds credence to my insistence on attention to particular details of history when collecting moral ideas for correcting societal wrongs. One of the lessons of this history of Christian brutality toward Jews is to remain vigilant in opposing Christian proclivities to foreground supposedly innate "Jewish characteristics" within any ethical critique of behavior by Jewish individuals. This vigilance does not preclude criticism of dehumanizing practices by certain Jewish employers, which were supported by societal notions of the innate inferiority of blacks. Rather than holding onto false claims of universality in homogenizing Christian theological notions, the moral enterprise of creating justice and fairness in our religiously pluralistic communities is enriched by an understanding of the sociohistorical contexts and forms of domination that are ensconced in those details.

A genuine clash of religious understandings can also arise when developing Christian ethics in a pluralistic society. Christian assumptions about the nature of God and sin sometimes clash with equivalent non-Christian views, yet we must still find a way to build justice and fairness across our communities.

Who Is God? Power, Sex, and Gender

The analysis of Harlem "slave market" conditions introduces concerns about how the non-Christian religious/cultural identity of the employers impacts Christian ethics. Building on that acknowledgment of differences and conflict rooted in religious plurality, how do the sensibilities of non-Christian black Harlem activists compare with Niebuhr's ideas?

As Niebuhr was working on a Christian vision of public ethics, simultaneously the Father Divine movement was actively developing a religious vision for creating social justice in our world. The Father Divine movement, sometimes pejoratively referred to as a cult, flourished during the 1930s and was based in Harlem after 1933. Father's Kingdom included well over fifty thousand followers (some say over a million) and spread to many cities throughout the United States and even a few abroad.[89] Their establishments were called Peace Missions.

Below, I juxtapose Niebuhr's Christian theological notion of sensuality as sin with some of the practices of women "angels" within the religious movement of Father Divine. I compare their understandings of what is necessary to generate more justice and fairness. Based upon these two perspectives, how does religion take into consideration the combined role of mind, body, and spirit in generating these values? In crafting Christian social ethics for a religiously pluralistic setting, how does the juxtaposition of these very different religious worldviews advance an understanding of the just use of power?

In both Niebuhr's theological discussion of sensuality and the activities of women angels in the Divine religious movement, spiritual and sexual needs are at issue.[90] Both cases offer insights into some of the ways that spiritual and sexual needs are informed by gender dynamics. The combined issues of gender and sexuality are so influential in shaping assumptions about human identity and God's identity that in any examination of the use of power in Christian social ethics they demand some attention. Moreover, it seems especially relevant to this discussion to note one of the instances where Niebuhr directly addresses gender. My adjoined consideration of Niebuhr and the Divine movement highlights familiar androcentric religious assumptions as well as ambiguities that belie simple judgments about male dominance in religion. As our attention moves from one perspective to the other, questions unfold about how spiritual and sexual needs shape the use of power for moral ends.

Niebuhr's concern with sin as selfish pride led him to engage the emphasis in much of Christian theology upon sin as sensuality.[91] He points out the parts of Christian theological tradition that link human proclivities toward sensual sinfulness with human sexuality. Although sins of sensuality include other problems like drunkenness or gluttony, Niebuhr mainly focuses upon sexuality because of the greater significance given to it in Christian tradition. He reconciles his theology with Christian tradition by explaining how sins of sensuality are an outgrowth of the sin of pride. With regard to sensual sin expressed in human sexuality, he states, "Once the original harmony of nature is disturbed by man's self love, the instincts of sex are particularly effective tools for both the assertion of the self and the flight from the self."[92] In heterosexual sexual acts, Niebuhr identifies the specific sinful temptations that arise as self-deification (the assertion of self) and deification of the other (the flight from self). He also discusses the gendered aspects of these human tendencies:

> While the more active part of the male and the more passive part of the female in the relation of the sexes may seem to point to self-deification as the particular sin of the male and the idolatry of the other as the particular temptation of the woman in the sexual act, yet both elements of sin are undoubtedly involved in both sexes.[93]

Although sinful elements of self-deification and deification of the other can be found in both sexes, he refers to specific gender role behavior. While having sexual relations, males with their "more active" part are not exclusively self-deifying, and females acting out their "more passive" role are not exclusively tempted toward idolatry. This reassurance, especially the latter part, may not really be necessary, for I wonder if there are many heterosexual women who would identify the sin of mistaking their male sexual partner for a god during sexual intercourse as a significant temptation.

Sexual mores within the Father Divine movement present quite a contrast to Niebuhr's assertions. No sexual intercourse was allowed within Divine's religious movement. Moreover, merging the deification of (one particular) male with the expression of one's sensuality seems to have been encouraged, especially for angels. Tiers of affiliation existed within the Father Divine movement, and becoming an angel meant abiding by the most stringent restrictions: followers had to not only renounce sexual intercourse and alcohol, but also relinquish their possessions, their ties to their families, and any belief in racial segregation.

This was a controversial religious movement. Its admirers stress its concertedly interracial gatherings, successful businesses, housing and feeding of great numbers of people at "Communion Banquets" (in the midst of the extreme economic hardship this community suffered during the Depression), and political work against racial discrimination. In 1930, for instance, the movement gathered some 250,000 signatures on a petition to pass antilynching legislation.[94] Critics of the movement, on the other hand, emphasize the autocratic leadership of Father Divine, who demanded absolute obedience and fawning devotion based upon his claim to be divine. He declared: "I AM here with you Personally for your own personal good and to appease your mortal concept concerning ME, but, with or without the Personal Presence, I will rule millions of homes and houses, for I AM DIVINE, and that is not merely a word, it is a Power."[95]

A large number of black women were attracted to this movement and became angels. Harlem Renaissance writer Claude McKay commented that he had "met several unhappy men in Harlem whose wives had left them to live in the kingdom of Father Divine."[96] Sexuality, at least heterosexual sensual expressions of it, appears to have occasionally been an element in the devotion to Father Divine offered by his angels. According to one 1950s account by a strong critic of the movement, Sara Harris, a ritual display celebrating Father Divine by women angels included physical "vibrating."[97] Harris describes this ritual being led by Divine follower, Holy Light:

> "I love you so much. You is my mate. You is beautiful, Father. You is so pretty, Father. Oh Father Divine, how cute you is."
>
> Father glances at Holy Light. His Face is imperturbable.
>
> She begins to walk toward him. "You is my husband, my one and only Father!" she says. "God!"[98]

If this description is accurate, sexual intercourse may not have been permitted in this religious movement, but an understanding of Father Divine as a surrogate mate was encouraged as part of the faith. The transition (escape?) from their ties to their former lives and intimate relationships meant embracing a relationship with Father Divine that may have included overtly sensual and sexual dynamics.

For Niebuhr, sensual sinfulness can be manifest in sexual interaction precisely in the sin of self-deification and deification of the other, in worshiping "the creature rather than the Creator."[99] Sexual relations can also be a foolhardy attempt to escape from the tension of life, "a flight not to a false god, but to nothingness."[100] For Niebuhr, the matter of human freedom is the central spiritual struggle in his discussion of sexuality. In his Christian understanding, freedom is frightening and anxiety producing for human beings, a problem rooted in the Hebrew Bible story about the freedom to choose between good and evil in the Garden of Eden, which ended with such disastrous consequences.[101] Freedom is something human beings try to escape or to hide from by getting lost "in the world's vitalities"[102] and turning down the path of sinfulness. Human freedom, Niebuhr asserts, must be found in the unfreedom of surrender to God's forgiveness and mercy.[103]

Father Divine's angels sought freedom in their religious quest and embraced the unfreedom of living under the dictates of Father. That is, they found a kind of freedom in their surrender to Father's acceptance and support for them. His religious vision offered a response to their quest for freedom by maintaining a vital link between spiritual and social needs. At least during the early 1930s, the black women angels seemed to find a degree of freedom in Divine's religious movement and some relief from the impoverished, disempowering conditions created by racial discrimination and the Depression.[104] Father Divine "ordered all of his illiterate angels to attend night school" and, interested in their political rights, he insisted "upon their exercising the right to vote."[105] The movement made sure that they were a politically educated electorate. The Righteous Government department of the Peace Mission held weekly lectures on government, civics, and local election issues. Active leadership roles by women as well as men were encouraged in these political forums.[106]

One prominent example of women's leadership was Faithful Mary, an angel who served as a primary leader in Father Divine's movement for several years. At first, she was placed in charge of a mission in Harlem where she successfully created a refuge for homeless women and single mothers. By 1935, she directed over a dozen establishments, among them an emporium for meat and vegetables, a coal store, and a tailor shop.[107] She had her own car and a chauffeur and often substituted for Father Divine when he could not make an appearance. Unfortunately, in 1937 she and Father Divine had a major dispute and she left the movement, making scandalous charges against him including descriptions of the sexual exploitation of women angels,[108] all of which she later recanted. When she eventually returned to the movement, her power and authority were never restored to what they had once been.[109]

The response to individual spiritual needs in the Divine movement included the goal of social morality, which meant changing the social and material conditions of oppressed people's lives. In contrast, the response to an individual's spiritual needs in Niebuhr's Christian theology remains mainly focused upon that individual with little attention to the relevance of surrounding social conditions. Niebuhr's discussion of individual spiritual neediness is linked to the goal of achieving personal morality. Though he does describe the social/sexual relations of a heterosexual couple, an explicit discussion of power relations between those persons drops out of Niebuhr's description of sensual, sexual sins. In this personal arena he analyzes only the individual male's or female's needs within a heterosexual marital relationship. An understanding of the use and abuse of power that can take place within these heterosexual couple relations, such as how intimate violence and psychological abuse might be manifested, has to be added to this aspect of Niebuhr's social ethic.

For Niebuhr, the notion of a will to power is an expression of the sin of pride, and sensual sin is a subsidiary part of the sin of pride. In sensual sin, self-deification and deification of the other can carry implications about one's spiritual struggle to gain a sense of control in a chaotic world. But the struggle is centered upon personal freedom and acted out within interpersonal relations, which Niebuhr often defined rather apolitically. Personal salvation from sensual sin is possible when Christian individuals surrender to the transcendent power of the Creator.

In Father Divine's movement individual surrender to the power of Father was a necessary occurrence. His movement offered the women angels social and political empowerment, but only after their submission to his authority. This was a somewhat ambiguous element in the exercise of his control over them. The movement enabled an improvement in their material circumstances and a degree of political empowerment in the broader society. The women's spiritual and sensual needs were restrictively focused upon Father, yet also constructively linked to broader social change. In addition, the leadership of Faithful Mary manifested its devotion to Father through programs targeting homeless single women and mothers. At least through Faithful Mary's leadership, acceptance of and support for single women was incorporated into the community's social/spiritual/sensual covenant.

A Christian social ethic like Niebuhr's that maintains sensuality as mainly a matter of personal, individual, spiritual needs is helpfully broadened by some of the assumptions in the Father Divine movement. The Divine movement demonstrated that even the intimacy of interpersonal sensual dynamics can be directly related to a divinely inspired mission of social justice. At the same time, Niebuhr's ideas about deification and sensuality provide a necessary critique of the Father Divine movement. Women's deification of a man involving sensual relations can feed his unbridled egotism and serve up the opportunity for autocratic control and possibly sexual exploitation of women.

A liberative social vision for linking sensuality and human freedom is found neither within Niebuhr's ideas nor the religiosity of the angels in the Divine movement. Yet jointly analyzing their contrasting perspectives is thought provoking for the task of constructing a liberative social ethic. One is compelled to contemplate a social ethic that stresses the expression of poor women's sexual/sensual power as a freeing form of empowerment and a potential resource for social change. Perhaps the true conditions of freedom from social subjugation for poor women and all subordinated groups must allow for "holy" expressions of sexual sensuality (though certainly not tethered to an autocratic male deity). Clearly, basic rights related to women's sexuality (including sensuality) should be added as criteria for measuring freedom in a liberative Christian social ethic, along with an interrogation of how the public protects against or endorses sexual violations of them.

To develop liberative Christian social ethics, Niebuhr's universalizing assertions about human pride, sin, and self-interested egotism need to be amended and challenged as they are utilized. Inspiration for a liberative ethical vision for society can be found in Niebuhr's courage to address contemporary social problems within the heart of his intellectual work on universal moral ideals. Inspiration for a liberative method is also found in confronting some of the limitations of his views. Particular ideas and experiences provide such expansion and correctives, as in: Petry's fiction, the protests about socioeconomic injustice offered by the 1930s Christian leaders of the Harlem YWCA, the circumstances of domestics at the "slave market" and in the homes of their employers, and perhaps even in some of the sociopolitical/spiritual/sensual leadership of Divine movement angels like Faithful Mary. The particular ideas and experiences of these Harlem community members function as more than mere supplements to Niebuhr. They independently generate ideas that can be resources for Christian social ethics.

In its critical relationship to the culture, for example, a liberationist ethic should include complex approaches to social dissent, like the oppositional work of struggling against socioeconomic injustice offered by the 1930s Christian leaders of the Harlem YWCA who separated themselves off from *and* engaged the culture. A liberationist method for Christian social ethics must incorporate "space" to conceptually pay attention to how oppressed community members, like those leaders, identify and confront oppressive realities. Conceptually paying attention to their ideas and experiences of resistance provides a kind of birthing space, like the 1930s Harlem YWCA did. Practically, for the YWCA, such space helped to generate courage to cope with, name, and resist destructive realities. For social ethics, birthing spaces of analytically paying attention to their stories helps to generate authentic knowledge of community sources and provide space to think about a wide range of ideas to help conceptualize what is needed for progressive social change.

A liberationist Christian social ethic should also be conceived in a way that recognizes exploitative conditions like those faced by the black women domestics, but appreciates acts of resistance too, like the gathering at Abyssinian Baptist Church during this period for a mass meeting of over three hundred people to demand rights for household workers.[110] This recognition allows for a complicated view of community members like the black domestics, as both victims and resisters of exploitation. The efforts by any whites, including Jewish women leaders who opposed practices at the "slave markets," are also a crucial source for learning about resistance efforts within the communities of those perpetrating exploitation.[111] Taking note of their oppositional efforts can help to counter the development of a Christian ethic that reinforces certain racial/ethnic prejudices as it attempts to dislodge others. From these examples, a communal ethic emerges that has differing, particular responsibilities for resistance to injustice. Producing this resistance could mean that one must take pride, mute one's pride, create space to find one's pride, or repent for one's pridefulness. The choice depends upon the moral context of communally reinforced power relations.

Reliance upon such guidance from specific Harlem women and their sociohistorical circumstances does not negate the need for universal moral claims. In a liberative method of developing Christian social ethics, more consideration has to be given to how universal moral claims can be included without disengaging them from particular moral concerns.

Chapter Two

Terms

Feminist/Womanist Ethics and Sexual Violation

It is not enough to broaden the sources of knowledge that count as significant for developing liberative Christian social ethics. The very tools of analysis must be drawn from the same, broadened understanding of social context as well. Formulating Christian ethics in the last chapter by decentering Niebuhr's ideas illustrated how creative possibilities can be generated when "great thinkers" are conceptualized as nonexclusive and contextual resources. There is an opportunity to discover more such possibilities through further experiments in assessing ethical responses to social problems. Could some of the specialized terminology utilized by scholars of Christian ethics be constructively reinterpreted by continuing to listen to stories about and by women engaged in struggle?

Besides taking account of the details in the interaction between community contexts and the claims of Christian social ethics, basic conceptual tools need to be revisited. The terms that name ethical concerns as well as the assumptions at the core of the Christian message greatly influence the process of creating a coherent ethical vision. In this chapter, I introduce basic conceptual terms for ethical ideas by placing them in dialogue with a concrete social problem: the sexual violation of contemporary women. Here a dialogical approach not only helps to specify a liberative method for developing Christian social ethics, but, perhaps more importantly, also explores the potential for getting help from scholarly resources in Christian ethics on a single urgent problem in varied contemporary settings. Basic terms in Christian social ethics are clarified or challenged through stories about the public consequences for individual women that sexual violation brings.

Racial dynamics that exist within public responses to sexual violation should impact articulation of social ethics related to public practices, but exactly how should it impact the discussion of ethics? What shifts in the conceptualization of Christian social ethics when its terms are applied to differing social contexts of sexual violation? Niebuhr's Christian ethical approach continues to be relevant to social issues in contemporary contexts, but I want to move beyond some of the limitations of his liberal vision. Feminist and womanist religious scholars offer more useful analyses of power relations for a liberative Christian ethic that is responsive to a range of settings where sexual violation has occurred.

Which Terms?

Interrogating the connection between particular and universal moral concerns is my major conceptual focus. This interrogation involves an examination of what it means for Christians to identify particular moral concerns as well as universal moral concerns when reflecting upon some of the circumstances surrounding the sexual violation of women. Particular moral concerns may include dynamics within an incident of sexual violation or surrounding issues of racism that arise in certain institutional practices where that violation has occurred. Moral concerns related to the particular details of the incident need to be considered together with universal moral concerns such as the woman's entitlement to basic human dignity and respect that fosters her sense of well-being in everyday life. Particular moral concerns can seem volatile and dependent upon varying circumstances. Universal ones seem like stable, unifying concerns that are completely independent from messy particularities. As Christians transform the ethical principles rooted in traditions of faith into daily actions that help to shape our society, exactly how is the link made between individual (particular) concerns and common (universal) ones?

When inviting discussion of universal Christian moral concerns, I hasten to reiterate my awareness that there is an extensive historical legacy of Christians violently imposing their beliefs on Jews, Muslims, and various indigenous populations who were practicing their own religious traditions before encountering Christians. This widespread legacy of coercion has included an assertion of the universality of Christianity for everyone, everywhere, interpreted to mean Christian superiority over other religions. This sense of superiority has justified Christian subjugation and even extermination of peoples. As we discuss the relationship between universal moral concerns and particular ones, remember that my focus on universal moral concerns for Christians probes beliefs about moral obligations that Christians might share in common. My inquiry is concerned with those moral beliefs that Christians might bring to the table of our religiously pluralistic world when reflecting upon the problem of sexual violation that is part of our shared communal life.

What Kind of Sexual Violation and Public Practices?

My understanding of sexual violation includes any unwanted, invasive contact with a woman's genitals, and any sexual act that she is coerced to perform or that is coercively performed on her body. My discussion highlights public practices surrounding sexual violation, by which I mean incidents where state officials play a key role either in the perpetration of the violation or in decision making about redress in the wake of its occurrence. In addition, the cases that I have chosen are public because they draw our attention to discussions that take place in response to incidents of sexual violation within public life, such as within the media, the courts, or official investigations by government agencies.[1]

Basic Goals of Christian Social Ethics

To begin with, ethics, particularly social ethics, is a normative project. Its major purpose is not only to analyze existing practices that inhibit and assault the social and spiritual well-being of persons, but also to specify how those practices should be transformed to provide or support socially just and spiritually nurturing relations among us. Attention to how we generate public perceptions of the moral and spiritual worth of women in conjunction with public practices that sanction their sexual abuse, assault, and harassment is especially salient in developing social ethics. In the situations of sexual violation described below, intimate, private aspects of women's selves are inescapably linked to public responses. This subject has a comprehensive quality, requiring consideration of private and public spheres, individual rights, and social relationships. The subject of sexual violation and its attendant public practices, therefore, provides a useful and rigorous test of the extent to which human dignity is a genuine social value within our communities.

Yet even when a close examination of this process of generating social values occurs, the ethical task remains unfinished. For some, it seems only natural (and not cynical) to conclude that the sexual violation of women may be unavoidable in a society like the United States with many diverse and conflicting cultural values. Social ethics should include analyses of how and why such viewpoints embracing the inevitability of the sexual violation of women seem to "make sense" and must also incorporate an alternative conclusion. It should offer a vision of what should be done to reduce the prevalence of sexual violation in our society.

If one hears a stranger announce that she or he is about to describe the Christian ethical perspective on an issue concerned with gender, sexual violation, and the public moral life of our society, it is impossible to predict which Christian viewpoint will be presented. Some may invoke their Christian faith as condemning sexual abuse by adult men of boys and girls under the age of ten, but assert that girls who are adolescents and teenagers can be temptresses with adult men, as in scriptural depictions of women's nature. When "things go too far" the girls make complaints of sexual abuse that are not legitimate, or in which they share some of the blame for behaving sinfully.[2] Other Christians would be diametrically opposed to any such victim-blaming distinctions and insist upon holding the perpetrator responsible in all cases for sexually violating God's precious child, whatever age the victimized person might be.

Similarly, for some Christians, a husband's sexual coercion of his wife, while wrong, should not be labeled a criminal act, nor should punishment for this behavior be pursued through the criminal justice system. Proponents of this view may explain that biblical passages about male headship in marriage and the requirement of obedience by wives to husbands make coercive sexual relations between them a problem of a husband needing to receive proper Christian guidance about handling his authority in an appropriate, responsible manner. Other Christians label any form that a husband's sexual coercion of his wife might take as a breach of the mutual covenant that forms the basis of Christian marriage, a crime against civil society that must be prosecuted by public officials, and an abrogation of a woman's basic human rights.

The proliferation of provocative, disparate articulations of Christian moral views creates confusion, and such divergent articulations seem to be especially abundant in discussions where gender, sexual violation, public scrutiny, and regulation are at issue. In a primary way, the confusion centers upon how to distinguish rudimentary, universal understandings of Christian moral positions from particular tangents, ideologies, or situational interpretations of Christian morality. A common understanding of the foundations of Christian social ethics and of the core Christian beliefs that support it cannot be taken for granted.

The word "Christian" marks social ethics as originating from a Christian faith commitment that can never simply be a matter of private spiritual introspection. As Christian social ethicist John C. Bennett pointed out, "We can start with the assumption that God is concerned about the public life of humanity and not only about the inner, private life of individuals."[3] For Christians, this necessitates an acknowledgement of ethics as constitutive of God's claim on and concern with each Christian's participation in the collective life of society—in their everyday decisions and interactions. It means relinquishing any contentment with merely being a social critic who decries the cynical acceptance of sexual assault and harassment of women, offering useful alternatives to that acceptance, but maintaining a detached, dispassionate stance.

Doing Christian social ethics also involves a process of discernment that is profoundly informed by the Bible and complex traditions of thought and action that have helped to produce that sacred text. The layers of moral meaning that one engages when identifying her or his work as Christian social ethics are weighted with biblical interpretations and an entire legacy of human activities that have borne the label of Christianity throughout history. Critical reflection on these traditions is necessary, and entails specific moral judgments about the actions and doctrines within that legacy. Most importantly, the mission and ministry of Jesus Christ that the traditions in the gospels identify are the core reference point for Christians and stimulate a commitment to persevere in justice-making, spirit-nurturing ethical work.

The gospels focus on how God's presence is located within human history and in a particular human body. This historical specificity, together with attention to how the lifework of Jesus concentrated on the concrete concerns of people in his community, makes Christianity an intrinsically materialist faith tradition. This tradition, where Jesus taught his followers to pray a prayer that petitions for "our daily bread" and performed many healing miracles of male and female bodies, is concerned with material realities of everyday survival and bodily wholeness.

Moreover, the material reality of the crucifixion of Jesus by ancient Roman authorities was an unmistakably brutal form of bodily torture and execution usually reserved for lower classes, such as slaves.[4] The public display of such brutality was a political tool that the Romans used to send a message to rebellious Jews that they are "no better than a slave population."[5] The gospel, with its culmination in the resurrection of Jesus that defiantly responds to this political execution, directs Christians toward a recognition of, and struggle against, public practices of state terror and humiliation, especially ones that reinforce social hierarchy and marginalization.

Political concerns in these pivotal events within the gospel narrative are fundamental for Christian faith and draw attention to abuse of power by the state. When Jesus' rebellious ideas and actions defied the constraints of his Jewish social identity, he became threatening to the power and authority of the rulers, and he was tortured and executed. The resurrection event manifests the transmission of miraculous, intervening, divine power. Collectively, these actions in the gospel story constitute political responses that take place (or intervene) in the particular circumstances of human history. This gospel tradition can guide Christians in the "incarnation" of political values and struggle against conditions that support the sexual violation of women, including public practices of the state.

Finally, and perhaps most importantly, this Christian social ethics work of critical reflection and social confrontation can never be adequately carried out as a solitary journey but must be waged within and through some form of Christian faith community that holds one another accountable and gives one another support.

Feminist/Womanist Christian Social Ethics: Embodied and Liberative

The many details of a Christian faith–based, ethical approach to challenging sexual violation require elaboration. Typically an inquiry in the field of ethics would concentrate on structuring and setting normative priorities to sort out the competing moral issues and address the destructive social patterns that perpetuate the problem. The moral priorities might be considered in one of the following two ways:

1. Are universal understandings about the nature and consequences of sexual violation needed that will transcend the particularities of the gender, race/ethnicity, socioeconomic class, sexual orientation, or national origin of the perpetrator and the victim? Is it indeed necessary to transcend such a particularistic focus for claims about sexual violation to be significant as one develops Christian social ethics?

2. Should we focus primarily upon understanding the particular circumstances within each case and abandon any claims about the universal significance of an individual woman's trauma? If so, we would assume that the extent and circumstances of violation in each case determine the appropriate ethical response and accordingly devise a situational Christian social ethic.

A feminist approach to liberative Christian social ethics embraces the importance of the moral concerns and questions that both of these approaches raise, but it eschews the false dichotomies that are presumed when they represent the universal as pitted against the particular. Feminist ethics rejects a rationalistic approach that attempts to impartially sort out moral problems into rigidly divided either/or categories of norms. Finally, a feminist method is dismissive of an ethical inquiry that would, in any way, be focused upon making additions to a moral lexicon of principles abstracted from their pragmatic implications for the everyday realities of life.

As Christian feminist social ethicist Beverly Harrison writes, "In the dominant ethical tradition, moral rationality too often is disembodied rationality."[6] A feminist approach compels us to resist the temptation to use the pursuit of rational categories to avoid the sensual implications that are present in the material relations we seek to understand and alter. This ethical work requires a visceral recognition of the meaning of body invasion, body assault, and body-demeaning speech, for women and the whole of society. Knowledge that we acquire through our bodily perceptions must not be discounted in ethics, for it is a crucial source of moral knowledge.[7] Moral knowledge about sexual violation includes our personal perceptions—what we feel about this subject of sexual violation; the impact of violation on those who are victimized, including women's self-perceptions related to the violation;[8] and our collective, societal perceptions about the victimization.

Some nonfeminist Christian social ethicists contend that because of the power of sin, circumstances within a particular context can only be morally judged by a wholly differentiated, absolute, and universal principle or force.[9] In this view, the universal represents moral obligations that are, as far as possible, disengaged from, and understood independently of, particular cultural contexts.[10] Particular concerns are seen as representing moral obligations that are contingent upon specific, culturally defined relationships and are enmeshed in social realities that are laden with conflicts and difficult to control.

In contrast, most feminist ethicists would argue in behalf of an intertwined, inseparable link between the universal and the particular. Universal moral obligations refer to common interests and capabilities that should be supported across cultural contexts, and are given meaning precisely by particular realities within particular contexts.[11] This integrated feminist ethical approach takes for granted insights stimulated by a linkage of the personal and political arenas of life as championed by activists in the women's liberation movements of the 1970s.

Activists and scholars in these movements insisted, among other things, upon greater attention to the domestic labor most often performed by women, such as family meal preparation and child care. Insights from some of the earliest radical black feminism (of the 1970s) highlight how essential it is for any analysis of our political economy to include as a base point the double contribution of domestic labor by many poor women of color and poor immigrant women across racial/ethnic groups.[12] These women perform domestic labor in the homes of wealthier families for minimal wages and benefits as well as within their own homes for "free."

Current recognition of the sexual violation of women also owes a debt to the arguments that heightened public attention to the issue of domestic violence by late-twentieth-century feminists. Activists and scholars have opposed the categorization of domestic violence as a personal or family concern dissociated from the political agenda of the whole community that is supposedly more appropriately focused on public concerns such as the sale of illegal drugs on the street or, more recently, international terrorist threats of violence to highly populated communities. On the contrary, political issues concerning social power and domination as well as the use of terrorism are at stake within the most personal, intimate relations when women are abused in their homes.

As in these broader community struggles related to our political economy and issues of crime and violence, my approach to Christian social ethics assumes that any attempt to sever universal moral concerns from particular ones will most often create an ethical analysis that ignores or disadvantages women by minimizing the significance of moral issues tied to concrete circumstances in their daily lives or related to their bodily integrity. Therefore, to identify moral concerns surfaced by a woman's experience of sexual violation, one must carefully consider that particular context and gather the sources of information embedded there as well as the broader social context. While our bodies, together with our minds, possess the common trait of interpreting moral knowledge, e.g., helping us to perceive what is harmful, they are also morally labeled on the basis of particular social criteria. In practices surrounding the sexual violation of women, particular, socially invented labels assigned to their bodies are directly linked, and sometimes conflated with what is considered to be common, universally known moral knowledge about the women's worth. Such practices that reinforce the valuing of human bodies according to sociopolitical labels demonstrate why and how the particular and the universal need to be understood as interlinked dynamics.

For example, long before the tragic events in the U.S. on September 11, 2001, and resultant concern about airport security, scrutiny of selected airline passengers occurred that seemed to be linked to their physical identities. In 2000, a United States General Accounting Office study reported that for fiscal year 1997 black women U.S. citizens were more likely to be strip-searched at airports by U.S. Customs agents than white men and women, Asian men and women, and Hispanic men and women passengers, regardless of whether they were U.S. citizens or non-U.S. citizens.[13] Incidentally, the second most likely group, after black women U.S. citizens, to be strip-searched in fiscal year 1997 was black women non-U.S. citizens. In fiscal year 1998, among U.S. citizens, black male, Hispanic, and especially Asian passengers tended to be strip-searched less often than whites, but black women were more likely to be strip-searched than all other types of passengers.[14] In one comparison of females in this GAO study, in 1998, black women U.S. citizens were nine times more likely than white women to be X-rayed after being frisked or patted down by U.S. Customs agents. But on the basis of X-ray results, they were less than half as likely to be carrying contraband as white women.[15]

Yvette Bradley, a black woman who filed a lawsuit complaining about these practices in the Newark, New Jersey, airport, explained, "Government agents have routinely singled out black females and treated us as if our bodies were worthless. . . . They rub their hands all over us. They strip-search us. They prod their fingers into our bodies. They even make us remove our tampons and pads, while menstruating, so that they can examine them."[16]

Patricia Appleton, a Chicago travel agent, was part of a lawsuit initiated by over one hundred black women complaining about these practices at Chicago's O'Hare Airport. Appleton commented about her experience of being strip-searched: "I felt raped. It's one of the lowest, most helpless feelings that I have ever experienced."[17] She also explained the long-term effect on her: "On a daily basis I think about it (the search). . . . I have stomach problems, headaches. I am fearful of traveling internationally."[18] These examples are evidence of moral knowledge about the specific damage that the unwanted physical invasion of women's bodies can inflict upon women.

In her liberative approach to Christian social ethics Katie Cannon points to "the role of the emotional, intuitive knowledge in the collective life of the people" as a crucial element for womanist scholars.[19] In her Christian ethics, she stresses the use of "intuitive faculties" by black female moral agents and contributes analysis of issues of race that are too often left out of Beverly Harrison's work and other embodiment approaches in feminist ethics and theology.[20] Assertions, such as Cannon's, within womanist ethics invite us to value the perceptions of black females like the women who were strip-searched as moral knowledge. Hence one might recognize that even though an official search of all of a woman's body cavities by a female government official may not be legally classified as sexual assault or sexual harassment, the woman's (Appleton's) perceptions of being sexually violated should count in an assessment of societal injustice. Furthermore, I would extend Cannon's womanist claims about embodied sources of moral knowledge beyond the moral process of black females and black communities to include the "emotional, intuitive knowledge" found in the larger cultural context. There is evidence in this U.S. Customs case of a type of intuitive knowledge about the social valuing of bodies that is operating as moral knowledge within the "collective life" of people in the wider culture.

This broader collective pattern of intuitive knowledge reveals lessons about how moral harm is generated. It is a pattern that attests to the cultural reproduction of moral knowledge about the worth—the violability—of black women's bodies, of white women's bodies, of white men's bodies, of Hispanic men's bodies, and so forth. The searches were not conducted in accordance with the results. Members of groups proven most likely to have contraband were not targeted as top-priority groups for future searches.[21] Defending the Customs Service, Customs commissioner Raymond Kelly explained that "racial bias is not the policy" of the Customs Service.[22] It seems that no deliberate policy of racial profiling was in place. In the commissioner's view, the agency slipped into discriminatory practices when selecting passengers for searches because the "whole process needed more management oversight than it was getting."[23]

It is apparent that the commissioner was relying upon the notion that the universal can be separated from the particular when he made this response. He appealed to the public to understand that, in general (universal) terms, there was no bias in the agency's policy, only particular incidents (of bias?) that occurred because of insufficient "oversight." He assumed that if the understanding of policy (universal guiding principles) was disconnected from the particular pattern of actual, discriminatory practices, the agency could be seen as having avoided a policy of bias. But at what point should the agency's practices be considered proof of their actual policy?

Moreover, there still seems to have been universal (?) intuitive knowledge operative in the choices that were made about whose bodies to X-ray and strip-search. The staff acted as recipients and reproducers of cultural learning, and did so most likely without any malice.[24] It appears that the U.S. Customs staff just "knew" that in comparison with the others they encountered, black women's bodies were more violable. We could, perhaps, even take the perceptions of Ms. Appleton literally and observe that black women's bodies were more "rapable."

This example illustrates how the particular and the universal cannot be disentangled by identifying a universal principle that supposedly lies outside of the combined cultural reproduction of race/ethnicity and gender identity. It is quite problematic to make a universal claim about how sexual violation constitutes a moral problem without attention to the role that the particularities of race/ethnicity and gender play. These black women's experiences of body violation help us to grasp the importance of recognizing how body-mediated knowledge,[25] such as affective perception, reveals moral knowledge. This is knowledge that may not only encourage the perpetration of such harmful public practices, but also for those victimized by these practices, their perceptions indicate cognizance of the harm the practices wreak. Finally, these women's experiences contribute moral knowledge about public practices that should undermine any inclination toward analytically dividing the universal from the particular in Christian social ethics.

Integrating Universal and Particular Moral Concerns

Besides feminist and womanist approaches in liberative Christian social ethics, other ethical approaches recognize the need for this integration. When compared to how some theological ethicists, for instance, maintain a link between particular and universal moral concerns, the explicitly political goals of liberative Christian social ethics are brought into view. Unlike social ethics, which concentrates on social relations, processes, and institutions, theological ethics focuses on theological claims about human existence and nature, as well as human consciousness and encounters with God. Theological ethics often engages Western philosophical traditions that have influenced such claims in the history of Christian theology.

For example, using a nonfeminist method, Christian ethicist Gene Outka explains how Christianity is essentially committed to maintaining both the historic particularity and the universal significance of its traditions. In addressing the need for theological assertions that support Christian universality and particularity, he explains that for Christian believers there is a "fear of redundancy."[26] This is a fear that Christianity only succeeds in telling us what we otherwise might have learned from philosophical sources and thus trivializes Christianity's historic particularity.

Outka also identifies the "fear of esotericism," where one is concerned that Christianity merely tells believers that "*they* are made in the image of God, for example, rather than that all people are thus made," which trivializes Christianity's universal significance.[27]

In response to those Christian fears and in conversation with selected philosophical sources, Outka explores a range of Christian perspectives that cumulatively have a unifying effect on the relationship between the particular and the universal. The theological positions he identifies "demonstrate that it is accurate (if a platitude) to say that the task in Christian theology and ethics is to take historic particularity and universal significance to heart without becoming theologically or philosophically undiscriminating in our account of each, or in our attempt to hold them together."[28] This approach within theological ethics takes seriously the spiritual longings of Christian believers for certainty about the truth of their moral beliefs. Christians long to have the communal traditions that have upheld their beliefs, and in which they have invested themselves, somehow validated as true. It is Christianity's distinctiveness and staying power that chiefly enhance its truth value.

Especially when focused upon its relationship to philosophy, theological ethics tends to take on a dispassionate, disembodied character that would seem to have little use for valuing perception as a crucial source for ethics in the ways I have stressed. Outka exemplifies a highly rationalistic distillation of the relationship between philosophical and theological knowledge that Christian ethics offers the believer who is fearful about the plurality of thought that she faces when seeking to ground her moral decisions. It is a nuanced, cogently presented range of Christian theological and ethical arguments about how to identify the staying power of Christian tradition that can help to replace fears with (rational) moral knowledge and maintain the universal significance of Christianity's particularities.

Within this framework, the sexual violation and racial/gender bias encountered by black women who were strip-searched by U.S. Customs agents would most likely be considered as merely representative of certain kinds of historical/contextual contingencies that may or may not be taken into account by theological ethics.[29] These occurrences would probably be regarded as any historical reality within Western Christian ethics would be. To directly address the role of racism or the historical biases and exclusions within European cultural systems would be optional in Outka's approach and dependent upon the method and point of the theological argument. The political dynamics within Christian history, which have generated Christian staying power, are ignored.

In this approach to studying ethics, one is trained to treat social inequities of power and privilege that are part of Christian history as if they were intractable features of human history. One is introduced to abstracted theological assertions and philosophical claims and implicitly encouraged to ignore questions about whose interests are served by generating those ideas or whose interests are served when those ideas are deployed within a particular social context (like an academic classroom). When Christians follow this presumably apolitical method, they uphold practices of domination that can erase or trivialize the ways in which Christian traditions of moral belief have participated in the oppression of peoples.

Feminist theological ethics, unlike nonfeminist versions, does take certain particularities about historical and political context into account in a primary way. As Christian feminist ethicist Margaret Farley describes in her feminist theological ethics, an understanding of the well-being of persons "includes considerations of persons as historical beings, living in social and cultural contexts, identified with yet transcending systems and institutions."[30] There is a focus on "women's experience," feminist hermeneutics, and a "concern for the lived experience of women precisely as disadvantaged."[31] Farley explains that this does not involve a claim for the universality of "women's experience" in relation to human experience, but rather a challenge to universal claims in theology that have been based upon "men's experience."[32] The emphasis on women is a "strategic priority" for a method of doing ethics that is concerned, in content, with the well-being of all persons and all of nature.[33]

The universal and the particular are joined together through a deliberate, analytical strategy where the particular experience of women helps to give meaning to the universal ethical principle about maintaining the well-being of all people. In other words, women's experiences bring to the surface important ideas about what is needed to achieve and maintain our common well-being. The particular (women's experience) is a vehicle to gain insight about the universal (common well-being).

As I make the sexual violation of women central to the discussion of social ethics in this chapter, I share Farley's methodological goal for feminist theological ethics of giving attention to women's experiences. But as I discussed in chapter 1, I would differ on the usefulness of the category "women's experience" (as well as "men's experience") because it masks inequalities and oppressive realities within it. A critique of power relations, including those that inform women's experiences with each other, must always be the starting point for liberative feminist and womanist social ethics. The emphasis on social particularities as one engages in a critique of power relations reflects a liberative strategy for the core concerns of social ethics with social relations, processes, and institutions.

Drawing attention to the dynamics of social power, liberative feminist and womanist Christian social ethics can guide moral discernment about public policy. We are guided, for example, to reject an understanding of the category "U.S. citizenship" as a morally neutral category, singularly conveying a universal meaning for designating rights and responsibilities that are separable from the particular political biases and injustices involved when the term is applied to U.S. citizenry. Otherwise, we might become complicit in concealing how the meaning of this category, "U.S. citizenship," can be encoded with social stigmas and acted upon in situations like the incidents mentioned earlier that the women experienced at airport U.S. Customs offices. The moral significance of the universal category is disclosed through the particularities of the context where it is in force. Maintaining this link between the broader universal category and the particular circumstances that convey its moral meaning is crucial for a liberative social ethics approach. This linkage ensures recognition of unjust practices that must be changed and of socially marginalized persons whose mistreatment must cease.

Liberation and Sexual Violation

I have repeatedly employed the term "liberative." Exactly what does a liberative approach to maintaining a link between particular and universal moral concerns entail? Let us consider sexual violations against women who undisputedly occupy a place at the margins of social acceptance: sex workers on urban streets. Delineating a link between particular and universal moral concerns with the sexual violations of urban sex workers as the focal point can help to clarify the distinctiveness of liberative Christian social ethics.

Because a Christian theological notion of liberation has to be rooted in the practices of Jesus, so must the definition of terms in liberative Christian ethics. Any ethical examination of how differing moral concerns are linked must be approached in a way that reflects the gospel stories about how Jesus challenged specific social practices and attitudes in his radical social and spiritual engagement of people. Therefore, attention to practical realities of this world is not optional but at the crux of liberative Christian social ethics. Harrison captures the essence of this ethical vocation, explaining, "We are called to confront as Jesus did, that which thwarts the power of human personal and communal becoming, that which denies human well-being, community, and human solidarity in our world."[34] But precisely what is meant by the terms "personal and communal becoming" that is so revealing about the liberative content of ethics? How does one recognize the thwarting of it? In the sexual violation of women, how are the women "becoming," and how is that "becoming" thwarted?

During the late 1990s, the *Hartford Courant* newspaper (in Connecticut) covered an investigation of police misconduct that involved sexual violations of women who worked as sex workers in the city. In this case, the public practices of newspaper journalism shape how sexual violation is recognized as a social problem. In addition, unlike the U.S. Customs situation cited above—where all of the women were African American and, to some degree, economically advantaged—the Hartford case involved women who were white, Hispanic/Latina, and African American. All of them were socioeconomically poor.

According to the newspaper accounts, police officers were sexually abusing and assaulting "prostitutes" in the city of Hartford. Six officers were indicted in a federal corruption probe. Three others were arrested by their own Hartford police department, and others made plea-bargain arrangements with prosecutors on related charges. The newspaper accounts explained that, in one instance, Officer Jose L. Pizarro admitted to providing Officer Jesus "Manny" Rivera with a police department camera to take pornographic pictures of "prostitutes."[35] The camera was supposed to be used to document injuries of persons who had been victimized in situations of domestic abuse. Officer Salvatore Abbatiello confessed "to being present when Officer Rivera forced a prostitute to perform sexual acts in the back of his police cruiser. . . . Among the allegations disclosed in court documents are that Rivera forced a prostitute to masturbate with his police baton and that Officer [Michael F.] Basile forced the same woman to perform oral sex seven different times."[36]

In its coverage of this scandal, the *Hartford Courant* quoted Robert Panzarella, a professor of police science at John Jay College of Criminal Justice, who explained that in large cities across the United States, "There's ample evidence that sexual assaults by police officers against prostitutes is not unusual."[37] Panzarella seems to describe an ongoing reality of tolerance. There is a kind of public malaise that tolerates physical assaults by these officials as the assaults are carried out against particular socioeconomically marginal members of the community.

Even if the public considered police officers' sexual assault of women sex workers to be a problem, it would probably not be considered a major public concern. These sexual violations do not constitute a major public concern (*read*: not of universal moral significance for the society) in the way that they would, if, for instance, sexual abuse and assault by police officers of nonpoor, suburban women receiving automobile traffic tickets were "not unusual." Isn't it likely that routine abuse and assaults by police of these women—especially nonpoor, suburban white women—would generate much more of a public outcry against the practice and, perhaps, some legislative redress? In order to even investigate the extent of public concern about police violations of the rights and bodies of poor women working as prostitutes, this subject would have to be included in poll questions created by mass media news agencies, academia, or political think tanks. These established institutions often designate what kind of important, universal moral concerns are of interest to the public. The apparent lack of a sense of urgency or public concern generated by such institutions helps to sustain the devaluation of these women, as well as their continued victimization. This absence of concern is, of course, predictable because they are morally marked women, doubly burdened with the stigma of being intrinsically "bad" and blameworthy because of their sex work, and with the shame and failure associated with their impoverishment.

In the *Hartford Courant* headlines and the text of the stories, the women who were assaulted were primarily referred to as "prostitutes." The women's names were not mentioned, most likely because it is customary for the press to protect those who have been victims of sex crimes by withholding their names. Yet, even the term "victim" was rarely used, either by the reporters or by the official spokespersons who were interviewed about the officers, to refer to the women who were violated. In fact, official spokespersons, such as the investigating U.S. attorney and the Hartford city councilman who chaired the City Council's public safety committee, identified these actions by police officers as a problem because they violate the "public trust" and place "the credibility of police officers" in jeopardy when they testify at trials.[38] Based upon accounts in the newspaper stories, public officials do not seem to have named the victimization of women citizens as a central concern.

It should be apparent that when they are sexually violated women's well-being is denied, and, in the language of liberative Christian ethics, their "personal and communal becoming" is thwarted. As their bodies are violated, their dignity and worth are demeaned on a personal level (here, by the police officers). They are further devalued on a communal level because of the insufficient manner in which their injury and victimization are considered the primary crime against society that the police have committed.

The Christian liberationist idea of becoming is an ethic that holds out hope while it instigates a critique of the context. It reflects hope about personal regard based upon respect, including a woman's right to exercise control and choice about intimate contact between her own body and that of other persons. This regard should be operative (*become* true) in her individual, interpersonal interactions, even if the woman is poor, and even if she is a sex worker, but it is not. Becoming reflects hope about solidarity that should inform (*become* a part of) our communal relations. This sense of solidarity should evoke public outrage about the sexual violation of women, especially when committed against some of the most socioeconomically marginalized women. But in the wake of such violations, solidarity with the women was not clearly demonstrated through broad-based community actions on their behalf, nor was very much outrage expressed about their treatment.

While projecting a normative vision for what personal and communal relationships consist of, the idea of becoming also depicts a process of struggle upon which this hopeful vision depends. It describes an ethic that is not concerned with achieving a finite goal or with a place that one aspires to reach in order to be finished with certain ethical problems. Instead, hope for ethical relationships is only found in one's participation in the process of becoming a more compassionate society, in confronting the multiple patterns of denial, devaluation, and abuse or assaults like those produced in the sexual violation of poor women sex workers. Becoming is a perpetually unfinished task. The punishment of some of the officers for their actions in the Hartford case and the local press attention it received is not satisfactory for liberative social ethics. A liberative approach to bringing together particular and universal moral concerns compels Christians to engage in an ongoing struggle for sustained, systemic changes in the universal moral agreements about social relations in our society as well as improvements in the material conditions that help to produce these particular problems.

Finally, liberative ethics reminds us to ask, what are we becoming? Or, to put it another way, what are the consequences of our actions or inactions for communal relationships with one another? The hopeful vision and ongoing struggle have to be accompanied by a critical assessment of consequences for individuals and for communities, with particular attention given to appraising the treatment of those with the status of the white, Hispanic/Latina, and African American Hartford "prostitutes." This assessment of consequences also includes concern for what we have become, for the consequences we have come to accept. In what ways have so many of us benefited from the marginalization of persons such as these women? An accounting is needed of unearned privileges that result from being the ones, like those of us who are middle and working class women, whose lives are seen as more valuable than street sex workers and therefore entitled to better treatment.

My emphasis upon socioeconomically marginalized persons is a familiar theme in liberative Christian theology and ethics. Yet, the particular situation of these women in Hartford reveals what a bizarre ethic it is, and how foolish one appears when calling for it. Instead of cleverly phrased, bold-sounding rhetoric that bestows "radical" credentials and acclaim (in certain circles) to their authors, its application to actual community realities like these opens liberation theory to ridicule. It is difficult to even make the complaints of violation seem credible. The following responses (from a trial transcript) by one of the women who testified against the police make this clear. The U.S. attorney prosecuting the police officers questioned her first.

Q. "What happened when you got out of the car?"
A. "I was upset."
Q. "Did you report this to anybody?"
A. "No."
Q. "Why not?"
A. "Who was I going to tell?"
Q. "Why didn't you report it to the police?"
A. "He is the police."
Q. "Were you concerned about reporting this incident to the police?"
A. "I was concerned because he is an officer. Who was I going to tell? Who was going to listen to me?"
Q. "Why were you concerned that nobody was going to listen to you?"
A. "Because I was a prostitute and he's law enforcement. Nobody's going to believe me."
Q. "I'm sorry?"
A. "Nobody was going to listen to me."[39]

And later when cross-examined by the defense attorney for the police officer, she responded to questions about her drug habit.

Q: "And how did the heroin make you feel? Why did you take it?"
A: "Made me feel numb."

Q: "Anything else?"
A: "Made me feel numb."
Q: "When you were feeling numb, could you read?"
A: "Yes, I can."
Q: "No, when you're feeling numb?"
A: "Yes, I can."
Q: "Could you talk?"
A: "Yes, yes I can."
Q: "Could you remember things?"
A: "I remember just fine."
Q: "Just fine, okay."[40]

Testimony such as this can have a disillusioning impact on attempts to make the linkage of universal and particular concerns a liberationist Christian moral priority. This ethical strategy seems weak and unconvincing when based upon the treatment of a woman who was using crack cocaine and heroin on a daily basis and standing on street corners selling sexual acts to men so that she could continue to purchase those drugs. Her low status infects the persuasiveness of the theory. It is hardly a simple demand that, for all Christians, concern about sexual violation of such women by police officers and the women's subsequent treatment by the rest of the community is a standard for authenticating a Christian ethical commitment to human well-being and dignity.

Courage and vigilance are required to uphold this ethic. There are continuously spawning forms of depoliticization and elitism that can hijack it. The task of keeping particular, socially marginalized lives directly linked to universal moral claims in public ethics can be easily distorted by a commitment to denying the significance of how social domination confers entitlement, power, and status, and identifies certain people as undeserving of equal treatment.

The Challenge of Racial Perceptions

Some day Christians might uniformly agree on the need for ethical thought and actions that keep the particular moral concerns of an individual's everyday life attached to universal concerns of the collective moral life of humanity. They could even embrace a liberative method for doing so, but racism would still get in the way.

Issues of race and racism can position universal and particular analytical concerns as separate and oppositional categories within liberationist social ethics. Christian social ethicist Katie Cannon poses the dilemma for liberative ethicists:

> On the one hand, my task as a *Christian social ethicist* is to transcend my blackness and femaleness, and draft a blueprint of liberation ethics that somehow speaks to, or responds to, the universality of the human condition. On the other hand, my assignment as a *womanist liberation ethicist* is to debunk, unmask, and disentangle the historically conditioned value judgments and power relations that undergird the particularities of race, sex, and class oppression.[41]

She concludes that it is absurd to try to sustain this dichotomy because claims about the human condition are always mediated by our historically and socially located perceptions. Accordingly, she crafts a basis of inquiry that integrates these dual goals for the development of a black liberationist ethic.

Sometimes, in womanist ethics, a refusal to sustain a dichotomy between the "universality of the human condition" and the particularities of oppression is developed through focused attention on a single historical person or movement. In her study of the black women's club movement at the turn of the twentieth century, womanist Christian ethicist Marcia Riggs asserts that the movement "had from its inception an ethical premise regarding an intrinsic interrelation of the particular and the universal as constitutive of the common good."[42] The programs by the groups that she studied addressed the needs of black women and black communities while also promoting reform and justice in the larger society.[43] Riggs posits this movement as a model of moral responsibility that provides a "mediating ethic for black liberation with larger implications for the moral vision of the church into the twenty-first century."[44] Her project highlights the agency of this particular group of women (in the club movement). They function not as mere objects governed and disciplined by universal rules about what constitutes civility in society, but as moral actors helping to generate principles of common good. Their work exemplifies an ethical approach that establishes the interrelationship between moral issues pertinent to a particular community and the goal of attaining universal justice across communities. I incorporate this womanist method for formulating liberative Christian ethics here, but my particularist lens includes the oppressive conditions and agency of women across varying groups who are socially marginalized by race/ethnicity and/or socioeconomic class and sexual identity.

When using her black female self as an example to describe womanist method, Cannon raises a troubling aspect of maintaining this interconnectedness. As her formulation of the two sides highlights, even if one develops a liberationist analysis that connects these two sides, transcendence of racial and gender particularity is still expected to be a defining ingredient of a cross-cultural universalism. Meanwhile particularities of racial and gender oppression that are to be "debunked and unmasked" stand on the other side of this bifurcation of ethical goals that one faces in liberationist ethics. I want to probe the issues of race that are foregrounded here. They remind us of how extremely difficult it is to achieve the integration of particular and universal moral concerns. How does one transcend race *and* pay attention to racial oppression?

Our thinking about conceptualizing ethics is strongly influenced by a steady flow of cultural messages reiterating racial distinctions and racism. Common understandings of virtuous, justice-oriented attitudes often incorporate racist assumptions and make the task of speaking to the universal human condition seem like it should be positioned as the primary goal in Christian social ethics. A commitment to white superiority as a norm and standard for behavior within our culture can become indistinguishable from a commitment to universal moral principles that are unhampered by particularity. This blurring of commitments can occur in the following way.

Remember that a major feature of white domination (the prevailing form of racism in U.S. society) is denial of the importance of race in the distribution of opportunities, rights, and privileges in U.S. society. Often attached to this denial is, first, erroneous logic about the reality of racism. Within this flawed logic one denies the significance of race by making claims like, "Race doesn't matter to me" or "I don't care what anybody's skin color is." With such assertions one supposedly proves that it is possible for some parts of society (namely the one making these claims) to genuinely uphold the position that race does not matter. This form of denial logic arrogantly asserts one's own capacity to control the effect of social labels that society assigns by simply claiming to have done so. It contains an arrogance that incorrectly assumes that there are exceptional instances in which racism and common perceptions about racial differences do not actually matter in those daily realities that shape an individual's sense of self and life chances, as well as the broader societal arrangements of power.

Second, a special moral claim is built into this denial, namely that denying the significance of race leads to justice because it represents racial neutrality and objectivity. It seems virtuous to deny the significance of race. Maintaining this denial and the fiction of racial neutrality covers up the ways that cultural resources and persons not classified as white and/or European are excluded and devalued.[45]

Racial logics based upon denial abound in our society, and they can have a profound impact upon one's ability to integrate universal moral concerns with particular ones in the way that I am suggesting is necessary for liberative Christian social ethics. When ideas and practices that reinforce white domination masquerade as racial neutrality, this fiction supports the need to recognize universal moral principles as detached from particular ones. Racial neutrality and detached moral principles can thus become mutually reinforcing notions. One is erroneously convinced that acting justly means detaching concern about the universal human condition from concern about particular human conditions like racism.

When, for instance, we make black women's experiences of sexual violation the subject of our ethical analysis, numerous barriers related to *how* race is taken into consideration must be confronted. The following example from a collection of black women's stories of rape is helpful here, in part because the narrative discusses how race functioned within one woman's experience. Her account also broadens our understanding of how assumptions about the meaning of race should inform a Christian social ethic that adequately addresses an experience like hers.

When she was eight years old, Yvonne was repeatedly sexually assaulted by a close and trusted family friend, "Mr. Hatcher." A few years later, when she was a twelve-year-old, a stranger grabbed her, pulled her into his car, and took her to a deserted house and raped her. Yvonne immediately reported it to her family and the police, and underwent a physical examination at the hospital. The police did not pursue the case, even though her childhood friend who had seen the man pull Yvonne into the car was a willing witness, Yvonne was bleeding, and her arm was dislocated. Years later, as an adult, Yvonne was shocked to learn from her grandmother that no one had believed her story. She reflected on her childhood ordeal of being raped with this new discovery in mind:

> To me it really seemed like [the police] were just going through the routine. They didn't care whether they got the guy or not. I think it was racial. I believe that if I *had* been white it would have been totally different. . . . I believe that they would have put out a description of the guy and actually made a composite, and put on the news that there's a rapist out there in our neighborhood. I don't think class

> would have mattered 'cause in that little town, class and race are pretty much the same—I mean, you're either rich or you're black. (She laughs.) I wish my grandmother had believed me.[46]

Yvonne described the racist encoding of public practices in the police response to her kidnapping and sexual assault at the age of twelve. Racist assumptions about the insignificance of her complaint seemed to inform the moral judgment of the police. Those assumptions were not merely underlying ones. They emerged as the concrete public practice of white domination when the police decided not to believe her and to do nothing. (Her grandmother told her, "The police said that it never happened—that you were never raped.")[47] By making a comparison with what the police response to the assault of a white child might have been, Yvonne was able to imagine a more moral (nonracist) response that could have occurred. Information about the kind of sexist racism that was present is also revealed in Yvonne's account when she says, "Where I lived in the South, any time a black woman said she was raped she was never believed."[48] In addition, her grandmother's participation in the disbelief of her story prevents a mistaken understanding that only whites uphold white supremacist cultural values. Yvonne's credibility and her status—as a citizen whom the police are obligated to serve, as a child who was vulnerable and innocent, and as a human being whose body and personhood were brutally violated—were all muted by her racial and gender identity.

What is most important about this story for the conceptualization of Christian social ethics? Racism is not only unavoidable in Yvonne's experience of seeking help from the police after being raped. As mentioned above, too often, it also shows up to confer its notions of white superiority within ethical analysis, especially through forms of denial. Racist denial can result in the formulation of differing ethical conclusions about Yvonne's story. The following rehearsal of how some of those differing conclusions might be constructed demonstrates the malleability and rational appeal of moral claims that serve the interests of white superiority.

Yvonne's story only contains universal meaning. One way that a racist filter may be encountered in ethical inquiry is through a dismissive attitude toward any story, like Yvonne's, that touches upon the topic of racism or even mentions black people. In such a dismissal, Yvonne's discussion of racism is seen as a familiar and thus an ordinary problem with obvious analytical implications. In other words, Yvonne's account is viewed as "just" another case of a black person complaining about racism, and thus should not be treated as a conceptually fertile resource, such as a Lacanian post-structuralist narrative (a psychoanalytic deconstructive approach).

This kind of response commodifies African Americans as synonymous with "the racism problem." It thereby maintains the pretense that race and racism are not at issue when, for instance, whites are discussed or "human" violent sexual behavior is examined. This response may also reflect the "weariness-with-hearing-about-racism" excuse that gives permission for avoiding the centrality of race in our public practices. Racism is understood to be a "known," particular problem "for blacks" that should be bracketed (or shed) as one analyzes Yvonne's testimony. Under this dismissive conceptual rubric, the most important point of her story for Christian social ethics could only be a universal point that ignores race. The universal point might be something like the following: Yvonne's story supports the conclusion that the police can sometimes be insensitive and unresponsive to victim-survivors of sexual violence. Insensitive behavior by police officials needs to be challenged in order to maintain a civil society.

Yvonne's story only contains a particular meaning. Another form of evasion finds the particularity of blackness completely overwhelming when it arises in a story such as Yvonne's. The uniqueness of black life becomes such an overpowering focal point that it invokes a marginal, often pitiable reality to which one (*read*: the "normal and average person") cannot fully relate. In this form of white supremacist denial, there is no universal point to draw from Yvonne's story. Only the particularities of the African American community experience are of concern. Those particularities may raise important moral issues for blacks and may contain an internal moral structure that provides an exotic site to analytically visit, even for a prolonged study. But the moral structures and issues found there are seen as irrelevant to the framework of Christian social ethics, which is, after all, focused upon norms for the human condition, and the human condition is understood to be the most appropriate subject for universal principles. Cases from black life represent ethical parentheticals. They are exceptions to the rule and do not have the cultural authority to bring the rule into question.

This way of viewing black life provides a justification for particularizing Yvonne's story and segregating it from a discussion of Christian ethical principles. One could conclude that the most important moral issues embedded in Yvonne's story are not relevant for the articulation of principles in Christian ethics, but do convey information about the particular circumstances of African American communities and how rape represents an important part of "their" problems with violence. Furthermore, in this approach it could even be asserted that the lack of police responsiveness to intimate violence against black women should be studied further and addressed.

Yvonne's story only contains Christian universal meaning. In still another form of racist dismissal, issues of racism and the sexual violation of black women invoke a familiar theme for Christians: the need for charity. From this vantage point, blacks occupy the status of a perpetual mission project within Christian consciousness, and whites (and Europeans) are seen as the central actors shaping the meaning of Christianity. This consciousness often pervades public perceptions across racial groupings (including those of African Americans). Yvonne's emotional and spiritual longing to be believed and cared about in the aftermath of sexual assault becomes a useful tool for diminishing her subjectivity and erasing the dynamics of racism and sexist objectification that contribute to her victimization. She represents a needy black: a receptacle for benevolences. In this paternalistic racism, Yvonne's testimony signifies the universal "other-in-need" that must be helped. Her case is ideal for carrying out love for neighbor, a fundamental tenet of Christian ethics, and provides a perfect invitation for this Christian response. This is, however, a distorted interpretation of neighbor-love when it relies upon paternalistic assumptions that objectify Yvonne as a needy black. It feeds a belief in the moral superiority of whiteness and hinders a Christian's ability to recognize her or his moral culpability in silence about racist practices that sanction rape. A universal notion of neighbor-love is seen as the best way to frame a Christian ethical response to Yvonne's story; it can delete the significance of the particular circumstances of racism that Yvonne describes.

These are examples of sympathetic approaches that I have encountered in liberal and/or feminist theoretical analyses of society and draw attention to the enculturated norm of denying the presence of racism and how it deters us from maintaining a connection between universal and particular concerns. These processes of denial hamper the capacity to perceive how universal moral concerns are changed by particular ones. We become both unable and unwilling to grasp how the particular problem of racism modifies universal concerns about violence, the particularities of black life can shape universal concerns about the human condition, or the particular racist circumstances related to rape can alter a Christian universal concept of neighbor-love. This comprehension is impeded by racialized perceptions in the dominant public sphere that include the places where we communicate with each other about our shared communal life, shaping and contesting our social values: newspapers, books, movies, university classrooms, courtrooms, public policy forums, and church worship services. When discussing social practices that sanction sexual violation, we participate in a dominant public sphere that is saturated with assumptions about white superiority that can warp comprehension of what constitutes an ethical response.

My reference to the public sphere is further clarified by incorporating the ideas of feminist social theorist Nancy Fraser, who calls for recognition of multiple, competing public spheres, instead of only one.[49] Public expression such as the book of narratives about black women's rape that contained Yvonne's testimony, the courtroom testimony of a sex worker against a police officer, and the actions of the women suing the U.S. Customs department constitute "publics" that are in conflict with more dominant "publics." The idea of multiple, contesting "publics" usefully directs ethical concern toward a vision that does not wait for the problem of white superiority in the public sphere to be fixed. The occurrence of a just valuing of women that opposes their sexual violation does not need to wait for sexism and white domination in the dominant ethos of the public sphere to be transformed. By delivering a testimony that reveals assumptions of white superiority and sexism in public practices, Yvonne creates a counterpublic voice. Her voice (speech-act) challenges racist perceptions that permeate the dominant public sphere, which can even include the conceptualization of Christian social ethics. The articulation of universal notions of morality must take account of particular challenges such as hers, resisting the ways that racist perceptions make it appear virtuous to sever this linkage.

The idea of multiple publics that includes counterpublic voices in liberative Christian ethics can be helpfully supported by analysis of multiple contexts. Multiple particular contexts of violation provide a helpful caution against making simplistic judgments about the role of social identity in liberative ethics. The goal is not to seek out persons with certain marginalized social identities in order to assign them superior, virtuous moral qualities based upon their social marginality, like being black, being women, being poor women. Women customs officers participated in the violations when strip-searches were conducted, and in Yvonne's story, a black woman joined with white police officers in disbelieving her granddaughter's testimony about being raped. Eschewing any inherent ties between social marginality and virtuousness, liberative ethical analysis relies upon contextual particularities to help find adequate methods for resistance and transformation of the socially marginalizing conditions.

"The affirmation of particularity tends to a type of universality, universal accountability, that precludes universally true interpretations of the human condition. . . . Particular stories call us to accountability," feminist social ethicist Sharon Welch explains.[50] Yvonne's story calls us to account, in our construction of ethics, for multiple forms of affective and systemic moral harm like the anguish of childhood sexual abuse, rape, and white supremacist denial conflated with socioeconomic class prejudice. These particulars not only help us to interrogate any assertion of norms in Christian social ethics, but also to shape those norms so that they reflect concrete problems of social hierarchy and state sanctioned abuse of the human body that are of such primary concern in the Christian gospel.

Although it is not directly communicated as such, Yvonne's testimony also raises a spiritual need that should not be overlooked. Her wish to have her story of violation believed—recognized as true—represents a spiritual concern. Beyond a desire for personal affirmation of her suffering, Yvonne's story indicates a need to be recognized as a bearer of truth. To be recognized in this way involves not just empathy for her, but also an honoring of the sufferer (Yvonne). Yearning for this kind of recognition represents one element in a common longing for supportive connections with others and reflects a spiritual aspect of our humanity. Public humiliation, like Yvonne endured in the reactions to her childhood rape, which may be part of the dismissive practices surrounding sexual violation, intensifies this spiritual longing. In response, public validation of such experiences of violation must take place with appreciation for the victim-survivor's contribution of a counterpublic voice as a valuable societal contribution.

Lessons from Prison on Autonomy and Relationality

Since universal and particular moral concerns must be understood as linked with one another, and even as overlapping so that the particular shapes the universal, we need to be even more precise about *how* a particular context of sexual violation could shape the conceptualization of universal moral concerns in liberative social ethics. In listening to a woman's perceptions about her experience of being labeled in stigmatizing ways, there are insights to be found there about the terms for conceptualizing ethical social relations that extend beyond merely illustrating the meaning of those terms. Women's particular experiences of sexual violation can possess the capacity to influence the meaning of concepts that tend to be applied universally in liberative social ethics, such as accountability, solidarity, autonomy, and relationality. For instance, how might women's autonomy and relationality, usually considered to be fundamental to human personhood (moral worth), be affected by the situation of sexual violation within a U.S. prison? The highly controlled and isolating environment of incarceration provides a rigorous challenge for scrutinizing the ethical significance of autonomy and relationality.

To differing degrees, most feminist and womanist ethicists make adjustments to the traditional emphasis on autonomy in Western philosophy and ethics. They accept the idea that autonomy—one's freedom to make her own choices, especially controlling intimate contact with her body, and participation in formulating and exercising rights and responsibilities in her society— is pivotal for every human person. However, feminist and womanist ethicists are also likely to stress that our relationships with others are of equal importance to and thoroughly enmeshed with individual autonomy. Autonomy and relationality are both inseparable and necessary for nurturing and confirming personhood (moral worth). When supposedly making our own choices, our dependent relationships to other persons and to the natural environment are at the center of how we learn, know, and experience what is moral and immoral. It is through these relationships that we even recognize the need for the freedom to make moral choices and come to learn what those choices might entail. Choices about exercising our freedom should infuse, enhance, or maintain respect in our relationships with one another.[51]

But conceptual assertions about autonomy and relationality that are devoid of context ought not to be the only means for understanding how these moral norms guide actions. Let us allow the particular circumstances of women prisoners to directly convey the meaning of autonomy and relationality for liberative Christian social ethics. How, one might immediately ask, is it even possible for liberative ethics to be generated from the vantage point of the lives of prisoners? After all, the primary goals of prisons are to withhold the inmate's ability to act as an autonomous agent in society and to reinforce punishment as the essence of her relational connection to the broader community. It may seem like this setting would too drastically limit reflection on these terms.

Sexual violation perpetrated against women prisoners by state officials is, however, precisely the kind of context that ought to be considered in a liberative Christian ethical approach to autonomy and relationality. The use of state authority for bodily torment is central to the climax of the Christian gospels. Jesus' relationship to his followers is definitively marked by the conditions imposed by the state after taking him prisoner (which the symbol of the cross represents). Humiliation (though it was not sexual) was certainly part of Jesus' sentence of execution authorized by the Roman state. His naked body was put on public display while he suffered from a physically brutal form of torture until death.

In addition, the prison context is perhaps most appropriate for a liberative Christian social ethic that maintains women's lives as normative sources. Torture of women prisoners by state officials constitutes some of the most subjugating social conditions that we can generate in U.S. society.[52] If such conditions are excluded from, or insignificant to, liberative Christian feminist and womanist ethics, the assertions in this ethical approach about having a fundamental concern with oppression are severely compromised.

In the 1990s Florence R., a Latina inmate, was held in an Illinois maximum security prison for women called Dwight Correctional Center, where she was assaulted. Her experience of assault was recounted in a study by the Women's Rights Project of Human Rights Watch, which included incidents of sexual abuse perpetrated by state officials against women inmates in California, Washington, DC, Michigan, Georgia, Illinois, and New York.[53]

> Florence R. was forced to perform oral sex on an officer because, in her view, she had identified herself as gay. . . . The officer who assaulted her had harassed her with comments like "Damn you need a good man." . . . As Florence R. walked from her assignment to the medical clinic, Officer Z. pulled up in a car and ordered her to get in. He told her he would report her for trying to escape if she refused. . . . [He] unzipped his pants, grabbed her by the back of the neck and forced her to perform oral sex on him.[54]

On the night that Florence R. was discovered with the officer, she was asked to prepare a written statement, questioned by several officers and given a polygraph test, which she failed. After the incident, she was repeatedly harassed about it by some of the guards. Florence R. described how one officer would say to her: "Who's going to believe you? You a fruit loop."[55] She explained how "they made me feel so small that I was beneath them. They'd say 'Who you think gonna stand behind you?'"[56]

Within three weeks after the incident, Florence R. attempted suicide by slitting her wrists. Shortly after the suicide attempt the officer who had assaulted her came to her unit and stood over her with a colleague (another corrections officer) and made further "harassing comments."[57] The harassment she faced in the aftermath of the incident also included the assistant warden calling her to his office and asking: "Why don't you stop this investigation? I get more paper from your people. . . ."[58]

When Florence R.'s story is our chosen road map, guidance for the meaning of autonomy is found in the conditions of her life. Her experience of sexual violation is a revealing source of information about those conditions and includes layers of social implications. For Florence R., the violation originated in the way in which her gay sexual identity was stigmatized. She bore the stigma of being seen as having a sexual identity that wrongly deviated from heterosexuality. This labeling of her identity invited sexual violation of her by certain officials with power over her. In addition, her gender identity as a woman meant that in prison, where full control over her person (body) was understood to belong to the state, the offending male guards could interpret enforcement of state control to mean that her body was any man's to use sexually. Sexism in our society with its attendant images of woman as sex object joined with heterosexism to reduce her social status in the eyes of the male perpetrator. Social labels attached to her sexual and gender identity thus helped to determine the basis for how her autonomy was restricted by prison officials.

The meaning of her relational connections was similarly impacted. The relational terms between Florence R. and the guards automatically mandated interpersonal disrespect for her because she was incarcerated. Her incarceration was the result of punishment by the state, which, according to the court, she deserved. Yet these relational terms of disrespect and punishment seem to have also been informed by her sexual and gender identity. The guard's expectation that she was to follow his order to get into his vehicle and perform oral sex on him represented abuse and violation that he believed she deserved because of who she was—a Latina lesbian, "a fruit loop" over whom he had power. His expectation was not merely due to the fact that she was sentenced to confinement in that institution. Distorted understandings of her sexual identity diminished her moral worth and helped to grant permission for this abusive treatment that was added to her punishment by the state.

In Florence R.'s ordeal, these dynamics related to social identity are helpful for an understanding of basic human rights. In defining the rights intrinsic to personhood, attention to devaluation based upon social identity shifts ethical thinking away from a typical starting point of focusing upon the rights to which each individual self is entitled. Instead, there is impetus in Florence R.'s story for moving the starting point for an ethical assessment of basic human rights to the role of the community in shaping rights for its members. Her story demonstrates how the politics of identity requires consideration. The power of labels like "heterosexual" and "homosexual" is found in the moral value our society attaches to them, like the common designations of heterosexuality as superior human identity and homosexuality as inferior human identity. Such routine value judgments represent evidence of how the broader society contributes to the torment of Florence R. Besides the perpetrator's institutionalized relationship to her as enforcer of her punishment, a broader, collective, and communal process supports his heterosexist and male entitlement to abuse and torment. A solely individualistic starting point that would examine the moral rights and freedoms of the self is unsatisfactory. Diagnosing to what extent one individual can make autonomous choices and measuring the quality of respect in that individual's relational connections will be insufficient for comprehending the social process at work here.

Florence R.'s particular context underscores the need for a communally centered approach to conceiving human rights. Any attempt to capture the meaning of autonomy and relationality for personhood must examine our communal assumptions. Her story suggests that we might, for example, need to interrogate how the rights and privileges attached to heterosexuality and maleness grant moral freedoms and impact the terms for respect in relationships. Questions about how we grant rights and privileges related to maleness and heterosexuality would have to be added, perhaps even emphasized to a greater extent than questions about what freedoms the individual self should have. Such questions should be integrated into any evaluation of the quality of respectful relations to which the individual is entitled. Florence R.'s story shows how certain definitions of collective rights, like the rights of males or heterosexuals, rather than individual rights, are more revealing about how intrinsic moral worth is generated. Our understanding of those collective rights needs to be altered in order to conceive of rights and terms for human personhood that lead to the just treatment of persons.

Because it was not named or explored in the reporting of her case, I can only speculate about the role of race/ethnicity. The fact that she bears the social label of "Latina" undoubtedly permeated her experience of harassment, and may have been part of the subtext reinforcing the guard's derogatory reference to her as a "fruit loop." (I don't know.) In another case, racial bias was specifically named when sexual violations were reported by Amnesty International in a 1998 lawsuit against the Federal Bureau of Prisons on behalf of three black women inmates in Pleasanton, California.[59] The lawsuit was based on what occurred in the official response to a group of women inmates after they filed a complaint. In their initial complaint the women revealed that the guards had been paid cash by male inmates in exchange for allowing the male inmates to sexually abuse them (the women). The white female prisoners who were part of this group of complainants were immediately removed from that prison setting after the complaint was filed, but the three black women in the group were left behind for several more days. Robin Lucas, "one of the three women, reported that she was beaten, raped, and sodomized by three men who in the course of the attack told her that they were attacking her in retaliation for providing a statement to investigators."[60] As this federal prison example indicates, social labels and institutional policy can work together to subject women to racially biased institutional practices in the wake of sexual violation. At least in this instance, the women's racial labeling as black appears to have made them unworthy of protection from retaliation after they complained about being sexually violated.

The collective, coordinated, and systemic anguish that these abusive practices extract are proof of their immorality and also an essential source for formulating liberative ethics. Every detail matters. The anguishing isolation, and as Florence R. described, the sense that "you feel powerless"[61] are indices of the emotional and spiritual assault that she suffered. The violations of her body and dignity have an overlapping effect. Because of the subordinating social messages and stigmas attached to her identity, the incident of physical violation, and demeaning behavior by guards and the assistant warden after her complaint, she faced relentless harassment. These public practices created an institutional ritual of torment.

Such practices make the inadequacy of ethical definitions exclusively highlighting autonomy and relatedness within each person's state of being more obvious. Mainstream definitions (ontic ones), to which we may be most accustomed when utilizing these ethical concepts to discuss personhood, most often steer our thinking to probe what it means to be autonomous and to be in relationships. Instead, Florence R.'s story compels us to give priority to examining practices rather than the person's state of being free and in relation to others.

When a focus upon practices is neglected we can, for example, get caught in the kind of Christian hypocrisy that often surfaces in relation to issues of sexual orientation. In describing their ethical commitments, Christians sometimes claim to believe in the intrinsic moral worth of all human persons, but at the same time insistently support practices of discrimination against persons whose sexual identity does not carry the societal label of heterosexual. Because the label of heterosexuality is understood as indicating a human identity God created as superior over others, practices of discrimination against all persons who are not considered heterosexual are seen as justifiable. Discriminatory church practices can range from denying ordination to lesbians and gay men to refusing baptism to the children of same-sex parents. Might this kind of religious permission for discriminatory treatment even extend, for some, to support for, indifference to, or even the commission of sexual violation of non-heterosexuals, as in the treatment of Florence R.? Particular institutional practices of discrimination contradict Christian assertions of the universal equal worth of God's human creation, emptying them of sincerity.

Our practices reveal our ethical commitments. The story of Florence R., the treatment of the women by U.S. Customs agents, the Hartford sex workers, and many similar stories demand a process for evaluating ethical commitments that begins with a review of social practices. This review would ask: What kind of social practices are necessary to foster one's autonomy, like the capacity to control sexual access to one's body? What core elements should just relational practices include (even for a prisoner)? What social values attributed to sexual, racial, and gender identity are assumed in public practices that place conditions on the right of certain persons to exercise freedom and to be recipients of respectful treatment? In such an approach to conceiving ethics, we can better understand how community practices shape the valuing of an individual's or group's moral worth. Conversely, the valuing of an individual's or group's moral worth in a society can be measured by examining community practices.

Especially if the anguish of Florence R. is indeed paramount criteria for constructing ethics, surely, in response to her story, we must do more than broaden our conceptualization of autonomy and relationality. There must also be a change in our public practices of torment and torture of women prisoners, and withdrawal of tacit public consent for punishment of women prisoners that includes sexual violation by state officials.

Within the context of our communities, historically rooted and particular moral concerns are entwined with historically rooted and universal moral concerns. These intertwined representations of our moral climate can be recognized in situations such as the ones that surrounded comments like: "Who you think gonna stand behind you?" made by the guard to Florence R.; "I wish my grandmother had believed me," written by Yvonne; or "Who was I going to tell? Who was going to listen to me?" made by the Hartford sex worker in her court testimony.

In response, a liberative Christian social ethic enhances one's recognition of the range of interconnected moral concerns that must be addressed.

It ignites a commitment to find ideas for resisting societal practices that violate bodies, devalue worth and dignity, and treat dismissively the gifts, hopes, and struggles of peoples. This ethical approach necessitates an investigation of multiple social contexts where the violations have occurred and includes the following list of components.

Embodied spiritual quest. In a liberative social ethic, Christians are drawn into a spiritually evocative quest where one is attentive to the moral resources of our bodies as well as the moral demarcations they are assigned by society. Spiritual reflection is evoked as one is required to engage in the dialogue between general assertions about Christian ideals by authoritative sources and the varied social contexts of bodily violation. Embarking on this quest to specify the meaning of Christian faith awakens a spiritual consciousness to human degradation and invites responsive, faithful practices in daily life. Beyond an exclusive focus on nurturing Christian faith, the discipline of concentrating on multiple contexts that this liberative ethic emphasizes also has potential for fostering respect for spiritually based values in diverse traditions and places.

Seeking out the margins. A requirement to seek out those among us with the least in status, privilege, and/or material resources must also be included. This approach means a refusal to create an ethical vision that confers most value upon those whose personal identities are just like our own or one that names as its starting point some fictional, generic "universal" individual. It opposes the continuous mass media celebration of those with advantaged status, privilege, and material resources (which plays such a dominant role in shaping our social values). A feminist/womanist liberative ethic always seeks out the sociopolitically marginalized women who are among those with the least and makes the conditions for them primary criteria for ethical judgment. Again, the goal is not to seek out persons with certain marginalized social identities in order to assign them special, valorized moral qualities based upon their social marginality. Instead, the goal is to find out what is required to resist the process of marginalization and dehumanization that such persons contend with, and to struggle against all the forms this process may take, like investigating how notions of white domination saturate our ethical thinking and social practices.

Historical consciousness. Any commitment to Christian ethical practices must be rooted in historical consciousness. There are too many crucial moral lessons to be found in both the concreteness and limitations of historical perspectives to ignore them. An awareness of historic constructions of social repression is indispensable for a liberative Christian social ethic, especially since the central reference point for Christianity is the historical God-human event of Jesus' life, arrest, execution, and resurrection. In addition, to conceive of an ethical response, for example, to the societal tolerance of sexual violations of women, this harmful social practice must not be treated as if it is an anomalous or new societal phenomenon. Such tolerance is embedded and accrued through centuries of culturally dominant, patriarchal moral frameworks found within Western societies. Also, repressive mores like tolerance for sexual violations of black professional women who were strip-searched by U.S. Customs agents are weighted by certain historical understandings of socioeconomic class, race, sexuality, and gender that must not be conflated in our ethical analysis with those surrounding tolerance for violations of poor women like the black, white, and Latina sex workers assaulted by police officers. Historical consciousness helps to promote an accurate reading of the nuances in our communal moral relations.

Strategic resistance. Identifying multiple, particular contexts of ethical problems can help to clarify precisely what the work of living out universal ethical principles involves. This integrated Christian ethical vocation critically appreciates bodily/sensory/emotional resources as sites of moral knowledge and harm. Recognizing multiple contexts when crafting ethics can also aid in avoiding a tendency to simplistically assume an oppositional stance to values in the dominant culture, thus diminishing the possibilities for genuine accountability and solidarity. Without strategic consideration of multiple contexts, there is a danger of inadvertently appropriating the dominant terms that the culture has set. This danger looms precisely when one rushes to claim values that seem to be at the opposite end of the spectrum from the dominant values. For instance, in the face of repressive public practices that control women's bodies, one might be tempted to promote public practices that consider independent, completely autonomous control by individual women over their circumstances to be a preeminent goal for human personhood. This kind of ethic dovetails with the erroneous but popular belief that a sign of an individual's moral fiber is complete self-sufficiency. Also, it would be an ethical position that is irrelevant to sexually abused women prisoners and likely to overlook the potential in an ethic that highly values care and interdependence.[62]

Scrutiny of institutions. Strategic resistance is only possible when accompanied by a critical awareness of how institutions structure our moral lives. We need to find ways to identify the collective rituals of torment that institutions can generate and spark some recognition of how institutions shape one's own moral perspectives. Government, media, education, health-care, business, and religious institutions continually interpret universal moral understandings. Their institutional practices provide a way of thinking about and acting out how we value one another in the many particular details of daily interactions. In a liberative Christian ethical approach, scrutinizing a range of contexts facilitates solidarity across institutional settings with differing groups who are marginalized, such as the various groups of women who are sexually violated. Based upon this scrutiny of institutions, adequate criteria for addressing distinct forms of marginalization can be established. They would need to address the insidious guises that, for instance, notions about the superiority of heterosexuals or of whites can take.

But honing one's ability to identify the moral concerns found in social realities such as those surrounding the sexual violation of women remains unsatisfying. We must explore how and why we continue to reproduce specific social practices that are so harmful and anguishing, and in need of so much resistance. Social practices of controlling and punishing socioeconomically poor women seem to be quite popular. When such practices are carried out through powerful, national institutions serving the public, some form of liberative Christian ethical approach must be able to adequately respond to their morally corrosive and indoctrinating impact on the public.

Part II

Liberating Practice

Chapter Three

Policy

The Bible and Welfare Reform

I am not sure if there is a more instructive subject than public policy for examining how major institutions that the general public relies upon can shape our moral values. Ideally, public policy is a formal expression of the moral priorities that we have commonly agreed upon as a society. This expression of moral priorities involves multiple public arenas and is formulated as politicians legitimate policy ideas in public comments and legislative actions, the mass media disseminates those ideas, and officials in government bureaucracies implement them through enforcement of rules.

In order to investigate the moral priorities established by certain policy initiatives related to poverty and then sketch out a Christian ethical response, a small shift is necessary. We shift from thinking about the formulation of basic concepts and method that occupied our attention in the previous chapters to focusing on the development of practices. We move away from a primary concern with the conceptualization of Christian social ethics—such as defining what autonomy and relationality might mean and identifying criteria for recognizing the unjust use of power—to concentrating more concretely on how to develop social practices that liberative Christian social ethics could support. This approach will mean only a slight shift in emphasis because integrating practice and thought remains crucial for every aspect of liberative ethics.

Public discussions about how to create a national policy in response to the problem of poverty provide a fertile basis for considering ethical social practices that have a direct impact on women's lives. Certain moral claims about poor women that were made by public officials when welfare reform legislation was developed in the 1990s require special scrutiny.[1] Major changes in the nation's public policy for responding to the plight of people who are poor took place at that time. In the enactment of the 1996 Personal Responsibility and Work Opportunity Reconciliation Act, it was decided that federally funded public assistance for them would be terminated after a limited period of time, and no further assistance would ever be available again, no matter what happens in their lives and families.

In terms of the theory that might inform this quest for ethical social practices, Christian scripture is, in many ways, the quintessential theory of Christianity. It serves as a common base point for Christian theological reflection. At the same time, scripture is most fundamentally concerned with the practice of faith. The Bible tells a myriad of stories about individuals and communities who face challenging social and political conditions as they struggle to be faithful to God, inviting its Christian readers to participate in that same struggle. Therefore, the Bible offers a kind of theory that encourages—more precisely, requires—of those who reflect on its meaning a serious concern with distinctive social conditions and practices. The Bible, particularly the gospels, is presupposed as a primary resource in the previous discussions of Christian ethical notions of power in society advanced by Niebuhr and liberative feminist and womanist ethicists. This chapter includes a more direct exploration of the Bible's claims about how the use of power in society is accountable to God's power. Most specifically, Mary of Nazareth (the mother of Jesus) is the focus here, with an examination of her portrayal in the gospel of Luke when she makes theological pronouncements about power within what is commonly called the Magnificat (Luke 1:46a–55).

Detailed consideration of how Mary's message in the Magnificat might critically engage the moral claims expressed in welfare reform policy holds potential for liberative Christian ethics. The Magnificat challenges our thinking about the treatment of the poor. It teaches a moral lesson about wealth and poverty by offering a radical theological understanding of political realities that create these inequities. Contemporary implications of this moral lesson can be garnered by asking how these ideas espoused by the pregnant, unwed Mary in Luke compare and contrast with the moral claims in welfare reform that affect the lives of so many poor, single mothers. How does the depiction of Mary in this gospel passage correlate with the depiction of poor women by contemporary news sources and officials that the public depends upon for information? Finally, perhaps the ideas in this gospel passage can be a helpful resource for churches to evaluate the social values that undergird public policies like welfare reform.

A conversation between the social context of welfare reform policy discussions and the text of the Magnificat scripture furthers an understanding of how collective moral values are generated. Through this conversation, we are able to envision scripture-based challenges of repressive values expressed in current social practices on a national level (beyond state and local public practices like the ones faced by Yvonne and Florence R. in the previous chapter). Similarly, an investigation of the values expressed in contemporary social practices can bring attention to possibilities for resisting repressive interpretations of scripture. This interchange between text and context is also revealing for certain issues related to race and gender, helping to identify the influence of racial and gender assumptions in shaping current publicly expressed responses to the plight of people who are poor.

There is, of course, no concept of race in the ancient world of Luke that reflects contemporary U.S. categories of race and ethnicity. There were, however, dominant cultural groups and dominated cultural subgroups in that ancient context whose influences should be sorted out when investigating Luke's message to and about women. In addition, all groups in that ancient context were governed by a rigid, hierarchical system of social class categories, which forms another major cultural influence to be considered.

Learning from the interplay of this ancient gospel text and the contemporary welfare reform context involves following a series of clues, a kind of ethical detective work. A review of claims about poor women's gender roles and sexuality in welfare reform discussions instigates questions about how similar cultural and political notions may also be present in relation to the text of Luke. Cultural and political ideas about women are found in the wording of Luke's text, the social context surrounding its author, and specific interpretations of Luke's presentation of Mary. We must sift through some of these ideas and analyze the messages about gender roles and sexuality offered by this passage. What are the implications of certain interpretations of Mary that emerge? For instance, do interpretations pointing to Mary as a role model who provides restrictive messages about women's sexuality and their appropriate social role diminish attention to Mary's prophetic utterance in the Magnificat about the rich and the poor?

The arena of public policy provides another opportunity to explore what it means to craft a Christian social ethic that does not simply mirror some of the most dehumanizing and unjust values of the culture but instead offers a critique of those values and an alternative moral vision for our shared social practices. Specific features of welfare policy enacted in the 1990s exemplify the morally laden quality of that federal legislation.

Although such specifics are the endpoint in the process of creating welfare reform policy, they are a good, concrete starting point for our ethical assessment of social practices.

Welfare Reform Policy

Public policy is supposed to address social problems, such as the consequences resulting from huge disparities in our communities between the resources accessible to the wealthy and those accessible to the poor.[2] Unlike members of wealthier communities, people who are poor face multiple, critical needs due to their lack of access to health-care resources, adequate housing, education, or enough food. In the face of ever-widening social disparities, what kind of social welfare policy was created by the government to guide U.S. society into the twenty-first century?

In the 1996 Personal Responsibility and Work Opportunity Reconciliation Act (PRWORA), the transference to the states of full responsibility for oversight and administration of welfare programs represented a historic shift in national public policy, which meant a dramatic change from a consistent federal policy concerned with the plight of the poor to a disparately allocated state block-grant program. Moreover, as the title of this new federal approach to poverty indicates, people who find themselves and their families in need of emergency economic assistance are now met by a government response that focuses on their personal responsibility.

One researcher, Sharon Hays, for three years accompanied applicants and chronicled the morally disciplining methods of welfare reform in a southeastern town. She describes the intake interview for the welfare recipient:

> By the time we got to the long-winded explanation of welfare-reform, we were nearly an hour into the intake, about half-way through. . . . Our caseworker, Gail, was speaking quickly now, partly because she knew how tiring this process can be. . . . [Hays quotes the caseworker as explaining:] The program TANF stands for Temporary Assistance to Needy Families. It was called AFDC before, welfare checks, lots of names for it. Now it's Temporary Assistance for Needy Families, and that's because of changes with welfare reform. With federal welfare reform, over the course of your lifetime, you can receive assistance for a total of 60 months. And what happens is that you have a big clock that ticks. Each time you receive a TANF check,

> one month of that clock is used up. . . . Okay, that's the federal requirements. In this state we have our own system of welfare reform, and what we have is another big clock that ticks. This clock says that you can receive TANF assistance for a total of 24 months. And when you hit that magic number of 24 months, there's then a two-year period where you cannot receive TANF checks at all.[3]

These complicated instructions reflect the emphasis in the policy upon ensuring that applicants give up any hope (it is believed they have) of permanent dependence on receiving public assistance.

Few aspects of the policy are more restrictive and complicated than those regarding the treatment of immigrants who are poor. PRWORA drastically restricted immigrant eligibility for assistance by denying impoverished legal immigrants (who are not yet citizens) the chance to receive welfare and medical benefits (TANF and Medicaid). It was left entirely up to state and local governments whether to make their funding available to legal immigrants who are now ineligible under federal law.[4] For immigrant benefit eligibility new categories were created: "pre-enactment immigrants" and "post-enactment immigrants" as well as predetermining categories of "qualified immigrants" (e.g., those who sign up for active duty in the military) and "unqualified immigrants" (e.g., international college and graduate students). Immigrants who are in crisis and seeking help must figure out which one of these categories applies to them.[5]

For citizens who want to receive some assistance, the policy allows a thorough invasion of one's personal and financial life. There is a threat of criminal prosecution if one does not submit to this government surveillance. Hawaii warns potential recipients: "If you lie, hide facts or fail to report changes within 10 days, you may be prosecuted. You must report all changes in your situation."[6] Punishment is an important aspect in welfare reform policy. As the Hawaii officials also warned in a policy update on their Web site: "A welfare recipient who does not engage in the required work activities without good cause will be sanctioned. Previously a benefit reduction for the adult would be the penalty for the violation. Now, the entire family will lose the cash assistance until the adult complies."[7]

These government-established public practices presume that poverty is a result of irresponsibility. To help them give up their supposed irresponsible ways, recipients in several states must sign a "Personal Responsibility Agreement Plan" to receive help. For example, in South Dakota the recipient must read and sign off on statements such as, "You will accept responsibility for yourself and your children."[8] Full disclosure to the government of any personal support that one receives is considered part of the personal responsibility that recipients need to learn. In South Dakota, as part of their personal responsibility plan, the applicant must reveal all sources of personal support that they receive from "family, in-laws? Friends? Church, Other organizations?"[9]

The parenting ability of the person seeking help is supposedly a key aspect of that person's irresponsibility and is specifically targeted by this law. The Mississippi Division of Human Services explains its federal requirement to create a Child Support Program, under Social Security law and PRWORA. In one of the four key points describing the purpose of the program, Mississippi's Web site explains that the program tries "to help families become more responsible and support their children."[10]

In sum, this policy demands moral reform of the applicant. The moral reform focuses upon parenting, work, sexuality, and family structure. The Oklahoma explanation of the four purposes of the TANF program includes the promotion of marriage alongside work as a way of ending a recipient's "dependence." Two of the four purposes focus upon sexual reproduction and family structure: "3. To prevent and reduce the incidence of out-of-wedlock pregnancies . . . 4. To encourage the formation and maintenance of two-parent families."[11]

The rules of "welfare reform" carry multiple assumptions about deficiencies in the character, families, and behavior of those who apply for assistance. The rules presume the government's right to play an aggressive, intrusive role in correcting these supposed deficiencies. How did this policy come to be popularly understood as the best way to treat mothers (and others) who are poor and who desperately need economic assistance? What would it mean to evaluate these governmental public practices utilizing Christian ethical principles? How can Christian scripture be a guide for such an evaluation?

Scripture as "Theory" for Moral Interpretation of Welfare Reform

The Magnificat is found at the beginning of the gospel of Luke, after Mary has given her consent to the angel Gabriel about her participation in God's plan. In this plan, Mary will become pregnant and give birth to Jesus even though she is unmarried and a virgin. She then goes to visit her relative Elizabeth, who has also suddenly become pregnant, though "in her old age." Mary responds to Elizabeth's greeting with the following words:

46 And Mary said,
"My soul magnifies the Lord,
47 and my spirit rejoices in God my Savior,
48 who has looked with favor on the lowliness of God's servant.
Surely, from now on all generations will call me blessed;
49 for the Mighty One has done great things for me,
and holy is God's name.
50 God's mercy is for those who revere God from generation to generation.
51 God has shown strength with God's arm;
and scattered the proud in the thoughts of their hearts.
52 God has brought down the powerful from their thrones,
and lifted up the lowly;
53 God has filled the hungry with good things,
and sent the rich away empty.
54 God has helped God's servant Israel,
in remembrance of God's mercy,
55 according to the promise God made to our ancestors,
to Abraham and Sarah and to their descendants forever."
(Luke 1:46–55)[12]

The particularities in scripture passages like this one must not be ignored. Interpreting how Bible passages are relevant to contemporary realities is part of everyday Christian practice in most local churches, and takes place in Bible study meetings, Sunday morning sermons, and even when scripture is offered at a hospital room bedside. In such settings, the process for discerning the ethical meaning of scripture too often follows an overly simplified formula. When scripture's moral meaning is sought, its universality is most highly valued because it does not seem to be contingent upon the details of the present circumstances or bound to the particular ancient cultural context in which the scripture was written. But the cultural particularities that inform the scripture passages make a difference in the theological and ethical meaning of the text. Ancient cultural references contain moral import. For instance, what did it mean in Luke's sociohistorical context for Mary to refer to herself as the slave/servant of the Lord (Luke 1:38, 48)? A better understanding of the accountability, rights, and role of a slave woman enables a better understanding of what kind of submission to the Lord is being described here.[13]

Such particularities in the text may be regarded as wrinkles that need to be smoothed over when scripture is applied to contemporary circumstances.

They are erroneously seen as details to be ignored or interpreted by a church leader who dictates their "proper" meaning without letting the scripture reader think for herself. In this search for the universal ethical point that must be separated from scriptural particularities, many possibilities for intellectual stimulation, spiritual nurture, and social change can be lost.

This troubling approach to interpreting and applying scripture can also impair moral perception of current realities. The moral value attached to particular groups may be diminished precisely because they seem to lack universal moral qualities. For this reason, single poor mothers who depend upon public assistance may seem unworthy of being lifted up as the most likely group that Mary's message in the Magnificat would champion. Seemingly, these women and girls do not possess moral qualities that have universal value, and they are frequently regarded as a particular problem group in the society to be either ignored or brought under control through stringent policies.

However, Mary's insistent words in the Magnificat carry a message about God's concern for the particular lives and needs of the lowly and poor. Her message stresses God's powerful actions on their behalf. Furthermore, in the canticle, salvation of this particular group, the lowly and the poor, is linked with the salvation of the broader faith community of Israel. Christians might be guided by this scripture to judge the morality of Christian faith communities, and even of the broader U.S. society, by assessing their public attitudes about and practices in the interests of poor mothers who need public assistance. To authentically reflect the scripture, a comparison of community attitudes about and practices in the interests of the rich would also have to be added to this assessment.

A Christian practice of interpreting scripture with attention to particularities is also instructive for an ethical reading of the role of contemporary public policy spokespersons. When studying Mary's Magnificat, we become mindful that any discussion about what is ethically significant in this passage refers to the author's viewpoint, not Mary's actual life. We only have access to Luke's representation of this historical person and her actions, and the moral message found in the representation of those details.

In Luke, Mary is identified as poor. As New Testament scholar Beverly Gaventa points out, this can be substantiated, in part, in the fact that she offered a religious sacrifice of turtledoves (or pigeons) at the temple after Jesus was born (Luke 2:24), rather than a sacrifice of a sheep prescribed for those who could afford it (Lev. 12:8).[14] Gaventa explains that "the poor and marginalized occupy a major place in Luke's Gospel, which might mean that he deliberately identifies Mary with the poor."[15] Evidence suggested by details of the gospel text, like the offering of pigeons, reminds us that the account of Mary found in Luke is explicitly shaped by certain theological clues that were important to this gospel writer, like identifying Mary with "the poor and the powerless."[16]

The lives of poor women were also represented by certain individuals and interest groups in welfare reform policy debates, yet do not receive the same treatment as Mary in Luke's narrative. This is exemplified in the 1995 Personal Responsibility Act, the welfare reform bill that became law as PRWORA in 1996. The 1995 Personal Responsibility bill, the centerpiece of the legislative successes in the Republican "Contract with America" plan, was launched under the leadership of Representative Newt Gingrich (R-GA). Through the use of statistics, it assigned responsibility for violent crime to poor black single mothers and illustrated the role that race played in helping to enact the policy. The statistics were cited in the introductory section of the bill titled "Reducing Illegitimacy." This section explained that "it is the sense of the Congress" that the sexual reproduction of single poor women and girls, together with a list of "negative consequences" the bill offers, represent "a crisis in our nation," which this welfare policy seeks to remedy.[17] The proposed legislation specifically asserted that "the greater the incidence of single-parent families in a neighborhood, the higher the incidence of violent crime and burglary."[18] In an even more explicit reference targeting black single mothers, the Act stated: "The likelihood that a young black man will engage in criminal activities doubles if he is raised without a father and triples if he lives in a neighborhood with a high concentration of single-parent families."[19]

Thus, the U.S. Congress promoted the absurd claim that the mere presence of single black mothers in high concentrations within a neighborhood causes crime to skyrocket. There is no explanation given for how these mothers induce high crime rates other than their mere identities and presence as single black mothers. Why is it tolerable for federal policy to be based on such a dehumanizing, prejudiced belief? Why is it so easy for U.S. political leaders to single out this group of citizens to objectify and insult? Where can one find a rationale for federal reform, written into congressional legislation, that refers to the impact on certain communities and on the nation of a high concentration of white males in a given vicinity? For example, would corporate regulatory legislation assert that when white men make up the majority of CEOs and managers of firms doing business with Wall Street stock exchange markets, there is a high likelihood that investors will be cheated and robbed? The creation of statistics for the welfare reform bill that linked violent crime to single black mothers obviously reflects an arbitrary decision. Crime statistics could also be linked with the degree to which people in a neighborhood suffer from hunger, or with the quality of schools or housing conditions. Formulating a correlation between single mothers and crime serves the particular agenda of targeting poor black single mothers as blameworthy for social ills and then leveling punitive policies against them.

In another version of this strategy of using inflammatory, stigmatizing rhetoric, the cause of welfare reform was advanced by convincing the public that poor single mothers are all sadistic, abusive parents. Representative Newt Gingrich based his call for welfare reform, in part, on the notion that mothers who receive welfare benefits are such awful parents that their children would be better off in orphanages. To promote his legislative remedy, Gingrich used horrendous examples to represent the welfare problem to the public:

> The little four-year-old who was thrown off the balcony in Chicago would have been a heck of a lot better off in Boys Town. . . . We say to a thirteen-year-old drug addict who's pregnant, you know, "Put your baby in the Dumpster, that's OK." . . . Now wouldn't it have been better for that girl, instead of dumping her baby in a Dumpster, to have had a place she could go to and say, "I'm not prepared to raise a child . . ."?[20]

Here the speaker of the House of Representatives offered appalling images of homicidally prone, poor mothers and children as typical of persons who are welfare recipients. This reasoning justified punitive public policy for poor mothers because of their own supposed tendency toward violent and criminal behavior.

The values in this social policy clash with the message in the Luke passage. Moral lessons about the worth of Mary and of others who are poor, on whose behalf she speaks, provoke a confrontation with the moral claims in public policy stigmatizing poor women. The pregnant young Mary boldly prophesies about God's reversal of the conditions for the lowly and the hungry, issuing a disruptive challenge with her body, mind, and faith. Her challenge compels scrutiny of, and resistance to, linked repressive ideas and societal practices that are useful for a liberative Christian social ethic.

Women's Virtues: Which Women? According to Whom?

It is not an effortless task to arrive at an interpretation of Mary that is liberating for women and others who are poor. It requires a journey down a path that is crowded with subordinating messages about women's autonomy, sexuality, and spirituality.[21] Many traditional theological interpretations of Mary that carry these subordinating messages are instructive for examining specific accusations about contemporary poor women's lives. Some of the same issues about gender and motherhood are raised in both places, but with differing conclusions.

Throughout centuries of Christian theological writings, art, and music, Mary has most often been celebrated as a model of faith-filled womanhood because she exemplifies passive, humble obedience based upon her sexuality and spirituality. Feminist theologian Rosemary Radford Ruether summarizes traditions developed by church fathers in late antiquity who understood Mary as the New Eve because she is "the obedient female who reverses the disobedience of the First Eve and thus makes possible the advent of the New Adam, Christ."[22] In addition, Mary is honored for being a virgin. She is worthy of veneration because she did not make use of her sexuality. Again, when contrasted with Eve, who is blamed for bringing sin into this world, Mary represents "a decisive break with carnal sexuality" and thus with sinfulness.[23] For some, Mary's sinlessness means that she abstained from having a sexual life throughout her entire life. Therefore, through the image of Mary, women are encouraged to link assertions of their sexuality with sinfulness and non-use of their sexuality with faithfulness to God. Passive subordination of her will and self-interests as well as a lack of embodied sexual activity is considered to be the ideal Mary holds up for women. As feminist biblical scholar Jane Schaberg succinctly notes, "Man exalts Mary for the virtues he would like woman to exhibit, and projects onto her all that he does not resolve to be."[24]

Few groups of women have been represented by media, politicians, and religious leaders as having strayed further from some of the virtues attributed to Mary than poor women and girls who are black and Latina and depend upon public assistance for the basic survival needs of their families. On the one hand, this cultural backdrop of patriarchal Christian interpretations exalting Mary's moral status because of the absence of her carnal sexual expression is clarifying. It fills in some of the unspoken cultural assumptions underlying the charges of poor women's immorality in public policy discussions. It helps to explain why poor women's assertion of their sexuality through sexual reproduction has been branded by many as a contagion that must be controlled. On the other hand, Mary has also been celebrated in a primary way within Christian tradition for fulfilling what much of the tradition has considered the quintessential vocation for women: motherhood. But the motherhood of poor women and their financial dependency that allows them to stay home while fulfilling this role is debased and scorned in popular images and political rhetoric.[25] When sorting out these contradictory representations of motherhood, issues of race and poverty seem to be determining factors for deciding when motherhood is and is not considered a virtuous quality for women.

Media images can instill the idea that the term "welfare recipient" refers to an individual with a moral problem, and that "welfare recipient with a moral problem" equals black woman. For instance, a degrading caricature of a black woman shown in the early 1990s on a *Boston Globe* opinion-editorial page depicted the "welfare mother" problem. A drawing of several blackened figures grabbing for cash appeared on this editorial page of the *Globe* beside an article written by columnist Ellen Goodman, entitled "Welfare Mothers with an Attitude."[26] The most prominent silhouette in the center of the illustration was a female with an Afro hairstyle, a wide nose, and a baby on her hip who was also reaching up to get some of the cash. In this instance, the public is literally drawn an object lesson on "the welfare problem" and taught to focus on black women. The news consumer viewing this page is led to believe that "the welfare problem" is mainly embodied in black, big-nosed females who are greedy for cash like this one, and who sexually reproduce similarly greedy offspring.

In the accompanying article, Goodman asserted the need to teach "middle-class values" to "welfare mothers." She proclaimed the importance of telling "AFDC mothers" that "no, we won't pay more for more children born onto the welfare rolls." This contention emphasizes the assumption that "AFDC mothers" are morally flawed in a manner that "middle-class people" are not. Again, without offering any proof, this argument about the need to tell them, "no, we won't pay," presupposes that these mothers are instinctively concerned with gaining welfare benefits when they have children. How do we know that they are? Why isn't some proof of this accusation necessary? In the logic used here, since the women are poor, they are also condemned as inherently immoral (without "middle-class values"), which leads one to deduce that by their very nature, they are greedily focused on birthing children to gain welfare money. This circular argument traps poor mothers inside of a degrading stereotype. They can never be seen as innocent mothers struggling to care for their children, since they are believed to be guilty of immorality the moment that they are born poor and black.

The tone of this analysis patronizingly treats these mothers like children who can perhaps be taught to do better. "We," the good people, presumably the middle-class people, who are repeatedly juxtaposed to the "welfare mothers," can try to teach them better values by saying "no" to them. Stripping "AFDC mothers" of the same human proclivities that "we" have in relation to mothering and morality in the ways noted above solidifies their inferior status. Therefore, it is taken for granted that the rights and privileges of "our" superiority to "welfare mothers" include exerting control over them. "We" have the right and even the responsibility to tell them how to behave. Who is this "we"? It is those who have "middle-class values" to teach, those who in no way resemble that black silhouette with the Afro hairstyle and wide nose.

These ideas about poor black mothers confound a common stereotyped notion of women that Christianity has reinforced. Feminist social critics often comment that Western cultures, steeped in Christian influences, cast women in one of two categories: madonna or whore. This appraisal is based upon the rigid cultural distinction between women who are preoccupied with motherhood (usually revered) and those who are preoccupied with being sexually active in exchange for financial reward (usually scorned). Expressed in the terms of more popular Christian interpretations of the gospels, there is a significant difference between sinless Mary, the mother of Jesus, and the sinner Mary Magdalene, who many Christian legends describe as a reformed prostitute.[27] However, in the derogatory characterizations of poor women in welfare reform debates, motherhood and prostitution are meshed together for poor women. This merger could have something to do with the way in which the Christian-based, sexist dichotomy has been altered when referring to black women. Instead of madonna or whore, black women have had to contend with being labeled stereotypically either as mammy or Jezebel. "Mammy" is a label derived from slavery, referring to enslaved black women who cared for the white children of slave masters. Could it be that when poor black women care for their own children, they lose their eligibility for the category of mammy and automatically fall into the category of Jezebel/whore/prostitute?

To create momentum for welfare reform in the 1990s, some proponents of regulating poor women asserted that single, poor women and girls become mothers for the purpose of attaining welfare money. Representative Tom

DeLay (R-TX) pointedly explained his assertion at a 1994 Republican press conference advocating passage of their welfare legislation:

> . . . the number one issue in welfare, and that's the enabling of illegitimacy in this country. Welfare is a major enabler of illegitimacy, and current policy presents young girls with a terrible deal. They make the best proposition that a young woman under the age of 18 can make. If you'll just have a baby out of wedlock, taxpayers will guarantee you cash, food stamps, medical care, and a host of other benefits.[28]

The language of DeLay and other proponents of this view evoked the image of prostitution. The state "propositions" poor girls, who then accept this deal and go out and engage in sexual activity, producing offspring in order to receive payment. In DeLay's scenario, it is as if the State acts as "pimp," inviting the girl into this way of life, and then sees to it that she gets paid. Especially with respect to younger poor girls, it is taken for granted that cash is the primary motivation for sexual/procreative activity. Do these assumptions make sense to the American public, in part, because it is assumed that he is referring to black girls and such racist racial logic is appealing to them?

This caricature of girls greedily viewing the performance of "illegitimacy" or the birthing of out-of-wedlock children as an opportunity to make money implicitly asserts that some advantaged lifestyle can be gained by this practice. Congressman DeLay completely misrepresented the quality of life that the supposed "host of benefits" ensures. All of the grinding economic and stressful emotional realities that poor mothers face are expunged from the picture and replaced by a dehumanizing portrait of a girl in search of cash who has found a way to thrive both sexually and economically.

From the highest levels of government the sexual reproduction of poor mothers was represented as an extraordinary crisis facing this nation. President Clinton sounded an alert when preparing to begin his second term in office. He dedicated his very first radio message for the New Year (1997) to the subject of teen pregnancy. In this speech he warned that there was a lot more for his administration and the nation to do in order to make the American dream a reality for all citizens in the twenty-first century. He noted that "We still have some pretty big problems in our society. None stands in our way of achieving our goals for America more than the epidemic of teen pregnancy."[29] The ensuing references in the radio address to the poverty conditions of teen mothers and to the welfare that they receive made it clear that the sexual reproduction of poor girls was the main subject of his concern. Their sexual behavior was preventing the nation from moving ahead to achieve its goals in the twenty-first century.

However, Clinton conveyed a sense of hope and efficacy when he boasted in this same speech about the "executive action" he took to deny welfare benefits to "young mothers" who do not remain in school. Punitive manipulation of access to the funds needed to support the livelihood of poor mothers and children was seen by this president as an outstanding achievement worthy of so much attention in his New Year's radio address. His speech reiterated a familiar linkage in popular political rhetoric about the key social problems facing the nation. Crime, welfare, and out-of-wedlock births were collectively cited as the most pressing national issues, with teen pregnancy (a subset of the out-of-wedlock birth issue) described as the number one problem. This selection of references placed the onus on a particular marginalized population, targeting, in a thinly veiled way, poor, urban, racial minorities. In explaining what impedes the progress of this nation, President Clinton selected problems of some of the very poorest communities. He lumped together the problem of (street?) crime, the government program of welfare benefits, and the birth of children to parents who are not married—all under the category of irresponsible behavior in this nation—and designated poor teenage mothers as the preeminent problem.

When the president of the United States argues that the power to hinder the nation's progress rests primarily upon the sexual reproductive behavior of the most economically and socially disenfranchised group of girls in American communities, a highly distorted notion of reality is portrayed. It is precisely the depth of their social vulnerability that makes the girls such good candidates for this distortion. Additionally, the selection of their sexual reproductive behavior creates an ideal tool for shaming and silencing them as well as any potential dissenters from this constructed reality. Placing mothering behavior in the same context as "other" shameful behavior, such as crime, equates or at least directly relates the birthing and raising of children by these girls with the victimizing of others by means of assault or the taking of life and property. The connection with such criminality annuls any claims poor women and girls might have to being innocent members of our community. Most importantly, Clinton together with other leaders enacted formal regulations for their lives based upon these shaming moral caricatures.

Ironically, politicians succeeded in creating these regulations by furthering an understanding of a critical link between universal and particular moral concerns. They argued that the particular (supposedly crime-producing) motherhood of poor girls and women represented a dire threat to the universal moral concern of the well-being of society. Here, the linking of particular moral concerns with universal ones signals dishonest, political manipulation of the public to create repressive public policy.

Finally, the outcome of these public policy characterizations of poor women and girls as non-innocent leads one in a similar direction as interpretations of scripture that hold up Mary as a model of passive obedience for women. In both instances patriarchal goals of reinforcing male control of families and communities are bolstered. Some contemporary welfare reform advocates are less than subtle in their support of such goals. As sociologist James Q. Wilson explained in his testimony at the 1995 congressional welfare reform hearings: "But once you have created a neighborhood in which all or most of the children are growing up in single-parent mother-only families, you are creating a neighborhood with men but no fathers. As a result, the social control that all communities try to maintain is weakened, because the people who primarily provide that order, fathers who take responsibility for their children and their neighborhoods, are absent."[30] The absence of father-ordered communities and families indeed threatens traditional means of social control.

Situating the Need to Control Women

What about male control and authority within the gospel of Luke and within the social context in which Luke wrote about Mary and the Magnificat? To declare that in liberative Christian social ethics the Magnificat is a statement by Mary of liberation for poor women, without some attention to the issues of gender and social control surrounding that text, would be deceptive. It would make it seem, quite erroneously, like the problem of patriarchy is not pertinent to Luke. Moreover, the aggressive use of power by contemporary leaders making moral claims about poor women invites questions about whether there are similar dynamics within Luke's text and ancient context. As Bible scholar Jane Schaberg asserts, Mary "represents the hope of the poor, but she represents that hope *as a woman* . . ."[31] What are the messages about gender and power that Luke intends with this text?

To fully grasp the gospel writer's intentions in his depiction of Mary it would be helpful to learn something about the lives of the women who surrounded him. There are important issues to consider about which sources should be relied upon and how they should be evaluated in order to cull credible evidence about women's lives. Another obstacle to overcome is the task of locating sufficient sources of information about women. With the help of feminist biblical scholars, we are introduced to this gnarled pathway of considerations. They contain clues about the need to exercise control over women that is so much at issue in contemporary policy discussions of the poor.

Gender and social class were significant factors during the first few centuries of the Common Era in the Greco-Roman world. For instance, in the household, the central unit of organization for their society, women's lives were restricted on the basis of gender. In general, women were subject to the control of men. In the family, daughters were subject to the authority of their fathers, wives to their husbands, fatherless daughters to their father's male relatives, widows to their own sons. Female slaves were subject to their masters, including the daughters of their masters. Slave women were thus subject to the authority of women as well as men. It should also be kept in mind that most men were also under the control of other men.[32] Under the Roman Empire, Greco-Roman society (the setting for the Lukan gospel writer) idealized and tried to enforce a rigidly hierarchical social and political system.

What cultural categories do we use to envision the lives of women who surrounded the gospel writer? As in our society, the first century eastern Mediterranean included multiple dominant and subcultural influences. Isolating the key cultural traits that defined the gospel writer's late, first century context is complicated. There were Hellenistic, Roman, Egyptian, and Jewish cultural influences.

Christianity initially emerged in first century Palestine as a movement within Judaism and then spread quickly throughout the Mediterranean region, where many Gentiles were converted. A distorted historical understanding results from setting Christianity against Judaism in order to prove that Christian women had more freedoms than Jewish women. Texts about women such as those found in Luke are sometimes heralded as evidence on behalf of a kind of ancient Christian feminism and are pitted against ancient Jewish sexism. This reasoning is not only anachronistic but also erroneous. In the first century Christian movement, some of the Christian women were Jewish. Thus, for some of the women in the movement, a dichotomous view of Jewish and Christian women is simply a mistaken one. In addition, the notion of ancient Christian feminism versus ancient Jewish sexism preserves an equally erroneous stereotyped portrait of (the non-Christian majority of) women within Judaism.

Especially when sorting out social problems related to gender and sexuality, current mores in contemporary discussions of religion and politics have made us accustomed to constructing analysis in terms of contrasting dynamics between rival cultural groups. For example, at a 1994 meeting of the largest black Protestant denomination, the National Baptist Convention, President Clinton received a warm response after he quipped to his audience: "Thirty years ago, one of forty white births was out of wedlock; now it's one in five. Thirty years ago, one in five African American births were out-of-wedlock births; now over half. But the white out-of-wedlock birthrate is growing much faster than the African American rate. So we're going to have equal opportunity for all before you know it."[33] Though injecting humor, he appears to be demonstrating an awareness of racial inequalities. Yet to make his point he relies upon a general acceptance of the faulty assumption that race is the most useful category for moral analysis and policymaking on this topic, as opposed to, for instance, socioeconomic class categories across racial groupings, e.g., rates for poor people across racial groups could have been rising. The president reinforces a notion of racial groups as separate cultural entities that produce distinctive moral patterns. Moreover, he supports the view that racial groups are morally competing. We are trained to uncritically accept this compartmentalizing form of racial logic as a way of thinking about contemporary culture and morality. This training impedes an ability to grasp the nuances of Luke's cultural context that is so necessary for understanding ancient women's lives.

When focusing on Judaism as the cultural context for at least part of the earliest Christian movement and trying to ferret out information about the content of women's lives within this minority group, sharp contrasts are sometimes made between Jewish women and Roman women. However, this approach is misleading. First, this focus may make it wrongly appear that differences between Jewish and Roman women would have been more significant than class differences between women across such groups. Such a view underestimates the overarching manner in which social class determined one's status in this ancient world.

Second, some biblical scholars rely upon the Mishnah (codified around 200 CE) to describe Jewish women in antiquity. They point out, for example, that in Jewish law, unlike in Greek and Roman law, a husband is permitted to take the life of his wife if she committed adultery.[34] Assertions about the lives of Jewish women and Roman women based upon such legal comparisons need further qualification. It is inaccurate to assume that teachings in Judaism such as those found in the Mishnah represent values that are distinctly different from other Greco-Roman societal influences. As biblical scholar Adeline Fehribach shows in her study of the way women were defined in the Mishnah, this is a problematic source for depicting Jewish women's lives in the first century. The Mishnaic framers combined elements of Hellenistic culture, Roman law, and scripture.[35] Moreover, the Mishnah represents writings of a particular rabbinic school; the sayings of the rabbis in the Mishnah reflect their vision for their communities. These writings were attempts by leaders to respond to current conditions facing their community rather than historical accounts of those conditions. Fehribach points out that the Mishnah was compiled at the end of the second century out of a need by survivors of the Jewish-Roman war to reorder their world following the destruction of the Temple. She asserts, "What the writers of the book described was what they wanted the world to be, not necessarily the world as it was."[36] Only in later centuries did the Mishnah become authoritative or normative for the majority of Jews.

Spurious characterizations of black women, as in the text of the 1995 Personal Responsibility Act linking them with the presence of high crime rates, mandate a cautious reading of legal artifacts. Similarly, easy moral conclusions about women based upon ancient legal texts have to be scrutinized. When one refers to the texts that constitute available sources of information about women in the Greco-Roman world, one enters a context of "male textuality."[37] We must be mindful that the ancient texts were written by men in the context of a society where education and literary production were primarily male prerogatives. The texts themselves functioned as tools of control. Statements in these texts that limit women's autonomy should not be interpreted as representations of women's actual lives in antiquity. As feminist theologian Elisabeth Schüssler Fiorenza reminds us, "Prescriptive injunctions for appropriate 'feminine' behavior and submission increase whenever women's actual socio-religious status and power within patriarchy increase."[38] She, too, comments upon both the Mishnah as prescriptive, rather than descriptive, of Jewish life, and the relentless male-centered nature of its vision. The Mishnah defines a woman's status, for example, not in terms of "whether she may have sexual relations, but 'with whom she may have them,' and what are the consequences for the natural and supernatural order."[39] To gain a sense of women's realities, Schüssler Fiorenza shows how important it is to launch an inquiry from the silences when analyzing a patriarchal text and context. In this vein, she poses the question of whether the Mishnah's androcentric prescriptions could have been a response "to a social-political current within the first and second century that allowed women to question and undermine" the patriarchal social order.[40]

In these explanations about how to interpret prescriptive first century religious writings, a theme arises that is also present in welfare reform discussions. As in many of the contemporary claims by politicians about the sexual reproduction of poor girls and women, first century religious leaders also associated the task of establishing order in the society through the control of women and their sexuality. In both periods the sexual autonomy of women seems to represent social disorder.

Evidently, to maintain order, certain rules are needed to penalize women. In the ancient context, the prescribed penalty for committing adultery may have even been death.[41] In our contemporary context, those who are economically destitute will be treated punitively in relation to their basic survival needs because they have sexually reproduced children without being married to a man. This is supposedly done, as Congresswoman Marge Roukema (R-NJ) said, as an expression of "tough love." When pressing for welfare reform measures that were ultimately passed, she explained the meaning of "tough love" for poor, single, pregnant women utilizing public assistance. To keep their benefits from being revoked, Congresswoman Roukema said, they "must cooperate by helping to establish paternity in the hospital at the time of [giving] birth. If cooperation is not there, support is cut off for the woman."[42]

Control and Resistance

Even if there appears to be overwhelming cultural consensus in the community about devising ways to control women, there are contradictions and venues of resistance. Examples of resistance in the context and text of Luke can perhaps inspire dissent amidst the contemporary Christian support for the shaming and punishment of poor mothers. In studying Luke, it becomes apparent that even scripture produced in a setting with a strong cultural bias for the primacy of male power and authority can carry a message supporting women's power and authority. Varied contradictions about women's power and authority have been uncovered in the ancient Jewish context inhabited by this spokesperson/mother, Mary of Nazareth.

Beyond an examination of the rules set forth by leaders, creative strategies are needed to recover a sense of women's real lives in the ancient world. Early Christianity scholar Bernadette Brooten suggests an alternative method of doing research on ancient women that includes the use of nonliterary cultural sources.[43] Though first century Palestine is not included in her material, Brooten utilizes nonliterary evidence (inscriptions) and finds that some women were leaders of synagogues during the Roman period.[44] Apparently a few high-status women exercised a degree of freedom and independence in leadership positions. These examples among elite Jewish women challenge sweeping generalizations about the rigidity of patriarchal restrictions over women's power and public leadership in the ancient Mediterranean world. Unfortunately, there is little direct nonliterary or textual information about the lives of more ordinary Jewish women, especially those at the bottom of the social hierarchy, such as enslaved Jewish women.

Though scholars disagree about the average age of first marriage for Jewish females, there does seem to be some consensus that it was often between the ages of twelve and eighteen.[45] Females became eligible for betrothal after the onset of menstruation, as early as age twelve.[46] When reviewing this cultural information about the social context of the Christian gospels, I cannot help but be reminded of the vociferous calls for removal of financial support by welfare reformers of the 1990s that was leveled against poor, pregnant teenagers and those who were already mothers. Many of these critics claimed that poor girls have a need for "moral values" that only Christian nurture can provide. In laying the groundwork for what would be called "charitable choice" in the 1996 law, poor mothers were generally represented as a kind of moral recovery project to be assigned to churches.

For instance, economics professor Glenn C. Loury invoked the need for church instilled values when he testified during the 1995 congressional hearings that prepared the way for the welfare reform law.[47] Loury advocated the restoration of moral teaching in the black community to help stem the tide of "illegitimacy problems and family breakdown." Without this change in the structure of black families, he argued, "the behavioral problems which Moynihan first noticed thirty years ago will persist, threatening the survival of the republic."[48] Necessary moral guidance, he argued, could occur most effectively through religious institutions. Since he identifies them as the most promising source of help, Loury suggests that checks be sent directly to churches, so that these women and girls can learn to "change their lives."

Similarly, in a 1995 speech given to leaders of the Progressive National Baptists, a predominantly black Protestant denomination, President Clinton sought the support and participation of these church leaders in his welfare reform agenda by linking the entire problem of poverty to teenage mothers. In this speech, he pronounced to black religious leaders that it would be viable to cut the poverty rate by more than 50 percent if, in part, "teenagers who are unmarried didn't have babies."[49] The enactment of disciplinary public policies regulating poor girls and women was repeatedly justified with arguments like these by academic consultants like Loury and political leaders like Clinton. Denial of public assistance, particularly for teenage mothers, was supported by varied rhetorical strategies often using (manipulating?) black churches as the public stage for invoking the need to instill Christian family values. Yet so central in launching the core Christian narrative of Jesus' life and ministry—at least in Luke's gospel account—is the one with whom God found favor (Luke 1:30, 48): an unwed, pregnant, Jewish female who may have been just a teenager, perhaps only twelve or thirteen years old.

In Luke's ancient cultural context, patriarchal control usually monitored the sexual status of teenage females. Fathers normally took control (though mothers may have frequently played an unofficial role).[50] Arrangements for marriage were most often negotiated between the fathers, or between the bride's father and her future husband. Citing a marriage contract where the dowry is related to the bride's status as a virgin, ancient Jewish studies scholar Ross Kraemer explains that "Jews, like their gentile neighbors, placed a heavy cultural and economic premium on virginity at first marriage."[51] Furthermore, though the data are minimal, we know that "enslaved Jewish women owned by non-Jews would almost certainly have routinely found themselves required to provide sexual services for their owners" and bear their children.[52] Thus in this ancient world, female sexual reproduction was an important matter for the community to regulate and control through a variety of customs. Of course, females with the least status and power in the society seemed to have endured the most coercive forms of this control, including overt violence.[53]

How does the depiction of Mary in Luke's text reflect some of these realities of women's status and autonomy in the Greco-Roman world? There is considerable scholarly discussion about how to interpret the author's intentions regarding gender. The Lukan author includes multiple references to women in Luke and Acts. Conflicting interpretations yield differing conclusions, but they consistently show how centrally the issues of gender and social control are at stake in this text.

Some interpreters celebrate Luke's inclusion of so many women characters as a sign of his support for broadening women's participation in religion and society.[54] However, some biblical scholars have concluded that Luke sought to limit the leadership activities of women in his early Christian audience.[55] As Mary Rose D'Angelo notes, after the speeches of Elizabeth, Mary, and Anna in the infancy narratives at the beginning of Luke's gospel, in the rest of the text "women speak in the Gospel only to be corrected by Jesus" (e.g., Luke 10:38–42; 11:27–28; 23:28) or disbelieved (Luke 24:10–11).[56] Luke's portrayal of Mary's delivery of the Magnificat must be examined in light of this concern about his possible objective of controlling women, and especially of restricting women's speech. We need to identify the message Luke conveys about women's prophetic vocation and how it might reveal his intentions with regard to the Magnificat passage.

Throughout Luke–Acts the author alternates stories about women with stories about men.[57] Precisely what this pattern indicates about the content of Luke's message about gender roles is, however, not generally agreed upon. Mary's prophetic speech (Luke 1:46–56) parallels Zechariah's prophetic speech (Luke 1:67–79). Both Mary and Zechariah are imbued with the Holy Spirit. With this parallel structure, Luke may have intended to make sure that both males and females are instructed by his gospel message. How? He may want them both to feel equally inspired by the prophetic speech of these characters. Therefore, Luke can be interpreted as supportive of women's equality, especially the equal importance of their prophetic speech.

On the other hand, he may have wanted to teach some kind of subordination of women's prophetic vocation to men's by means of this parallel structure. Mary is not explicitly named as a prophet in Luke's text, while Zechariah is named as one. In Luke's infancy narratives, of the three prophetic women presented, Elizabeth, Mary, and Anna, only Anna is labeled a prophetess. Her prophetic words are only briefly summarized with no reference to her being imbued with the Holy Spirit, unlike Simeon with whom she is paired, who is anointed by the spirit three times.[58] Therefore in the gender pairing included in the infancy narratives, where Mary's Magnificat is found, Luke may be teaching women in his audience, who aspired to it, the subordinate, restricted nature of women's prophecy. In this understanding, women such as Mary are presented by Luke as a means of "edification and control" of women in the early Christian community.[59]

The relationship between the text and its ancient social context may reveal attempts to exercise patriarchal control over women's lives through the use of sacred texts, but it does not reveal the extent to which these attempts succeeded. There are also some indications of resistance. For some women, even with the varying social restrictions on it, their sexual status could be a means of empowerment. In Luke's text, women who enjoy the "charismatic privilege" of prophecy are usually either widows or virgins (in both cases maintaining their celibacy).[60] This analytical point about the gospel of Luke serves as a reminder of how the sexual/marital status of women impacted their autonomy and of how Luke's prophetic women characters may have reflected women in his social context. Within their ancient world, a woman's widowhood or choice to live a celibate, ascetic life defied the cultural ethos that emphasized matrimony and childbearing as most important for women.

Jane Schaberg comments on this trend in the early Christian movement: "Already in Corinth in the mid-first century there existed a movement of considerable proportions of unmarried virgins 'consecrated in both body and spirit' (1 Corinthians 7:34)."[61] But over the next few centuries as Christianity evolved from a missionary movement and became more institutionalized, the value and role of this ascetic lifestyle chosen by women was increasingly interpreted by male authorities. Celibate, ascetic women became excluded from the official power structure of the church. In this process "male power was exercised through the power to define women's sexuality" and its meaning for the organizational structuring of the church.[62] The status of celibate, ascetic women in the church decreased as the status of celibate, ascetic fathers of the church increased.[63] Mary's prophetic speech as a virgin may represent a historical, momentary defiance of gendered cultural constraints, albeit short-lived.

Sorting through these interpretations of Mary and her prophecy demonstrates how Bible study can provide training in reading for resistance. To study the context of Luke in this way teaches vigilance about recognizing both the control of women asserted in texts and practices of Luke's culturally pluralistic society, as well as possible venues of opposition to that control within the actual lives of ancient women. Reading the text of Luke–Acts for its gender message to women leaders of the Christian movement teaches the reader how to interpret Mary and her prophecy in a liberative way for contemporary women, perhaps in spite of the author's agenda. It also provides a model of disruptive strategies for critically analyzing public policy related to gender and sexuality in a contemporary religious and political climate where the control of women who are poor and "lowly" is seen as a moral imperative.

Moreover, we must not become so singularly focused upon how and for what purpose the representation of Mary was controlled that the details of her speech-act recede from view. Feminist biblical scholars who provide such valuable insights about accurately identifying ancient restrictions of women (in texts and practices) as well as women's defiance of those restrictions neglect the bold content of the speech Mary delivers. Even when mindful of Luke's possible motives related to controlling the impact she might have, the message within the text of Mary's prophetic speech deserves an attentive listener. Attentive listening can, perhaps, allow Mary to have liberative significance in the midst of restrictive intentions and could open the way for the listener to be affected by her challenging message.

As she serves God's interests, Mary prophesies about God's power. The significance of her pregnancy is asserted with this pronouncement about how God exercises divine power in society. Mary explains that God is concerned with the poor and the lowly as well as the rich and the powerful. Her prophecy indicates a direct relationship between what the rich and the poor deserve, and what the powerful and the lowly deserve. This message guides Christians to look for this kind of parity in contemporary public policies. For example, when welfare reform goals for the poor and lowly consist of ideas such as, "the birth rate among welfare recipients should be zero," as asserted by House of Representatives leader Tom DeLay, what analogous policies do the rich and powerful who receive a host of benefits and breaks from the government (related to taxes, investments, business) deserve?[64] In keeping with the emphasis on parity in this scripture, shouldn't one also ask, for pregnant women in this privileged group who want to continue receiving such benefits, what kind of "tough love" is in order for them as they give birth in the hospital to dependent children?

Finally, gathering cultural information about marriage and women's sexuality in Luke's ancient context also enhances one's ability to envision the betrothed girl, possibly only a teenager, who would have been the referent for the author, and to fathom the humiliation that would likely have been attached to her pregnancy. This pregnancy, as womanist ethicist Cheryl Kirk-Duggan puts it, is "a scandalous blessing."[65] Some knowledge of ancient cultural expectations permits the scripture reader to be attuned to the extraordinary defiance simultaneously represented in her joyous, pregnant bodily self and her prophetic assertions about the lowly and the powerful in her society. Rather than adhering to the popular rhetoric and restrictive policies for the poor offered by contemporary political leaders, the church could be inspired by her example. Insofar as it is possible to reconstruct and imagine them, Christians could find courage for countercultural support of poor women from these particular ancient realities of the historical Mary's life.

Interpreting the Real Lives of Poor Women and Girls

To formulate public policy that does not consist of so many demeaning and disciplinary measures for poor women, we need to pay attention to the current sociohistorical circumstances of their actual lives. The act of truly listening to their stories is held hostage by the politics of representing their actual lives.

Just as scholars have provided clues about the historical Mary and the lives of women in the communities of gospel writers such as the author of Luke–Acts, so, too, current researchers have unearthed a mountain of evidence about the real lives of poor women and girls. While feminist biblical scholars have sought to escape the limitations of "male textuality," many feminist and liberal social scientists have sought to undermine and refute racist and inaccurate caricatures of poor women in public policy discussions. In relationship to written texts, however, there is an important difference between these two pursuits. One group primarily probes written texts for evidence while the other creates textual evidence. The feminist *biblical* researchers scour texts and sometimes other sources documenting women's subversive responses to the prevailing patriarchal social order. The feminist *social policy* researchers create texts in response to debasing, punitive social practices aimed at poor women. The strategy by some of the feminist biblical scholars of suspiciously probing scripture texts to inquire how and why they may have upheld the ancient social order offers guidance for contemporary studies.

As well-intentioned, skillful researchers create texts about the lives of poor women and girls, how is their work affected by the degrading views articulated by officials in our society? Researchers and activists valiantly dispute viewpoints by our political leaders, such as those I have mentioned accusing poor women and girls of hindering the nation's achievement of its goals in the twenty-first century, of greedily producing babies in order to get welfare funds, or of being homicidally prone mothers who put their children in Dumpsters. Dedicated scholarly efforts to challenge such ideas may also produce an unintended effect that undermines those efforts. When refuting these ideas, there is a danger of becoming too accommodating to the assumptions one is trying to oppose, that is, of becoming entrapped by the terms that those degrading assumptions set. I realize that there is a critical need for accurate information. When Christian ethical choices are made about supporting specific public policy initiatives regulating access for people who are poor to resources necessary for their survival, their perspectives should matter. The church and others in our society should listen to them. And in light of how distorted claims about poor women and girls have been, someone needs to make sure that their actual perspectives are truthfully reported, but must the goals of the reporting be tethered to those distortions?

The work of some researchers and scholars seeks to establish the importance of hearing from poor women and girls whose lives are directly affected by welfare policy. For instance, Elaine Bell Kaplan writes about the lives of black teenage mothers because she believes that this knowledge will create change. In her study of black teenage mothers in Oakland, California, Kaplan explains, "The only way to reduce the number of teenage pregnancies or to improve the lives of teenage mothers is to understand the societal causes by examining the realities of these girls' lives."[66] Authors such as Kaplan argue that a better understanding of the lives of poor mothers can lead to a more adequate policy to address the problems that they face.[67] It is imperative to hear from those "who are seldom invited to speak what they know."[68] The women's testimonies demonstrate the consequences for society of "not listening to the needs of the recipients of welfare services," writes Meredith Ralston in her study of homeless women *Nobody Wants to Hear Our Truth*.[69]

Some researchers work on documenting countervailing evidence in response to particular caricatures of welfare recipients. Journalist-researcher David Zucchino proved that instead of "Cadillac-driving, champagne-sipping, penthouse-living welfare queens," women recipients of welfare checks were destitute, their daily lives filled with suffering and struggle as they foraged for food, clothing, and safe housing for themselves and their children.[70] In short, proof was located that shows extraordinary suffering accompanies poverty. Also, there is documentation that poor women utilize Medicaid coverage for serious medical problems.[71] Some of the racial stereotypes about blacks in the arguments of those who successfully advocated for a public policy of "ending welfare" are addressed in studies that concentrate exclusively on white women welfare recipients, such as studies in Oregon and Michigan.[72] Not only is the existence of poor white mothers receiving welfare benefits noted, but some of those white mothers can appear to be "irresponsible," with filthy, naked children running around.[73]

Researcher Lisa Dodson summarizes the adverse conditions that poor mothers face. As her Boston-based, cross-racial study of low-income women and girls explains:

> [The interviewees] spoke of little erosions which finally wear you down into someone you don't want to be. They spoke of having no

> car, no warm coats, no baby clothes, no functioning laundry in the building, no elevator and many stairs, no heat sometimes, no pampers, no tampons, of long lines at clinics, and of being able to go only to stores which accept food stamps, and above all, of having no one to "offer a kind word."[74]

In their low status and desperate circumstances, the desire for "a kind word" can be understood as a desire to be looked upon with favor rather than scorn. Similarly, the need to find favor in her lowliness is identified in the opening sentences of Mary's Magnificat. But Mary announces the fulfillment of that need in the divine favor she has found, which is also bestowed upon all the lowly and hungry. If their actual life circumstances were better known, would poor women and girls receive a more favorable public response and would more supportive policies be developed?

Some studies try to counter popular opinion by proving that black teenage mothers who have received public assistance benefits do indeed transition off of welfare benefits.[75] On the issue of the blameworthiness of poor mothers, Kristin Luker's study of teenage pregnancy argues that teenage childbearing should be seen as "a *measure*, not a cause of poverty and other social ills."[76] Other researchers take on the challenge of making a case for the disabling role of systemic structures of power in addition to exposing the details of poor women's struggles.[77] Focusing on predominantly black homeless women who lived in a temporary residential facility in New York City, Alisse Waterston was

> compelled by an ongoing politic of "blaming the poor" to offer intimate portraits of the women and to reflect on political and economic processes that contextualize the lives of the women and the institution in which they reside. . . . Listening to Woodhouse [the temporary residence] women recall their experiences, sharing their memories and hopes, I sense ways larger social forces circumscribe their lives: the intersection of poverty, gender, and race, and the cultural construction of sexuality, mental illness, and homelessness.[78]

Through their varied methods the researchers function as interpreters, transmitting the pleadings of poor women and girls so that they may be viewed in a more just and caring manner. The pleas are directed to anti–welfare state theorists, to policy makers, and to the general public, including churches. Through the researchers, the mothers ask us to believe that they are already truly suffering in the midst of impoverishment and dire conditions, which they have not willfully chosen as a preferred lifestyle, and that they are hardworking people.[79] One wonders why their pleas are necessary, why there is so much public doubt about and indifference to these realities. I find that the sympathetic arguments about the morality of the poor generate an uneasiness that lingers even though it is clear these researchers and activists are focused upon defending the moral fiber of poor women and girls. While contesting the nature of the problem, even defenders seem to be caught within a troubling perspective that only identifies people who are poor as having the problem that needs to be addressed.

I do not mean to suggest that the detailed defense of contemporary poor women and girls that has been offered is expendable. Evidence is needed on the effects upon human lives and dignity not only of poverty, but of welfare policies as well. Feminist studies offer details about how badly women feel they are treated in the offices that dispense public assistance.[80] Women's stories describe how they are treated like children who need to be corrected after doing something wrong. For instance, one woman with a twelve-month-old son who applied for assistance had to struggle with two different social service offices to get shelter, and then had to agree to eight hours of meetings each week, including parenting classes, as well as individual counseling that included sessions with a family life advocate and a child specialist.[81] This mother who received all of these mandates sought public assistance because she faced a crisis when her apartment building was suddenly burned down.

Testimonies about women's resistance to infantilizing or degrading treatment by the social service bureaucracy have also been gathered. Researcher Lisa Dodson tells the story of Margarita, who sang songs from her Puerto Rican cultural background and joked with the other mothers as she waited two to three hours each time she needed to see her caseworker.[82] Margarita consciously used this tactic because she did not want her daughter "to remember Mommy with her head down."[83] Margarita also tried to counter the attitude of the welfare office, "which teaches that poor mothers are lazy, that they have babies for money, and that in the case of Puerto Rican women like her, they shouldn't even be here anyway."[84] Some studies show that whites find caseworkers more helpful in finding potential jobs than blacks do; blacks are removed from enrollment for noncompliance with welfare rules at higher rates than whites; and Latino/a applicants, unlike white applicants, have to submit documentation of marriage and citizenship before receiving appointments.[85] Besides racially discriminatory treatment by welfare office workers, there is confirmation of the compounding impact of racism that is generally present in the lives of poor women of color utilizing the welfare system. For instance, Dana, a homeless thirty-seven-year-old Native American welfare recipient, talks about what she encountered when she left the reservation. She describes how debilitating it can be to cope with the attitude that "All Indians are thieves. . . . All Indians are no good. Nothing but drunken Indians."[86]

Sometimes there is also a detrimental internalization and reproduction of the values in welfare reform rhetoric by the women. Activist/author Grace Chang describes Asian immigrant and refugee women who were able to receive some public assistance and their feelings of deep shame about it. In addition, some of these women seem to have "absorbed, wholesale, the dominant negative images of black Americans as welfare abusers and positive images of Asian Americans as 'model minorities.'"[87] In another instance, a young male El Salvadoran refugee whom Chang interviewed, who was poor and economically struggling himself, described Mexican immigrants as "pregnant women coming over to have babies and get welfare right away."[88] The negative impact on women's own self-perceptions as well as the learned behavior of competitive, racial/ethnic devaluation of others that takes place among poor persons of color should be counted among the costs of this kind of public policy.

Whereas accounts of the damaging effects of racism may not be compelling to many in our society, the stories about sexual violence in the lives of poor mothers might be.[89] Again, the aim of many of these studies is to persuade those who construct welfare policy to do so in a manner that is responsive to the problems poor women actually confront. After offering several women's testimonies, social theorist Meredith Ralston asserts that besides experiences of racism and sexism, the childhood physical and sexual abuse of women must be taken into account in order to understand "why women are homeless, addicted, and on welfare."[90] Sometimes women become homeless because of the emotional trauma of having been assaulted in their homes. For instance, Linda, who was gang-raped by five men in her apartment, and Hattie, who was raped and tortured for many hours by two men in her apartment, both found that they just could not go back to their homes.[91] It is also a frequent occurrence for women who are homeless to be raped when trying to find a safe place to sleep or looking for shelter in bad weather.[92]

In addition to having to face the traumatic impact of sexual assault by strangers, intimate assaults on women who are poor that directly affect their need for assistance also occur within their ongoing intimate relationships.[93] In defense of women who are stigmatized for failing to marry the fathers of their children or punished if they refuse to name them and stay in contact with them, researchers present evidence of violence and abuse that women are fleeing. There are many women like Patsy, who was trying to develop a relationship with the father of her thirteen-year-old daughter when, as she explains, "One day he took me into the basement and he raped me. He hurt me. He put a broom up my vagina."[94] Researcher Jody Raphael studies one African American woman who was a welfare recipient, Bernice Hampton, and her struggles with an abusive male intimate partner. This study reveals Bernice's persistent efforts when trapped by both life-threatening domestic violence and poverty. Bernice suffered as a result of being repeatedly raped and badly beaten by her boyfriend and the father of her children with whom she lived while trying to keep her family together. The most violent incidents usually occurred just as Bernice was about to succeed in a job or educational program that would have allowed her to get the financial stability she needed.[95]

In these and many other cases of intimate-partner rape and domestic violence, the researchers demonstrate that marriage is probably not the answer to the problems of poor mothers, as President Clinton and the Congress asserted when initially enacting the 1996 welfare reform law that stands as current policy. The first sentence of this U.S. law to address poverty pronounced that "marriage is the foundation of society." President Bush built upon this theme in subsequent additions to it during its reauthorization. As part of his Healthy Marriage Initiative in 2004, Bush added $1.5 billion over five years for promoting the idea that women who are poor and seeking public assistance should get married or reunite with their husbands (if separated).[96] Bush excluded from this initiative federally mandated waivers for recipients who face domestic violence. Increasingly, studies are being generated on the marital expectations and desires of poor single mothers who have sought public assistance to document that most of them highly value the ideal of a healthy, stable marriage and that heterosexual marriage would not solve the problems that make them seek public assistance.[97]

The prevailing assumptions of the social order are neglected in arguments that contradict accusations about a poor single mother's intrinsic faults, the pleadings for some compassionate concern about the brutal realities facing homeless women, and other defensive claims based upon the most intimate and painful details of their lives that the researchers get the women to reveal. These arguments leave intact a social order where the morality of those with the most privileges, power, and status in society is not questioned. Specifically, the morality of *their* choices to use their power, privilege, and status to create or uphold social policy that denies those with the least in our society full support for basic survival needs is not even under consideration. Thankfully, the disruptive message of Mary's Magnificat does not allow this omission.

What Would It Mean to Listen to Mary?

Blessing the particular. Mary's Magnificat, which begins with a focus on her particular circumstances and lowly status, speaks to the particular circumstances and treatment of poor mothers. Mary announces her joyfulness over God's salvation. Considering the racist caricatures of contemporary poor mothers, the blaming distortions, desperate conditions of poverty, and most importantly the disciplinary public policies imposed upon them because they are poor, the idea of God's salvific blessing and favorable attention to them would certainly be a reason for joyful celebration.

No more humiliation. The assertiveness in the wording of the Magnificat shows Mary, as Jane Schaberg says, to be "one who has triumphed over her enemies, one to whom God was merciful, one for whom there was a radical overturning of social expectations."[98] Surely these ingredients are needed in the situation of contemporary poor mothers who seek public assistance. In Luke 1:48, when Mary proclaims that God has looked with favor upon her, she is not describing her insignificance compared to a mighty God; rather, this verse "refers to an attitude that arises out of an experience of injustice."[99] The passage specifically points to the humiliation that Mary endured as a woman and the victory over that humiliation found in the favor with which God looks upon her. Mary's humiliation has to do with her pregnancy while she is a betrothed virgin and may even pertain to how she became pregnant.[100]

Women and girls in our contemporary context are also humiliated when they are poor, unwed, and pregnant. Differing forms of degrading treatment extract that humiliation in the welfare office, in the media, and in legislation enacted by the government. Further humiliation is generated not only by tolerance of their suffering under impoverished conditions, but also by outright indifference to it by most of their neighbors (the public) as well as most of their political leaders. Mary's words represent a greatly needed challenge to this treatment and indicate support for rebellion against such humiliation. Resonating with Mary's attitude in the text are outspoken voices of protest by these targeted mothers and other groups of people who are poor and have "already" publicly affirmed the rightful importance of their well-being and dignity through the organized efforts of groups such as the Kensington Welfare Rights Union of Philadelphia or Grassroots Organizing for Welfare Leadership (GROWL).[101]

Mary's words offer a vision of God's power as having already been used unequivocally with regard to the pretentious human rulers and the lowly who have been degraded. Her speech provides a key ingredient for struggle: imagination. It preserves images of what political and socioeconomic justice that has already been achieved looks like.

Reversal? The Magnificat links God's concern about Mary's particular situation with God's delivery of justice in the broader society. Her prophetic speech about how just community relationships come into being advocates a dramatic change in the social order and a confrontational approach by God. There is a battle-like tone to her words that echoes biblical passages like Psalm 89:10, where it is said of God, "You scattered your enemies with your mighty arm."[102] Mary's speech also recalls the tradition of liberation hymns by biblical women such as Hannah.[103] Using language that stresses the reversal of social conditions in similar ways as Mary does in the Magnificat, Hannah proclaims: "The bows of the mighty are broken, but the feeble gird on strength. Those who were full have hired themselves out for bread, but those who were hungry are fat with spoil" (1 Sam. 2:4–5). When Christians acknowledge Mary's speech as a prophetic proclamation of God's judgment, what steps must they take to adhere to it? What measures should be enacted to achieve the parity between rich and poor, lowly and powerful in her prophecy?

Heeding the approach offered by Mary in the Magnificat would mean some kind of reversal in the political situation, wouldn't it? The Magnificat could be suggesting a reversal of conditions for our leaders who proudly create policies rewarding the rich and powerful with ever-increasing benefits so they can acquire more wealth and power, while endlessly studying, negatively labeling, and disciplining the morality of those struggling with the least resources and under the most destitute of conditions. Agreement with the biblical theme in Mary's song could require Christians to support policy regulating the lives of all elites with status, power, and wealth, especially policy makers. This regulation could be based upon, for instance, probing and analyzing the charges of extramarital sexual liaisons made against Newt Gingrich,[104] the charges of sexual harassment and extramarital sexual liaisons against President Clinton, and Glenn Loury's sexual liaisons that resulted in children by a woman he never married and his alleged physical assault of his extramarital female partner.[105] If public policy is to be created on the basis of "personal responsibility," such as sexual behavior (as it has been in welfare policy), wouldn't just public practices mandate scrutiny and regulation of those who actually wield political and economic power in this nation, rather than targeting those with little or none?

I would not advocate establishing public policy based upon certain examples of personal sexual behavior. But Mary's confrontational approach stresses the reversal of unjust political and social conditions and prompts us to envision, in concrete terms, what God's intervention might encompass. The role of the prophet is to stir up her audience's concern about God's judgment of their unrighteousness. Applying not only the same moral scrutiny, but also the same legislative remedy of regulation to policy makers and public opinion shapers as they have implemented for the poor may best illustrate what Mary's prophetic call might mean within our social context. The enactment of public policy regulating the family and financial lives of all policy makers and public opinion shapers receiving any public funds or benefits (such as salaries, grants, tax breaks) on the basis of alleged moral failures in the personal choices of certain individuals among them would be controversial. It would no doubt create indignation about the unfairness of collective punishment as well as assertions about the entitlement of this group to privacy in matters strictly related to their families and personal lifestyles. This indignation about fairness and respect for privacy could, perhaps, then be extended to poor black and Latina mothers and others who seek public assistance.

Might such a reversal approach be a more effective step toward a just welfare policy than begging and pleading with leaders to believe that poor mothers and their children are actually suffering under destitute conditions that they do not choose or desire? I don't know.

Churches breaking their primary allegiance to the state's agenda. The church's role has to be identified in a liberative ethical response to the Magnificat's pronouncement of God's harsh judgment of the political leaders who rest upon "their thrones" of power. If the response from the churches were to be guided by this biblical injunction, they would probably find themselves in conflict with the political establishment. Biblical scholar Richard Horsley reminds us of the ancient political setting that the Magnificat refers to: "In the very structures of the imperial situation, imperial regimes ruled through local aristocracies and client-kings, and the latter were dependent on the imperial regime for the maintenance of their privileged position at the head of their own people. . . . To assert the only true, divine rule, God had to put down the pretentious human rulers."[106] Thus the Magnificat speaks to the oppression suffered by the lowly and hungry at the hands of both local and imperial leaders. The "charitable choice" provision in the 1996 PRWORA legislation may place churches in the midst of a similar political situation. In particular, as they struggle to respond to the needs of people who are poor in their communities by participating in programs receiving funding under welfare reform provisions, many black churches may be caught delivering the state's moral message when functioning in the state-designated role of service provider.[107]

This assignment for churches by political officials in welfare reform policies is comparable to what political scientist Cathy Cohen calls secondary marginalization. Though she uses this term in her study of black politics and the AIDS crisis, it can be usefully applied to welfare reform policy as well. As Cohen explains, "Dominant elites, refiguring the process of regulation of and service to marginal groups, come to depend on a stratum of and service to marginal group members expected or allowed to staff those dominant institutions and that directly affect the quality of life of the most vulnerable in marginal communities. . . . Indigenous leaders risk assimilation or cooptation through such a process."[108]

Cohen's description allows us to recognize a concerted strategy that is routinely used by national political leaders. It is a political strategy that enlists a certain sector of socially marginalized communities to implement regulations and deliver certain services for others in that community. Most germane to this discussion, moral values about who deserves to occupy the "thrones" of power and who deserves to be shamed for being "lowly" are maintained in the enforcement of those regulations and delivery of services. The configuration of bureaucratic personnel and procedures helps to preserve the interests of those with the most privileges, advantages, and material resources in our society.

In welfare reform policy, regulations connected to "charitable choice" as well as certain governmental "faith-based initiatives" sponsored by churches in poor communities of color may reflect this kind of political strategy. Some churches face the dilemma of how to maintain services for socioeconomically vulnerable persons in their communities by utilizing some state sponsorship but without adopting the state's values. If faith-based groups do not adhere to the rules and regulations of the state—upholding specific, predetermined values—they risk the loss of their funding.

The economic policies of George W. Bush drew upon the widespread acceptance of welfare reform ideology established in the 1990s by Newt Gingrich, Bill Clinton, and others. In a 2003 speech to a group of Christian leaders in which he affirms the key role of the church in meeting the needs of the poor, Bush explained, "Welfare policy will not solve the deepest problems of the spirit."[109] He then offered an analogy, further explaining, "You don't fix the crack in the wall until you fix the foundation."[110] President Bush's comments and policy reflect the viewpoint that people lack socioeconomic resources and need assistance because their "foundation" is broken, and fixing it (them?) is most appropriately the role of the church. Further, when describing Bush's plans to visit local communities touting his marriage promotion policy as a remedy for the poor, one White House aide told the press, "The president loves to do that sort of thing in the inner city with black churches, and he's very good at it."[111]

Black churches are continually targeted as crucial audiences for supporting and carrying out welfare reform policies. There are undoubtedly benefits for leaders of these local churches, such as media attention, the possibility of desperately needed resources, and status rewards of publicly receiving approval from the "thrones" of power (of the empire). Agreeing to hand over their churches to the president and others as a stage for their pronouncements about what is wrong with the poor churches may, however, lead to abandoning their advocacy of any gospel values that are in opposition to the state's, but those gospel values characterize the church's distinctiveness.

It is not only churches in poor communities of color that face an ethical challenge in this social and political climate. In some ways white Christians, within varying economic groupings, face one of the hardest challenges. They must choose to resist the comfort they can find in supporting values that point to the superiority of their own white racial group. When black and Latina poor single mothers who need public assistance are depicted as having a cracked foundation and innate tendencies toward laziness, criminality, and prostitution, whites receive an unearned reward of being excluded from this depiction. This is comforting for them. A sense of the superiority of whiteness is reinforced because, based upon their white racial identity, they are not and will never be known as lazy-criminal-whore-broken blacks and Latinas. Not surprisingly, whites will most often cling to this superior status attached to their racial identity, and to public policies that reinforce this understanding.

Moreover, distributing "tough love" or supporting the goal of "fixing" the impaired moral foundation of welfare recipients can make white Christians feel especially good about themselves. These strategies reenact a familiar scenario of white Christian paternalism mentioned earlier. One performs charitable acts for objectified others that fit into a universalized Christian notion of the other-in-need of help. Welfare recipients may easily be seen as another set of needy persons of color who are receptacles for benevolent attention that whites bestow upon them to help them.

However, Christian practices can offer alternatives. Studying scripture passages like the Magnificat proclamation by Mary of Nazareth could be a public practice of the church that helps Christians make decisions about the church's role in welfare reform. As Latin American liberation theologians Ivone Gebara and Maria Clara Bingemer declare:

> It is from the mouth of a woman that this song of the battle against evil emerges, as though a new people could only be born from the womb of a woman. The image of a pregnant woman, able to give birth to the new, is the image of God who through the power of God's Spirit brings to birth men and women committed to justice, living out their relationship to God in a loving relationship with other human beings.[112]

To live out this distinctive Christian commitment to justice, churches need to carefully identify which of their routine practices indeed break with social values and policies that help to marginalize and degrade people.

Chapter Four

Liturgy

Church Worship and White Superiority

The rituals of Sunday worship enable Christians to publicly rehearse what it means to uphold the moral values they are supposed to bring to every aspect of their lives, from their attitudes about public policy to their intimate relations. Christian worship should provide ritual reminders of how these moral values can be distinctively rooted in their Christian faith. As God's powerful presence and sanction for certain attitudes and behavior is liturgically invoked, Christian worship practices also reinforce or challenge cultural norms of our society. This tradition of ritually representing cultural behaviors and attitudes as endorsed by God makes the public venue of Christian worship so crucial for liberative ethics.

One of the persistent cultural norms in the United States that needs to be closely examined and challenged is a commitment to the superiority of white people (usually those of European heritage) and their cultural contributions, traditions, and history. As we have seen in earlier chapters, ideas that support white superiority can surface in the formulation of Christian ethical thought, whether expressed in the work of figures such as Niebuhr or a contemporary feminist approach. Examples of the competition between ideas supporting the superiority of white middle-class people and ideas about poor people in the Christian gospel were also apparent in the creation of welfare reform policy.

To be a valuable resource in this morally competitive climate, a liberatory social ethic based upon the Christian gospel has to be fostered within the concrete practices of Christian faith communities. The weekly practice of communal worship holds promise for providing Christians with a space to cultivate their ability to recognize and contest repressive cultural norms like white superiority. While appreciating this constructive potential in worship, one must also acknowledge the unlikelihood that repressive, pervasive cultural norms can be completely abandoned when segments of the public gather for Christian worship. How might a commitment to white superiority be manifested and sometimes encouraged within weekly worship practices?

Theories about white privilege and multiculturalism are especially useful for investigating racially repressive cultural norms within Christian worship. Theoretical understandings of the cultural dominance of "whiteness" by sociologists, legal scholars, and Christian ethicists describe deeply embedded rituals of racism in the broader society. Multicultural approaches to racial/ethnic justice can help to break up the simplistic white-black dichotomy too often assumed when racism is discussed, and support a religious sensibility within Christian worship practices that views God's power and mystery as multiply located and shared. Theoretical discussions of white privilege and multiculturalism can, therefore, not only aid in identifying a commitment to white superiority in worship practices, but also help to suggest liturgical strategies for relinquishing that commitment.

Just as it is possible to make choices about which ethical values are espoused in the communal practices of the broader society (e.g., addressing unjust conditions of wealth and poverty in the formulation of governmental public policy), it is also possible to make choices about which values are supported in the communal practices of the church, such as public worship. For Christians to make conscious choices about reversing their commitment to white superiority, or at least occasionally reneging on it, an intense scrutiny of worship practices is required. This includes provocative and speculative questioning about racial messages in Christian worship practices that individual worshiping communities would need to explore together and tailor to reflect their racial/ethnic composition. Racial messages do not need to be intentionally placed within the service to be present and have a powerful impact on the spiritual and moral formation of the worshiping community, and thus must be deliberately investigated. To begin, I share a few personal experiences. Like the stories in earlier chapters, my stories are offered to highlight some of the complicated dynamics of ordinary life that are part of the construction of liberative Christian social ethics.

Welcome to Our Church, White Church

I am a black member of a predominantly white Protestant denomination, a tradition in which I was raised from infancy.[1] The following account includes some of my visits to predominantly white congregations, mostly within my own denomination, and take place in various locations in the United States. My experiences can assist in reflection about how whites may culturally assert themselves within the worship setting of a Christian faith community, through a routine, initial encounter with an "outsider."

> I am embarrassed to admit that I sometimes fall prey to some of the most naive and idealistic longings about what it means to participate in local church life. I can induce especially maudlin desires about attending Sunday morning worship services. On several occasions, filled with spiritual cravings and theological ideals about worship, I've popped into the nearest church I could find only to be reawakened to the racial realities present within the Christian worship context and have my spiritual longings and questions deepened.
>
> For instance, on one very snowy morning, when I was living in a northeastern suburban community, I decided to visit a church that was close by. As I drove, I traveled on slippery roads and had to stop a few times to clean the ice off of my windshield wipers. When I entered the large church building, relieved to have made it there, it was bustling with people. I began to surmise that this was probably not a racially integrated church when not only was everyone that I saw white, several people seemed to gape at me in a rather obvious way when I encountered them, almost making me feel like an intruder. When I said "Good morning," most of them answered with, "Welcome to our church." I toyed with the idea of obnoxiously giving a response to their welcome that asked how they knew that I was a visitor and not a lapsed member. (I guessed that there were probably hundreds of families affiliated with this church.)
>
> I sat down in the sanctuary and began my personal meditations. Because I had been anxiously preoccupied with the snow and ice on the roads, I needed a little extra time to settle down and prepare myself for worship. Just at that moment, I looked up at a woman who was walking down the center aisle. She was probably volunteering as an usher for those arriving at the service. She approached me, peered into my pew, and asked in an assertive tone, "Where do you live?" I was very startled and unsure of how to respond. I wanted to know why she was inquiring. I glanced around quickly at all of the white faces and started thinking that maybe this really is a concertedly segregated white church! In a tentative, questioning tone, I told her that I lived in the neighborhood. She said, "Oh," and walked away. I never did figure out the meaning of that inquiry. Later, after becoming

acquainted with a white woman who was a long-standing member of that church, I told her about my initial experience of her church. She explained that it was impossible for members of her congregation to be unwelcoming on the basis of race, and supported this claim with a description of their participation in a successful annual choir exchange with a black congregation located in a nearby city. I could not convince her that issues of race might be a component in my experience of her church as less than friendly when I visited.

On another occasion, when visiting relatives in the South, I decided that I wanted to attend a local church in town because it was part of my own Methodist denomination. Along with several members of my extended family, I had come to gather around an uncle who had been recently diagnosed with terminal lung cancer. We were enjoying a happy occasion with him, knowing that all too soon our visits would be focused on his suffering and pain, and then our sadness about his death. On this particular Sunday morning, I felt like going off on my own for a little private time and to worship with what I (naively) regarded as another kind of extended family. My relatives gave me puzzled and somewhat amused glances as they prepared to go to their own black Baptist church, and remarked to one another, "Traci's going to the white church."

When I entered this huge church in the center of town and realized that my face was the only brown one amidst a sea of white ones, I was a bit worried, but tried not to make cynical assumptions about how I would be accepted at that worship service. In fact, most people were quite friendly to me, which would have been okay except for the nature of some of their comments. For instance, after the service, one smiling woman who had been in the choir came up to me and warmly greeted me with a handshake. She informed me that she had picked me out during the worship service and guessed that I was a visitor. She further explained, "I said to myself, *Now I just know that that gal can sing. We ought to get her up here to do it.*" I was not sure how to respond to her. To be honest, I repressed the urge to burst out laughing and mumbled something about the fact that I am actually a dreadful singer. When I told my family about this exchange at lunch that day, one of my relatives suggested a wonderful retort to the woman's comment. She said that I should have given the widest grin that my lips could stretch into and said, "I does dance too!"

At one point, I was almost starting to think that this singing theme might be a special greeting that white churchgoers save for black

> visitors, because when I was a guest at another predominantly white church in the Northeast, I almost got into a big argument with another white woman over this same issue. This time, in an attempt to make me feel welcome after the service, a white woman came up to compliment the sound of my singing. Because I am very aware of my inability to sing well, I tend to sing in a fairly self-conscious, quiet way. I explained to this woman that she had definitely mistaken my voice for someone else's in the congregation, but she maintained that she had indeed heard the almost operatic quality of my voice booming out above the others during the hymns. "That wasn't me," I repeated, gently but firmly. She continued to insist that she *knew* it was me that she had heard singing so beautifully. I soon realized that no matter what I said, it was a futile effort to try to convince her otherwise, for "just looking at me" confirmed her statement about my extraordinary singing abilities.
>
> In varying ways, in these encounters my worship experience was profoundly affected by my growing awareness of being a racial outsider, an awareness that was tentative at first but grew progressively stronger. My ability to focus upon worshiping God during the service, and in some instances my reflection following the service about my communal experience of worshiping God, were saturated with messages about race. My pursuit of a holy gathering of people in a holy space was infiltrated with a cognizance of what it means for me to spend time with white people in white organizations.

Of course, my reactions should be further explored and questioned in ways that I do not include here. Even without more explanation, these stories introduce some of the intense spiritual, emotional, and cultural issues that a racial interrogation of worship practices might bring. They also point to the need for clarity about the definition of white racism and how it functions in order to effectively identify worship practices that uphold it.

Analyzing White Privilege: The Basics

Issues of race were not the only factors at work in my encounters as a visiting worshiper. A variety of other cultural dynamics were part of those interactions and could also be considered, such as gender, class, or ethnicity (e.g., exploring which white ethnic groups were involved and how they differed). It would be erroneous, however, to deny that race was one of the factors present. A basic starting point for understanding white dominance is the reality that issues of race are at play in all interactions. When there are only white people in the room, issues of race are still there. Whites contest, reinforce, and create the meaning of their racial identities even when they exclusively engage each other in conversations and activities. Likewise, when there are only people of color in the room, issues of race, including white dominance, are there. Even when they exclusively engage each other, people of color are always contesting, negotiating, and creating the meaning of their racial identities, especially in reaction to the boundaries and stigmas marking them as inferior.

White dominance is perpetuated through varied forms of denial—that is, by ignoring racial realities, pretending they are not relevant in certain kinds of social interactions, like the dynamics within Christian worship services. There is widespread consensus that Sunday morning is the most segregated hour of the week for Christians, and that this high degree of segregation is an indication of racial problems in the United States. But reinforcement of racial divisions and inequities that takes place within that Sunday morning hour continues to be largely ignored or denied. Examining the content of worship practices for their racial messages represents acknowledgment that a problem exists and takes a small step forward in challenging the stranglehold of white dominance. Racism analyses focusing on critical studies of "whiteness" can provide valuable tools for probing racial messages in worship, but these resources tend to be underutilized by Christian churches and seminaries. Discussions of white supremacy (or dominance) and white privilege are more commonly understood as useful for studying social attitudes and stratification in secular society, but rarely seen as applicable to internal church practices.

White privilege is derived from white supremacy (or white dominance). White supremacy is characterized by the manner in which access to power and resources in U.S. society is structured.[2] Whites tend to be favored with greater access to money, property, education, health care, and environmentally healthy conditions. White supremacy is also maintained by the ways in which cultural expressions and patterns are valued, such as notions of "classic" art and music, stable families, proper speech and language. The cultural expressions and behavioral patterns of whites (and Europeans) are usually valorized as the most worthwhile aspects of civilization. White privilege is a concrete manifestation of how whites benefit from white supremacy. The need to recognize white privilege provides a specific starting point for opposing white supremacy that further clarifies what it means to acknowledge the presence of racial dynamics in daily interactions. Many theorists emphasize the freedom to choose whether or not to think about race as one of the main features of white privilege.[3] For instance, in most places in the United States white Christians who go off to visit a worship service probably do not think about the racial dynamics ahead of time. Unless they consciously decide to attend a service with a majority nonwhite congregation (which would be an unusual choice), they are most likely to simply assume that they do not need to be concerned about race.

Racist socialization privileging whites is revealed in ordinary matters that may be part of our daily routine. A variety of cultural sources teach us that whites are to be seen as those who are "just human beings" or as the normal ones who do not project a particular racial identity and perspective. This understanding may be reinforced when reading a novel and the characters whose racial group remains unidentified are assumed to be white, listening to a news report that only reveals the race/ethnicity of a group or individual if they are not white, or attending a big church gathering in a predominantly white denomination where it is exuberantly announced that "diversity is here," which is meant as an announcement that more than just white people are present. When, over and over, in so many different arenas of our culture, whites are treated as the normal group of human beings that do not need to be racially classified, this status comes to be taken for granted. It seems like something to which whites are naturally entitled.

This entitlement aspect of white privilege could be communicated or inculcated in predominantly white worship services, especially among those with socioeconomic advantages. In congregational prayers or announcements about mission activities, for example, ideas might be conveyed about who the normal, regular (white) people are, and who should be assumed to be the (racial) others. Racialized understandings of "us and them" can be strongly conveyed in prayers about those who are "less fortunate than we are" or projects to reach out to help "them." These practices exemplify ritualized responses to local community and global needs, and teach the congregation to recognize its distinctive Christian identity on a weekly basis. They also link Christian identity to a sense of privilege that easily merges with racial messages about privilege in the broader culture.

Similarly, special rituals in church services surrounding outreach projects might be a central way of celebrating key Christian events, like the birth of Jesus. These rituals might provide a routinized confirmation that the distinctiveness of being an active Christian lies in the obligation to help those "others," who are not the normal, independent, regular (white) people. However, in predominantly white congregations, where do congregants learn about what kind of "help" white people need with giving up privileges they enjoy at the expense of other people's exploitation?[4] Besides problematic intercessory prayers for the unfortunate dependent "others," prayers of thankfulness for what "God has given to us" can undergird a sense of entitlement to material "blessings." Such prayers of thanksgiving by whites as well as prayers about "our" entitlement to God's grace and forgiveness because "we are God's children" could get confused with entitlement to white privilege or seem to be confirming entitlement to white privilege. When giving thanks, where do these white congregants learn to recognize privileges to which they are not entitled, but receive anyway? Said differently, how do they learn to distinguish between privileges they receive from the racist cultural elevation of their racial group and the "blessings" they receive as children of God?

To garner nuanced insights about whiteness and white privilege in a Christian worship context, the considerable complexity in the meaning of these racial terms must be noted. In the United States, the identification of an Irish immigrant during the 1840s and 1850s as white, and the identification of a citizen of Irish descent in the twenty-first century as white, involve considerably different cultural descriptions and experiences. Classification as white would have been highly contested for the person in the former case, but would be unquestioned for the person in the latter one. Moreover, in our contemporary period, white people experience whiteness and white privilege in multiple ways. A socioeconomically destitute and homeless white woman, a working-class Jewish white man, an openly gay white male Christian couple, and a wealthy, white, Spanish-speaking immigrant woman from Spain each experience whiteness and white privilege in differing ways and degrees. Yet, all of them benefit from some degree of white privilege. A very basic aspect of whiteness and of race in general is that it is socially constructed, not biologically determined.

The fact that all racial classifications have been constructed on the basis of historical and social conditions may be erased in church worship. A contrary lesson is frequently conveyed in church settings where culturally dependent markers of social identity are merged with theology. Rather than learning that God created humankind with a range of biological and social capabilities and then humankind created social labels and racial categories to assign to those traits, some expressions of Christian creation theology may lead one astray. They may propagate divine endorsement of the social formula of using biology as a means for defining race. In liberal church settings, for instance, the supposed fact that "we are red and yellow, black and white" may be celebrated as evidence of racial differences that God created. This is well-intentioned theology about racial diversity but problematically linked to biology, and is, unfortunately, often taught to children in worship celebrations.

Complications in the social construction of race presented by socioeconomic class differences also must be taken into account when strategizing about how to recognize encouragement for the entitlements of white privilege in worship. Definitions of white privilege that point to an individual's material "blessings" will be inadequate. As Christian social ethicist Elizabeth Bounds argues, "White working-class persons generally do not experience themselves as privileged, and are likely to feel that this idea adds insult to class injury."[5] For working-class whites struggling to maintain basic material comforts, assumptions about the nature of white privilege that are linked to assumptions about the material "blessings" of whites may only fuel a stronger denial of the existence of white privilege. For poor whites, like those who receive welfare benefits, distinguishing oneself from blacks and Latinos and more transparently embracing the superiority of whiteness may seem more important than for economically advantaged whites who tend to have less daily contact with racial others as peers.[6] Bounds cites the example of a white woman secretary who had, at an earlier time in her life, needed to receive public assistance funds. The woman's account of this difficult time refers to black women "on welfare," depicting them as lazy, and to her own, contrasting, superior qualities.[7]

In worship services, prayers of thanksgiving by white congregants, a sense of one's "blessings and blessedness" linked to a sense of one's white superiority, could be supported by widely ranging social status and economic needs. Liturgical strategies that intervene in this sense of blessedness would have to attend to the distinctive socioeconomic class circumstances that might inform the spiritual and social identity of these congregants. Such strictly individualistic perspectives on the construction of whiteness through denial and entitlement do not, however, satisfactorily depict how white superiority is collectively sustained.

As a systemic concept, white privilege also uncovers the basis for acts of racial discrimination by individuals or groups in our society. Cultural historian and theorist George Lipsitz stresses the "systemic, collective, and coordinated" group behavior of whites.[8] He describes how environmental racism protects the health and welfare of whites by placing health-endangering facilities, such as those for garbage incineration, toxic waste dumping, and nuclear waste storage, in predominantly black, Latino, and Native American communities. As a result of their proximity to these sites, members of these communities, especially the children, suffer from serious health problems (e.g., phenomenally high rates of reproductive organ cancer for exposed Navajo teenagers).[9]

There are harsh penalties for endangering the environment where white citizens live. Lipsitz cites findings from a study of the Environmental Protection Agency's response to toxic waste polluters, disclosing how "polluters of sites near the greatest white population received penalties 500 percent higher than penalties imposed on polluters in minority areas."[10] The interests of whites, in this case, their health and especially the health of the more vulnerable members of their communities—white children—are given governmental priority. These examples clarify how white privilege is extended through the consequences of discriminatory actions. The white beneficiaries of racial discrimination may or may not participate in those discriminatory practices. Thus, even if whites claim that they do not personally engage in racially discriminatory acts, the salient point is that, in reality, they benefit from and are advantaged by a persistent, historic pattern of such acts.

In what ways might these systemic aspects of white privilege be preserved in predominantly white worship settings? Within their worship, this systemic priority of treating whites as a group deserving of protection may not be distinguishable from the designation of Christian people as deserving recipients of special protection under the new covenant Jesus established. Christian worship celebrations deliberately foment a sense of Christian peoplehood, of being collectively called by God, and of being God's people. Power relations in the society that reward an "investment in whiteness," in maintaining the privileges and protection of whites, could be subtly reaffirmed in liturgical pronouncements by white congregational members about their special status as God's people. What message in the service interrupts, for instance, liturgical language such as "This is the Word of God for the people of God" (that may be said after scripture is read), from undergirding the existing strong cultural investment in maintaining the privileges of the society for the central people (whites) of the society?

An investment in whiteness prioritizes the group interests of whites through systemic discrimination, and also involves the elements of denial and entitlement described above. All three—denial, entitlement, and systemic investment—are aspects of white privilege that rely upon each other, upholding one another. Denial of the fact that issues of race and racism are significant in white people's self-expression and interactions protects their entitlement. Conversely, the entitlement of whites to be seen as the normal group, or as "just human beings" who do not need to be classified, rests upon denial. Entitlement employs denial, gives it a purpose: to keep the benefits of white privilege from being acknowledged. Finally, the systemic assertion of the racial group interests of whites, by means of discriminatory policies favoring whites, requires both entitlement and denial. This systematic assertion of group interests is propped up by a sense of white entitlement—that is, whites, as opposed to others, are naturally entitled to have their human worth considered incontestable and of paramount importance. In addition, systemically discriminatory policies seem rational and fair because of various forms of denial about their existence. When historic, institutional patterns that advantage whites are covered up with denials, it can seem reasonable to minimize or dismiss individual claims of racism (such as the pollution examples above) as isolated phenomena.

The denial of white privilege, entitlement to white privilege, and systemic investment in it all dance together to create a form of cultural ritual that helps to supply meaning and order for living together in our society.

Rituals and Ritualizing

We need rituals. They celebrate, promote, and create patterns of behavior. Rituals provide a sense of stability and of possibility. On Sunday mornings, in the lived experiences and attitudes of the worshipers, cultural rituals that preserve white privilege encounter rituals of Christian faith. A commitment to the superiority of whites supplies meaning and order in the broader society, and thus offers clear moral guidance about the status and worth of people in our shared communal lives. At the same time, a commitment to Christian faith is difficult if not impossible to maintain without some ritual reminders of the distinctive substance of Christianity. Worship rituals of gathering people and sending them off, receiving sacraments like Communion and baptism, as well as listening to preaching about the meaning of scripture, help to provide spiritual and moral guidance for a Christian's daily life.

Theologian Tom Driver helpfully differentiates the meanings of "ritual" and "ritualization."

> Like art ritualization involves both improvisation and the establishment of repeatable form. These two elements provide a way of distinguishing the words "ritualization" and "ritual" in reference to human activity. The former (ritualization) emphasizes the making of new forms through which expressive behavior can flow, while the latter (rit-

> ual) connotes an already known, richly symbolic pattern of behavior, the emphasis falling less upon the making and more upon the valued pattern and its panoply of associations. . . . Without its ritualizing component, ritual would be entirely repetitious and static.[11]

Christian worship includes both of these ritualizing and ritual functions as it links contemporary cultural events and attitudes to ancient Christian symbols and texts. In its ritualizing function, new forms are created that allow the worshiping community to engage in behavior that recognizes or celebrates the events, needs, and concerns continuously arising from the faith community. In its ritual function, symbolic and repeated acts of naming and silencing in Christian worship may preserve and even sacralize established patterns of behavior and attitudes of the gathered community as well as the broader society.

Messages about denial, entitlement, and systemic investment in white dominance function in a ritualizing manner, creating new adaptations to social changes in economic conditions or in response to varied forms of anti-racist resistance. The ritualizing function performed by that triumvirate of white dominance can adhere to the ritual function of Christian worship, to the repeatable forms of worship that lend a sense of stability and order and conserve social patterns. Thus, a syncretistic fusion between the meaning of Christian worship and cultural expressions of white dominance may occur in the worshiping congregant's experience of this comfortable liaison.

The maintenance of white dominance exhibits its own religious qualities. It can be understood as a system of beliefs that assigns moral worth and functions through symbols and spokespersons. As sociologists Joe Feagin and Hernán Vera demonstrate in their research chronicling a series of antiblack incidents in the 1980s and 1990s—sometimes through brutal violent acts by private groups or by police officers,[12] and at other times through pronouncements by state officials who assign stigmatizing labels—persons of color are routinely treated as inferior in ways that have symbolic meaning for every member of the broader society. Feagin and Vera argue that there are "racialized rituals" such as hostile acts of discrimination and violence against blacks that "broadcast to the entire community the racial mythologies held by many in the dominant white group."[13] Through such racist rituals, unspoken understandings about the status and worth of white people and of black people "are maintained and propagated to present and future generations of Americans in all racial and ethnic groups."[14]

These rituals bolster faith in the myth that peoples not considered to be white have innate deficiencies as well as accompanying fictions about the superior qualities of whites. Feagan and Vera identify the central participants in these incidents/rituals as "officiants" and those who willingly or unwillingly carry out racist policies as "acolytes." There are also a host of passive white participants who choose not to intervene or protest the racially hostile acts and statements that are usually part of these rites. Most importantly, racist rituals deprive their victims of basic human rights, and have a destructive impact on their lives, their energy, and their talents. Feagin and Vera explain:

> The millions of people of color in the United States who have been and continue to be sacrificed to the mythological needs of white superiority are in certain ways like the sacrificial victims of religious rites of some ancient societies: alien others who may be compelled to forfeit their lives or well-being in the name of compelling dominant-group interests.[15]

How might lessons about the "alien other" that racist rituals teach be reinscribed within Christian worship rituals?

In predominantly white cultural contexts, there are some ways in which the ritual of Communion might absorb the kinds of cultural meanings related to whiteness that Feagin and Vera depict. When they enter the worship service having been "acolytes" or passive observers of the ways persons of color are "sacrificed to the mythological needs of white superiority," what does it mean for whites to repeatedly rehearse this ritual of giving thanks for the fact that Jesus suffered, sacrificed, and died to take away their sins? Does this ritual encourage whites in taking for granted the suffering of others, and maybe even the deaths that benefit them (whites)? To some degree, atonement theology expressed in church rituals like Communion could merge with and inform white people's sense of entitlement. It could teach them that reaping the benefits of forgiveness and absolution that is due them because of God's intentional sacrifice of a person for their sake. Communion could function as a kind of liturgical reinscribing of the privileges of whiteness, possibly fostering a lack of concern for the systemic ways they may benefit from the sacrifice of the health, safety, and well-being of "alien others."

Christians may resist an investigation of worship for such particularized social messages about white privilege because worship is considered an important expression of universality in Christianity. The universal quality of Christian liturgy has usually been understood as providing Christians with common practices such as baptism and Communion that are not fundamentally shaped by the particular cultural contexts where those rites are performed. A major reason for stressing this universal quality has been to promote Christian unity across national boundaries, differences in structure and polity of church bodies, and theology and methods of interpreting scripture. A Christian theological emphasis on how rites like Communion are a celebration of unspecified divine mystery also contributes to this characterization of Christian liturgy's universality.

If instilling a notion of universality means that Christian ritual is unaffected by cultural particularity, then worshiping congregants are encouraged to pretend that race and culture do not matter in this worship space, practicing one of the major characteristics upholding white privilege: denial. Though beyond the scope of this discussion, it might be helpful to review the origins of Christian liturgy in elitist Greco-Roman culture and the historical development of its capacity to function as a mechanism of social control within culturally pluralistic contexts.[16] The problem of how routine Christian liturgical practices preserve the denial of sociopolitical inequalities within the faith community may be rooted in the social origins of Christianity.

Participation in worship practices falsely labeled culturally neutral constitutes a specific practice of denial that can foster white dissociation from the reality of racist inequality, how people are implicated in it, and what its costs are. White denial provides insulation from the pain caused by sacrificing persons of color to the need for a sense of superiority. In another point of mutual reinforcement between rituals of white dominance and rituals of Christian worship, the true virtue (perhaps divine ingredient) of Christian worship may seem to be found in its distance from and inability to be shaped by ongoing, discrete (painful) sociopolitical realities. Christian worship may be aided in taking on this socially distancing (absolving?) function by ongoing cultural rites in the broader society that abet the denial of painful social arrangements advantaging whites.

Mary Hobgood, a white Christian social ethicist, points out the moral costs to whites of this kind of dissociation. She describes the fear of their own vulnerability and dependence that fuels white projections of negative characteristics onto people of color, the need "to split off the vulnerable and dependent self onto racialized and impoverished others."[17] There are moral costs to whites in this behavior "because white status depends on denying the deepest parts of the relational self, our humanity is impoverished, and our capacity to be moral—in right relationship with others—is diminished."[18] Such alienation from self and others can produce a psychic and spiritual numbness that needs to be shattered for change to occur.[19]

Christian worship practices frequently invoke an emotional and spiritual sense of relational dependence, and nurturing this sense of dependence presents an opening for both consenting to and contesting white privilege. A student in an ethics class that I taught, Sally Wilson,[20] helpfully analyzed white privilege in a written account of her experience as a participant-observer at a Protestant worship service in Massachusetts made up of fairly affluent whites (middle and upper-middle-income households). Her report drew attention to messages about dependence that were part of the liturgy.

> On the one hand, phrases in the invocation ("make us ready to hear your good news") and the doxology ("praise God from whom all blessings flow") suggest human dependence upon God, challenging white elite assumptions about independence and inherent or personally achieved wisdom, strength, and wealth. . . . At the same time that the (primarily white) congregants are called upon to see themselves as dependent upon God, we are called upon to see others (those outside of the congregation) as dependent upon us and persons to whom we give, (the invocation calls upon God to "touch us so that we may touch others with your love").[21]

These are community-building rituals that affirm the congregation's sense of common purpose in coming together before their God. Remembering their dependence upon and need for God can challenge the white privilege of these congregants or support it when their sense of neediness is attached to a hierarchical theological understanding of relating: God (down?) to us, us (down?) to others in need.

For faith communities such as the one that Sally Wilson visited, social hierarchies might be ritually supported through some of the following dynamics. Habitual practices that maintain social dominance and exploitation surround congregants in daily life, especially within their economic relationships, and are uncontested in regular enactments of Christian spirituality in church. The broader culture consists of socioeconomic relations where richer people with more material wealth who are disproportionately whites have higher status and more privileges than poorer people, disproportionately blacks and Latinos. When denial about certain unfair realities is maintained, this ordering of society seems deserved. For example, these congregational members might have mortgage loans upon which they depend in order to afford their housing, thereby benefiting from the frequent incidence of discrimination favoring white housing-loan applicants.[22] When they get dressed each day, in most cases, they rely upon the labor of the poor who have produced their clothes, often under sweatshop factory conditions in Asia and Latin America.[23] When eating their meals they probably depend upon fruits and vegetables picked by economically exploited U.S. immigrant workers from Mexico or South America. These worshipers may cling to the myth that they are economically advantaged—better off than those "below" them, because they are economically independent and self-sufficient members of society.

Concealing their dependence upon varied forms of socioeconomic exploitation and racist privileging may be upheld rather than challenged by well-intentioned Christian prayers asking God to "touch us so that we may touch others." The moral and spiritual message these congregants receive from such prayers might not only protect their social dominance from being questioned, but also imbue it with righteousness in the following manner. First this kind of liturgy could convey a need for them to replace their sense of self-sufficiency with recognition of their dependence upon God's blessed "touch" for the wealth and comfort they enjoy. Second, it could also convey a need to reach out with caring to "others" below them in social status and privileges, fulfilling the role that God intends for those to whom God has given so many "blessings." In this prayer the social hierarchy is therefore left intact and appears to be part of God's plan. In a different church setting, one where there are more working-class and poor whites, such Christian rituals may give members an opportunity to symbolically inhabit a position of superiority and advantage that is not realized materially in their daily lives.

As a corrective response to the demands of racist rituals in society, Christians cannot abandon their own rituals. Christians need worship rituals that destabilize rituals of white dominance and confront its entangled religious and political veneer. Especially for predominantly white faith communities, liturgical acknowledgment of dependence upon both God *and* upon other people could lead to an awakening, instigating a cognizance of the rituals of white dominance in the broader community in which they also participate. Not everyone, however, in such Christian worship settings is white. We must also inquire about how people of color might negotiate overlapping messages about faith and race that support white dominance.

White Dominance and the Practices of the Rest of Us

Focusing our discussion only on whites within predominantly white settings can maintain the privileges of whiteness, that is, the centrality of whites in precisely the manner I have been criticizing. Persons of color can internalize notions of white superiority and of their own inferiority in multiple ways, and these notions can surface in the context of Christian worship, especially within predominantly white Protestant churches and denominational gatherings. They can also be present in worship settings that are predominantly composed of persons of color.

As I emphasize problematic dynamics of racism for persons of color within predominantly white worship settings, I am definitely not covertly advocating racial separation during worship. On the contrary, I am urging the formulation of probing questions about existing social dynamics in order to enable the discovery of more liberative practices. Persons of color enter the worship space with well-learned cultural lessons from having been victims of, passive observers to, and sometimes even "acolytes" for racist rites of white dominance in the broader society. Their socialization also includes the messages about moral worth in the highly rewarded practices of denial, entitlement, and systemic investment in white domination. Why wouldn't the distortions of personhood that these experiences produce, merge with, and hence also distort, their corporate experience of worshiping God? The following examples explore varied forms of racial silencing and misrepresentation of self and community as well as taboos about openly criticizing repressive practices in one's own community.

"Presenting an acceptable face, speaking without a Spanish accent, hiding what we really felt—masking our inner selves—were defenses against racism passed on to us by our parents to help us get along," comments legal scholar Margaret Montoya.[24] Montoya describes this process of *máscaras* (masks) as she reflects on her law school education. This process is a response to white denial that pressures persons of color to silence parts of their identities and self-expression. In spite of these costs, *máscaras* is also learned as a way of coping, surviving, and generally "getting along." As Montoya points out, "Silence ensures invisibility. Silence provides protection. Silence masks."[25] Silence is a helpful tactic to avoid looking, as her mother chided her against when she was a child, *greñudas* (uncombed). Besides a reference to her hair looking messy, this term protectively conveyed, "Be prepared, because you will be judged by your skin color, your names, your accents. They will see you as ugly, lazy, dumb, and dirty."[26]

In predominantly white worship settings, the avoidance of looking *greñudas* might mean consciously attempting to be "the exceptional" racial/ethnic minority person, the one who evades the stereotypes of ugly-lazy-dumb-dirty racial minorities. For a Latina, this conscious attempt may involve trying to excel in speaking English without an accent when offering prayers, singing a hymn, or reading scripture. For a South Asian male, it may mean trying to look and behave in a manner that makes it obvious that he is not a "terrorist." For an African American, it could mean a preoccupation with attempting to be seen as always impeccably neat and clean, arriving on time, and speaking in a manner that is extremely articulate in order to prove one is an exception to racist white expectations. In numerous ways, one may participate in the denial that is commonly assumed to be part of Christian worship rituals—that race does not matter in this space. But, at the same time, the constraints of race are always looming, so that the approval of whites may remain, implicitly, almost as important as the approval of the God one has come to church to worship.

Even in predominantly black worship spaces, where rituals may be created to celebrate "our people and heritage," pursuit of the status of the exceptional black may still be nurtured. Undeniably such ceremonies of recognition in predominantly black churches can be an innovative tactic for ritualizing resistance to the racist exclusion that occurs elsewhere, creating a place for valuing and celebrating black life in opposition to its devalued status in mainstream society. For instance, recognizing the educational achievement of black youth in worship services can defy more popular images of black youth that do not emphasize their interest in education.

Those who are celebrated as the achievers in whom "we can take pride" rarely include the economically destitute. Instead, those who are commended in such black worship rituals can be seen as "exceptional" blacks and cherished for being unlike "the others" who are, it seems, a source of embarrassment. As a result, some of those popularly labeled as deficient by white racist judgments in the broader public sphere may face that same stigmatizing treatment within church practices. Community members such as poor black single mothers who have achieved amazing feats of struggle and survival on public assistance will most likely not be among those celebrated for accomplishments or for gifts of courage and tenacity. Indeed, the salvation that may often be preached and prayed about them will be focused on helping them repent of their allegedly ugly-lazy-dumb-dirty ways. These worshipers may learn that earning God's approval is exactly the same as earning the approval of white politicians and media spokespersons who make racist assessments of them. For example, Elder Smith of the predominantly

African American Temple Zion Church of God in Christ in Mississippi explains how he preaches about welfare in his sermons:

> I tell them this. "It is not God's will for you to be on welfare. And it insults God for Him to be our Father, [for] us to trust Him, and we have to have a handout every day of our lives." So, therefore, I teach it is essential to us growing, to being proper witnesses, that we don't find ourselves on welfare.[27]

The problem for Christian public assistance recipients who hear this message is not merely that this preacher compounds their social stigma by adding religious authorization to it. Heeding this message that it is insulting to God and a sign of Christian failure to receive public assistance (welfare) can endanger women who are trying to escape the terror of life with an abusive male partner (as is the case for many applying for welfare benefits).[28]

Besides rewarding or punishing proclamations by worship leaders, a different response by worship participants to the endless task of fending off white racism may be a kind of surrender to the protection of silence. The easiest response, for some, may be to simply accede to white dominance by performing the discrete tasks of taking care of one's self, family, and church family, and never bringing up anything about racism. Even if, for instance, one does argue a little when a white person greets her during worship with insistent comments that reflect a racial stereotype about all blacks being able to sing, pretty quickly one just lets it go. One silently allows that white-centered definition of reality and of one's self to merge with all of the other ways that the centrality of white people and their cultural understandings reign in our society as dominant and superior.

For some persons of color, this struggle with acquiescence to white dominance may compel them to claim inaccurate self-definitions in order to fit one of the acceptable racial classifications.[29] If their physical appearance does not immediately indicate to strangers how their racial classification conforms to one of the societally prescribed categories, they frequently have to respond to some form of the racial question, "What are you?" In their response, any choice these persons of color make from the limited options available demands a distorted and truncated representation of their cultural identity. And often, they must also make a decision about whether or not to claim some degree of the superiority of whiteness as part of their identity. Lisa Kahaleole Chang Hall, a native Hawaiian, describes her experiences of continually having her identity questioned as she moved to different regions of the United States while growing up.

> Throughout my childhood, anyone telling racial/ethnic jokes always questioned me to make sure that I wasn't one of the "them" they were about to degrade. Depending upon where we were stationed, I was offered many chances to be one of the good colored/(not Bad Black) people and sometimes I took them.[30]

She mutes the particularity of her native Hawaiian racial/ethnic identity in order to be accepted, lessening the worth of her own identity and of other "others" (blacks). Even in childhood, she clearly understood the moral currency in distancing herself from a black racial identity. Later, in high school in Virginia, she admits that she "became white exotica," rather than a black girl, apparently the only two options she had.[31]

This racial classification system of the broader culture and the moral climate it nurtures is too often mirrored in church life. Especially in predominantly white Protestant denominations, persons of color who are not African Americans may be offered the limited options of identifying with "regular" church worship (among whites), black worship and preaching, or "one of our" ethnic church worship styles resulting from "our foreign missionary work." This spectrum may be the only one available in predominantly white church organizations, only a monocultural, monolithic identity is permitted, and the centrality of whiteness as reference point is undisturbed. The spiritual implications of acquiescence to this unsatisfactory choice can involve wrestling with white-centered definitions of culture and self in order to recognize one's self as part of the people of God.

An assertive, rather than yielding, expression of this wrestling with self-definition might include generalized, celebratory claims by persons of color about worship practices from their "own" culture or tradition, accompanied by requests for inclusion of such practices in predominantly white worship settings. These claims are intended to counter the stranglehold of European influences represented as classical and authentically universal in most Western Christian liturgy and hymnody.[32] Requests for multicultural resources are, therefore, a creative and useful intervention by persons of color in predominantly white contexts. But the outcome can be a strange distortion when such requests are fulfilled by efforts like adding the "Korean worship style" to one service or "Latino rhythms" to the hymnody. The diversity within the Korean and Latino traditions being introduced is lost. Moreover, even as it is celebrated, cultural particularity is recognized as only a characteristic of those who are not Euro-American. An eighteenth-century British hymn writer like Charles Wesley ("O for a Thousand Tongues to Sing") remains a symbol of culturally universal worship resources. In addition, issues of power, domination, and exploitation within and among the religious traditions of peoples of color are avoided when acting out this type of liturgical multicultural tourism. A preference for denial about injustices and inequalities that is so prevalent in the dominant ethos of the society may also be reproduced within non-dominant racial/ethnic communities.

Discriminatory treatment of women in the worship practices of certain predominantly black churches illustrates this problem of reproducing inequality and is sometimes even treated as a reasonable strategy to offset racist treatment of black men.[33] In these churches women are denied access to full pastoral leadership and may be physically barred from the pulpit area—as if the mere presence of a female body constitutes a desecration of it. The preaching/pastoral role in worship may be treated as a province of authority and status to which black males are solely entitled because of the white racism that they encounter in the broader society. In other words, for some, black women should be denied full participation in the preaching/pastoral role because racism in the society prevents black men from assuming their (rightful?) roles as patriarchal figures of authority. Within this sexist logic, in order to counter racism in the broader society, the worship space of black churches becomes the one public space where black males who function as preachers and pastoral leaders can claim a supposed patriarchal male entitlement to exert dominating authority over women. Unjust treatment of women is institutionalized in Christian worship and justified by the realities of white domination.

When claims about the nature of worship in "the" black tradition are made in the presence of whites (any public sphere of dominant society), this problem of discrimination against women is not often acknowledged by black Christians as one of its core components, even by many scholars of African American religion.[34] There is a concern that such open criticism of black religious tradition undermines its historic role of maintaining unity and cohesion in the black community that enables resistance to white domination. (Remember that "black community" does not refer to a geographic grouping, but a political one; it includes African Americans in diverse community settings.) Assertions about worship in "the black tradition" that strongly criticize the sexism that has been and continues to be so thoroughly a part of that tradition is often seen as divisive.

What is really at stake in the fear of divisiveness is the concern that whites will take the criticisms of blacks and use them as evidence of black inferiority or as a means to escape self-criticism. This is hardly a trivial concern. Some whites will use such criticism of blacks to further rationalize the subjugating treatment of them or simply to feed an insatiable appetite for entertaining themselves with the curiosity of black objects, and when those objects are in conflict with each other, the excitement of the spectacle is heightened. Discussing the problem of sexism in black churches may provide whites with a way of evading criticism of similar patterns among predominantly white church groups with comparable exclusions of women's ordained leadership in Roman Catholicism, Orthodox Christianity, or among Southern Baptists.

The concern for avoiding divisiveness provides a helpful reminder that one's sense of performing "in front of whites" even surfaces in racially homogeneous settings. Because the response of whites matters so much, to a certain extent, one is always in front of whites. The white gaze can take root in black psyches even when whites are not physically present. But acceding to their dominance comes with costs that are too high—such as sacrificing black women's gifts of preaching and leadership to the myth of male superiority. When some demonstration of "our black tradition" is uncritically performed in worship, it can take on a warped form that will not trouble white dominance, and even reproduces some of its characteristics of denial and entitlement.

Building blocks for creating more liberative practices can be found in an understanding of the inseparability of form and content. The content of Christian practices, such as the language or words charismatically preached in worship, cannot be separated from the form guiding those practices, e.g., the rules that define who can speak from the pulpit. There is a powerful moral message in preaching and teaching about God's inclusive love within exclusive traditions that rule out certain groups of people as innately ineligible to do that preaching and teaching. This worship practice conveys moral hypocrisy, and cultivates a spiritually comforting routine for denying that hypocrisy.

White supremacy, namely the benefits of white privilege, can produce a numbing effect on everyone. For whites, there may be a deadening of empathy for persons of color and a diminished capacity to be in right relation with them. For persons of color, this dehumanizing relationship can produce a deep hunger for affirmation. Hence, rituals that provide self-affirmation are necessary, but not just any self-affirming ritual will be adequate. Within Christian worship, a conscious choice has to be made for inclusion of affirming rituals that stimulate a faithfulness to God that opposes rather than replicates a loss of empathy for persons of color in groups other than one's own as well as for low status members of one's own racial/ethnic group.

Multicultural Methods for Making Liturgical Choices

More specific ideas are needed to boost Christian imagination about how to gain some measure of freedom from this preoccupation with white dominance.

Potential for change lies in the fact that choices are always made about appropriate elements of worship. Deliberations take place for the selection of instrumental and choral music or the design of stained-glass windows and wall banners in the sanctuary. In the desire to inspire meaningful silent meditation by individuals and heartfelt hymn singing by the whole congregation, a decision-making process about how to do so occurs. The scripture texts that are given emphasis and the words that are used to encourage people to offer their prayers and testimonies also reflect certain choices. In the many details of preparing a worship service, choices are made about how public, communal expressions of Christian worship nurture or challenge existing mores about white dominance.

Multicultural theoretical approaches can assist Christians in making liturgical choices that enhance their recognition of human diversity as good, as well as their intolerance for unjust social relationships among diverse human communities. Multicultural understandings can offer guidance in creating worship rituals where Christians are more likely to be offered the chance to participate in disrupting a commitment to white dominance than encouraged in going along with it and similar repressive social practices.

To recognize human diversity as good requires some understanding of varying cultural patterns. Cultural variations display the distinctive ways human beings express their thought and creativity. As advocates of multicultural education in U.S. schools have argued, increasing cultural literacy about the broad spectrum of racial/ethnic identities, traditions, and experiences provides a more accurate and thorough understanding of how this nation's history and culture have evolved.[35] Indeed this kind of multicultural literacy can unleash a sense of plurality (in cultural perspectives) as norm rather than exception, as valuable rather than a problem to be overcome. It can break open binary categories that mute the racial/ethnic pluralism that exists and insist on the racial identity question, "Are you black or white?" A basic understanding of a range of cultural traditions and experiences can encourage appreciation for interwoven cultural identities like those of persons of mixed racial parentage or who have been cross-racially adopted.

This multicultural emphasis can also shift our identification of white Americans and Europeans as the central agents of history. It allows greater awareness of patterns of discrimination and racial prejudice among, for instance, the varying groups lumped together under the category of "Asians" or "Hispanics/Latino/as." This form of historical literacy also includes cognizance of patterns of solidarity between nondominant racial/ethnic groups as well, like historical examples of relations between Native American tribes and African American slaves in Florida, or Mexican American and Japanese American farm workers in California at the turn of the twentieth century.[36]

James Banks, a multicultural education scholar, stresses how multicultural competency "helps students expand their conception of what it means to be human . . . Because cultures are made by people, there are many ways of being human."[37] In Christian religious terms, learning about multiple cultural patterns needs to be valued not only because it can expand an understanding of what it means to be human. It also offers worshipers the spiritually enlivening opportunity to grow in their views about how God's creative power and justice-seeking interacts with the social adaptations human beings create.

Ritualizing diverse, nondominant, cultural expressions of faith may provide an affirmation of human diversity with the potential to expand the conception of God that Christians gather to worship. Such practices can perhaps develop recognition of God's blessed presence amid the wide spectrum of cultural patterns developed by God's human creations. Filipino theologian Eleazar Fernandez celebrates Asian American preaching that speaks to Asian American congregations "of a God who affirms their color, a color that has been devalued in white racist society . . . God is colorful and delights in the variety of colors. . . . God transcends not by becoming colorless; rather God delights and takes cognizance in a variety of colors."[38] As Fernandez suggests, theologically expressed, direct attention to issues of race/ethnicity within worship can address the combined spiritual and social needs of the people. But the particularity of the message is essential. In communities of color, this theology about God's cognizance of a variety of colors might enable the faith community to resist the poisonous effects of racism that surround them and deepen their understanding of God as well.

An emphasis on multicultural patterns and experiences as reflective of diverse ways of being human might be theologically nourishing in yet another way. It may help worshipers engage and reflect upon key, historic theological understandings of God within Christianity. Similar to human cultural identities, core theological descriptions of God are also fundamentally pluralistic, such as the Trinitarian notion of God as Creator, Redeemer, and Holy Spirit, or the understanding of Jesus as simultaneously fully human, fully divine, and fully divine/human. For Christians, contemporary heterogeneous cultural understandings of our communities may be understood in a way that is directly relevant to historic expressions of faith. Hence the content of worship celebrations of Christian faith could be guided by the assumption that consciousness of human plurality can enrich one's ability to perceive plurality within the very nature of the divine, and vice versa.

The possibilities that break open when nondominant multicultural perspectives are incorporated in worship are abundant, but my purpose is not to simply extol the virtues of such an approach.[39] The pull of white dominance and its destructive patterns of relating still present a formidable challenge for Christian worship in the U.S. context, even when a focus upon including nondominant cultural traditions and theology is secured. As noted earlier, representations of these nondominant traditions can be inserted into worship in a static way that unintentionally promotes racial stereotypes. Especially in predominantly white settings, celebrations of multiple cultural identities can be a means for avoiding and thus denying the presence of racism. A racially integrated congregation or a liturgy with culturally diverse expressions of faith is not necessarily an indication that racism is being addressed. There is still a need to clarify how multiculturalism can provide guidance on what it means to disrupt that consuming social commitment to white supremacy which can seep into the ritual practices of the church.

An assessment of what it means to expand the cultural assumptions in one's worship practices certainly could be a starting point for addressing racism. Banks created a grid for analyzing multicultural education that might be useful to congregations for generating ideas about how to evaluate the inclusion of multicultural content, beyond dominant white (and European) centered cultural sources, in their liturgical traditions. Banks describes four levels of integration for ethnic content in schools.

Level 1: Contributions Approach—Focuses on heroes, holidays, and discrete cultural elements.

Level 2: Additive Approach—Content, concepts, themes, and perspectives are added to the curriculum.

Level 3: Transformation Approach—The structure of the curriculum is changed to enable students to view concepts, issues, events, themes from the perspective of diverse ethnic and cultural groups.

Level 4: Social Action Approach—Students make decisions on important social issues and take actions to help solve them.[40]

Besides offering churches an instructive tool for assessment, the precedence given here to decision making as the culminating goal is key for addressing white supremacy, particularly the numbing effects of white privilege. Churches that are already committed to inclusion of nondominant multicultural expressions of faith in their liturgies are likely to employ some combination of these approaches, and the categories Banks suggests could help to organize their evaluation of how racial messages are conveyed in their practices.

For example, in a predominantly white church, the congregation may have an annual recognition of Martin Luther King Jr. during worship. They acknowledge the fact that one special individual who is not white has made contributions to church and society that should be honored by their congregation within worship (contributions approach). Or a predominantly black congregation may host a guest Korean choir in their worship service. The choir may come and sing a song in Korean with references to ideas popularly known in Korea that are translated and explained to their hosts. This church thereby adds a cultural perspective on worshiping God through music that it would not have otherwise experienced (additive approach). In another approach, a church might change its Communion ritual. As a way of commemorating the execution of Jesus by the Roman state, his suffering that preceded it, and resurrection that followed it, the Communion ritual could highlight a range of cultural contexts where suffering due to state sponsored terrorism and killing has occurred in the past or present (transformation approach).

Unless congregants reflect on the daily choices they make related to issues of race/ethnicity and power, these worship rituals will not represent a meaningful shift in practices for either the church or society (social action approach). An emphasis on cultural diversity that leaves out an examination of how issues of power and status have shaped relationships between racial/ethnic groups fails to accurately reflect social realities and certainly does not challenge white dominance.[41] For instance, it would be misleading if one were to describe U.S. history by equating the cultural perspectives of the indigenous nations of people and the perspectives of the people from European nations who came and settled on the lands of the indigenous peoples. Attempting, with the best of intentions, for a more inclusive understanding of cultural history, one might tell stories in, for example, a Thanksgiving worship service about the distinctive cultural traditions that the Europeans brought, alongside of a description of the unique cultural traditions of the indigenous peoples that Europeans encountered. But the genocide, rape of Native women, and theft of Native lands that was part of the cultural perspective asserted by European Christians and their descendants would be rendered morally neutral in this form of multiculturalism. An antiracist consciousness that is alerted to how cultural rituals can so easily merge with and corrupt corporate experiences of worshiping God will reject liturgy that renders all social particularities relative.

Another way to trivialize the peculiar, differing circumstances oppressive conditions create could be overgeneralization in the form of prayers about "celebrating the blessedness of *all* of our diversity in age, race/ethnicity, sexuality, gender, abilities/disabilities." Similarly, a universal call for repentance from "our" complicity in sinfulness may help to reproduce injustice rather than repair it. These appeals to universality lump what it means to perpetrate or benefit from sinful acts together with what it means to be "the sinned-against."[42] Just as the social circumstances differ for those whose identities are given privileged status from those whose identities are devalued, so too should the theological message for each that is offered in worship.

In a liberative Christian ethic, multicultural awareness must include theological attention to the choices that have been made in our society which result in some people being granted status and privilege on the basis of their racial/ethnic identity. Especially in predominantly white congregations, to destabilize patterns of social dominance will mean deliberately making choices that risk diminishing one's access to certain benefits of social privilege or status. In Christianity, where the incarnation of Jesus and the church's embodiment of Christ are such central beliefs, a liturgy that is unrelated to the concrete, embodied practices of the worshiper's life is inadequate. A liberative ethic enjoins participatory expressions of this faith within the worship practices themselves as well as the practices of the broader society that one engages within daily life.

In congregations with varied racial/ethnic configurations as well as predominantly white ones, engendering a breach in their embrace of white dominance and similar social patterns will necessitate choices that comprehensively break with exclusive and excluding patterns within religion. As liturgical studies scholar Janet Walton argues when defining feminist liturgy, "Whereas in a patriarchal ritual one or a few men traditionally mediate power to and from God and to and from the people," feminist liturgy must be participatory where "leadership is reordered as collective authority, and power is imaged in new ways."[43] In liberative Christian ethics, power can be imaged in new ways in worship by interfering with all of the status quo hierarchical arrangements of it. Mixed messages, like a contradictory insistence on confronting white supremacy together with claims and practices that assert the superiority of heterosexuals in God's sight will be counterproductive. Contradictions in the Christian group's opposition to varying forms of exclusion and devaluation based upon identity will rob the truthfulness from any ritual of dissent with white dominance that is included in worship. Eric Law, author/activist specializing in a multicultural approach to Christian ministry, suggests that living the good news at the "crossings" requires a vigilant commitment to power analysis in order to know how "the gospel challenges the powerful to let go of power, to pick up the cross and follow Jesus," and how it "empowers the powerless to speak and act, because they are blessed, and God will liberate them."[44]

What if, within the worship service, there was an opportunity for testimonies of spiritual courage about confronting an everyday practice of privileging some people over others on the basis of their identity? Individuals could be invited to stand up and testify about instances of white privilege that they notice in the details of their daily life and the decisions that they made to resist those cultural practices. They could include details like their response to a store's selection of "nude" panty hose or an author's novel where the race of the white characters is assumed to be the normal one that does not need to be identified by the author. No detail would be too insignificant for this ritual of testifying.

What if, in worship of multiracial congregations, the cultural location of "classical" music was identified, such as German composer Ludwig van Beethoven's (1770–1827) "Hymn to Joy" ("Joyful, Joyful, We Adore Thee"), by reminding congregants of multicultural understandings within the composer's own sociohistorical German context? Through reminders as simple as bulletin inserts or as elaborate as a play preceding the music, contemporary ideas in the composer's setting could be cited, like German anthropologist Johann Friedrich Blumenbach's pioneering 1770s notion of five races of the human species—Caucasian, Mongolian, American, Ethiopian, and Malay—with Caucasian (originating from Mount Caucasus) as the primary race whose physical characteristics prove their loftier mentality and generous spirit.[45] As they sing Beethoven's tune, congregants could be asked to morally reflect on whether they perpetuate any of the same supremacist ideas about race as those surrounding this German musician when he chose a poem emphasizing "all human beings as brothers [and sisters]" to adapt for his Symphony No. 9 in D minor (from which the tune comes).[46]

What if, in predominantly white, economically advantaged congregations, there was a "God asks who is supposed to dispose of your trash" week during Advent? Every household could hold onto its trash for a week.[47] Youth could investigate the racial/ethnic and economic "geography" of trash and toxic waste disposal for their communities as well as the health and environmental consequences, and adults could find ways to minimize their household's accrual of trash. Sunday worship would include a ritual utilizing some representative piece of trash that each member brings to church, acknowledging sinful privileges and naming the costs passed onto others in disposal of household trash, as well as celebrating the need to do one's own work of building (environmental) justice when preparing the Way for Christ's advent, using noisemakers made out of the pieces of trash the children, youth, and adults brings forward.

We need many more concrete ideas about what liberative ethical practices might entail.

Chapter Five

Leadership

Dissenting Leaders and Heterosexism

Besides internal church practices of Sunday worship, liberative Christian ethics should be generated in the ongoing work of ministry and activism. Multiple forms of Christian thought and practice that dissent with cultural commitments to the superiority of certain groups are essential, but someone has to deliberately instigate and nurture them.

The stories with which we began in the first chapter focused on activist leadership in the 1930s by women like Cecelia Cabaniss Saunders of the Harlem YWCA and activist/journalists Ella Baker and Marvel Cooke. Those Harlem women demonstrated how knowledge that contributes guiding principles and assumptions to a Christian ethical vision for society is not just found in written texts like those authored by Reinhold Niebuhr. We can also learn from another kind of theoretical text, one created by the lives of those who make constructive changes in our common moral life through their leadership.

The contemporary testimonies of ministers and activists with which we conclude in this chapter add another demonstration of how guiding principles are generated, analyzed, and tested in the practice of leadership within local communities. We listen to the defiant responses by certain women leaders to the current climate of sweeping claims and institutional policies promoting the innate superiority of heterosexuals, claims and policies that easily fuse with the entitlement and systemic aspects of white privilege pointed out in the last chapter. In the leadership of the black women whose voices are included below, theory and practice merge and foster dissent in public life. These ministers and activists exhibit tenacity when facing what can seem like an overwhelming societal commitment to shaming and discriminatory treatment of people who openly identify themselves as lesbian, gay, bisexual, or transgendered. Particular liberative expressions of religious outreach, like these, boldly refuse to consent to the commitment to heterosexual superiority that appears to be so universal, proving that this commitment is not universal at all.

The conditions that these ministers and activists face are reminiscent of the debasing public practices related to sexuality that we saw in the sexual violation of women airline passengers, women prisoners, and Yvonne's rape experience (chapter 2), or in caricatures of the sexuality of poor single mothers receiving public financial assistance (chapter 3). Here ministers and activists create oppositional as well as alternative ethical habits. They help to initiate a breach with both the denial and the currency of racism in public practices related to sexuality that would support the body invasion, body assault, and body-demeaning speech we have previously discussed. In particular, these ministers and activists develop antiracist resistance to body-demeaning public practices that are based on sexual identity.

Their strategies for confronting heterosexism are highlighted. Though homophobia may be a more familiar term to some of us, heterosexism draws attention directly to the need for ethical social practices. Heterosexism and homophobia are related but not identical social phenomena. Heterosexism comprises acts and practices that confer superior worth, status, and power upon heterosexuals and heterosexuality. Homophobia is primarily a fear of same-sex desire, attraction, and physical expressions of intimacy; this includes fear of the same-sex desire of another as well as of one's own feelings of same-sex desire. The articulation of homophobic fear ranges from ignorant statements and attitudes to violent crimes. Heterosexism in church and society is certainly fueled by homophobic fears and ignorance, but it takes the further step of maintaining rules and regulations that guarantee the perpetuation of homophobia. Most importantly, heterosexism comprises cultural and institutional rewards for persons who identify themselves as heterosexual and penalties for anyone who refuses to claim this label for their sexual identity.

Christian heterosexism incorporates a wide spectrum of teachings and practices. There are extremist teachings by Christian leaders like Pastor Pete Petersen, whose ministry asserts that the Bible compels Christians to make sure that the death penalty is instituted for all gays and lesbians.[1] Christian heterosexism also includes Protestant denominations that oust any clergy member who does not agree to either be celibate or enter a heterosexual marriage.[2] Some Protestant groups oust any heterosexual clergy member who will ceremonially bless and function supportively of monogamous, covenantal unions between two Christian intimate same-sex partners (even if the couple belongs to the congregation where the clergy member is supposed to serve as their pastor). In this way, the institution's severest penalties also extend to heterosexual clergy who offer their lesbian or gay church members the same pastoral support they would offer their heterosexual members. Like church rituals that reinscribe broader societal rituals of white superiority, Christian heterosexism adds God's sanction to bias-based social practices. But, in contemporary life, Christian heterosexism sanctions the sacrifice of the equal treatment, human worth, and dignity of lesbians, gay men, bisexuals, and transgendered persons with more explicit policies than the rewards for demonstrating a commitment to white superiority.

Christians often encounter this insistence on maintaining prejudice and discrimination as an assertion of the right thing to do, the right way to be a Christian. Yet, at the same time, it is possible to take exception to this insistence. There are, hopefully, many strategies to lessen the prejudice, discrimination, bigotry, and sometimes even violent assaults fostered by Christian heterosexism. It is also possible to actively differ with heterosexist social policies that can include the denial of someone's right to be at her life partner's hospital bedside and informed about the medical treatment that her partner is receiving only because they are same-sex spouses. Discriminatory government policies are sometimes expressed through the courts and may deny children the right to be raised by their lesbian mother, severing all of her parental rights based solely upon her sexual orientation.[3] Christian heterosexism merges with government policy in, for example, the attachment of welfare benefits for poor single women to their participation in heterosexual marriage promotion classes taught by Christian groups (as recommended by the U.S. Department of Health and Human Services).[4] Through such policies, heterosexual behavior, based upon heterosexist interpretations of Christian teachings, may be coercively foisted upon poor women who need to receive assistance.

Clues about what dissent might involve can be found in these interviews that I conducted with eleven African American women leaders who are heterosexuals and lesbians, living in differing parts of the United States and with backgrounds that constitute a range of Christian Protestant traditions.[5] Six of them have served as pioneering lesbian pastors who helped to found churches primarily comprising black gay and lesbian Christians.[6] The work by all of these women displays an ethical approach that refuses to reinforce a hierarchy of moral worth based upon sexuality, race, gender, or any other category of social identity. Their stories document a liberative struggle in our social history and offer liberative moral knowledge that develops ethical communal practices.

Listening to Living Texts

Theoretical and practical knowledge merge together in the living texts that these ministers and activists create. Several of the women are clergy or commissioned ministers who generate what might be considered evolving Christian ethics "texts" for us to explore. As Christian theology, reflection upon the meaning of Christian faith in God, is articulated in their roles as teacher, preacher, counselor, or community advocate, they produce living texts of theology and ethics through their leadership. Their discussions demonstrate how these ministers uphold certain theological traditions and seek to transform others. The nonclergy activists who work with church groups similarly contribute to the development of Christian theological and ethical norms. Through their advocacy with clergy and church groups they also provoke important discussions about the meaning and transformation of Christian tradition. All of the women construct liberative Christian social ethics that includes alternative and innovative approaches alongside resistance to oppression.

In each section below I place two interviews together (that were conducted separately) and arrange them in an alternating pattern to highlight the connections between the method and vocational starting point of each person. Like the engagement between differing sources in the other chapters, the "conversations" here draw attention to the contrasts and similarities between viewpoints offered by the interviewees. These "conversations" are offered in the following sequence. "Walking into the 'Firewall'" illustrates the courage and confrontation necessary for liberative praxis. "I Help Lay Down the Foundation for Those Who Come after Me" contains more examples of confrontation but shifts the focus slightly to the hope and patience that is so crucial for communal ethics. "Jesus Pushed the Parameters Away" emphasizes some of the theological assumptions that create a foundation for liberative leadership. It shows how this leadership can emanate from two very different life experiences. "What Would God's Church Look Like?" offers the testimony of local church pastors about what it means to build a supportive, trustworthy faith community that is centrally composed of black gay, lesbian, bisexual, and transgendered Christians. In "Raised Up . . . and Sent Out with a Purpose to Help," ministers of similarly composed predominantly black churches continue the description of church communities that affirm their members, but it concentrates on the design of antiracist, gay-affirming church outreach, witness, and mission. The interviewees are Rev. Irene Monroe, Dr. Sylvia Rhue, Ms. Mandy Carter, Rev. Dr. Youtha Hardman-Cromwell, Bishop Leontyne Kelly, Rev. Lynice Pinkard, Rev. Wanda Floyd, Rev. Ruby Wilson, Rev. Lisa Robinson, Rev. Alma Crawford, and Minister Janyce Jackson.

Walking into the "Firewall"

Dissenting with homophobia and heterosexism in church and society demands multiple, courageous confrontations of prejudice, discrimination, and hate. The testimonies of Dr. Sylvia Rhue and Rev. Irene Monroe specify some of the misunderstandings and illusions about scripture, race, and sexuality that must be clarified in those confrontations.

Sylvia Rhue, a documentary film producer and activist/educator, was raised a Seventh-day Adventist. She coproduced the documentary All God's Children,[7] *which focuses on homosexuality and religion within African American communities. She lives in southern California.*

Sylvia Rhue I go around the country to show these films in churches and community settings, to talk about these issues. . . . Religion has been such a firewall of ignorance on homosexuality and of resistance, and I do mean firewall.

If you get too logical, some people get turned off because they have a vested interest in hating homosexuality, as part of their identity. It's part of their identity as a religious person, and that could be as a Christian, a Jewish person, a Muslim, Hindu, whatever. But, mainly I work with Christians. . . .

We expanded our agenda [in one workshop with a predominantly white group of about twenty-five ministers in Charleston, South Carolina] to deal with issues of racism, sexism, and homophobia among people of faith.

Now, there were these two ministers there, and our argument to them began with issues of sexism, pointing out: "See where Paul said that women should be silent in the church?" And we discussed with them how all these things that Paul said about women have impacted women negatively in the church. They said that they don't believe in those statements about women. We also talked about Paul's statements telling slaves to obey their masters. We said, "Why do you reject those statements and not what Paul said about homosexuality?" And their argument back to us was, "Those other things were cultural. And, this [issue of homosexuality] is not cultural, this is scriptural." And we sat there stunned. Everything stopped for a minute. We didn't push them too much farther, because after all, they didn't have to show up for this workshop. . . . I said to one of them afterwards that I don't often get a chance to talk to conservative white people about these things. He said, "Oh, I'm not conservative."

They also explained to us that they could not vote yes within their denomination to support gay marriage. So I put on the chalkboard: "Reasons why heterosexuals get married." The group called out a lot of reasons why heterosexuals get married. Then I said, "Why do gays and lesbians want to get married?" We listed a lot of things there. And both lists had all the same reasons. Then one of the ministers pointed out that men and women were made for each other. And I brought up the fact that the clitoris wasn't made for a penis, and the clitoris is the primary sexual organ in women. And if your primary sexual organ wasn't made for the opposite sex, why did God do this? What is the function of the clitoris? You know, he almost fainted for a minute there. . . .

Now these two men said that maybe in five to ten years they would come around to seeing things differently, to seeing what we see, but that right now they were not going to vote to support the ordination of gay people or for "gay marriage."

[At another workshop on the AIDS crisis and its impact on gay people:] One man told me, "Let them die, if they're not going to follow God's Word, then just let them die." What do you say when somebody says something that hateful? How do you respond? You know, I don't want to be in the same room with this man again. He also said that he felt that gay people were possessed by the devil. It's mind-boggling, you know—how people can make these statements and think these thoughts.

Most of my work has been with black churches, black Christian churchgoers, and I find it's not the lesbians as much as the gay men who are in the closet, are being tortured, and torturing themselves. They believe these hateful statements. In my work, I've met so many, like one black gay man who was in the closet and he was suicidal, partly because of what he's been going through with the church. Especially for black gay men in black churches, church so often reinforces self-hatred, it's tormenting. . . .

But, sometimes in black churches, some of the male clergy preaching the loudest and sometimes even the most viciously against gay people are in fact having gay sex. I don't know how they define themselves. Well, they define themselves as heterosexuals who, in the closet, have sex with other men.

Irene Monroe is a Christian activist clergy member and black feminist public theologian. She has been a religion columnist for The Witness *and* In Newsweekly *and writes and lectures in many other national venues on issues of sexuality and religion. She lives in the Boston, Massachusetts, area.*

Irene Monroe When I moved, I had to go find the black folks. I had to find out: where are the black folks up here in Boston? I just went out to meet people. A lot of my time was spent seeking out people, getting involved in their community agendas and then also just building trust. I was an outsider and this person from Harvard. I am black and I am queer. So how do you develop trust? It developed out of my work, doing funerals, baptism, same-sex unions. I was working as an assistant pastor at a black church in Boston.

I began doing work around AIDS with black churches on how we needed to protect our black community. . . . We were at epidemic rates in terms of AIDS. In that ministry, I was visiting people at the hospitals. I was there at the jails and at the funerals. I was giving them information. I was talking about sex openly. I was giving out condoms. I was helping them to access medical services and telling them, "You have the right to ask for this. Do *not* be ashamed." I was working on destigmatizing the whole idea of having AIDS. I explained that "the sin is not that you have AIDS. The sin is that our community is sick because we have not come to your aid. That is what the sin is, not that you are sick." I kept asking: how do I, what is the best way, to reach this population of people, because they are not coming into the churches. Because they are so stigmatized—drug addicts, prostitutes, people with AIDS, this population is just not coming to church.

Also, I decided that what I needed to do was to talk with black ministers and develop some sort of trust with these guys. Did I develop any trust? Not really, but they know who I am. Most of them are dismissive of black women in ministry. At some point they have had to hear me or listen to me, because now I have become a voice in the community just as they are. I am representing the needs of not just queer people that they don't want to hear about. I have also won trust among straight black women, and among folks who are infected with this AIDS epidemic.

In [a workshop with a group of black church leaders] I said that we needed to deconstruct within our community this notion of a hierarchy of oppressions. I draw a diagram on paper. I try to explain it in a way that all the folks can get it. . . .

Then I go on and I say that as black people we are not as wedded to every letter of the biblical text. There are passages that are damning and damaging to black people. We have been very intentional about constructing a different kind of theology and ethics around those troubling texts in order to move us out of slavery. I say to them, we are still enslaved by virtue of our lack of understanding that we also have to take the shackles off of our women, and off of our lesbian, gay, bisexual, and transgendered people. The church has always had this hierarchy . . . this conceptual trap that we have to break ourselves out of, this intractable web. As much as it is our aim to be faithful Christians, we are also engaging in forms of spiritual abuse.

Sylvia Rhue What's most challenging is the belief that God says homosexuality is an abomination. The word "abomination" is rather liberally sprinkled throughout the Bible. Heterosexual homophobic people like to run with the word "abomination" because it is associated with feelings of disgust, loathing, and filth. But, to them, is it disgusting, loathsome, and filthy to eat shellfish, use weights and measures improperly, or to do all the other prohibitions in the Bible that are abominations? No, what it comes down to is the idea of anal sex, of men's fears about being raped, of being available to be raped. For homophobic heterosexual people, it really comes down to men's fears about being penetrated, especially against their will. For them, to be penetrated would be an abomination.

Many of these folks have to have a demonized sexual group to project all of their sexual fears and loathing and disgust upon. That's the function of this false division of people into homosexual and heterosexual beings. It sets up a false dichotomy. In my view, we all have the same sexual preference. It's genital stimulation to the point of orgasm. Now, with whom we want to experience this sexual stimulation is a matter of orientation.

Irene Monroe In black church contexts, one of the biggest challenges is sexuality. But if we can find a way to talk about sexuality, we will be able to talk about wife abuse, about rape, about child abuse. We can talk more freely about the construction of black heterosexuality. We can talk about the way in which black bodies are constructed within this American context.

The United States is constructed on a powerful racial ideology. Even the welcoming church movement[8] is shaped by a white notion of queer oppression. Clearly we're oppressed as queer people but how that factors into also being black or Latino or Asian or Native American is not part of the movement. A lot of times there may be interest by whites in hearing about it, but with an attitude of "Let's talk about it, but let's not do anything about it." There is no move toward changing the power dynamics related to racism that would bring about effective change. That's the problem even in the welcoming church movement. . . .

I don't really stand alone or in a vacuum, as much as it looks that way. I am really rooted in a black woman's tradition. I really stand on the shoulders of black preachers and leaders like Julia Foote, Jarena Lee, Rebecca Cox Jackson, Ida B. Wells. These women picked up the pen and wrote our lives into existence. They had a lot more tenacity and strength and guts than I do. I am of that tradition.

"I Help Lay Down the Foundation for Those Who Come after Me"

In the confrontational process of dissent, the courage to have hope and patience about the possibility of change toward more just social practices is also a crucial ingredient and is highlighted in the following testimonies of Mandy Carter and Rev. Dr. Youtha Hardman Cromwell. Their leadership includes strategies within the differing venues of citywide public policy campaigns, one-on-one work with students in a classroom, and internal denominational church politics.

Mandy Carter has had a lifelong primary commitment to social activism, especially to the peace movement, spending over twenty years working with the War Resisters League. More recently, she has worked on gay rights campaigns across the United States. Though she was raised Protestant and her family attended church regularly, she does not now consider herself particularly "religious." However, she is deeply committed to the importance of spirituality as a resource in "our movement," and the vocational direction of her life was deeply influenced by nonviolent teachings of Quakers she encountered as a teenager. Carter lives in the Durham, North Carolina, area.

Mandy Carter My work went in the direction of grassroots activism, especially related to electoral politics. I started paying more attention to the Christian radical right. When the Christian Coalition and other groups first started to think it was strategically important to outreach to the black churches to get them on board with an anti-gay agenda in the 1980s I took notice. I said, "Wait a minute. You're going to do what now? You're going to come into our black churches and try to get them into this whole anti-gay thing, to push them to get on board with you? I don't think so."

Specifically in Cincinnati, there was a group called the American Family Association, and they decided to do something different (tactically).[9] Rather than trying to be the face and voice of the anti-gay effort to roll back a city ordinance protecting the rights of gay and lesbian city employees, they decided to go the route of trying to get a black minister to become the face and voice of the black church in Cincinnati. They found someone named Reverend K. Z. Smith, who said that gay people were just trying to hijack the civil rights movement of the 1960s. I had previously met Smith on the *Phil Donahue Show*. By engaging this one black minister they tried to pit the black community against white gays and lesbians, as if there were no black gays and lesbians. Black gays and lesbians were there in Cincinnati, but not out. Anyway, it was amazing how Christian right-wing groups did it. And, by the way, their anti-gay measure won. The media said "the black churches of Cincinnati" supported it, but that wasn't true. There was one black church that got involved. The media made it seem like all of the black churches in Cincinnati were organized against gay rights.

From that day forward, I decided that I have got to figure out how I work with black churches to, at least minimally, counter the radical right, to counter them as they try to come into the church to do this anti-gay stuff.

At one point, in order to share the video *All God's Children* with churches and show the faces and voices of black Christian lesbians and gay men, I went to see a number of black ministers. Probably one of the worst experiences or most painful was at one Seventh-day

Adventist church. I sat and looked at this black minister across from me, and he shared this story about this brother in "our congregation" and said that "the good news is we got him turned around. He's married now with four children." I asked him, "Is he married now with four children because that's what he wanted or because his church said this is how it's supposed to be?" He didn't answer me. But I thought, *I wonder if that guy is really happy. . . .*

After he made additional anti-gay statements using the Bible, I said, "You know, that's exactly what folks said about us. Wasn't it the Bible that was used to justify slavery for 350 years? Why would you buy into this? I don't understand it." He said, "You don't want to be going there, Miss Carter. We can't *even* talk about comparing blackness to gayness." To hear that black man sit there and justify discrimination against gay people, using the same kinds of arguments that were used against blacks, that hurts. I left almost in tears. The man basically said, "Being gay is wrong. Not only is it wrong, but who you are is wrong. I'm never going to change my mind." And I looked at him and I thought, *How many people do you influence in this church and this community, every day, with this attitude?*

Youtha Hardman-Cromwell is an ordained United Methodist minister, a seminary professor and administrator, and a social activist in church and society, especially on issues of racial justice and equal rights for lesbians, gay men, bisexuals, and transgendered persons. She lives in the Washington, DC, area.

Youtha Hardman-Cromwell My cousin Johnny was gay, and his gay friends had been to my grandmother's house before and they were treated with respect just like everybody else was. So I was used to people who were gay being accepted for who they were. Even though I really didn't intellectually know a whole lot about what it means to be gay, you know, I loved my cousin Johnny. And then Johnny started losing weight. During that one particular summer, everybody in the family started asking what's wrong with Johnny. If you asked the aunts who were closer to him, they would respond with all of these statements like, "Oh, Johnny is having problems with this, Johnny is having problems with that." But he was looking more and more to me like the people that I knew of who had AIDS. And so when our part of the family got together we began to say that we thought Johnny had AIDS. Once when Johnny came to my grandmother's—I always made homemade ice cream for family get-togethers—and as I was preparing the ice cream he came over. He began to ask me about where he could find a congregation that he could be a part of. I said to him, "You go to Shiloh, right?" But apparently Shiloh had had a change in pastors and something had happened with the new pastor. I didn't know anywhere to tell Johnny he could go because all of the churches I came up with, he had tried and had had negative experiences of rejection.

To make a long story short, Johnny died and he had stopped going to church. But before, for years, he had sung in the choir, and had been a really active church person. His sister said that she could not even begin to think about taking him back into the church where he was not welcome when he was alive. She told me that he had asked if I would be the person who helped put his funeral together. And so I did his funeral at the chapel at Howard [University] because that's where I was working. The choir he sang with came to the funeral, and they sang. They sang the song that he had been the major soloist for. Well, it was clear to me that there was something really, really wrong with this picture. Johnny had invested years in his congregation. Yet, when he died, he was no longer welcomed there by the pastor, and he couldn't be buried out of the church where he had given his resources and his talents and his time. There was something really, really wrong with this picture.

Mandy Carter [In a community campaign by white Christian right organizers in Ypsilanti, Michigan[10]] once again their tactic was to try to impact the black church by getting a couple of black ministers who were anti-gay to join forces with them. The most high-profile thing that they did was, literally a week before the election, they had a big rally and brought in Elveta Celeste King (the niece of Dr. Martin Luther King; all of a sudden she was being employed by every radical right group you can think of), the two Winan sisters who wrote that very anti-gay song, and the football player Reggie White. The anti-gay group, that was predominantly white, was bringing in all of these black folk. This was going to be their big rally. These white folks were afraid of doing something that they thought would come off like it was antiblack.

But then some black sisters who lived there said, "Wait a minute, we've got to do something." I got a phone call from a sister with the

American Friends Service Committee in Michigan. She called me and said, "Mandy, what do you think we should we do?" I said, "You know what we need to have is some people of color, gay and straight, to come out and have some kind of presence outside that stadium. They can challenge what's being done there by saying, 'As people of color, we don't like the idea of you bringing these people in and we're standing up for equality.'" So she gathered some people together. They held a nonviolent prayer vigil in front of that arena and they named their group African Americans Say No to Discrimination. It was a powerful, powerful thing that occurred. Also, Coretta Scott King wrote a letter that was sent to all the voters opposing discrimination on the basis of sexual orientation. When the election occurred, the anti-gay forces lost. So even though I wasn't physically there, I was able to at least say here's some thoughts, some suggestions, and it worked.

So what sustains me is realizing that things are changing. I just can't believe how much progress we've made. I might not see it all in my lifetime, but I help lay down the foundation for those who come after me so that they get to see the fulfillment of the dream of equality.

Youtha Hardman-Cromwell In my course on sexuality, whenever I'm working with people around this issue of homosexuality, I start off by letting them know that I have not always been where I am on this issue today. I say, "I want you to know that wherever you are is okay. But we need to use our minds. We need to think." I talk about how we, as Christians, are on a journey. And I say: "I probably won't be where I am if you meet me in a few—I hope I won't be in the same place as I am today— if you meet me a few years down the road. I hope I'm growing." Okay, so I try to set up that kind of dynamic, one that has the anticipation, the expectation that you can move from where you are, you know, and still be a Christian. Also, I own where I am, that I do not believe that homosexuality is a sin. I explain that some of us can live out heterosexuality in a sinful manner and some of us can live out homosexuality in a sinful manner, but who we are does not make us sinful.

I try to lift up for them the diversity of God's creation that we have evidence of different flowers, different trees, and so forth. . . . I also use videos to help me to talk about children when they're born, and how we determine the gender of a baby, how sometimes at birth, that's not clear. For example, I have a video about a woman who externally appears to be a female. At first she feels that she is a female and she functions as a female in terms of gender, but when she was unable to have children, then they found out that internally (her internal organs), she is a male. Okay. I show this to kind of broaden their perspectives. The students see the medical people talk to her and tell her about her physical situation and they learn the story of her life. This can open up their minds about the fact that things aren't as simple as we would like them to be.

I talk about other issues in my class, like medical findings about some females that have testosterone at the levels of a male, and about some people that we call males who have estrogen at the levels of females. I present all of this kind of information, sharing it with students. I point out that these are facts; these are people's experiences. You know, we can't just say that they don't exist. I explain that there is variety in what people are in terms of their gender.

Mandy Carter I try to figure out: how do you make an impact, how do you make some change? At least, how do you start with churches? But in my opinion we also need someone who is straight, black, committed. There's just a different conversation that will happen than if it's me, a black lesbian who is not so much into the church, we need a range of folk.

Youtha Hardman-Cromwell I'm a black woman who's been divorced, and God still called me. You see, as a black woman, I could never be who I am in the church today if it hadn't been for the people who stood up for me, who stood up for black people, who stood up for women, when I wasn't even around. And so I have an obligation.

I will stand up [at statewide, annual Methodist church meetings in Virginia, in support of gay rights and their full inclusion], and I will challenge them. Okay, I am disliked by many people. But also, there are people who say to me: "I'm so glad you said that, I wish I could," or, "You know my daughter or my son is . . . "

Usually the legislation that comes forward is negative legislation. So there has to be something said. You know—very few will, and I'm known as someone who is going to say something. I don't feel defeated when my position does not hold, and sometimes it does. Sometimes, the thing that I speak against gets voted down. I can't say that it's just because I spoke, of course. I don't think that I'm that powerful.

Oh, I'm not called to be successful, I'm called to be faithful. You know. It's not my responsibility how other people vote. That's not my responsibility. My responsibility is to try to be faithful to who I feel God has called me to be. That's what God presses on my heart. Sometimes I say, "I'm not going to say anything, I'm going to sit here and I'm not going to say anything," and the next thing I know my orange card is up in the air [requesting permission to speak].

Mandy Carter Most Protestant denominations have some kind of pro–gay rights members and organizations, right? The Lutherans do, the Methodists do . . . but still, gays and lesbians can't be ordained in the Methodist Church, is that right? I keep thinking, *How is that possible? How can you have welcoming and accepting congregations, yet you won't let people—won't let gays and lesbians who are there become ordained?* There's a disconnect there, and I don't understand it. But I think people are working on changing that church policy, is that correct?

"Jesus Pushed the Parameters Away"

What theological and pastoral understandings affirmingly attend to the spiritual needs of gay and lesbian Christians, whom so many church bodies are fighting to exclude? With vastly different personal journeys, the testimonies of Bishop Leontyne Kelly and Rev. Lynice Pinkard offer Christian ethical perspectives on the theology and church practices needed to address the betrayal, void, and "disconnect" created by Christian heterosexism.

Leontyne Kelly retired after serving as the first black woman bishop in the United Methodist Church.[11] Over eighty years old and living in northern California, she spoke out of her deep commitment to social activism and Christian evangelism. Bishop Kelly lifts up her experiences of racial segregation and the struggles against racism within her predominantly white denomination as a resource in describing her faith and encouraging support for gay rights.

Leontyne Kelly The thing that you are called to do is to be faithful. I'm eighty-one, eighty-one, you're young, you can't lose hope. The hope is not in the system. The hope is in the Lord. . . . It is very clear why you have to do battle in relation to a church that is going to take measures to cut anybody out and still call itself the church. . . . I think that for us as black people, to be drawn into that kind of complete hatred—and that is what it is, hatred—it violates our own history and the way God has worked with us.

I have to go back to the context of our home when I was growing up, and to issues of race, when talking about gay rights issues (and we didn't use the term "gay" back then; that term meant "happy"). Anyway, I remember when my father came back from the Uniting Conference. Now that meeting was about the last real schism over slavery, when the Methodist Church North and the Methodist Church South had split over slavery.[12] That Uniting Conference wasn't until 1939. Yes, I remember that. We were living in Cincinnati. My father went to that conference when the Central Jurisdiction was established as a compromise. For the white southern church to come back and be united with the north, they would not accept the inclusion of blacks. . . . I remember when he came back and we were having dinner together and I asked my father, "Papa, why do you stay in this segregated church? You can be Christian without being Methodist."

My father's answer was, "You don't win a battle by leaving a battlefield. You've got to stay there. We have more battling to do because if the Central Jurisdiction is going to ever be dissolved it is going to have to come from within. Nobody from without is going to come. They have already decided who is acceptable and who is not. . . . If I am going to be a Christian, I am going to be where I can battle. The church cannot be Christian without us."

Rev. Lynice Pinkard is a religious scholar and minister who grew up in the African Methodist Episcopal Church. She has worked with interdenominational ministries and helped to found an independent ministry and outreach program in Oakland, California. Her outreach ministry specialty included drug and alcohol addiction counseling and support for persons living with HIV-AIDS. Still in northern California, she spoke to me while completing a PhD in religion and society and working as a noninstitutionally based minister who preaches, teaches, and counsels.

Lynice Pinkard I began to think about issues of gender and sexuality in the context of the AME Church as a teenager. That's when I first came to know that sexuality was an issue for me. I was still working those things out, but I was beginning to have questions about, for instance, a church that supposedly had a liberationist stance with respect to the plight of black people, on race and class issues. Historically, these were things that concerned AMEs. They broke away from the Methodist Church and formed their own structure. I began to see some disparity in terms of what they espoused on an ideological/theological basis and what I saw them doing about those ideas, which was essentially nothing.

I saw an absence of celebration of the lives of people who were gay and lesbian. And it was interesting to me, being a singer, how we who were gay and lesbian musicians were so useful to the church in terms of bringing the church life. But when it came to really acknowledging who we were, there was none, no acknowledgment. It was a kind of "don't ask, don't tell" situation. People knew, but it wasn't talked about, so I began to experience, first, in that context, a kind of invisibility. I began to notice the discrepancies in, for example, the celebration of the cycles of people's lives in their heterosexual contexts: their deaths, their marriages, their anniversaries, even sometimes having rituals related to their separations and divorce, while there was no acknowledgment whatsoever of the lives of people who were lesbian/gay/bisexual.

When I was fourteen or fifteen years old, I began to see these things and wonder: what happens to the little girl who doesn't fit within those parameters? I always thought of myself as a good girl, in the sense that I was very much into my relationship with God, with Jesus Christ. I was ready to give my life to the church in the sense that I wanted to serve the church. As a young girl, I wanted to be in ministry, and I began to wonder about how that would work out. I was coming to know who I am and who I was at that time.

Then, as a college student in Virginia, I was very involved in churches in the Tidewater area, and there you would get lots of statements like, "God created Adam and Eve, not Adam and Steve." That sort of message was conveyed. There was an equation of nastiness, dirtiness, impurity, and perversion with homosexuality, and an emphasis on making a connection between the molestation of children and homosexuality. The teachings were consistently conveying that homosexuality was "dirty and it's ugly and it's nasty and it's abominable, and God hates it." Lots of that.

Also, churches often preached what I call the patriarchal bargain. In both white and black church settings there was an emphasis on remembering that "men of God rule their homes, protect their women, and provide for their women," and in exchange, the woman is to take care of her husband, her children, and the home, creating a place of safety for her husband. That was the first time I was really exposed to that ideology in quite that way. Those were the teachings about gender and sexuality across class lines, among people who had money and education and those who did not. Their theological perspective was very narrow. Growing up AME in California, I had never confronted the kind of fundamentalism I encountered in the Bible Belt. I had come from an African Methodist Episcopal context where there was an emphasis on social justice, even if I didn't see it fully actualized. It was the underpinning of the whole theological structure of the church. And I didn't see that when I went to the South. Black people were very religious and pious, which I was accustomed to, but more disengaged from issues of poverty and homelessness.

I was also preaching in a few places. I preached in Hampton (Virginia). One of the responses from some older, straight men was their attempt to sleep with me. It was kind of a way in which they wanted to sublimate me, to kind of press—it's almost archaic and draconian to think of this—but it was like a need to penetrate me to undermine my sense of authority, push me down, keep me down, make me feminine.

Also, on campus I became aware that people were getting all kinds of negative stuff from their families. A lot of the men who were struggling with their sexuality felt like they were feminine, or people had told them they were feminine and they were trying to squelch that. In so many ways, there was a connection between gender and sexuality issues in the community and on the campus.

I started feeling more and more like an alien and trying, really struggling within myself at that point to figure out: how does the deep passion that I feel for God and the whole vocation of ministry and my wanting to do that square with the fact that I really do like women? How does it make me feel about me, about who I am? I not only thought, *How is this going to work?* but also, *Who am I?*

Leontyne Kelly One of the things that women should have learned is that they can't rear their children with that same junk. They must help their children to feel secure and to be whoever God intends them to be, help them to utilize their abilities. No good mother is going to train a child to believe that they can't do or be anything they want to be.

Lynice Pinkard My mother was very instrumental in my life and probably set the course and tone of my life with respect to sexuality. Now, my mother was definitely not identifying herself as bisexual or lesbian or anything like that when I was growing up. She told me that the only thing a woman could do for her was lead her to a man. But my mother did such a beautiful thing for me when I was thirteen. She had separated from my father, and we moved to Los Angeles. I fell in love with this young woman who was eighteen or nineteen. We developed a friendship, nonsexual, but a really tight, thick one. One day I was at her house. She had a couch in her bedroom and she had her head on my lap. Her mother came into the room and just started screaming, "I knew something was the matter. You're funny. I knew it. You're trying to change my daughter into one of those funnies." Her mother called my mother at home and said to my mother, "Your daughter, I knew something was funny about her, she's trying to change my daughter." Remember, I was thirteen or fourteen years old, and the young woman I was with was nineteen years old.

My mother brought me home. When we got there, my mother said, "Come here, Baby. Mommy wants to talk to you." I came in the room and she said, "Do you know some people are crazy?" Then she asked me, "Do you love Sandy?" I said, "I do, I love her." My mother said, "Do you know there is nothing wrong with that, and that love is beautiful? Love is powerful, and love comes in many forms. You haven't done anything wrong, and you don't have to feel ashamed." She encouraged me to date and she did other little things that I think straight parents do, but it was almost . . . prophetic. It was almost like God chose that parent for me at that point in time. I didn't have a lot of the struggles other gay and lesbian people did. Yes, some people were projecting onto me the message, "You're sick and dirty," but I didn't feel sick and dirty.

Later, when I was in college I also encountered any number of gay and lesbian people who were closeted. I haven't thought about this in a long time, but as I look back on it now, I started counseling people back then. People would come to me. They sensed that I shared it, that I understood it, identified with it. I was president of the Student Christian Association. . . . But it's interesting that that's where God started calling me, connecting me to those issues. Most times, I was reassuring people of God's love for them, lots of that, for people who came from really rigid religious family environments, and whose religion had developed in the cauldron of southern racism. . . . I remember praying with people. There were some who really wanted God to deliver them from these feelings. They may not have even had a sexual experience, but they wanted to be delivered because they wanted to be right with God. They wanted to please God. They asked: Is there some way to change it? If I pray more, if I fast more, how can I change it? So people were looking for ways to change. But I was reframing "the problem" in my own mind and thinking, *What is it about homosexuality that brings about such rabid hatred and venom from people?* I wasn't answering these questions at that time, but kept asking them. *Why it is that we're so hated? What is it that people are so afraid of?*

Leontyne Kelly You can't say all of this good stuff about Christianity and about Jesus Christ and at the same time decide who Jesus is going to accept. Jesus pushed the parameters away and there is evidence of it in this world. . . . For instance, I know a young man who belongs to the Metropolitan Community Church.[13] He's a black man, a very able young man. He is going to be ordained in Houston, and I am preaching at his ordination service. . . . But you see, it is not because I am retired that I am doing things like this; it is because it fits into what I believe. He is like a son to me. On another occasion, because he invited me, I did go to preach for a Metropolitan Community Church group, and the Holy Spirit didn't have a bit of trouble falling on that crowd of gay Christians. . . . There was a powerful movement of the Spirit because the people were sincere in what they were saying and doing. It was the same God and the same Spirit. You see, you can't say that you can't accept them. If you do, you cut the spirit of God. . . .

Lynice Pinkard Later when I served in the Bay Area, as part of the Love Center[14] ministry, we established an agency in that church that was called Ark of Love. It was a separate agency that served people with HIV and AIDS, and early on it was predominately serving gay men. We had an educational component, a housing component, a support services component. Interestingly though, what happened was, there was this kind of retrenchment around the internalized homophobia in the people we served, and it went way up when gay men started dying in droves.

We needed to develop a ministry of full acceptance, based on the belief that God made you and created you and you're beautifully and wonderfully made. Joining with Rev. Yvette Flunder, who was associate pastor at Love Center, we started our own ministry (in 1992), City of Refuge ministry in San Francisco. It started as a small gathering in a house, and then it moved out and now there are probably over one thousand members. . . . What happened with City of Refuge is that for the first time in my life and the first time in many people's lives, there was a ministry that said that sexuality is nothing for you to change. It reaffirmed you as a gay/lesbian/bisexual/transgender person, as you are. What immediately happened was that people who had been addicted to crack and cocaine and on other drugs began to get into programs, began to recover, people who were estranged from their families, estranged from their children. The minute we said, "No, you are the apple of God's eye," men were living for years. We began to see people partnered with people. They brought their partners to church. We celebrated the cycles of their lives.

I've worked very hard at decolonizing my spirit and trying to help other people decolonize theirs, starting by just giving voice to the pain, to the struggle. It's fatal to love a God who does not love you. It's fatal to any person to love a God or to perceive of a God that does not love you and to worship that God. . . . So, my life, my ministry is about healing, about God's love of the human person, the whole person. That's freeing. It means being able to hold the ambiguity of the power of the church, the power of ministry, the power of the example of the life of Jesus Christ, while acknowledging and speaking to the limitations, the abuses, the violence that is also done in the church, the subjugation, the manipulation, disempowerment, and disenfranchisement. Because I'm honest about it, that's freeing for me.

Leontyne Kelly One of the ways that you help is with the doctrinal and theological work that has to be done. You've got to ask: How do your attitudes toward persons affect your theology? It's like teaching evangelism. Some of the ministers told me, "You can't teach evangelism together with social action." That was one of the courses that I taught: "Evangelism and Social Witness." So I said to those ministers, "What do you mean I can't teach it? If Jesus had not been a social activist, I could not be a Christian."

Lynice Pinkard I really have a relationship with Jesus Christ. I believe in the life, the message, the ministry, the teachings of Jesus Christ, and I want to embody that. I've experienced the freedom of my own sexuality in the context of my relationship with Jesus Christ. It was soothing and empowering.

And so I see myself as a subversive. What I do is that I throw sand into the machine. I clog up the wheels that work to preserve the status quo and move in the way of business as usual. . . . That's what I do from the outside. I throw sand with love and humility, in the sense that I'm constantly trying to deal with my own pain as a first act of resistance, constantly examining myself, critiquing myself and what I'm willing to do, what I'm not willing to do, where I want to stand, and understanding how difficult and complex the work is.

"What Would God's Church Look Like?"

Building a faith community that is supportive and affirming of gay, lesbian, bisexual, and transgendered Christians requires subversion of heterosexist practices as well as the creation of alternative models of what it means to embody Christ. What does this ongoing work of healing, counseling, community building, preaching, and other tasks of ministry involve? Liberative Christian theological traditions and church practices are given expression in the routines of the pastoral ministry offered by Rev. Wanda Floyd in North Carolina and the joint ministry of Rev. Ruby Wilson and Rev. Lisa Robinson in Brooklyn.

Ruby Wilson and Lisa Robinson are life partners who jointly provide the ministerial leadership at Safe Haven United Church of Christ (UCC), a small black congregation in Brooklyn, New York. They started this ministry in 1995, and officially became a part of the UCC in 2002. The church background of Wilson (the primary interviewee below) is Pentecostal, chiefly in the Church of God in Christ.

Ruby Wilson Rev. Robinson here is actually the visionary for the creation of this ministry. Her vision was of a place where people from all walks of life would be able to come and have their spiritual needs met, a place that would address all of the other needs that make us who we are, that make up our personhood.

Lisa Robinson That's the main theme of the ministry. I envisioned a place where she [Ruby Wilson] could stand before the people and declare the Good News of Jesus Christ. You know, you'd have people just hanging out, really with no place to go. And God spoke to us and said, "These people need a place of worship." And that's how Safe Haven began.

Ruby Wilson What would God's church look like? What would it mean if we understood who we are but did not accept the derogatory labels attached to us? One person comes in as a straight black female, someone else comes in as a white gay male, but how do we see God in each other? What if we came together to honor God and to worship the God who created not only me and all that I am, but you as well? Yes, we all come with our baggage. But how can we find the will to say, "Lord, you created us. Help us to be one. Make us one"? What if our differences are not points of division, as it is in the world, but when we come together, we're God's children? What would that church look like? Safe Haven has gay members, straight members, married people, gay/lesbian couples who are living together, gays and lesbians who are single. We try to reach out and be the church as we understand Jesus established it: open to whosoever, let him come, let her come.

Wanda Floyd spoke about her work as founding pastor of Imani Metropolitan Community Church in Durham, North Carolina, when it was just over four years old. Her denomination, the Metropolitan Community Churches (MCC), is a predominantly white Christian group founded in 1968 and that now has over forty thousand members. MCC is a "worldwide fellowship of Christian churches with a special outreach to the world's gay, lesbian, bisexual and transgender communities."[15] Floyd serves one of the few predominantly black congregations in her (MCC) district, which includes North Carolina, South Carolina, Georgia, Alabama, Mississippi, and Tennessee.

Wanda Floyd I was at a social gathering—well, actually, it was a hoochie-cootchie bar. There were these women doing a strip-tease act. And a whole bunch of women were there, watching and dancing, women of all colors, and from all walks of life. And there were also a few men there. I felt this overwhelming sense of God—I don't know if it was God's voice or the sound of God's strong presence—but I clearly heard a voice say, "Come Sunday morning, these people will not have anywhere to go. They are not going to hear me. They are not going to know me." As I was standing there, my partner says that she was talking to me, but I wasn't hearing her. You know, I don't usually talk about listening to "voices," or go into religious trances. I don't do any of that stuff. I grew up Baptist, a conservative Baptist. We just sat there in our worship. We didn't clap our hands, didn't shout "amen." But, at that moment in that bar, my partner said that I was crying, and that for two or three minutes it was like I was just gone. I was physically there but I wasn't there. So, she knows, even if nobody else knows it: Imani came into being because of God. . . . God called this church into being.

Ruby Wilson I remember a class I taught once in the church on basic fundamentals of what it means to be the church: Who is the church? Who are we? Who are we becoming? Who are we supposed to be becoming? Someone in the class raised their hand and said, "Look here, I'm a gay woman, and I need to fellowship with God's people. And I want to know if Safe Haven is the kind of place where that can happen. Because if it's not, I'm gonna leave. But if it is, then I just want you to know this is who I am. Is this the kind of church that will understand that?" And we said, "Of course. What do you mean? Of course it is." And that was a very telling moment.

A while ago, there was a transgendered person who wanted to attend the church, and some church members were really quite concerned about how she would be perceived by other church members. So, Rev. Robinson got up one Sunday, and said, "If we're Safe Haven, if we are the church, then our mission is to acknowledge the dignity and worth of all God's people. And we endeavor to show the love of Jesus Christ with the help of the Holy Spirit by being a haven of help and healing for people. That's our mission. And there is someone who desires to come into this fellowship and she is transgendered. How will we receive that person?" And one of the deacons said, "Wait a minute! We receive anybody that comes. We go out, and we spread the Good News. Someone hears that Good News and comes in. We cannot turn anybody away, because God never turned us away." Those are the kinds of moments that have always been a source of encouragement in this ministry.

Wanda Floyd We have Bible studies for adults on Wednesday nights at the church, and then we have small-group Bible studies in different areas all around Durham, Raleigh, down to the Hillsboro area, that are meeting needs of our folks on a smaller scale. People get fed in the Bible studies. I sit back and look at folks who grew up in the church and are just now beginning to read the Bible, just now beginning to have a real, active, prayer life. I've got people who are going out and buying Bibles for the first time in their lives at the age of forty-five.

Of course, pastoring this particular congregation is challenging because it is predominantly female. The challenge has to do with issues around internalized oppression, internalized homophobia. This became very clear when we did a Bible study on self-esteem a couple of years ago. One of the things that I wanted to do was have the group say an affirmation together based on Psalm 139:14 that talks about how "I am fearfully and wonderfully made. . . ." I asked the group to say aloud, "I am fearfully and wonderfully made in the image of God," to own that. Then, in the back corner of the room, one hand went up, and a woman raised her hand and said, "I can't do that." At first, I was stunned. I said to myself, "*Okay, regroup.*" Everybody's eyes went to her when she raised her hand to say something, and then everybody's eyes went back to me as soon as she said that. "Okay," I said, "I'll tell you what we'll do. We'll do it together. You all close your eyes, bow your heads—I'll say it out loud. . . ." And after that Bible study session ended, she came up to me and said, "I want to apologize for disrupting the Bible study." I told her that it was okay, but that I had to ask her why she felt that way about saying the affirmation. She said, "Because I'm not sure if I really believe that." And I took a moment to think about what she was telling me, and then I said, "You know, I thank you for your courage. There were probably other people here who felt the same way. I appreciate it that you were willing to raise your hand and say that."

From our very second worship service, we have been a congregation that is predominantly women. It's just been amazing to see some of the transformations that have happened among some of the women. They're beginning to be okay. I mean, I have women parishioners who tell me how they grew up in the church, and are only now beginning to understand that God really does love them.

Ruby Wilson You have to know it, deep inside yourself, to know it in that great way that Jesus puts it, "You will know the truth and the truth will set you free." I tell this to our church members, and that's how it is for me as well. I want to know the truth about myself. I want to know the truth about God. I want to know the truth about the world I'm living in. And when I realize the truth, recognize it, embrace it, and can still say, "God loves me!" that's liberation. That's freedom.

Lisa Robinson I'm very big on having a personal relationship with Jesus Christ, and I'm free within myself because I know God loves me. I know that God created me so I can stand firmly on that. I will preach that kind of freedom as long as I have a breath in my body. So my personal relationship with Jesus Christ is what sustains me.

Ruby Wilson In our ministry, there are people who are "coming out." It can involve the following: you say to someone "this is who I am," and if it's someone who hasn't known you in that particular way, it's hardest when that person goes to the same place where you've been struggling all the time. Like, when people in the church talk about homosexuality and say, "Oh, I can't agree with this. I can't go there." They should understand that anybody who's gay or lesbian, particularly if they were raised in church, has been right there, thinking and feeling that rejection at some point in their journey, and has struggled through that. It's often a constant fight to know, "I'm God's child, and I know God loves me." That's one of the biggest issues in our congregation.

We did a seminar on Psalm 139, which happens to be one of my favorites. The theme of the seminar focused on the question: "How does God feel about me?" Well, when you get to that verse that says, "When I awake, I'm still with thee . . ." [Ps. 139:18b KJV], we looked at it as saying to us: when we get up in the morning, it's almost as if we're birthed at that moment. You see, God looks at us just like a mother or father seeing their baby for the first time. The baby doesn't have to clean up her room or graduate from college in order to be loved. The baby doesn't have to do anything to receive love, except to be born into that family. Every day when we wake up, God just looks at us as if we were newborns and loves us, just like that.

Wanda Floyd When someone tells me that all their life they have heard that they are going to hell because they're gay and they don't know what to do with that, for me that is the most painful thing. I'm working with a fifteen-year-old girl right now. When her father found out she was gay, he raped her. Not only did he rape her, but he also gave her an STD [sexually transmitted disease]. Now she's living in a foster-care household with two other lesbians. She's black and the other two are white. They're a wonderful young group.

That girl who was raped by her father grew up Pentecostal and heard throughout her life that she's going to hell because she's a lesbian, so I've been working with her and we have a regular date to do something together once a month. We have dinner, we talk, and we do something fun. This past month we went out in the paddleboats at one of the local lakes. While we eat and talk, we talk about these things—how are you doing today, you know, how are you feeling about who you are? I'm not necessarily trying to take away all the negative stuff that she grew up with, because that's so much a part of who she is right now, but I am trying to give her another perspective. I'm trying to help her know that she's not going to go to hell in a handbasket because she's gay.

I heard another kid say a couple of weeks ago that he knows that one day God is going to change him, and he described how often he was told while growing up that he "was going to go to hell." Then, he said, "I don't believe God wants me to go to hell, so therefore I believe God is going to change me and make me straight." He doesn't live at home. His mom and dad kicked him out because he's gay, and I think he lives with a relative. His father hates him, and he hates his father.

I really don't think that ministers truly understand the depth of telling somebody they're going to go hell for this or for that—fill in the blank. It's amazing. There are a lot of youth around here that are going through so much anguish right now, and of course the greatest challenge comes with helping them with the self-esteem issues and all that that entails.

When people come through the doors of our church, they feel something different. I have had people literally cry from the time they walked in the door to the time they left, all throughout the service, because they felt God's love and God's presence all around them. They didn't know what to do with that, except cry, because they've heard that they can't receive that, that God doesn't love them and so how can they dare to feel God's presence. They sit there and sob all service long, and by the time Communion comes, it's like the floodgates are really opened up. We have Communion every Sunday, and as people gather for it I talk about how this one symbol shows us God's unconditional love for us. Period. Nobody has a right to tell you that you're not worthy to take this meal. Our belief is that if you have a relationship with Jesus Christ, you may partake of this meal. So I try to be very empowering in my message and very positively focused. But I don't let them off the hook, because, you know, God expects some things of us.

Ruby Wilson Just because we know that we're loved by God, and that God's grace covers us all, do we have a right to continue certain patterns of hurtful behavior? No, God forbid. That's not how we must behave. We should be bound by an ethic of love. This ethic should be at the core of our community: because I love you, then there's no way I would violate what this relationship means to me. We tell our members, "You are part of a community of faith. And there's a certain way you behave when you're part of a community of faith. So, when you read things like the Ten Commandments, whether you are gay or straight, our community is bound together by them. And this is what we do as a faith community: we don't sleep with somebody else's partner, or with somebody else's husband or wife. We don't steal from each other. We don't slander one another. And if someone comes into our community who doesn't understand this, you don't follow where they're going. You help them to understand, saying, 'Hey, wait a minute. Wherever you've come from, maybe that was the norm, but when you're part of this community, this is how we behave.'"

Wanda Floyd As a pastor, I'm not afraid to deal with the issue of sexual immorality within the gay community. I'm not afraid to deal with those things that people think don't have anything to do with us because we're not straight. . . . I believe that the Bible is written for everyone who calls themselves Christian. It is our guide to how we live our lives. Yes, nine times out of ten, in our intimate relationships, we may have more of a tendency to live together with our partner and not have commitment ceremonies. But whether you're straight or gay we still need to pay attention to the issue of sexual immorality.

I preach to my congregation: "Yes, God loves me. Yes, God knows I'm gay. Yes, I'm created in God's image. But, God also cares about my salvation and God cares about your salvation. Let's get to that. Let's get to the nitty-gritty. Are you living your life as God wants you to, and if you're not, what can we do to rectify that? If you're not sure of where you are going to go when you die, we need to talk about that. You don't need to leave this church today without grabbing somebody on the prayer team, the pastoral team, or me, and saying, 'We need to talk.' Because none of us are guaranteed tomorrow, and yes, God cares about who we sleep with, in the sense of how we treat that person."

That message is challenging to some folks who come here, because I think they have this misconception about our denomination. Some think that because we outreach to the gay-lesbian community that we're not going to tackle the hard issues or we're not going to deal with things that they heard being dealt with as they were growing up in the church. I challenge people on that. For example, I talk about adultery.

I say, "Adultery is adultery. Y'all know that we cannot legally be married, but we are still in intimate relationships with partners. When you are in a relationship with somebody though not able to be legally married, but you are in a monogamous, same-sex relationship and it's been going on for a while, if you decide to step out on that relationship with somebody else, that's adultery. Let's call it what it is." This shook a few folks up, but people appreciated it. I think a lot of times our MCC folks do not hear much of that kind of preaching. They hear the feel good stuff. They hear, "God loves you, it's okay to be gay, etc." Well, you know, that's true, but there's more to it than that.

The last time I preached about this, it was in connection with a message on temptation. There was a woman in our congregation, who just happened to be white, and she was married, still living at home with her husband. Her husband knew she was gay. They were trying to maintain a household for their daughter, who was twelve at the time. After I gave that message, she went home and decided she couldn't do this anymore. She started divorce proceedings with her husband and began moving out. Because she was seeing somebody at the church she began working on moving out. We had talked about this long before that day. But she said there was "something you said that Sunday. I must have been in the right place to hear it, because at that point I realized what I was doing wasn't right. I had to go home and make some hard choices that night." And her husband was fine with it, and now her daughter lives with her, I think, on a weekly basis.

Ruby Wilson Since we are leaders, I think it is very important for the two of us [Reverend Wilson and Reverend Robinson] to set an example. We have to be an example that sends the message: "I'm a lesbian. You don't see me sleeping with anybody else's partner." There are ethical standards we must maintain because we have young people in the church, as well as the older saints. So, if I'm a minister who's running around, what can I preach to my parishioners about being ethical?

You see, we're trying to develop a model that is not so dependent upon the heterosexual model, that does not just imitate the heterosexual model. There is a difference. It's almost like what it means for women preachers to develop their own models of preaching. It's like what my brother often says when he is listening to women preaching. We taught a preaching class together. In his critique when he was listening to some of the women preach, he said, "I want you to feel honored in your right as a woman, and not feel as if you have to follow the male preaching model in your presentation. There are distinctions. Female preachers bring something to the pulpit that males cannot. . . ." Whatever it might be, there are things that we bring as women to the pulpit that are just very different. In the same way, in our relationships [romantic relationships of LGBT Christians] there's a model being created that breaks out of the heterosexual model with which we are so familiar. And, for example, there's one idea that I really like to challenge, that I like to say to my heterosexual brothers and sisters: "You're not saved because you're heterosexual. It's wonderful that you're married, and it's wonderful that you have children . . . but that is not what saves you. You're saved by God's grace. You're saved by faith alone."

Wanda Floyd The message that is preached in our congregation is the good news of Jesus Christ. When people come through the doors, we don't ask them if they're gay. We don't ask them if they're straight. We see people coming in looking for the love of God. They are looking for something they can take away with them on Sunday so when Monday morning gets here and they've got no gas in their car, or they don't have money to put food on the table for their kids, they know they're going to be okay because there's something out there greater than they are that will make a way for them to make it that day.

Ruby Wilson And so there's almost this hierarchy—and that's what you've gotta call it—this hierarchy of how we see each other. For instance, there's an attitude of "Well, I may be black, but at least I'm not dark-skinned"—that's how some of our lighter brothers and sisters would look at it. Or, for some, "I may be black, but at least I have money, or at least I have education." And when it comes to homosexuality, I find that to be the characteristic that is the most discriminated against. Of course, as a black female, there's going to be discrimination, but as a lesbian too—forget it! There have been centuries of learning this stuff. So in response to it, you know, we have to remember what Jesus said to Nicodemus, "You must be born again." I think Jesus hit the point on the head when he said this. This scripture means that all that stuff, all of those oppressive structures you have built for all of these years, passed down for all of these years, they have to be torn down, and "you must be born again."

"Raised Up . . . and Sent Out with a Purpose to Help"

Building upon the creation and sustenance of a nurturing community of faith that dissents with heterosexism, liberative ethical leadership also involves ongoing communal outreach. What does this church-based outreach look like? What are some routinized ways to engage the broader community, including heterosexuals? Beyond a general openness, how can support be organized to continually respond to the needs of those who are among the most marginalized in local communities? Examples are found in the antiracist, gay-affirming Christian witness and mission of Minister Janyce Jackson in Newark, New Jersey, and Reverend Alma Crawford in Chicago, Illinois.

Janyce Jackson is an ordained minister in the Unity Fellowship Movement, a predominantly black church movement founded in 1982.[16] *She served as coordinator of the Open Door Drop-in Center, a ministry of the Liberation in Truth Church in Newark, New Jersey. The Drop-in Center began in 2002 and served homeless street people, injection drug users, sex workers, and those infected by HIV/AIDS or who are at high risk of contracting the virus. It provided them with immediate access to a variety of services, including a shower, laundry facilities, food, and a space for temporary rest and respite. It also offered people access to a range of HIV prevention and treatment services.*[17]

Janyce Jackson It all started in the church, with the Unity Fellowship Movement, which was founded in order to provide gay and lesbian people with a safe space to worship, a place to worship as they are—without being stigmatized. People were being put out of churches, and not allowed to worship. . . . That's how I got started in all of this. I'm a new minister, just ordained a couple of weeks ago. When I first got involved in the Unity Fellowship Movement, I got involved as a trustee and I worked as treasurer. I've been in the movement for ten years, so for about six of those years, that is the kind of work that I did. I worked on committees, raising money, bookkeeping, and handling finances. I never thought I would do anything else. Then, I don't know . . . It just happened one day. I just became more interested in talking to and working with the people who came to church. As a trustee, I was more on the inside of how the ministry was organized. I became more interested in working with the people.

Alma Crawford was cofounder and copastor of the Church of the Open Door, which began its ministry in 1996. The church functioned as a community organizing and social service center serving the black LGBT community of the Chicago metropolitan area and the mostly Mexican immigrant community in its surrounding neighborhood. The pastors were politically active in their community on a range of issues from immigrant rights to marriage equality across differences in sexual orientation. The church outreach services included programs such as a computer center, domestic violence and substance abuse intervention, voter registration and education, American Sign Language and English as a Second Language classes, and extensive health advocacy related to HIV/AIDS, women's cancers, and wellness strategies.[18]

Alma Crawford What kind of a world do we want to live in? What kind of a world is God calling for? And what is God giving birth to *now*? God led Karen and me to respond to this challenge. Karen Hutt is my life partner and copastor and cofounder of this congregation. The congregation is affiliated with the United Church of Christ and the Unitarian Universalist Association. In our theological orientation God is imminent but also transcends a lot of our theological, liturgical, and denominational boundaries. Sometimes I have kind of an eschatological perspective about the Church of the Open Door, viewing it as a posthomophobia, postheterosexism, post-AIDS community.

Christ is seeking us out to reorder every dimension of who we are, of who we are as parents, who we are as participants in the political life of our communities, and then it's up to us as people who are experiencing this liberating action of Christ to get beyond the questions: Am I going to hell? Could God love me? Will God hear my prayers? All of this kind of ridiculous stuff keeps us sidelined. But instead, empowered by Christ, we must ask, where am I being sent out to? At Church of the Open Door, we get into an Acts of the Apostles kind of orientation: we are people who have been raised up, filled up, and sent out with a purpose to help all of us to live in a new way, with a whole new sensibility about relationships.

Janyce Jackson We started this outreach project in 1998 as an HIV-prevention program funded by the state of New Jersey. It grew out of one of many different ministries in our church. Basically, the goal was to target women, especially lesbians, because that was the population that was not targeted by other programs. Since we had that population in church, we felt that we needed to reach out to this particular group of women and get the message of HIV prevention out to them. I think we started out with just three people on staff. The congregation was open and supportive of this ministry. They told their family and friends about it; women did come! We called the program "health education risk reduction." We'd come together for six sessions and talk about some ways in which we can be safe. We'd talk about: What are the behaviors that we do? What makes us do what we do—makes us not be safe, sometimes? How can we change that, if necessary?

Later, we were located right next door to a jobs center, and a lot of men went there looking for jobs. Soon, some of those men began to come in to see us for information and condoms. We have always had a sign on the door that says "free condoms." So, we find the population coming in has changed, and our goals have changed. We now focus on outreach to women and men, to men who have sex with men, to transgendered persons. That's the population that we target. The Drop-in Center is a new concept in New Jersey. We're one of the few places in the state providing these services that is open to all people. I wouldn't say we're the only one because there must be another one out there somewhere.

Alma Crawford I think the best thing about Chicago is that—well, I see us as sort of the heart of black America. This is where *Ebony* and *Jet* are based. The black experience here is sort of a combination of the urban North and the rural South, all together. For the generic, garden-variety, indigenous black people of the South and North, this is the place. There are around two million black people in Chicago, thousands of whom are gay, and a large proportion of them call us pastor. So we have something sort of like a Catholic parish ministry. We're the religious institution that people turn to, calling us to be ready do their funeral or maybe help them negotiate with their parents. We also get a lot of calls from people we never meet. That's when I hear a lot of what's going on in some of these other churches and the spiritual abuse they're experiencing in those churches. In most of black Chicago, same-gender-loving folks go to churches that are either at one end of the spectrum where they're condemned and told they're going to hell, or at the other end, in supposedly liberal churches, where they're tolerated and told we'll bury you but we won't marry you, so they have second-class membership.

And of course, there's the stigma about AIDS that so many people face and the fertile ground surrounding it of homophobia and the antisex culture and so forth, so they're afraid to get tested. Or they may think that they're not worthy of doing the work involved in keeping up a regimen of medication, or they're afraid to bring their drugs home because then people will know they have AIDS and ostracize them because the stigma is so big and humiliating. That's an example of how it kills people. I talked with one guy on the telephone who is a music minister at a Pentecostal church and his partner is a music minister at another Pentecostal church. They live together. They both have full-blown AIDS, but they have never even discussed it with one another.

Janyce Jackson People have gone to church for years with their partners, but never really told the congregation or the minister who they are to each other. Then once they make a decision that they want to be open and they tell, they're not accepted. As people grow they decide they don't want to live like that anymore, don't want to hide anymore, saying "this is my sister" or "my cousin." They want to be open about the person they love. I know in the case of one couple, one of them who had gone to her family church for years and years, she was all excited about the special woman that she met and loved. They had been together for two or three years. She went to her pastor and, although she didn't tell me what he said to her, whatever it was, she was devastated. She could not believe that he could treat her so badly. She was devastated.

I think the reputation of our church draws people to the Drop-in Center. At Liberation in Truth, we are a place for everybody. We embrace gays and lesbians. We talk about it. We do an affirmation every Sunday that affirms all people: "No matter what you look like, whether you are tall or you're short or you're fat or you're bald or you're gray-haired, or you're gay or you're lesbian, God loves you." I think that the success of the Center started from this kind of ministry in the church.

Here at the Drop-in Center, there are more issues about people struggling to survive. We're not only a place that is concerned about supporting you if you are gay or lesbian. We are concerned about whether you have something to eat and some place to live. . . . The people who come here don't ask the people who work here, "Are you a lesbian?" They ask, "Do you have something to eat? Can I take a shower?" That's more important. Those who are gay or lesbian or transgender feel comfortable here. . . . This feels like a place that's a catch-all for everybody, which is good.

Alma Crawford One of the reasons that I'm in the United Church of Christ (UCC) is because it provides me with an ecumenical link to other churches. As a UCC clergywoman at a National Council of Churches meeting, for example, I can sit at the table with people from the Church of God in Christ or African Methodist Episcopal Zion, some of whom would not normally interact with somebody like me who is openly gay. And we're all "reverends." They may be aware of one perspective that has been put out there labeling me as something foreign, but I'm still familiar to them. I love the Lord, I eat barbecue, I vote Democratic, I pray before I eat . . . we're such ordinary, recognizable black people. They can see we're not some foreign species. They've heard a lot of lies about us, a lot of which have been put out there by white evangelicals who just want to dilute black voting strength, and that's why these white evangelicals are using these wedge issues. And when [black clergy at ecumenical meetings] find out that gay people—they find out that we're regular people, you know, that we pay our taxes, we take care of Mamma, we love our children and our families, hold all of those real core values, and that we come from them. We really do. We're from the exact same stock. We're not exotic or fundamentally different except we're same-gender-loving people, and even that is familiar to them if they really are truthful.

You know, a lot of the people who are the most vocal about keeping this homophobic stuff in place are, of course, closeted gay people. Often the ones who are the main enforcers of heterosexist policies are closeted gay preachers. I see them across denominations. But *I'm* talking about a gay life that is out in the open, respectful, loving, covenantal, Spirit-filled, responsible, compassionate, fun, and that's not "on the down low," not about nasty sex in the park exploiting people. But again, I believe that if they can taste and see the goodness of the Lord, see what God can do with us and what's possible for them, something that is better than a depressing existence where you are just chasing sensation and hiding and lying, I think that ultimately they may come out from under it.

Janyce Jackson The work is mostly done in a group setting. We try to do health education and risk reduction. . . . It gives people an opportunity to talk openly about where they are and what they do. The major premise of our work is to offer a relaxed, casual atmosphere. And so we want to create a safe space where people can talk about themselves. Everybody's different, so the words that we use and the tone of each group is different. We are sort of led by where the group participants are. We encourage them to talk about, for example, what do you do when you go out? And for the younger people: Will you go out on the club scene? When you see someone that you like, where does that lead you? What are you thinking? How do you respond? Talking about sex is not comfortable for most people we come across. We just continue the conversation and give them an opportunity to know that it's okay to talk about it. Sometimes, the facilitator will encourage them by telling her own story or by giving an example. I think that because the people on the staff don't feel ashamed, the participants are not worried about the stigma that usually comes from Christian people. They feel more comfortable talking about themselves.

It starts with one conversation, and then another conversation, and another one. Trust doesn't happen all at once in the group. The group has to get to know each other. So, it's usually six weeks of sessions with the same people in the group, and they become comfortable with each other. You'd be surprised, by the third week, people are really talking.

Alma Crawford We're in a neighborhood that is made up of African Americans and Mexican immigrants. We have a lot of community ministries that are in partnership with our neighbors immediately surrounding the church, like ESL classes, computer labs, the kinds of things that help to meet people's immediate needs, help build up the people of the neighborhood so that we can become people who are less likely to be completely exploited. Rather than have a full food pantry, we built a computer lab so people could move out of the lowest rung of the economic ladder.

Instead of a very bureaucratic church structure with committees, committees, committees, resolutions, Robert's Rules, all of this kind of stuff that is part of a certain cultural orientation to church life that is very, very paper oriented, we found that what people responded to and what worked best for us was a much more organic kind of a structure where a lot of things are done by affinity groups. Groups are formed when people are interested in a particular concern or when particular kinds of constituencies emerge—like we have a men's ministry called Brothers of the Open Door, and we have a women's ministry called New Women in Christ. Part of my model is really to believe in the people, trust what they have to say. There is tremendous wisdom and brilliance and creativity among regular people.

A church presumes that the Word became flesh and dwelt amongst us full of grace and truth so that in becoming flesh Christ has a purpose and offers the possibility of redemption for our financial lives and our physical health. You know, everybody knows—hears from the pulpit, when I've had a Pap smear. They know that Pastor Tom is openly HIV positive, that he takes his meds, and that he goes to the doctor. We rejoice over each "T cell" somebody in the congregation grows . . . throwing off all of the shame and denial about living in our bodies. It's a constant struggle to do this, but that shame and silence about our bodies is killing us. So we value black life enough that we're going to struggle through all of that old programming and extend our lives.

Janyce Jackson There are so many different medicines that people who live with HIV can have. But there is still the money factor. The medicine is still so expensive. People from all walks of life are HIV positive and some are working, some are not. Some are on drugs. Some are homeless. When a homeless person or a person who is on drugs decides that they want to do something different, often that's when we get a chance to see them. It is so hard. I mean, one of our goals is to connect people with services, connect them with the medical attention that they need, try to get them housing, or try to get them some counseling. But what's available is so limited. . . . Like with Section 8 housing, supposedly there is this pot of money to provide housing, but where is it? If I have someone at my desk who needs a place to live, who has been sober x amount of time, what does he do to get it? We can't take him somewhere today. Or, if I have a person who needs mental health counseling . . . the system is so inadequate.

Alma Crawford When they think about issues like adoption, foster care, and so forth, white gay people are so often worried about their right to adopt and to fully actualize their freedom as white people in leadership positions or as white people in the middle and upper-middle class. So they'll say, "Well, there's so many children out there waiting to be adopted, so we should be able to adopt them."

Meanwhile from our perspective, we think about the current welfare system. We're thinking about, first of all, why are all these children in foster care? We're thinking about the fact that a lot of these mothers have lost their children because of heterosexist assumptions about what a family is supposed to look like, and thinking about the role of heterosexism, along with the economic exploitation, in why so many of those children are in the system at all. We look at what happens to gay kids who are in the foster-care system and how they get treated, how this issue affects poor black gay kids. The white gay movement doesn't even raise some of these issues. Sure, we're concerned about our right to adopt, but the people whom we are likely to be fighting for the right to adopt are our nieces and nephews and so forth. The goal is to keep family together. It's not to say that these families don't matter and nobody wants those children. We're likely to say that this child who may have been drug-exposed, may have HIV or whatever, isn't someone we're taking because we're so noble, but we're taking them because they're so precious and we're grateful to have them. That child is our first choice, not one we've settled for. So we come at these things from vastly different points of view. So much of the media looks to the white gay perspective as the norm, as representative of gay perspectives, and there is so often an inherent racism in that white gay perspective. I think that's part of what a lot of black people are responding so negatively to, and that reaction can become homophobia. There's an assumption that what these white folks are saying is what gay people think. But in fact, it's another shading of what some white people think. So, that's why it's so critical for gay people to speak up as part of our communities, whether gay people who are in Korean communities or African American communities or Puerto Rican communities or whatever. We have to have these conversations among ourselves. . . .

But we also have to remember that there is a lot of nonhomophobic behavior in our African American community. I think the values that counter homophobia in our community in particular are ones that value the sense of extended family. Even though, now, we all feel obligated to give lip service to this nuclear family model, our reality in this country has never been that. So, to the degree that we are resisting this hetero-patriarchal model that is coming from white European Western modernist values is the degree to which we are able to keep our extended family covenant alive.

Janyce Jackson A church that accepts gay, lesbian, transgendered persons, I mean, it's necessary. Our cities have churches on every other corner almost. And that is good. That's okay. But there has to be a place where I can go with my partner, where she can wear her pants because she's not wearing a skirt, where we can praise God and pray, and be okay. There has to be a place like that, and I wanted to be a part of making that happen. That's how I got started, that's what made me get so involved. . . . this Drop-in Center has to be available.

I'm so new in the fight. I worked in the police department in the City of New York for twenty-eight years. I've only been full-time coordinator of the Center for this past year. I'm just getting into it. I feel like I'm just getting into the fight. There are people who have been working so hard, for so long. I'm picking up the reins now. I can work and help somebody else, and then somebody else can pick up the reins.

Notes

Introduction

1. Steven Greenhouse, "Federal Suit Accuses City of Not Acting on Harassment Complaints in Workfare Jobs," *New York Times*, July 15, 2001, 27.
2. Ibid.
3. Ibid.
4. Katia Hetter, "Workfare Workers' Rights in Question," *New York Newsday*, July 27, 2001, A49; Thomas J. Lueck, "Judge Rejects Harassment Lawsuits for Women on Workfare," *New York Times*, March 12, 2002, B2.
5. Greenhouse, "Federal Suit."
6. Jill Nelson, "These Women Work, But Aren't Protected," *USA Today*, March 22, 2002. Also see *Doe v. Commissioner of Human Resources Admin.*, No. 160981302, EEOC, filed March 1998.
7. The USS *Corpus Christi*, PF 44, was launched in 1943 and decommissioned in 1946; the USS *City of Corpus Christi*, SSN 705, was launched in 1981. The naming of the city (Corpus Christi, Texas) as well as the naming of a nuclear submarine both make the religious significance of the term "body of Christ" indistinguishable from its civic meaning.

Chapter 1

1. Patricia Hill Collins, *Fighting Words: Black Women and the Search for Justice* (Minneapolis: University of Minnesota Press, 1998), xiii.
2. I limit my study to Niebuhr's attention to domestic issues. His writings on international issues are also relevant to the Harlem community, but I have found more than enough material and challenge for this one project in a focus limited to domestic social issues.
3. Also see Ruth L. Smith, "Reinhold Niebuhr and History: The Elusive Liberal Critique," *Horizons* 15, no. 2 (1988): 263–98.
4. John C. Bennett, "Reinhold Niebuhr's Social Ethics," in *Reinhold Niebuhr: His Religious, Social, and Political Thought*, ed. Charles W. Kegley and Robert Bretall (New York: MacMillan Co., 1956), 46.
5. Richard Wightman Fox, *Reinhold Niebuhr: A Biography* (Ithaca, NY: Cornell University Press, 1996), 135.

6. See Robin W. Lovin, *Reinhold Niebuhr and Christian Realism* (New York: Cambridge University Press, 1995); Larry Rasmussen, "The Contours of Niebuhr's Mind," in *Reinhold Niebuhr (1892–1971): A Centenary Appraisal*, ed. Gary A. Gaudin and Douglas John Hall (Atlanta: Scholars Press, 1994), 144. Rasmussen comments: "The basic structure of Niebuhr's habit of mind was set early on and remained remarkably consistent, especially for someone whose reflection always arose from his engagement and whose engagement ranged across a broad spectrum of social issues over five tumultuous decades"; Bill Kellerman, "Apologist for Power," *Sojourners* 16, no. 3 (1987): 14–20; Michael Novak, "On Needing Niebuhr Again," *Commentary* 15 (September 1972), 52–62; idem, *The Spirit of Democratic Capitalism* (New York: Simon and Schuster, 1982), 313–29; Robert Benne, *The Ethic of Democratic Capitalism: A Moral Reassessment* (Philadelphia: Fortress Press, 1981).
7. Robin Lovin, "Introduction," in Reinhold Niebuhr, *The Nature and Destiny of Man: A Christian Interpretation*, vol. 1, *Human Nature* (1941; repr., Louisville, Ky.: Westminster John Knox Press, 1996), xiii.
8. Niebuhr was described as a Christian prophet, wherein the "philosopher moves from the particular to the universal, the prophet is to exploit universals to cast light upon the particulars. . . . While [Niebuhr] has been friendly to many a secular prophet, he has been distinguished from them by his use of the Christian rather than secular perspective." Robert Fitch, "Reinhold Niebuhr's Philosophy of History," in *Reinhold Niebuhr: His Religious, Social, and Political Thought*, ed. Charles W. Kegley and Robert W. Bretall (New York: Macmillan Co., 1956), 309.
9. I am grateful for a conversation about this point with feminist ethicist Ruth Smith, who pointed out the need for ethicists "to see the world as more than simply examples." Also see Ruth L. Smith, "Morals and Their Ironies," *Journal of Religious Ethics* 26, no. 2 (1998): 367–88. I am building upon Sharon Welch's discussion of Reinhold Niebuhr and her critique of Dennis McCann's defense of Niebuhr's Christian realism at the expense of Latin American liberation theologians in *Christian Realism and Liberation Theology: Practical Theologies in Creative Conflict* (Maryknoll, NY: Orbis Books, 1981), in Sharon D. Welch, *A Feminist Ethic of Risk* (Minneapolis: Fortress Press, 2000), 109–10. For another feminist challenge of how Niebuhr has been interpreted by critics of liberation theology, see Rosemary Radford Ruether, *Sexism and God-talk: Toward a Feminist Theology* (Boston: Beacon Press, 1983), 215.
10. Larry Rasmussen, "Niebuhr's Theory of Power," in *Reinhold Niebuhr (1892–1971): A Centenary Appraisal*, ed. Gary A. Gaudin and Douglas John Hall (Atlanta: Scholars Press, 1994), 161. Also see Ronald Stone, *Professor Niebuhr: A Mentor to the Twentieth Century* (Louisville, Ky: Westminster/John Knox Press, 1992), 119, n.49. Stone asserts that with this 1935 passage in *Moral Man*, Niebuhr predicted the nonviolent strategies that would prove most useful in the civil rights movement.
11. Reinhold Niebuhr, *Moral Man and Immoral Society* (1932; repr., New York: Charles Scribner's Sons, 1960), 254.
12. I have a longer discussion of Niebuhr's supposed predictions of the Negro civil rights movement in my essay "Constructing Ethics: Reinhold Niebuhr and Harlem Women Activists," *Journal of the Society of Christian Ethics* 24, no.1 (Spring/Summer 2004): 24–49.
13. Cheryl L. Greenberg, *Or Does It Explode? Black Harlem in the Great Depression* (New York: Oxford University Press, 1991), 116.
14. Ibid., 117.

15. In fact, because of his own comments during the civil rights movement era, I am reasonably certain that Niebuhr was not influenced by these boycotts. It seems that he was unaware of the boycotts in Harlem during the 1930s. In a sermon at Union Theological Seminary in 1963, he said, "When I first came to New York, I tried to organize a boycott in Harlem, among some of my Negro minister friends. And they were shocked at this. They said that wasn't the Christian thing to do. . . . Now they have boycotts." Reinhold Niebuhr, "Double Love Commandment," April 28, 1963, Reinhold Niebuhr Papers, Sermons, Box 41, Manuscripts Division, Library of Congress, Washington, DC. He did, however, study the tactics of Gandhi's nonviolent movement in India, and perhaps some of the ideas on this list may have been influenced by his familiarity with that movement. See references to Gandhi in this same chapter where this statement about Negroes and boycotting is found, *Moral Man and Immoral Society*, 241ff.
16. Department of Commerce, Bureau of the Census, *Sixteenth Census of the United States: 1940, Population Vol. II, Characteristics of the Population, Sex, Age, Race, Nativity, Citizenship, Country of Birth of Foreign Born White, School Attendance, Education, Employment Status, Class of Worker, Major Occupation Group, and Industry Group*, Part 5: *New York–Oregon* (Washington, DC: GPO, 1943), 178.
17. Ibid., 177.
18. See Jervis Anderson, *This Was Harlem 1900–1950* (New York: Farrar, Straus, Giroux, 1981), 244.
19. Nat Brandt, *Harlem at War: The Black Experience in WWII* (Syracuse, NY: Syracuse University Press, 1996), 41.
20. Ibid., 42; also see Frederick M. Binder and David M. Reimers, *All the Nations under Heaven: An Ethnic and Racial History of New York City* (New York: Columbia University Press, 1995), 179.
21. Sarah and A. Elizabeth Delany with Amy Hill Hearth, *Having Our Say: The Delany Sisters' First 100 Years* (New York: Kodansha International, 1993), 125.
22. Ibid.
23. Ibid., 137–38. E. Franklin Frazier was a frequent visitor who organized demonstrations at her office.
24. Ibid., 138.
25. Ibid., 160.
26. Ibid., 159.
27. Ibid., 161.
28. Hilary Holladay, *Ann Petry* (New York: Twayne, 1996), 10.
29. Ibid.
30. Ann Petry, *The Street* (Boston: Houghton Mifflin, 1946), 430.
31. Marika Sherwood, with Donald Hinds, Colin Prescod, and the 1996 Claudia Jones Symposium, *Claudia Jones, A Life in Exile* (London: Lawrence and Wishart, 1999), 20. Also see Claudia Jones, *An End to the Neglect of the Problems of the Negro Woman* (New York: New Century Publishers, 1949).
32. Sherwood et al., *Claudia Jones*, 30–31.
33. "Woman Communist Leader Is Arrested for Deportation," *New York Times*, January 21, 1948, 1. Sherwood et al., *Claudia Jones*, 25.
34. Niebuhr, *Moral Man and Immoral Society*, 254.
35. Some of Reinhold Niebuhr's topical articles on race (up to 1960) include: "The Race Issue in the Church," *Detroit Times*, February 1, 1930, 18; "Meditations from

Mississippi," *Christian Century* 54 (February 10, 1937): 183–84; "The Race Issue in Parochial Schools," *The Messenger* 12, no. 21 (October 14, 1947): 7; "The Sin of Racial Prejudice," *The Messenger* 13, no. 3 (February 3, 1948): 6; "Sports and the Race Issue," *The Messenger* 14, no. 3 (February 1, 1949): 6; "The Perils of Complacency in Our Nation," *Christianity and Crisis* 14, no. 1 (1954): 1–2; "School Segregation Situation Illustrates Difficulty of Applying Abstract Principles," *The Lutheran* 38, no. 8 (November 23, 1955): 18; "Race Problem in America," *Christianity and Crisis* 15, no. 22 (1955): 169–70; "Why Do We Explode When Communists Accuse Us of Colonialism or Race Bias: Judgment by Evildoers," *New Leader* 39, no. 8 (February 20, 1956): 8–9; "If Races Mix, Won't There Be Intermarriage," *The Lutheran* 38, no. 45 (August 8, 1956): 17–18; "School, Church, and the Ordeals of Integration," *Christianity and Crisis* 16, no. 16 (1956): 121–22; "The Civil Rights Bill," *New Leader* 40, no. 37 (September 16, 1957): 9–11; "Bad Days at Little Rock," *Christianity and Crisis* 17, no. 17 (1957): 131; "Civil Rights and Democracy," *Christianity and Crisis* 17, no. 12 (1957): 89; "The States Rights Crisis," *New Leader* 41, no. 35 (September 29, 1958): 6–7; "Drive to Overcome Racial Prejudice Is Complicated by Genuine Cultural and Economic Problems: The Negro Dilemma," *New Leader* 43, no. 14 (April 11, 1960): 13–14.

36. Niebuhr, *Moral Man and Immoral Society*, 253.
37. Reinhold Niebuhr, *An Interpretation of Christian Ethics* (New York: Harper and Brothers, 1935), 228.
38. Since I am not offering a biographical study of Niebuhr, several details about Niebuhr's personal involvement with blacks and issues of race relations are beyond the scope of this chapter. During the 1930s, Niebuhr was president of the board of trustees for the Delta Collective Farm in Richdale, Mississippi. This project supported a racially integrated collection of poor families cooperatively farming together within the environment of a hostile, active Ku Klux Klan as well as the desperate rural poverty of the Mississippi Delta. In addition, Myles Horton, the founder and director of the Highlander school for social change in Tennessee (founded in 1932)—legendary for its nurturing progressive activism in the labor and civil rights movements—gives Niebuhr credit for influencing his ideas and helping to get Highlander started. Myles Horton to Ursula Niebuhr, April 1, 1989, Reinhold Niebuhr Papers, Letters, Manuscripts Division, Library of Congress, Washington, DC. Niebuhr repeatedly came to the defense of the Highlander School when it was under attack for its work on racial integration in the 1950s. See John M. Glen, *Highlander: No Ordinary School, 1932–1962* (Lexington: University Press of Kentucky, 1988). A Union Theological Seminary course called "Ethical Viewpoints in Modern Literature" that Niebuhr taught in 1931 included texts by W. E. B. Du Bois and James Weldon Johnson on the syllabus. Scott Holland, "First We Take Manhattan, Then We Take Berlin: Bonhoeffer's New York," *Cross Currents* 50 (Fall 2000): 371.
39. Niebuhr had been pastor of Bethel from 1915 to 1928. Also, biographer Richard W. Fox reports that Helm's efforts were "so judgmental," even supporters of the admission of Negroes were alienated, and that Helm "vilified those willing to compromise with prejudice." *Reinhold Niebuhr: A Biography* (New York: Pantheon Books, 1985), 118–19. Based upon his characterizations of Helm, it seems that Fox, as well as Niebuhr, may have believed a gentle approach against the racist exclusion of blacks was necessary.

40. Also, in keeping with his commitment to addressing racism, Helm apparently invited Du Bois to speak to an evening adult forum at the church. When Helm was forced to resign, the church rescinded the invitation to Du Bois. W. E. B. Du Bois to Office of the Bethel Evangelical Church (Detroit, MI), February 27, 1930, Reinhold Niebuhr Papers, Correspondence, Box 4, Manuscripts Division, Library of Congress, Washington, DC. Du Bois also wrote to Niebuhr to complain about this insult (Du Bois to Niebuhr, February 27, 1930, Reinhold Niebuhr Papers, Correspondence, Box 4, Manuscripts Division, Library of Congress, Washington, DC).
41. As quoted in Fox, *Reinhold Niebuhr*, 119.
42. When he served as a pastor in Detroit, Niebuhr was chairman of the Mayor's Race Committee that issued a 1926 report on race relations in Detroit. The report summarized an extensive study of "The Negro in Detroit" by university social scientists. Although it did not endorse integration with whites, the report was sympathetic to many of the inequalities faced by "the colored community" in Detroit.
43. Fox also notes that Niebuhr wrote that not more than twenty churches (presumably white ones) in the whole nation could receive Negroes without suffering great losses in membership or complete disintegration (*Reinhold Niebuhr*, 120).
44. Reinhold Niebuhr, "The Civil Rights Issue and the Democratic Convention," unpublished article, June 21, 1956, Reinhold Niebuhr Papers, Correspondence, Box 15, Manuscripts Division, Library of Congress, Washington, DC.
45. "What Resources Can the Christian Church Offer to Meet Crisis in Race Relations?" *Messenger* (April 3, 1956), cited in *Love and Justice: Selections from the Shorter Writings of Reinhold Niebuhr*, ed. D. B. Robertson (Philadelphia: Westminster Press), 155.
46. Ibid.
47. See Oscar Cole Arnal, "A Canadian Socialist Christian Looks at Reinhold Niebuhr" in *Reinhold Niebuhr (1892–1971): A Centenary Appraisal*, ed. Gary A. Gaudin and Douglas John Hall (Atlanta: Scholars Press, 1994), 82. He comments on this same tendency in Niebuhr in relation to issues of class: "[Niebuhr] puts himself above and beyond the fray. . . . He becomes the prophetic arbiter beyond class arrogance, pointing out the sin of both oppressor and oppressed."
48. Reinhold Niebuhr, *Reflections on the End of an Era* (New York: Charles Scribner's Sons, 1934), 268, 275.
49. Niebuhr, *Moral Man and Immoral Society*, 268.
50. Ibid.
51. Niebuhr, *Reflections on the End of an Era*, 253. Even when he recognizes the positive leadership of Negro leaders, he asserts that the educational advantages which allow them to "battle for the freedom of their race have come largely from the schools established by philanthropic white people" (idem, *Moral Man and Immoral Society*, 252).
52. She was also a church activist in the civil rights movement. As coordinator of special projects for the Commission on Religion and Race of the National Council of Churches, Hedgeman was the only woman to serve on the administrative committee for the March on Washington in 1963, and is credited with recruiting tens of thousands of church people to participate in that march (Brian Lanker, ed., *I Dream a World: Portraits of Black Women Who Changed America* [New York: Stewart, Tabori and Chang, 1989], 90). Also see Anna Arnold Hedgeman, *The Gift of Chaos: Decades of Discontent* (New York: Oxford University Press, 1977).

53. Anna Arnold Hedgeman, *The Trumpet Sounds: A Memoir of Negro Leadership* (New York: Holt, Rinehart, and Winston, 1964), 41.
54. By 1935, the director reported that the Harlem YWCA was 87 percent self-supporting. Judith Weisenfeld, *African American Women and Christian Activism: New York's Black YWCA, 1905–1945* (Cambridge, MA: Harvard University Press, 1997), 170.
55. Ibid., 164.
56. As quoted in ibid., 174 n.50.
57. Niebuhr, *Moral Man and Immoral Society*, 252.
58. Greenberg, *Or Does It Explode?* 3–6.
59. Weisenfeld, *African American Women and Christian Activism*, 177.
60. Reinhold Niebuhr, *Moral Man and Immoral Society*, 130.
61. Ella Baker and Marvel Cooke, "The Bronx Slave Market," *The Crisis: A Record of the Darker Races* 42 (November 1935): 330–31, 340.
62. Ibid., 330.
63. Ibid.
64. Brenda Clegg Gray, *Black Female Domestics during the Depression in New York City, 1930–1940* (New York: Garland Publishing, 1993), 61; also see Judith Rollins, *Between Women: Domestics and Their Employers* (Philadelphia: Temple University Press, 1985), 191.
65. Anna Hedgeman was warned about this trick during her investigation of the Bronx slave market. See Hedgeman, *The Trumpet Sounds*, 69.
66. Brian Lanker, interview, "Queen Audley Moore," in *I Dream a World: Portraits of Black Women Who Changed America*, 103; also see Alana J. Erickson, "The Bronx Slave Market" (draft), 1996, http://www.columbia.edu/~aje4/bronx.html (retrieved August 2004).
67. Gray, *Black Female Domestics*, 84; Baker and Cooke, "The Bronx Slave Market," 331.
68. As quoted in Gray, *Black Female Domestics*, 85.
69. Ibid., 61.
70. Niebuhr, *The Nature and Destiny of Man*, vol 1:208ff.; also see Niebuhr, *An Interpretation of Christian Ethics*, 124–25, where he admits that sin is present "even in the most individual and personal relationships."
71. Niebuhr, *The Nature and Destiny of Man*, 1:226.
72. See Beverly Harrison, "The Role of Social Theory in Religious Social Ethics: Reconsidering the Case for Marxian Political Economy," in *Making the Connections: Essays in Feminist Social Ethics*, ed. Carol S. Robb (Boston: Beacon Press, 1985), 59. She explains: "When power is conceived, as Niebuhr and other realists conceived it, as an inevitable dynamic of individual and group self-assertion endlessly reiterating itself, the particularity of historical process and the shifting history of institutions largely drops out of the picture."
73. Valerie Saiving Goldstein, "The Human Situation: A Feminine View," *Journal of Religion* 40 (April 1960): 100–112, reprinted in Carol P. Christ and Judith Plaskow, eds., *Womanspirit Rising: A Feminist Reader in Religion* (Harper and Row, 1979); Susan Nelson Dunfee, "The Sin of Hiding: A Feminist Critique of Reinhold Niebuhr's Account of the Sin of Pride," *Soundings* 65 (Fall 1982): 316–27; Judith Plaskow, *Sex, Sin and Grace: Women's Experience and the Theologies of Reinhold Niebuhr and Paul Tillich* (Lanham, MD: University Press of America, 1980); Judith Vaughan, *Sociality, Ethics, and Social Change: A Critical Appraisal of Reinhold Niebuhr's Ethics in Light of Rosemary Radford Ruether's Works*

(New York: University Press of America, 1983); Catherine Keller, *From a Broken Web: Separation, Sexism and Self* (Boston: Beacon Press, 1986), esp. 38–43; Daphne Hampson, "Reinhold Niebuhr on Sin: A Critique," in *Reinhold Niebuhr and the Issues of Our Time*, ed. Richard Harries (Grand Rapids: William B. Eerdmans, 1986): 46–60. For a critical evaluation of feminist perspectives on Niebuhr, see Aurelia Takacs Fule, "Being Human before God: Reinhold Niebuhr in Feminist Mirrors," in *Reinhold Niebuhr (1892–1971): A Centenary Appraisal*, ed. Gary A. Gaudin and Douglas John Hall (Atlanta: Scholars Press, 1994), 55–78. Although her essay is not a discussion of sin, see Barbara Hilkert Andolsen's criticism of Niebuhr's emphasis on self-sacrificial love on similar grounds as other feminists, citing the neglect of "female experience" and the challenge it represents to this notion of Christian love. "Agape in Feminist Ethics," in *Feminist Theological Ethics: A Reader*, ed. Lois K. Daly (Louisville, KY: Westminster John Knox Press, 1994): 146–59.

74. Hampson, "Reinhold Niebuhr on Sin," 55.
75. See Susan Nelson Dunfee, "The Sin of Hiding," *Soundings*, 324.
76. Plaskow, *Sex, Sin and Grace*, 3.
77. Ibid., 151.
78. Not all feminist theologians have agreed with this interpretation of "women's experience." See Sheila Greene Davaney, "Limits of the Appeal to Women's Experience," in *Shaping New Vision: Gender and Values in American Culture*, ed. Clarissa W. Atkinson, Constance H. Buchanan, Margaret R. Miles (Ann Arbor, MI: UMI Research Press, 1987): 31–49; Mary Grey, *Feminism, Redemption and the Christian Tradition* (Mystic, CT: Twenty-Third Publications, 1990), 22.
79. Rebekah L. Miles, *The Bonds of Freedom: Feminist Theology and Christian Realism* (Oxford and New York: Oxford University Press, 2001), 173 n.154, 87.
80. Ibid., see 34–50, 80.
81. For examples of interdisciplinary discussions see Joan Scott, "A Reply to Criticism," *International Labor and Working Class History* 32 (1987): 39–45; idem, "The Evidence of Experience," *Critical Inquiry* 17 (1991): 773–97; Christine Stansell, "A Response to Joan Scott," *International Labor and Working Class History* 32 (1987): 24–29; Donna J. Haraway, "Reading Buchi Emecheta: Contests for 'Women's Experience' in Women's Studies," *Simians, Cyborgs, and Women: The Reinvention of Nature* (New York: Routledge, 1991): 109–24; bell hooks, "Essentialism and Experience," in *Teaching to Transgress: Education as the Practice of Freedom* (New York: Routledge, 1994): 77–92; Chandra Talpade Mohanty, "Feminist Encounters: Locating the Politics of Experience," *Copyright* 1 (1982): 30–44; Jacqui M. Alexander and Chandra Talpade Mohanty, "Introduction: Genealogies, Legacies, Movements," in *Feminist Genealogies, Colonial Legacies, Democratic Futures*, ed. Jacqui M. Alexander and Chandra Talpade Mohanty (New York: Routledge, 1997): xiii–xlii; Dorothy Smith, "Sociology from Women's Experience: A Reaffirmation," *Sociological Theory* 10, no. 1 (Spring 1992): 88; Judith Grant, *Fundamental Feminism: Contesting the Core Concepts of Feminist Theory* (New York: Routledge, 1993); Shari Stone-Mediatore, "Chandra Mohanty and the Revaluing of 'Experience,'" in *Decentering the Center: Philosophy for a Multicultural, Postcolonial, and Feminist World*, ed. Uma Narayan and Sandra Harding (Bloomington: Indiana University Press, 2000), 110–27; Rosemary Hennessy, *Materialist Feminism and the Politics of Discourse* (New York: Routledge, 1993). For a white Christian theological discussion relevant to this topic of sin and women's experience, see Serene Jones, *Feminist Theory and Christian Theology:*

Cartographies of Grace (Minneapolis: Augsburg Fortress, 2000), especially 108–15. For a womanist theological discussion of sin that is also relevant here and specifically mentions the Baker and Cooke article, see Jacqueline Grant, "The Sin of Servanthood and the Deliverance of Discipleship," in *A Troubling in My Soul: Womanist Perspectives on Evil and Suffering*, ed. Emile M. Townes (Maryknoll, NY: Orbis Books, 1993): 199–218.

82. LeRoy Jeffries, "New York's Slave Markets," *Opportunity: Journal of Negro Life* 17, no. 3 (March 1939): 85–86.
83. See Irma Watkins-Owens, *Blood Relations: Caribbean Immigrants and the Harlem Community, 1900–1930* (Bloomington: Indiana University Press, 1996).
84. See Greenberg, *Or Does It Explode?* 126–27; Claude McKay, *Harlem: Negro Metropolis* (New York: Harcourt Brace Jovanovich, 1940), 198–200, 205; Adam Clayton Powell writes critically of Negroes, "Here we are a disenfranchised group trying to solve our problem with prejudice toward another group," but also that "It is the task of the Jewish people, not the Negro, to condemn the slave market in the Bronx. . . ." Powell, "Soap Box," *Amsterdam News*, 1939(?), from New York Public Library Schomburg Center Clipping File 1925–1974, "Domestic Workers." Murray Friedman quotes a Jewish woman who was an adolescent in New York during the 1930s who commented about the "slave markets" that she felt "infuriated," "sorrowful," and "ashamed" that she could not alter anything about them. Friedman, *What Went Wrong? The Creation and Collapse of the Jewish-Black Alliance* (New York: Free Press, 1995), 87–108. In a 1941 publication of the American Jewish Congress, Marie Syrkin writes five years after the publication of the Baker and Cooke article: "Another sore point has been the existence of the notorious 'slave markets' of the Bronx, where housewives would engage domestic workers on street corners or park benches. Frequently the pay offered was shamefully low. . . . LaGuardia's establishment of employment stations, as well as the rise in employment opportunities has remedied this evil. But the resentment at exploitation by some Jewish women has had unfortunate after-effects. The fact that the great majority of Jewish women are as fair and considerate as any other group of employers has not prevented the formulation of unjust generalizations," in Marie Syrkin, "Anti-Semitic Drive in Harlem," *Congress Weekly* 8, no. 35 (1941): 6–8, as quoted in Maurianne Adams and John Bracey, eds., *Strangers and Neighbors: Relations between Blacks and Jews in the United States* (Amherst: University of Massachusetts Press, 1999), 382.
85. Baker and Cooke, "Bronx Slave Market," 330–31.
86. For analysis on the attainment of white status for Jews, see Karen Brodkin, *How Jews Became White Folks and What That Says about Race in America* (New Brunswick, NJ: Rutgers University Press, 2002).
87. For a discussion of social conditions for Jews during this period, see Beth S. Wenger, *New York Jews and the Great Depression: Uncertain Promise* (New Haven, CT: Yale University Press, 1996). Unfortunately, Wenger's comprehensive treatment of Jewish economic life in Harlem and in the Bronx during the 1930s does not include the struggles with Negroes related to the slave markets. For a historical discussion of social conditions of Jews that covers a broader period and context than just New York City, but pays closer attention to gender issues and conditions for Jewish women, see Riv-Ellen Prell, *Fighting to Become Americans: Jews, Gender, and the Anxiety of Assimilation* (Boston: Beacon Press, 1999). Prell explains that "although it was difficult to manage, many Jews still idealized the middle-class family that kept women out of the workplace," 126.

88. Hedgeman, *The Trumpet Sounds*, 69.
89. Robert Weisbrot, *Father Divine: The Utopian Evangelist of the Depression Era Who Became an American Legend* (Boston: Beacon Press, 1983), 59. Some of Father Divine's followers still gather together in this century; see David B. Caruso, "Followers Age and Dwindle, But Some Still Believe Father Divine Was God, Not Fraud," *The Washington Afro-American*, June 7–13, 2003, D7.
90. The differences in my sources for each of these affects my analysis. I am comparing the primary views of Niebuhr with secondary accounts depicting the actions of the "angels" in Father Divine's movement. I have to be much more tentative in my description of the "angels," especially their viewpoints, than in my discussion of Niebuhr.
91. See Miles, "Sensuality: The Denial of Freedom," in *The Bonds of Freedom*, 84–89, where she offers a discussion of the complex nature of Niebuhr's understanding of sin as sensuality.
92. Niebuhr, *Nature and Destiny of Man*, 1:236–37.
93. Ibid., 1:237.
94. Weisbrot, *Father Divine*, 7.
95. As quoted in Jill Watts, *God, Harlem U.S.A.: The Father Divine Story* (Berkeley: University of California Press, 1992).
96. Claude McKay, *Harlem: Negro Metropolis*, 166. However, Divine claimed that wives asked their husbands for permission to come and submit themselves to him (Watts, *God*, 196, n.15).
97. Sara Harris, with Harriet Crittenden, *Father Divine: Holy Husband* (New York: Doubleday and Company, 1953), 114.
98. Ibid.
99. Niebuhr, *Nature and Destiny of Man*, 1:237.
100. Ibid.
101. Ibid., 1:258.
102. Ibid., 1:236, 1:179.
103. Ibid., 1:260.
104. Jill Watts notes a shift in the status of women that occurred at the end of the 1930s as the movement became more institutionalized. Specific orders and creeds were developed that emphasized obedience and submissiveness for women. See Watts, *God*, 161–62.
105. McKay, *Harlem*, 167.
106. Watts, *God*, 136–37.
107. Ibid., 123–24; Weisbrot, *Father Divine*, 123.
108. See Faithful Mary's exposé, *"God": He's Just a Natural Man* (New York: Gailliard Press, 1937); "Young Angel Tells Weary Tale of Woe," *Amsterdam News*, July 10, 1937.
109. Watts, *God*, 153–54, 159.
110. Gray, *Black Female Domestics*, 104; Eugene Gordon, "300 Demand for 60 Hour Week, Pledge Fight for Higher Wages, Abolition of 'Slave Markets,'" March 5, 1939, (n.p.) New York Public Library Schomburg Center Clipping File 1925–1974, and in the same file "Domestic Workers" (n.p., n.d.).
111. See "Would End Abuse in Job Soliciting," *New York Times*, March 12, 1939, D5. Also, rabbis were part of citizens' groups working to bring about change; see "'Slave Markets' in Bronx Decried," *New York Times*, December 1, 1939, 25.

Chapter 2

1. Just as the array of contemporary scholars in Christian ethics whose work is mentioned here is not representative of the breadth of the field, so too the examples of sexual violation and related public practices that I cite do not adequately represent the vast range of incidents that occur.
2. Chicago's Cardinal Francis George commented on the abuse of females by male clergy: "There's a difference between a moral monster like Geoghan who preys upon little children and does so in a serial fashion and someone who, perhaps under the influence of alcohol, engages in an action with a 17 or 16 year old young woman who returns his affection." Geoghan was a predator protected by the church while he abused many boys in the Boston Archdiocese. Alan Cooperman, "'One Strike' Plan for Ousting Priests Has Catholics Divided," *Washington Post*, May 19, 2002, A1ff. Also see Kathy Shaw, Thomas Farragher, and Matt Carroll, "Church Board Dismissed Accusations by Females," *Boston Globe*, February 7, 2003, A1.
3. John C. Bennett, *The Radical Imperative: From Theology to Social Ethics* (Philadelphia: Westminster Press, 1975), 12.
4. For a study of the political significance of crucifixion in antiquity, see Martin Hengel, *Crucifixion in the Ancient World and the Folly of the Message of the Cross* (Philadelphia: Fortress Press, 1977). Also, for a discussion of New Testament writings by Paul that recognize the political significance of the cross, see Neil Elliott, "The Anti-Imperial Message of the Cross," in *Paul and Empire: Religion and Power in Roman Imperial Society*, ed. Richard A. Horsley (Harrisburg, PA: Trinity Press International, 1997), 167–83.
5. Gerard S. Sloyan, *The Crucifixion of Jesus: History, Myth, Faith* (Minneapolis: Augsburg Fortress, 1995), 19. Sloyan discusses the political circumstances surrounding the torture and crucifixion of Jesus on pp. 9–23. For an argument about the element of sexual humiliation that may have been present in the political execution of Jesus that is linked to the use of state terror in Latin America, see David Tombs, "Crucifixion, State Terror, and Sexual Abuse," *Union Seminary Quarterly Review* 53, nos. 1–2 (1999): 89–109. Also see Rita Nakashima Brock and Rebecca Ann Parker, *Proverbs of Ashes: Why Jesus' Death Didn't Save Us* (Boston: Beacon Press, 2001). Their critique of atonement theology and the ways that it supports violence, including sexual abuse of children, influenced my argument.
6. Beverly W. Harrison, "The Power of Anger in the Work of Love," in *Making the Connections: Essays in Feminist Social Ethics*, ed. Carol S. Robb (Boston: Beacon Press, 1985), 13.
7. Harrison explains: "We recognize that all of our knowledge, including our moral knowledge is body-mediated knowledge. . . . *Perception* is foundational to *conception*. Ideas are dependent on our sensuality. Feeling is the basic bodily ingredient that mediates our connectedness to the world" (ibid.).
8. I discuss the impact of intimate violence on women's self-perceptions in *Wounds of the Spirit: Black Women, Violence and Resistance Ethics* (New York: New York University Press, 1999).
9. See, for example, Max Stackhouse, "Christian Social Ethics in a Global Era: Reforming Protestant Views," in *Christian Social Ethics in a Global Era*, ed. Max L. Stackhouse, Peter Berger, Dennis P. McCann, and M. Douglas Meeks (Nashville: Abingdon Press, 1995), 11–73. For a feminist critique of universalism in Stanley Hauerwas, see Gloria

Albrecht, *The Character of Our Communities: Toward an Ethic of Liberation for the Church* (Nashville: Abingdon Press, 1995), especially related to sexuality, 125–30.

10. Gene Outka, "The Particularist Turn in Theological and Philosophical Ethics," in *Christian Ethics: Problems and Prospects*, ed. Lisa Sowle Cahill and James F. Childress (Cleveland: Pilgrim Press, 1996), 96.
11. For a capabilities approach that underscores the need for universal ethical principles, see Martha C. Nussbaum, *Women and Human Development: The Capabilities Approach* (Cambridge: Cambridge University Press, 2000), especially chap. 1, "In Defense of Universal Values."
12. See The Combahee River Collective, "A Black Feminist Statement" (1977), in *Words of Fire: An Anthology of African-American Feminist Thought*, ed. Beverly Guy-Sheftall (New York: The New York Press, 1995), 235, which states, "A political contribution that we feel we have already made is the expansion of the feminist principle that the personal is political . . . we are dealing with the implications of race and class as well as sex." Also see Pauli Murray, "The Liberation of Black Women," in the same volume, especially 195.
13. "U.S. Customs Service: Better Targeting of Airline Passengers for Personal Searches Could Produce Better Results" (Letter Report, 17 March 2000, GAO/GGD-00-38), 12. Senators Carol Moseley-Braun (D-Ill.) and Richard Durbin (D-Ill.) requested an investigation in June 1998. They called for a nationwide review of the U.S. Customs Service after Chicago-based WMAQ–Channel 5 revealed that many more women than men, including at least fifty innocent black women, were strip-searched by agents looking for contraband at O'Hare Airport. In response to the request by Senator Durbin, the GAO conducted a study of the policies and procedures of the U.S. Customs Department for fiscal years 1997 and 1998. The report was issued to Durbin in March 2000 and released by his office in April 2000.
14. Ibid.
15. Ibid., 2.
16. Statement of Yvette Bradley, ACLU Client Challenging Racial Profiling at Newark Airport, Press Release, May 12, 2000, http://www.aclu.org/news/2000/bradley-statement2.html (retrieved November 2000).
17. Maureen O'Donnell, "O'Hare Searches Still Haunt Women," *Chicago Sun-Times*, April 11, 2000, 3.
18. Ibid.
19. Katie G. Cannon, "Hitting a Straight Lick with Crooked Stick: The Womanist Dilemma in the Development of a Black Liberation Ethic," in *Katie's Canon: Womanism and the Soul of the Black Community* (New York: Continuum, 1995), 126.
20. Janet R. Jakobsen, "The Body Politic vs. Lesbian Bodies: Publics, Counterpublics, and the Uses of Norms," in *Horizons in Feminist Theology: Identity, Tradition, and Norms*, ed. Rebecca S. Chopp and Sheila Greeve Davaney (Minneapolis: Fortress Press, 1997), 116–36; Carole R. Fontaine, "Disabilities and Illness in the Bible: A Feminist Perspective," in *A Feminist Companion to the Hebrew Bible in the New Testament*, ed. Athalya Brenner (Sheffield, England: Sheffield Academic Press, 1996), 286–300; Margaret D. Kamitsuka, "Reading the Raced and Sexed Body in *The Color Purple*: Repatterning White Feminist and Womanist Theological Hermeneutics," *Journal of Feminist Studies in Religion* 19, no. 2 (Fall 2003): 45–77; Lisa Isherwood and Elizabeth Stuart, *Introducing Body Theology* (Cleveland: Pilgrim Press, 1998); Lisa Isherwood, ed., *The Good News of the Body: Sexual Theology and Feminism* (New York: New York University Press, 2000);

Elisabeth Moltmann-Wendel, *I Am My Body: A Theology of Embodiment* (New York: Continuum, 1995).

21. The GAO report recommends "that Customs compare the characteristics of those passengers subjected to personal searches with the results of those searches to better target passengers carrying contraband" (U.S. Customs Service, "Better Targeting," 2).
22. When the GAO report was presented in the spring of 2000, the commissioner insisted that the problems that the report revealed had already been addressed by changes he had put in place. Stephen Barr, "Customs Says It's Changed; Agency Says Racial Disparities in Drug Searches Diminished," *Washington Post*, April 11, 2000, A21.
23. Ibid.
24. I am grateful to Sue Houchins for helping me to clarify this discussion of the role of the agents.
25. Harrison, "The Power of Anger," 13.
26. Gene Outka, "The Particularist Turn in Theological and Philosophical Ethics," in *Christian Ethics: Problems and Prospects*, ed. Lisa Sowle Cahill and James F. Childress (Cleveland: Pilgrim Press, 1996), 93–118.
27. Ibid., 95.
28. Ibid., 115.
29. Even when more philosophically oriented religious ethics focuses upon a concrete issue including a direct reference to a "minority" person, the implications of race and racism may still be left without interrogation. For example, when British ethicist Joseph Runzo asserts the universal wrongness of torture, he gives an example of a scenario involving a "minority resident" in order to account for the particular, or as he puts it, the "relative" circumstances that might test that assertion. The "simple but well meaning minority resident" is a "simpleton" who refuses to tell the police about a terrorist bomb plot that threatens thousands of lives, hatched by a gang of "terrorists from the same minority" to which the "simpleton" belongs and feels loyalty. Runzo considers the reasonableness of police using torture to extract information to save thousands of lives. He opposes "a false dichotomy between ethical relativism and the universality of the moral prohibition on torture. Morality can be relative, yet torture universally wrong." Runzo pays insufficient attention to the injurious political implications of referring to a "minority" group member as a simpleton. Joseph Runzo, "Reply: Ethical Universality and Ethical Relativism," in *Religion and Morality*, ed. D. Z. Phillips (New York: St. Martin's Press, 1996), 171–87 (quote on 173).
30. Margaret Farley, "Feminist Theology and Bioethics," in *Feminist Theological Ethics: A Reader*, ed. Lois K. Daly (Louisville, KY: Westminster John Knox Press, 1994), 203. Also see Farley's "Feminism and Universal Morality," in *Prospects for a Common Morality*, ed. Gene Outka and John Reeder Jr. (Princeton, NJ: Princeton University Press, 1993), 170–90; Farley, "Feminist Ethics," in *The Westminster Dictionary of Christian Ethics*, ed. James F. Childress and John Macquarrie (Philadelphia: Westminster Press, 1986), 229–31.
31. Farley, "Feminist Theology and Bioethics," 203.
32. Ibid., 202.
33. Ibid., 203.
34. Harrison, "The Power of Anger," 18.
35. Josh Kovner and Edmund Mahony with contributions to the story by Eric M. Weiss and Mark Pazniokas, "Sexual Assault Scandal Hits Police Officers: 2 Accused of Abus-

ing Prostitutes," *Hartford Courant*, April 8, 1999, A1. In March 2000 Basile pled guilty to lying about sexual misconduct involving women he encountered while on duty. In exchange for this plea, prosecutors dropped a series of other charges including an allegation that he aimed his gun at a woman while sexually assaulting her. Josh Kovner, "Guilty Plea in Police Probe, A Hartford Officer Admits He Lied to Federal Officials about Sexual Misconduct; A Plea Agreement Allows Him to Avoid Prosecution on Other Felony Charges," *Hartford Courant*, March 25, 2000, B1.

36. Kovner et al., "Sexual Assault Scandal Hits Police Officers."
37. Josh Kovner, "Officers Accused of Misconduct, Prostitutes' Allegations Prompt Investigation," *Hartford Courant*, October 1, 1998, B1.
38. U.S. Attorney Stephen C. Robinson, as quoted in Kovner et al., "Sexual Assault Scandal Hits Police Officers," A1. City Councilman Louis. Watkins as quoted in Kovner, "Officers Accused of Misconduct."
39. *United States vs. Salvatore Gallo*, U.S. District Court for the District of Connecticut (Hartford, CT), jury trial transcript excerpt—examination of Latoya Grasser, October 24, 2000, 31.
40. Ibid., 61–62.
41. Cannon, "Hitting a Straight Lick," 122.
42. Marcia Y. Riggs, *Awake, Arise, and Act: A Womanist Call for Black Liberation* (Cleveland: Pilgrim Press, 1994), 79.
43. Ibid., 79, 95.
44. Ibid., xi. The emphasis on black liberation in womanist ethics provides a point of distinction between feminist and womanist Christian ethics. Womanists are concerned with survival and liberation of black women that is always linked in a primary way to the survival and liberation of the black community. Although this concern with black community liberation may be part of a feminist (including black feminist) agenda, it is usually not primary in the same way that it is for womanists. Such distinctions between feminist and womanist Christian ethics should be made cautiously, however, mindful of the goals and methods they share. For instance, Riggs cites the seven stages of liberation social ethics method created by feminist ethicist Beverly Harrison as foundational to her own liberationist method.
45. My use of the term "cultural resources" refers to the centrality of European history and Euro-American writers in the education of children in most U.S. schools and as the primary intellectual traditions taught and researched in higher education.
46. Charlotte Pierce-Baker, *Surviving the Silence: Black Women's Stories of Rape* (New York: W.W. Norton, 1998), 138–39.
47. Ibid., 138.
48. Ibid., 124.
49. Nancy Fraser, "Rethinking the Public Sphere: A Contribution to the Critique of Actually Existing Democracy," in *Habermas and the Public Sphere*, ed. Craig Calhoun (Cambridge, MA: MIT Press, 1992), 116; also see the critique by Iris Marion Young regarding reason and affectivity in Jürgen Habermas, "Impartiality and the Civic Public: Some Implications of Feminist Critiques of Moral and Political Theory" in *Feminism as Critique: Essays on the Politics of Gender in Late-Capitalist Societies*, ed. Seyla Benhabib and Drucilla Cornell (Cambridge: Polity Press, 1987), 56–76, especially 67; Iris Marion Young, *Inclusion and Democracy* (New York: Oxford University Press, 2000).
50. Sharon Welch, *A Feminist Ethic of Risk* (Minneapolis: Fortress Press, 2000), 139.

51. As Margaret Farley asserts, "autonomy is ultimately for the sake of relationship," and "relationships without respect for individuality and autonomy are destructive of persons"; thus, respectful, enduring "relationships make an autonomous self ultimately possible." "Feminism and Universal Morality," 182; also see idem, "A Feminist Version of Respect for Persons," *Journal of Feminist Studies in Religion* 9, nos. 1–2 (Spring/Fall 1993): 183–98. My thinking about autonomy and relationality has benefited from this work by Farley. Also see Ruth L. Smith, "Relationality and the Ordering of Differences in Feminist Ethics," *Journal of Feminist Studies in Religion* 9, nos. 1–2 (Spring/Fall 1993): 199–214.
52. International standards established by Amnesty International and the United Nations Commission on Human Rights, UN Doc E/CN.4/1992/SR.21, February 21, 1992, recognize rape and sexual assault of women while being held in detention as a form of torture.
53. Human Rights Watch, *All Too Familiar: Sexual Abuse of Women in U.S. State Prisons* (New York: Human Rights Watch, 1996, distributed by Yale University Press). Human Rights Watch is an international nongovernmental organization that monitors human rights, founded in 1978. Also see "Deterring Staff Sexual Abuse of Federal Inmates," Office of the Inspector General, U.S. Department of Justice, April 2005, www.usdoj.gov/oig/special/0504/final.pdf.
54. Human Rights Watch, *All Too Familiar*, 188.
55. Ibid., 210.
56. Ibid.
57. Ibid., 211.
58. Ibid.
59. Amnesty International, *"Not Part of My Sentence": Violations of the Human Rights of Women in Custody*, AMR 51/01/99 (New York: Amnesty International, 1999), 41.
60. Ibid., 59.
61. Human Rights Watch, *All Too Familiar*, 210.
62. See Virginia Held, ed., *Justice and Care: Essential Readings in Feminist Ethics* (Boulder, CO: Westview Press, 1995).

Chapter 3

1. This chapter includes ideas from my essays: "Agenda for the Churches: Uprooting a National Policy of Morally Stigmatizing Poor Single Black Moms," in *Welfare Policy: Feminist Critiques*, ed. Elizabeth Bounds, Pamela K. Brubaker, and Mary E. Hobgood (Cleveland: Pilgrim Press, 1999); "Policing the Sexual Reproduction of Poor Black Women," in *God Forbid: Religion and Sex in American Life*, ed. Kathleen Sands (New York: Oxford University Press, 2000).
2. Christopher Jencks, "Does Inequality Matter?" *Dædalus* (Winter 2002): 49–65; idem, "Our Unequal Democracy," *American Prospect* 15, no. 6 (June 2004): A2–A4; Rakesh Kochhar, "The Wealth of Hispanic Households 1996–2002," Pew Hispanic Center, October 2004; Barbara Hagenbaugh, "Nation's Wealth Disparity Widens," *USA Today*, October 10, 2004, A1.
3. Sharon Hays, *Flat Broke with Children: Women in the Age of Welfare Reform* (New York: Oxford University Press, 2003), 47–48.
4. Audrey Singer, "Welfare Reform and Immigrants: A Policy Review," in *Immigrants, Welfare Reform, and the Poverty of Policy*, ed. Philip Kretsedemas and Ana Aparicio (Westport, CT: Praeger, 2004), 22.

5. Ibid. As in most industrialized democracies in the world, prior to the enactment of this law, legal immigrants in the United States had equal access to public assistance benefits as citizens had.
6. www.state.hi.us/dhs/ (acessed August 2004).
7. Ibid.
8. www.state.sd.us/social/TANF/applying.htm (accessed August 2004).
9. Ibid.
10. www.mdhs.state.ct.us/pubs/index.htm (accessed August 2004).
11. www.okdhs.org/childsupport/formspubs.htm (accessed August 2004).
12. This version is based upon the NRSV translation in *The New Testament and Psalms, An Inclusive Version*, ed. Victor Gold, Thomas Hoyt, Sharon Ringe, Susan Brooks Thistlethwaite, Burton Throckmorton, and Barbara Withers (New York: Oxford University Press, 1995).
13. See James Malcolm Arlandson, *Women, Class, and Society in Early Christianity: Models from Luke-Acts* (Peabody, MA: Hendrickson, 1997). An example of a linguistic pattern that signals a moral message to the reader is found in the question of whether the Magnificat was a hymn of a particular outcast community. See Raymond Brown's discussion of the canticles of the Jewish Christian Anawim in *The Birth of the Messiah: A Commentary on the Infancy Narratives in Matthew and Luke* (1977; repr. New York: Doubleday, 1993). Also see Richard A. Horsley's dispute with Brown's analysis of the "Anawim," *The Liberation of Christmas: The Infancy Narratives in Social Context* (New York: Crossroad, 1989).
14. Beverly Roberts Gaventa, *Mary: Glimpses of the Mother of Jesus* (Columbia: University of South Carolina Press, 1995), 4.
15. Ibid. For another theological concern about Mary's portrayal, see Vasiliki Limberis, "Mary 1," in *Women in Scripture: A Dictionary of Named and Unnamed Women in the Hebrew Bible, the Apocryphal/Deuterocanonical Books, and the New Testament*, ed. Carol Meyers et al. (Boston: Houghton Mifflin, 2000). Limberis explains, "That God takes a virgin, Mary, to be the mother of his son reveals Luke's Greco-Roman hermeneutic. Although the idea that a mortal woman could conceive and bear the son of God is foreign to all Jewish writings, it is a familiar Greco-Roman theme in explaining the origin of many 'Divine Men': Heracles . . . Plato. In fact, such a genealogy would be a minimum requirement for legitimating a new god in the Greco-Roman world" (117).
16. Gaventa, *Mary*, 57.
17. Personal Responsibility Act of 1995, 104th Cong., 1st sess., H.R. 4.
18. Ibid., Title I, Sec. 100, Para. 3(P).
19. Ibid., Para. 3(O).
20. *Meet the Press*, NBC, December 4, 1994.
21. For a good summary of feminist theological discussions of Mary, see Els Maecklberghe, *Desperately Seeking Mary: A Feminist Appropriation of a Traditional Religious Symbol* (Kampen, Netherlands: Kok Pharos, 1991).
22. Rosemary Radford Ruether, *Sexism and God-Talk: Toward a Feminist Theology* (Boston: Beacon Press, 1983), 150.
23. Ibid.
24. Jane Schaberg, *The Illegitimacy of Jesus: A Feminist Theological Interpretation of the Infancy Narratives* (San Francisco: Harper and Row, 1987), 13.

25. For a critical discussion of their "improper" dependency, see Elizabeth M. Bounds, "Welfare as a Family Value: Conflicting Notions of Family in Protestant Welfare Responses," in *Welfare Policy: Feminist Critiques*, ed. Bounds et al., 157–74.
26. Ellen Goodman, "Welfare Mothers with an Attitude," illus. Barrie Maguire, *Boston Globe*, April 16, 1992, 19.
27. See Jane Schaberg, "How Mary Magdalene Became a Whore," *Bible Review* 8 (October 1992): 30–37, 51–52.
28. Press conference with Representative Bob Michel (R-IL), Senator Bob Dole (R-KS), and others, Washington, DC, June 14, 1994 (Dialog File 660: Federal News Service).
29. Bill Clinton, "Radio Address of the President to the Nation," January 4, 1997, www.presidency.ucsb.edu.
30. House Committee on Ways and Means, *Contract with America–Welfare Reform: Hearing before the Sub-Committee on Human Resources, Hearing on Illegitimacy and Welfare*, 104th Cong., 1st sess., January 20, 1995, 152.
31. Schaberg, *The Illegitimacy of Jesus*, 101.
32. Ross S. Kraemer, "Jewish Women in the Diaspora World of Late Antiquity," in *Jewish Women in Historical Perspective*, ed. Judith R. Baskin (Detroit: Wayne State University Press, 1991), 61.
33. President Bill Clinton, "Remarks to the 114th Annual Session of the National Baptist Convention USA," New Orleans, Louisiana, September 9, 1994 (Dialog File 660: Federal News Service).
34. Ben Witherington, *Women and the Genesis of Christianity* (New York: Cambridge University Press, 1990), 6.
35. Adeline Fehribach, "Between Text and Context: Scripture, Society and the Role of Women in Formative Judaism," in *Recovering the Role of Women: Power and Authority in Rabbinic Jewish Society*, ed. Peter J. Haas (Atlanta: Scholars Press, 1992), 43. See also Bernadette Brooten, "Early Christian Women and Their Cultural Context: Issues of Method in Historical Reconstruction," in *Feminist Perspectives on Biblical Scholarship*, ed. Adela Yarbro Collins (Chico, CA: Scholars Press, 1985), 79.
36. Fehribach, "Between Text and Context," 43.
37. Averil Cameron, "Women in Early Christian Interpretation," in *A Dictionary of Biblical Interpretation*, ed. R. J. Coggins and J. L. Houlden (Philadelphia: Trinity Press International, 1990), 729.
38. Elisabeth Schüssler Fiorenza, *In Memory of Her: A Feminist Theological Reconstruction of Christian Origins* (New York: Crossroad, 1983), 109.
39. Ibid., 57.
40. Ibid., 59.
41. Undoubtedly, socioeconomically advantaged women fared better in situations where there was the possibility of facing the death penalty for committing adultery.
42. Press conference with Representative Bob Michel (R-IL), Senator Bob Dole (R-KS), and others, Washington, DC, June 14, 1994 (Dialog File 660: Federal News Service). For more recent tough-love arguments by Representative Roukema favoring higher work requirements without allocations for child care in welfare reform, see Charles Dervarics, "Black, Hispanic Caucuses Take Aim at Welfare Bill," *Black Issues in Higher Education* 19, no. 9 (June 20, 2002): 8.
43. Brooten, "Early Christian Women," 67. For other examples of this nonliterary approach, see Ross Kraemer, "Hellenistic Jewish Women in Greco-Roman Egypt: The

Epigraphical Evidence," in *Society of Biblical Literature 1986 Seminar Papers*, ed. Kent Harold Richards (Atlanta: Scholars Press, 1986), 183–200; and Matthew S. Collins, "Money, Sex and Power: An Examination of the Role of Women as Patrons of the Ancient Synagogues," in *Recovering the Role of Women: Power and Authority in Rabbinic Jewish Society*, ed. Peter J. Haas (Atlanta: Scholars Press, 1992), 7–22.

44. Bernadette J. Brooten, *Women Leaders in the Ancient Synagogue* (Chico, CA: Scholars Press, 1982), 1.
45. Kraemer, "Jewish Women in the Diaspora World of Late Antiquity," 55–56; idem, "Jewish Women and Women's Judaism(s) at the Beginning of Christianity," in *Women and Christian Origins*, ed. Ross Shepard Kraemer and Mary Rose D'Angelo (New York: New York University Press, 1999), 58. Also see Tal Ilan, *Jewish Women in Greco-Roman Palestine* (Tübingen: J.C.B. Mohr [Paul Siebeck], 1995), esp. 65–69.
46. Schüssler Fiorenza, *In Memory of Her*, 124; Leonard Swidler, *Women in Judaism: The Status of Women in Formative Judaism* (Metuchen, NJ: Scarecrow Press, 1976), 141; Léonie J. Archer, *Her Price Is Beyond Rubies: The Jewish Woman in Graeco-Roman Palestine* (Sheffield: Sheffield Academic Press, 1990), 151–53; Ilan, *Jewish Women in Greco-Roman Palestine*, 65–69. Ilan argues that the sources depict an ideal of a very young age for marriage for girls, but no firm indication that twelve was the customary age.
47. House Committee, *Contract with America–Welfare Reform*, 146.
48. Ibid. Loury is referring to a report by Daniel Moynihan, submitted when serving as a policy advisor to President Lyndon B. Johnson, that described the Negro family as dysfunctional and disintegrating, entitled "The Negro Family: The Case for National Action," Office of Policy Planning and Research, U.S. Labor Department, March 1965.
49. President Bill Clinton, "Remarks to Progressive National Baptists Convention," Charlotte, NC, August 9, 1995 (Dialog File 660: Federal News Service).
50. See Ilan, *Jewish Women in Palestine*, 84. If the father was deceased, the marriage was arranged by a mother or brother.
51. Kraemer, "Jewish Women and Women's Judaism(s) at the Beginning of Christianity," 59. Also see Ilan, *Jewish Women in Palestine*. Such concerns would have been most important for families with money and property (229).
52. Kraemer, "Jewish Women and Women's Judaism(s) at the Beginning of Christianity," 57.
53. Arlandson, *Women, Class and Society in Early Christianity*, 99–102.
54. For examples, see Constance Parvey, "The Theology and Leadership of Women in the New Testament," in *Religion and Sexism*, ed. Rosemary R. Ruether (New York: Simon and Schuster, 1974), 136–46; Eugene H. Maly, "Women and the Gospel of Luke," *Biblical Theology Bulletin* 10, no. 3 (July 1980): 99–104; Jane E. Via, "Women, the Discipleship of Service, and the Early Christian Meal in the Gospel of Luke," *Saint Luke's Journal of Theology* 29 (December 1985): 37–60; idem, "Women in the Gospel of Luke," in *Women in the World's Religions, Past and Present*, ed. Ursula King (New York: Paragon House, 1987, 38–55); Jane Kopas, "Jesus and Women: Luke's Gospel," *Theology Today* 43 (July 2, 1986): 192–202; and Alesana Eteuali, "The Persistence of Women in Luke's Gospel: In Response to Elisabeth Schüssler Fiorenza," *The Pacific Journal of Theology* Series II, no. 22 (1999): 73–81.
55. Schüssler Fiorenza, *In Memory of Her*, 49, 160–62. Also see idem, *But She Said: Feminist Practices of Biblical Interpretation* (Boston: Beacon Press, 1992), esp. 65–66; Barbara Reid, *Choosing the Better Part? Women in the Gospel of Luke* (Collegeville, MN: The Liturgical

Press, 1996), 52–53; Mary Rose D'Angelo, "Women in Luke-Acts: A Redactional View," *Journal of Biblical Literature* 109 (1990): 441–61; idem, "(Re)Presentations of Women in the Gospel of Matthew and Luke-Acts," in *Women and Christian Origins*, ed. Ross Shepard Kraemer and Mary Rose D'Angelo (Oxford: Oxford University Press, 1999): 171–95; and F. Scott Spencer, "Out of Mind, Out of Voice: Slave-Girls and Prophetic Daughters in Luke-Acts," *Biblical Interpretation* 7 (April 1999): 133–55. For a womanist discussion of the Luke–Acts author, see Clarice J. Martin, "The Acts of the Apostles," in *Searching the Scriptures*, vol. 2, *A Feminist Commentary*, ed. Elisabeth Schüssler Fiorenza (New York: Crossroad, 1994), 763–99.

56. D'Angelo, "Women in Luke-Acts," 452.
57. For a foundational account of this literary technique, see Charles Talbert, *Literary Patterns, Theological Themes, and the Genre of Luke-Acts* (Missoula, MT: SBL and Scholars Press, 1974). For a feminist analysis of this pattern, see Turid Karlsen Seim, *The Double Message: Patterns of Gender in Luke-Acts* (Nashville: Abingdon, 1994).
58. F. Scott Spencer, "Out of Mind, Out of Voice," 135.
59. D'Angelo, "Women in Luke-Acts," 461.
60. Turid Karlsen Seim, "The Gospel of Luke," in *Searching the Scriptures*, vol. 2, *A Feminist Commentary*, ed. Elisabeth Schüssler Fiorenza (New York: Crossroad, 1994), 756.
61. Jane Schaberg, "The Infancy of Mary of Nazareth," in *Searching the Scriptures*, 724. For other discussions of women, virginity, and Christianity in this period, see Kate Cooper, *The Virgin and the Bride: Idealized Womanhood in Late Antiquity* (Cambridge, MA: Harvard University Press, 1999); Margaret Y. MacDonald, *Early Christian Women and Pagan Opinion: The Power of the Hysterical Woman* (New York: Cambridge University Press, 1996), esp. 127–82. For an example of this same discussion in later antiquity, see Virginia Burrus, "Word and Flesh: The Bodies and Sexuality of Ascetic Women in Christian Antiquity," *Journal of Feminist Studies in Religion* 10, no. 1 (Spring 1994): 27–57.
62. Schaberg, "The Infancy of Mary of Nazareth," 724.
63. See Burrus, "Word and Flesh."
64. Press conference with Representative Bob Michel (R-IL), Senator Bob Dole (R-KS) and others, Washington, DC, June 14, 1994 (Dialog File 660: Federal News Service).
65. Cheryl A. Kirk-Duggan, "Proud Mary: Contextual Constructions of a Divine Diva," in *Blessed One: Protestant Perspectives on Mary*, ed. Beverly Roberts Gaventa and Cynthia L. Rigby (Louisville, KY: Westminster John Knox Press, 2002), 76.
66. Elaine Bell Kaplan, *Not Our Kind of Girl: Unraveling the Myths of Black Teenage Motherhood* (Berkeley: University of California Press, 1997), 26.
67. Virginia E. Schein, *Working from the Margins: Voices of Mothers in Poverty* (Ithaca, NY: Cornell University Press, 1995), 156; Jody Raphael, *Saving Bernice: Battered Women, Welfare, and Poverty* (Boston: Northeastern University Press, 2000), 9.
68. Lisa Dodson, *Don't Call Us Out of Name: The Untold Lives of Women and Girls in Poor America* (Boston: Beacon Press, 1998), x. Also see Elliot Liebow, *Tell Them Who I Am: The Lives of Homeless Women* (New York: The Free Press, 1993).
69. Meredith Ralston, *"Nobody Wants to Hear Our Truth": Homeless Women and Theories of the Welfare State* (Westport, CT: Greenwood Press, 1996), xii.
70. David Zucchino, *Myth of the Welfare Queen: A Pulitzer Prize Winning Journalist's Portrait of Women on the Line* (New York: Scribner's, 1997), 13. Also see Schein, *Working from the Margins*, 108–10.

71. Zucchino, *Myth of the Welfare Queen*, 196.
72. See Deborah R. Connolly, *Homeless Mothers: Face to Face with Women and Poverty* (Minneapolis: University of Minnesota Press, 2000); Catherine Pélissier Kingfisher, *Women in the American Welfare Trap* (Philadelphia: University of Pennsylvania Press, 1996). Also see Valerie Polakow, *Lives on the Edge: Single Mothers and the Children in the Other America* (Chicago: University of Chicago Press, 1993), 81–97.
73. Connolly, *Homeless Mothers*, 11.
74. Dodson, *Don't Call Us Out of Name*, 115.
75. Kathleen Mullan Harris, *Teen Mothers and the Revolving Welfare Door* (Philadelphia: Temple University Press, 1997), 129.
76. Kristin Luker, *Dubious Conceptions: The Politics of Teenage Pregnancy* (Cambridge, MA: Harvard University Press, 1996), 133.
77. See Kingfisher, *Women in the American Welfare Trap*. Also see Ruth Horowitz, *Teen Mothers: Citizens or Dependents?* (Chicago: University of Chicago Press, 1995). Horowitz studies the relationships between the personnel and participants in a program for inner-city teenage mothers who are welfare recipients in order to provide a microlevel analysis that exposes the dynamics of social control.
78. Alisse Waterston, *Love, Sorrow, and Rage: Destitute Women in a Manhattan Residence* (Philadelphia: Temple University Press, 1999), 2, 12.
79. Succinctly stated: "As the women's stories indicate, they applied for public assistance out of necessity, not out of choice" (Schein, *Working from the Margins*, 105). For descriptions of hardworking mothers in the post–welfare reform era, see Griff Witte, "Poverty Up as Welfare Enrollment Declines, Nation's Safety Net in Tatters as More People Lose Their Jobs," *Washington Post*, September 26, 2004, A3; Jason DeParle, *American Dream: Three Women, Ten Kids, and a Nation's Drive to End Welfare* (New York: Viking, 2004).
80. See Dodson, *Don't Call Us Out of Name*, 125; Schein, *Working from the Margins*, 107; Kaplan, *Not Our Kind of Girl*, 134–38; Polakow, *Lives on the Edge*, 68.
81. Donna Haig Friedman, *Parenting in Public: Family Shelter and Public Assistance* (New York: Columbia University Press, 2000), 157.
82. Ibid., 193.
83. Ibid.
84. Ibid. Also see Ralston, *"Nobody Wants to Hear Our Truth,"* 86.
85. See Susan Gooden, "Examining Racial Differences in Employment Status among Welfare Recipients," in *Race and Welfare Report* (Oakland: Grassroots Innovative Policy Program, 1997); Steve Savner, "Welfare Reform and Racial/Ethnic Minorities: The Questions to Ask," *Poverty & Race* 9, no. 4 (2000): 3–5; Kenneth J. Neuback and Joel A. Cazenave, *Welfare Racism: Playing the Race Card against America's Poor* (New York: Routledge, 2001), 189.
86. Ralston, *"Nobody Wants to Hear Our Truth,"* 82. Also see Lucie White, "'That's What I Growed Up Hearing': Race, Redemption and American Democracy," in *Who Will Provide? The Changing Role of Religion in American Social Welfare*, ed. Mary Jo Bane, Brent Coffin, and Ronald Thiemann (Boulder, CO: Westview Press, 2000), 238–65; Fran Leeper Buss, comp., *Dignity: Lower-Income Women Tell of Their Lives and Struggles: Oral Histories* (Ann Arbor: University of Michigan Press, 1985), 37, 111–28.
87. Grace Chang, *Disposable Domestics: Immigrant Women Workers in the Global Economy* (Cambridge, MA: South End Press, 2000), 44.

88. Ibid., 206.
89. See Martin Gilens, *Why Americans Hate Welfare: Race, Media, and the Politics of Antipoverty Policy* (Chicago: Chicago University Press, 1999); Neuback and Cazenave, *Welfare Racism*.
90. Ralston, *"Nobody Wants to Hear Our Truth,"* 88.
91. Waterston, *Love, Sorrow, and Rage*, 34–35.
92. Ibid., 53–54.
93. See Patricia Tjaden and Nancy Thoennes, *Extent, Nature, and Consequences of Intimate Partner Violence: Findings from the National Violence Against Women Survey*, NCJ 181867 (Washington, DC: National Institute of Justice and Centers for Disease Control, 2000); Richard M. Tolman and Jody Raphael, "A Review of Research on Welfare and Domestic Violence," *Journal of Social Issues* 56, no. 4 (Winter 2000): 655–81; Jody Raphael, "Keeping Battered Women Safe during Welfare Reform: New Challenges," *American Medical Women's Association Journal* 57, no. 1 (Winter 2002): 32–35; Noel Bridget Busch and Terry A. Wolfer, "Battered Women Speak Out: Welfare Reform and Their Decisions to Disclose," *Violence against Women* 8, no. 5 (May 2002): 566–84; Ellen K. Scott, Andrew S. London, and Nancy A. Myers, "Dangerous Dependencies: The Intersection of Welfare Reform and Domestic Violence," *Gender and Society* 16, no. 6 (December 2002): 878–97; Joan Meisel, Daniel Chandler, and Beth Menees Rienzi, "Domestic Violence Prevalence and Effects on Employment in Two California TANF Populations," *Violence against Women* 9, no. 10 (October 2003): 1191–1212; Beth Silken Catlett and Julie E. Artis, "Critiquing the Case for Marriage Promotion: How the Promarriage Movement Misrepresents Domestic Violence Research," *Violence against Women* 10, no. 11 (November 2004): 1226–44. For women's statements about fleeing domestic violence, see www.legalmomentum.org/issues/wel/marriagediaries.pdf.
94. Waterston, *Love, Sorrow, and Rage*, 80.
95. Raphael, *Saving Bernice*, 31, 43.
96. "Working toward Independence: Promote Child Well-Being and Healthy Marriages," http://www.whitehouse.gov/news/releases/2002/02/welfare-book-05.html (accessed October 17, 2004); Robert Pear and David D. Kirkpatrick, "Bush Plans $1.5 Billion Drive for Promotion of Marriage," *New York Times*, January 14, 2004, A1.
97. See Kathryn Edin, "What Do Low-Income Single Mothers Say about Marriage?" *Social Problems* 47, no. 1 (2000): 112–33; Avis Jones-DeWeever, *Marriage Promotion and Low-Income Communities*, Briefing Paper no. D450 (Washington, DC: Institute for Women's Policy Research, 2002); Daniel T. Lichter, Deborah Roempke Graefe, and J. Brian Brown, "Is Marriage a Panacea? Union Formation among Economically Disadvantaged Unwed Mothers," *Social Problems* 50, no. 1 (2003): 60–86; Daniel T. Lichter, Christie D. Batson, and J. Brian Brown, "Welfare Reform and Marriage Promotion: The Marital Expectations and Desires of Single and Cohabiting Mothers," *The Social Service Review* 78, no. 1 (March 2004): 1–25; and Maureen R. Waller, "High Hopes: Unwed Parents' Expectations about Marriage," *Children and Youth Services Review* 23, no. 6 (2001): 457–84.
98. Schaberg, *The Illegitimacy of Jesus*, 95.
99. Ibid., 98.
100. Schaberg argues that it is possible that Mary's humiliation may have occurred because she was sexually assaulted and became pregnant (ibid., 95).

101. For a good discussion of a range of activist groups, see Vijay Prashad, *Keeping Up with the Dow Joneses: Debt, Prison, Workfare* (Cambridge, MA: South End Press, 2003), 144–77; Neubeck and Cazenave, *Welfare Racism*, 238–41. Also see "Poor People's Human Rights Report on the United States," Kensington Welfare Rights Union, 1999, www.kwru.org.
102. See Horsley, *The Liberation of Christmas*, 111. He points out that this wording is also repeated in Ps. 89:13.
103. The tone of Mary's Magnificat is also often compared to Miriam's (Exod. 15), Deborah's (Judg. 5), and Judith's (Jdt. 13:14, 16).
104. Gail Sheehy, "The Inner Quest of Newt Gingrich," *Vanity Fair*, September 1995, 147–54, 217–22.
105. See Peter J. Howe, "Loury Bows Out of US Job Bid, Arraigned on Assault Charges," *Boston Globe*, June 6, 1987, 1; Robert Connolly, "Harvard Prof 'dragged me down stairs,'" *Boston Herald*, June 6, 1987; Diane Alters, "Loury: Public View vs. Private Life," *Boston Globe*, July 6, 1987, 1.
106. Horsley, *The Liberation of Christmas*, 113.
107. See Samuel K. Roberts, "On Seducing the Samaritan: The Problematic of Government Aid to Faith-Based Groups," in *New Day Begun: African American Churches and Civic Culture in Post-Civil Rights America*, ed. R. Drew Smith (Durham, NC: Duke University Press, 2003), 278–91.
108. Cathy J. Cohen, *The Boundaries of Blackness: AIDS and the Breakdown of Black Politics* (Chicago: University of Chicago Press, 1999), 63.
109. "Remarks by President George Bush at the National Religious Broadcasters' Convention," February 10, 2003, http://www.whitehouse.gov/news/releases/2003/02/20030210–5.html.
110. Ibid.
111. Pear and Kirkpatrick, "Bush Plans $1.5 Billion Drive for Promotion of Marriage," A1.
112. Ivone Gebara and Maria Clara Bingemer, *Mary Mother of God, Mother of the Poor* (1987; English trans., Maryknoll, NY: Orbis Books, 1989), 73.

Chapter 4

1. The discussion of church practices in this chapter largely focuses upon Protestant worship.
2. For examples of studies on racial inequality, see Melvin L. Oliver and Thomas M. Shapiro, *Black Wealth/White Wealth: A New Perspective on Racial Inequality* (New York: Routledge, 1995); Thomas M. Shapiro, *The Hidden Cost of Being African American: How Wealth Perpetuates Inequality* (New York: Oxford University Press, 2004); Major G. Coleman, "Job Skill and Black Wage Discrimination," *Social Science Quarterly* (December 2003): 892–903; Robert D. Bullard, Charles Lee, and J. Eugene Grigsby III, *Residential Apartheid: The American Legacy* (Los Angeles: CAAS Publications, 1994); Robert D. Bullard, *Unequal Protection: Environmental Justice and Communities of Color* (San Francisco: Sierra Club Books, 1994).
3. Peggy McIntosh, "White Privilege: Unpacking the Invisible Knapsack," in *White Privilege: Essential Readings on the Other Side of Racism*, ed. Paula S. Rothenberg (New York: Worth Publishers, 2002); Richard Dyer, *White* (New York: Routledge, 1997); Ruth Frankenberg, *White Women, Race Matters: The Social Construction of Whiteness*

(Minneapolis: University of Minnesota Press, 1993); Christine E. Sleeter, "How White Teachers Construct Race," in *Race, Identity, and Representation*, ed. Cameron McCarthy and Warren Crichlow (New York: Routledge, 1993), 157–71; Stephanie M. Wildman with Adrienne D. Davis, "Making Systems of Privilege Visible," in *Critical White Studies: Looking Behind the Mirror*, ed. Richard Delgado and Jean Stefancic (Philadelphia: Temple University Press, 1997), 314–19.

4. I recall a friend of mine telling me about a black pastor of a predominantly poor black congregation in New Haven, Connecticut, who preached a sermon to a predominantly white wealthy congregation telling them that it was ironic how both congregations (his own and this white wealthy one) prayed about the same material conditions with very different prayers. He said that his congregation prays to God to be relieved from the misery of the very same material conditions for which this white congregation gives God thanks and regards as the blessings that God has provided. He was referring to the white landlords who financially profited from charging high rental prices for substandard housing units in the city's poor neighborhoods.
5. Elizabeth M. Bounds, "Gaps and Flashpoints: Untangling Race and Class," in *Disrupting White Supremacy from Within: White People on What* We *Need to Do*, ed. Jennifer Harvey, Karin Case, and Robin Hawley Gorsline (Cleveland: Pilgrim Press, 2004), 137.
6. For examples of studies of white racist attitudes, see Eduardo Bonilla-Silva, *Racism without Racists: Color-Blind Racism and the Persistence of Racial Inequality in the United States* (Lanham, MD: Rowman and Littlefield, 2003); Joe Feagin and Eileen O'Brien, *White Men on Race: Power, Privilege, and the Shaping of Cultural Consciousness* (Boston: Beacon Press, 2003); David Roediger, *Towards the Abolition of Whiteness* (London: Verso, 1994); Jon Hurwitz and Mark Peffley, "Playing the Race Card in the Post–Willie Horton Era: The Impact of Racialized Code Words on Support for Punitive Crime Policy," *Public Opinion Quarterly* 69, no. 1 (Spring 2005): 99–112; Jonathan Knuckey, "Racial Resentment and the Changing Partisanship of Southern Whites," *Party Politics* 11, no. 1 (January 2005): 5–28.
7. Bounds, "Gaps and Flashpoints," 124; also see my "Agenda for the Churches: Uprooting a National Policy of Morally Stigmatizing Poor Single Black Moms," in *Welfare Policy: Feiminist Critiques*, ed. Elizabeth Bounds, Pamela K. Brubaker, and Mary E. Hobgood (Cleveland: Pilgrim Press, 1999), 143.
8. George Lipsitz, *The Possessive Investment in Whiteness: How White People Profit from Identity Politics* (Philadelphia: Temple University Press, 1998), 20.
9. Ibid., 10. For discussions of environmental racism, see Laura Westra and Peter S. Wenz, eds., *Faces of Environmental Racism* (New York: Rowman and Littlefield, 2001); Rachel Morello-Frosch, "Discrimination and the Political Economy of Environmental Inequality," in *Environment and Planning: Government and Policy* (August 2002): 477–96; Michael Ash and Robert T. Fetter, "Who Lives on the Wrong Side of the Environmental Tracks? EPA's Risk Screening Environmental Indicators Model," *Social Science Quarterly* 2, no. 85 (June 2004): 441–62; Manuel Pastor, James Sadd, and Rachel Morello-Frosch, "Waiting to Inhale: The Demographics of Toxic Air Release Facilities in 21st-Century California," *Social Sciences Quarterly* 2, no. 85 (June 2004): 420–40.
10. Lipsitz, *The Possessive Investment*, 8.
11. Tom F. Driver, *Liberating Rites: Understanding the Transformative Power of Ritual* (Boulder, CO: Westview Press, 1998), 30.

12. The beating of Rodney King by Los Angeles police officers or the sodomizing of Abner Louima by New York City police officers are examples of brutal, racially significant, highly publicized events that can be understood as this kind of white supremacist ritual.
13. Joe R. Feagin and Hernán Vera, *White Racism: The Basics* (New York: Routledge, 1995), 10.
14. Ibid.
15. Ibid., 9–10.
16. Richard K. Fenn cautions us to remember how liturgy gave legitimacy to the ruling families and provided services to people in the Greco-Roman world as a means of social control. He continues to trace this history of Christian liturgy and pluralism: "As the church expanded throughout Europe after the fall of Rome, it enjoyed the patronage of aristocratic families and regional warlords. . . . The church proved itself a particularly useful institution in subduing local leaders and in incorporating diverse communities within the larger society. To be sure, the church often allowed local languages and devotions to find a place within the liturgy. In the long run, however, these expressions of local culture were gradually replaced by a liturgy that was increasingly uniform over large stretches of territory." Richard K. Fenn, "Diversity and Power: Cracking the Code," in *Making Room at the Table: An Invitation to Multicultural Worship*, ed. Brian K. Blount and Leonora Tubbs Tisdale (Louisville, KY: Westminster John Knox Press, 2001), 65–66.
17. Mary Hobgood, *Dismantling Privilege: An Ethics of Accountability* (Cleveland: Pilgrim Press, 2000), 47.
18. Ibid., 58.
19. Ibid., 49.
20. Sally Wilson was a student in a class that I taught at Harvard Divinity School in the fall of 2000.
21. Sally Wilson, "Christian Ethics in Context: Analysis of Worship Service," unpublished paper, December 12, 2000.
22. Lipsitz, *The Possessive Investment*, 13. Also see Mitchell Zuckoff, "Mortgage Gap Still Exists for Minorities," *Boston Globe*, September 27, 1992, Metro sec., 1; Rob Wells, "Fleet Unit's Lending Practices Under Fire in Georgia," *Chicago Tribune*, January 10, 1993, M1; *Los Angeles Times*, "Blacks Rejected More Often than Whites for Home Loans, Survey Shows," January 23, 1989, Business sec., 2; Margery Austin-Turner, Erin Godfrey, Stephen L. Ross, and Robin R. Smith, "Other Things Being Equal: A Paired Testing Study of Discrimination in Mortgage Lending, Working Paper," University of Connecticut Economics Department, 2005; Guy Stewart, *Discrimination Risk: Mortgage Lending Industry in the Twentieth Century* (Ithaca, NY: Cornell University Press, 2003).
23. Pamela Brubaker, *Globalization at What Price? Economic Change and Daily Life* (Cleveland: Pilgrim Press, 2001); Human Rights Center, University of California Berkeley and Free the Slaves, Washington, DC, "Hidden Slaves: Forced Labor in the United States," September 2004; Robert J. S. Ross, *Slaves to Fashion: Poverty and Abuse in the New Sweatshops* (Ann Arbor: University of Michigan Press, 2004).
24. Margaret E. Montoya, "Máscaras, Trenzas, y Greñas: Un/masking the Self While Un/braiding Latina Stories and Legal Discourse," in *Critical Race Theory: The Cutting Edge*, ed. Richard Delgado and Jean Stefancic, 2nd ed. (Philadelphia: Temple University Press, 2002), 516.

25. Ibid., 521.
26. Ibid., 515.
27. As quoted in John Bartkowski and Helen A. Regis, *Charitable Choices: Religion, Race, and Poverty in the Post-Welfare Era* (New York: New York University Press, 2003), 105.
28. See chap. 3, n. 93.
29. Discussions of the struggle to challenge these categories are found in Heather M. Dalmage, ed., *The Politics of Multiracialism: Challenging Racial Thinking* (Albany: State University of New York Press, 2004).
30. Lisa Kahaleole Chang Hall, "Eating Salt," in *Names We Call Home: Autobiography on Racial Identity*, ed. Becky Thompson and Sangeeta Tyagi (New York: Routledge, 1996), 245.
31. Ibid.
32. Examples of such classic church music would be Isaac Watts's "O God, Our Help in Ages Past," Wolfgang Amadeus Mozart's "Requiem," or Johann Sebastian Bach's "Magnificat."
33. In their landmark study of the black church, C. Eric Lincoln and Lawrence Mamiya explain: "Hence, the roadblocks to preaching for black women were further compounded by the complex problem of black male identity in a racist society. If the ministry was the only route to even a shadow of masculinity, the inclusion of women seemed very much like a gratuitous defeat for everybody." C. Eric Lincoln and Lawrence Mamiya, *The Black Church in the African American Experience* (Durham, NC: Duke University Press, 1990), 278. For a more critical perspective than this one on sexism in black churches, especially related to preaching, see Teresa Fry Brown, "An African American Woman's Perspective: Renovating Sorrow's Kitchen," in Christine Marie Smith, ed., *Preaching Justice: Ethnic and Cultural Perspectives* (Cleveland: United Church Press, 1998): 43–61; Katie Cannon, "Womanist Interpretation and Preaching in the Black Church" in *Katie's Canon: Womanism and the Soul of the Black Community* (New York: Continuum, 1995), 108–11, 113–21. For criticism of the exclusion of women from ministry and preaching in black churches by black preachers, see Ella Pearson Mitchell's "Introduction: Women in Ministry," in *Those Preachin' Women: Sermons by Black Women Preachers*, ed. Ella Pearson Mitchell (Valley Forge, PA: Judson Press, 1985); idem, *Women to Preach or Not to Preach? 21 Outstanding Preachers Say Yes* (Valley Forge, PA: Judson, 1991). For a historical perspective that stresses biblical arguments, see Demetrius K. Williams, *An End to This Strife: The Politics of Gender in African American Churches* (Minneapolis: Fortress Press, 2004), especially chap. 4, "Pulpit, Power, Prohibitions," 107–33. Also, I offer a discussion of sexist practices in black churches in "Mind, Body, Spirit: Sexism and the Role of Religious Intellectuals," in *The Crisis of the "Negro Intellectual" Reconsidered*, ed. Jerry G. Watts (New York: Routledge, 2004).
34. For example, see James H. Cone, "Sanctification and Liberation in the Black Religious Tradition, with Special Reference to Black Worship," in *Speaking the Truth: Ecumenism, Liberation, and Black Theology* (Grand Rapids: William B. Eerdmans Publishing Co., 1986), 17–34. See also James Melvin Washington, "Editor's Introduction," in *A Testament of Hope: The Essential Writings of Martin Luther King Jr.* (San Francisco: HarperSanFrancisco, 1991). He summarizes, "For all their personal foibles and disad-

vantages, black preachers managed to create and sustain the only consistent tradition of prophetic ministry in America," xvii; James H. Harris, *Preaching Liberation* (Minneapolis: Augsburg Fortress, 1995); Albert J. Raboteau, *Canaan Land: A Religious History of African Americans* (New York: Oxford Press, 2001); Peter J. Paris, "The Linguistic Inculturation of the Gospel: The Word of God in the Words of the People," in *Making Room at the Table: An Invitation to Multicultural Worship*, ed. Brian K. Blount and Leonora Tubbs Tisdale (Louisville, KY: Westminster John Knox Press, 2001), 78–95.

35. See James A. Banks, *Teaching Strategies for Ethnic Studies* (Boston: Allyn and Bacon, 1997); James Banks and C.A. Banks, eds., *Handbook of Research on Multicultural Education* (New York: Macmillan, 1995); C. E. Sleeter and C. A. Grant, *Making Choices for Multicultural Education: Five Approaches to Race, Class and Gender* (Columbus: Merrill, 1988); C. E. Sleeter and P. L. McLaren, eds., *Multicultural Education, Critical Pedagogy, and the Politics of Difference* (Albany: State University of New York Press, 1995).
36. Lipsitz, *The Possessive Investment*, 4; Carmen Luz Valcarcel, "Growing Up Black in Puerto Rico," in *Challenging Racism and Sexism: Alternatives to Genetic Explanations*, ed. Ethele Tobach and Betty Rosoff (New York: Feminist Press, 1994).
37. Banks, *Teaching Strategies for Ethnic Studies*, 27.
38. Eleazor S. Fernandez, "A Philipino Perspective: 'Unfinished Dream' in the Land of Promise," in Smith, *Preaching Justice*, 77.
39. For discussions of multiculturalism in liturgical studies, see Kathy Black, *Culturally Conscious Worship* (St. Louis: Chalice Press, 2000); Blount and Tisdale, eds., *Making Room at the Table;* Gordon Lathrop, *What Does "Multicultural" Worship Look Like?* (Minneapolis: Augsburg Fortress, 2004); Eric H. F. Law, *Inclusion: Making Room for Grace* (St. Louis: Chalice Press, 2000); James R. Nieman and Thomas G. Rogers, *Preaching to Every Pew: Cross-Cultural Strategies* (Minneapolis: Fortress Press, 2001); and Kathy Black, "Promises and Problems of a Multiethnic Church," in *The Conviction of Things Not Seen: Worship and Ministry in the 21st Century*, ed. Todd E. Johnson (Grand Rapids: Brazos Press, 2002), 141–52.
40. Banks, *Teaching Strategies for Ethnic Studies*, 26.
41. Cameron McCarthy makes this point about the need to include information about relationships between groups when he offers a critique of approaches by James Banks and others to multiculturalism in education, in "After the Canon: Knowledge and Ideological Representation in the Multicultural Discourse on Curriculum Reform," in *Race Identity and Representation in Education*, ed. Cameron McCarthy and Warren Crichlow (New York: Routledge, 1993), 295.
42. The term "sinned-against" is used by Andrew Sung Park and Susan L. Nelson to describe a critical need for such distinctions in Christian theology in "Introduction: Why Do We Need Another Book on the Subject of Sin?" in *The Other Side of Sin: Woundedness from the Perspective of the Sinned-Against*, ed. Andrew Sung Park and Susan L. Nelson (New York: State University of New York Press, 2001). They explain, "Every Sunday Christians come to church to worship and hear a minister proclaim the good news of salvation. . . . Demanding repentance of sin from the abused, the hungry, and the humiliated is not good news, but absurd news. . . . It is time for the church to think about the salvific path for the sinned-against" (1–2). For an elaboration of this theme of

constructing theology for those sinned-against, specifically as it pertains to worship, see Ruth Duck, "Hospitality to Victims: A Challenge for Christian Worship," in *The Other Side of Sin*, ed. Park and Nelson, 165–80.

43. Janet R. Walton, *Feminist Liturgy: A Matter of Justice* (Collegeville, MN: The Liturgical Press, 2000), 46.
44. Eric H. F. Law, *The Word at the Crossings: Living the Good News in a Multicultural Community* (St. Louis: Chalice Press, 2004), 93.
45. Reginald Horsman, *Race and Manifest Destiny: The Origins of American Racial Anglo-Saxonism* (Cambridge, MA: Harvard University Press, 1981), 47.
46. See Esteban Buch, *Beethoven's Ninth: A Political History*, trans. Richard Miller (Chicago: University of Chicago Press, 2003).
47. This idea is based on exercises in Amy E. Ballin, with Jeffrey Benson and Lucille Burt, *Trash Conflicts: An Integrated Science and Social Studies Curriculum on the Ethics of Disposal* (Cambridge, MA: Educators for Social Responsibility, 1993).

Chapter 5

1. For a detailed analysis of Pastor Pete, see Ann Burlein, *Lift High the Cross: Where White Supremacy and the Christian Right Converge* (Durham, NC: Duke University Press, 2002).
2. My own United Methodist denomination serves as an example of this form of discrimination. See Neela Banerjee, "Methodist Jury Ousts Lesbian Minister," *New York Times*, December 2, 2004; Neela Banerjee, "United Methodists Move to Defrock Lesbian," *New York Times*, December 3, 2004.
3. For examples of legal cases, see Ex parte H.H., 830 So. 2d 21 (Ala. 2002)—D.H., lesbian mother who was denied custody of her children, in part for allegedly violating Alabama sodomy laws; Bottoms v. Bottoms, 249 Va. 410, 419 (Va. 1995)—Sharon Bottoms, lesbian mother who lost custody of her son for allegedly violating Virginia sodomy laws; and Ex parte D.W.W., 717 So. 2d 793, 796 (Ala. 1998)—R.W., lesbian mother who lost custody for allegedly violating sodomy laws, stating that "the conduct inherent in lesbianism is illegal in Alabama."
4. See U.S. Department of Health and Human Services Healthy Marriage Initiative Web site, www.acf.hhs.gov/programs/region2/index.htm. For analysis by advocacy groups, see www.legalmomentum.org/issues/wel/statemarriage.shtml; nowldef.org/html/issues/wel/marriagepromotion.shtml.
5. The women are part of the following Protestant churches: Baptist, United Methodist, Unitarian Universalist, Metropolitan Community Church, Unity Fellowship, and United Church of Christ. They lived in Boston, Chicago, Los Angeles, Oakland, Raleigh-Durham, New York City, and Newark.
6. The discussions I have collected are based only upon the early years of these ministries (the first four to five years), and in no way offer a comprehensive picture of the breadth of these ministries.
7. *All God's Children*, 26 minutes, Woman Vision Productions, 1996, videocassette.
8. The welcoming church movement includes Christians from a range of groups including Catholics, Protestants, independent churches, and individual practitioners of Christian spirituality. Some of the largest gatherings of members of this movement have occurred at the biannual national Witness Our Welcome Conferences that began in 2000.

9. See Edward Walsh, "Challenge to Gay Rights: Opponents Test Strategy in Cincinnati," *Washington Post*, October 30, 1993, A1; Donald Suggs and Mandy Carter, "Cincinnati's Odd Couple," *New York Times*, December 13, 1993, A17.
10. See "Crucial Referendum: Ypsilanti Votes on Discrimination Ordinance," Editorial, May 5, 1998, www.freep.com/news/metro/qypsi1.htm, accessed March 20, 2005; Niraj Warikoo, "Ypsilanti's Human Rights Ordinance Prompts Rallies," May 1, 1998, www.freep.com/news/metro/qypsi1.htm, accessed March 20, 2005.
11. She was elected bishop in 1984 in the Western Jurisdiction where she served as bishop in California until she retired in 1988. See Angella Current, *Breaking Barriers: An African American Family and the Methodist Story* (Nashville: Abingdon Press, 2001).
12. See James Thomas, *Methodism's Racial Dilemma: The Story of the Central Jurisdiction* (Nashville: Abingdon Press, 1992); Grant S. Shockley, ed., *Heritage and Hope: African American Presence in United Methodism* (Nashville: Abingdon Press, 1991).
13. The Metropolitan Community Churches is a Protestant denomination primarily made up of gay, lesbian, bisexual, and transgender Christians, based in the United States and founded by Troy Perry in 1968.
14. Love Center Church (Oakland, California) was founded by Walter Hawkins in the 1970s.
15. See www.mccchurch.org.
16. See www.ufc-usa.org.
17. See www.litufc.org/sjcenter.htm.
18. See www.urbandisciples.org/members.htm.

Index

97096256R00134

Made in the USA
Lexington, KY
26 August 2018

Use Bee Notebook/Form for note taking. Data collection forms.

First Lessons in Beekeeping

Bee Arrival Date - May 14 @ noon
Installation Date - May 14 @ noon

April 24th - Hive Placements

What to bring *1:1 ratios by weight of white granulated

Additives to syrup: Honey B Healthy

*Feeder
* protective Equipment

Fall 2 sugar: 1 ratio (Start August)

OTHER DADANT PUBLICATIONS

American Bee Journal

The Hive and the Honey Bee

Contemporary Queen Rearing

Mites of the Honey Bee

Honey in the Comb

The Classroom

First Lessons in Beekeeping

by KEITH S. DELAPLANE
in the tradition of C.P. Dadant's 1917 original

Earlier Editions Revised and Rewritten by
M. G. DADANT, J. C. DADANT,
DR. G. H. CALE, JR., AND HOWARD VEATCH

DADANT & SONS • HAMILTON, ILLINOIS

Published by DADANT & SONS, INC.,
51 South 2nd St., Hamilton, Illinois 62341
Phone: (217) 847-3324 • Fax: (217) 847-3660
E-mail: dadant@dadant.com • Website: www.dadant.com

Library of Congress Cataloging-in-Publication Data

Delaplane, Keith S.
First lessons in beekeeping / by Keith S. Delaplane, in the tradition of C.P. Dadant's 1917 original.
p. cm.
Includes index.
Summary: "Introduces the prospective beekeeper to the basics of beekeeping through easy-to-understand text and numerous color photos on honey bee biology, beekeeping equipment, management, honey production and processing, as well as disease diagnosis and treatment"--Provided by publisher.
ISBN 978-0-915698-12-7 (pbk. : alk. paper) 1. Bee culture. I. Title.
SF523.D38 2007
638'.1--dc22

2007017208

ISBN Number 978-0-915698-12-7

TYPESETTING AND GRAPHIC DESIGN BY
AMY LEEBOLD

Preface to the 2007 Edition

In another book I have told the story of my beginnings in beekeeping. It was not remarkable in any particular way, but for this author its memory is suffused with a glow akin to the landscapes of the Greek myths, Tolkien's Middle Earth, and Lewis' Narnia. I suppose most of us have a golden memory of some kind, usually from childhood, when time stood still and we were young enough to be wholly absorbed in something instead of ourselves. For me, that thing was beekeeping, and its beginning involved a Christmas present from my father consisting of a bee hive, a certificate for bees to arrive in the mail, and a book. That book was the 1968 edition of Charles P. Dadant's *First Lessons in Beekeeping*. Its pages opened to me a golden world of honey bees and beekeeping and guided my stumbling steps that first spring season. My story is but one of thousands who have passed through the door opened by Dadant's little book, the first edition of which appeared in 1917. It is an honor to be asked by Dadant's heirs to rewrite it for the 2007 edition. I offer this work in hopes that it will honor the tradition of Charles Dadant and keep the door open for thousands more.

The chiefest cause, to read good bookes,
That moves each studious minde
Is hope, some pleasure sweet therein,
Or profit good to finde.
Now what delight can greater be
Than secrets for to knowe
Of Sacred Bees, the Muses' Birds,
All which this booke doth showe.

Charles Butler, *The Feminine Monarchie*

Table of Contents

Chapter 1
The Place of Honey Bees in the World

"Of course they answer to their names?"
the Gnat remarked carelessly.
"I never knew them do it."
"What's the use of their having names," the Gnat said, "if they won't answer to them?"
"No use to THEM," said Alice; "but it's useful to the people who name them, I suppose. If not, why do things have names at all?"

Lewis Carroll, *Through the Looking Glass*

This book is about the western honey bee *Apis mellifera* L and the ways it is managed in North America. The generic name *Apis* means "bee-like," and students of Romance languages will note in the specific name *mellifera* echoes of the word "honey." Thus the Latin translates loosely to bee-like-honey-loving-insect. The "L" stands for the 18th century taxonomist Carolus Linnaeus who named the western honey bee along with hundreds of other plant and animal species. The adjective "western" is necessary to distinguish our bee from its eastern cousin *Apis cerana* from Asia. The genus *Apis* is distinctive for its fascinating biology, ecologic preeminence, and pervasive importance to agriculture. Its natural range extends from Portugal to Japan, from the cape of South Africa to near the Arctic circle, and in that vast range are at least five member species. But we must limit our attention to just one.

For starters, that one species, *Apis mellifera*, is further subdivided into at least 20 recognized subspecies, races, or locally-derived biotypes ranging naturally from northern Europe, the Middle East, and all of Africa. None is native to North America, but was introduced to that continent, most significantly during the centuries of European colonization. I will limit my discussion to those races of enduring historic or practical interest to North American beekeeping.

Apis mellifera mellifera

Called variably the German black bee or north European bee, this race is thought to be the first to make landfall in North America, most likely in the year 1622 on the coast of Virginia. It is this bee which Native Americans famously called "white man's fly," a newcomer to the neighborhood and a signal that European settlers were not far behind. Encountering flora and temperatures similar to back home, the German black bee flourished along the east coast, so much that by the end of the next century naturalists were debating whether in fact *A. mellifera mellifera* was alien to the continent. Practically speaking, the German black bee was the only honey bee in eastern North America until the mid-19th century when improved steam technology made possible rapid ship transit across the Atlantic. This development heralded a wave of diverse and unregulated honey bee imports to a degree never seen before or since. The German black bee, in spite of its suitability for northern latitudes, never really won the hearts of American beekeepers. It tended to sting a lot and was prone to serious diseases like American foulbrood (see **Chapter 8**). So beekeepers were on the lookout for "better" bees, some of which were successfully introduced and are described below. In speaking about the German black bee I tend to speak in past tense because it is doubtful whether *A. mellifera mellifera* exists anymore in North America. Although its genetic ghosts remain in the melting pot that has become North American *A. mellifera*, its supplanting, begun in the 19th century, was complete by the late 20th when exotic parasites (see **Chapter 8**) wiped out what remained of German black bee populations, by then abandoned by beekeepers to the woods and hollow trees.

I consider it a blessing to have memories of this bee as a boy catching wild swarms in Indiana in the 1970s. I was also a partner in its demise. Whenever I could I'd replace a German queen with a "better" one.

Apis mellifera ligustica

By far the most enduringly popular bee in America's history is the Italian. Like cream rising to the top, its numerous assets became apparent during the Great Importations of the 19th century and before long it predominated over other imports and became the standard against which others are judged. This preeminence is justified. The Italian bee is relatively gentle, and it is not far-fetched to say that the Italian bee is the most productive honey bee on Earth with colony populations and honey yields regularly exceeding comparison groups. Its body color tends toward lighter golds and browns. I once had the opportunity to observe an apiary of imported Italian bees in the country of Azerbaijan near the Caucasus Mountains, native range of the Caucasian honey bee. It was not a scientific observation, as the sample size was one and I cannot exclude the possibility that this beekeeper was unusually skilled and progressive. But after days of observing apiaries of lackluster native bees, I was astonished at this Italian apiary in which bees were foraging like crazy and colonies at least twice as populous as their neighbors.

I must hasten to add that Italian bees are not perfect from a beekeeping point of view. Their rapid spring buildup and productivity come at the cost of what is best described as reckless spending. This is seen in late winter/early spring when colonies begin expanding their populations, a growth fueled by honey and pollen stored from the previous season. Italians initiate early and expansive brood production at levels far in excess of the food stores they possess to support this activity. Unless the beekeeper intervenes, the outcome can be colony death from starvation. Another problem with Italians, most apparent since the parasite introductions of the 1980s, is a general susceptibility to pests and diseases.

Apis mellifera caucasica

This subspecies is native to the trans-Caucasus region between the Black and Caspian Seas and was imported to North America beginning around 1882. Its body color is grey/black. It is best known as a gentle bee, and for this reason was a favorite of beginners in the United States for a long time. I remember advertisements for this bee in the beekeeping magazines as late as the 1970s. But Caucasian bees have fallen out of favor, and there are few if any providers of this stock remaining in North America. For one thing they are not as productive as Italians, and they have a propensity to heavily coat the interiors of their hives with *propolis* – a natural glue derived from tree resins. North American beekeepers have an historic intolerance of propolis, but I have come to think this is a misguided prejudice. There is evidence to suggest that propolis possesses anti-microbial properties and aids bees in defense against nest invaders, traits increasingly important in this age of exotic pests and chemical-based pest control. There may come a day when Caucasians, or at least their propolis habits, are looked on favorably again.

Apis mellifera carnica

In contrast to the Caucasian, the Carniolan bee has enjoyed a rise in popularity in recent years. *Apis mellifera carnica* is native to east-central Europe. It is the darkest of the popular races, and for this reason one sometimes has trouble finding Carniolan queens while working a hive because they blend so completely into the background of black bees surrounding them. Carniolans are thought to express a measure of resistance to the parasitic varroa mite (see **Chapter 8**). But perhaps their most consistent feature is the conservative way in which they spend their food resources and expand their brood nest in spring. In this regard one might think of them as the antithesis to Italian bees.

Russian bees

In the 1990s the US Department of Agriculture began a cooperative project with researchers in eastern Russia to locate, test, and import honey bees from that area into the United States. The motivation behind this was the varroa mite crisis in the US and the search for bees that would have genetic resistance to this pest. The USDA researchers reasoned that genetic resistance was most likely to be found in that area of the world where the ranges of *Apis mellifera* and varroa mites had overlapped for the longest period of time, thus providing a chance for natural selection to confer resistance to the bees. In eastern Russia there was a long-established population of honey bees originally imported by rail from European Russia in the early

20th century. It is assumed the original bees were predominately Carniolan. Subsequent studies revealed that the east Russian bees are indeed resistant to varroa mites, and ultimately the bees were introduced into the United States where today they comprise a growing fraction of the commercial bee stocks. The bees display a measurable degree of varroa mite resistance while maintaining levels of productivity comparable to Italians. The Russian bees also exhibit the Carniolan feature of conservative spring buildup.

Apis mellifera scutellata

This is the so-called Africanized, or more sensationally, "killer" bee. During the centuries of European New World colonization, as in North America there were repeated introductions of European bees into the southern continent. However, European bees transported into tropical regions of South America did not flourish and by the mid 20th century beekeeping in Brazil and other South American countries was considered below world standards. The solution, it was believed, was to import honey bees from tropical Africa, and this objective was accomplished in the late 1950s. The new bees were indeed splendidly suited to the conditions they encountered in Brazil and soon began a rapid territorial expansion, eventually reaching the southern US by 1990. For most of their history in the US, Africanized bees restricted their range to the American Southwest; however this changed in 2005 when reproducing populations of Africanized bees were confirmed in Florida. The extent of their eventual range in North America is uncertain, but there is evidence that they are limited by temperate latitudes.

During their 50-year history in the New World the Africanized bees have established a reputation as extremely defensive insects. There have been thousands of mass stinging incidents with these bees, some lethal, involving humans and animals. In spite of this infamy, *Apis mellifera scutellata* has been the engine for improved profitability in Brazil's beekeeping industry. Under good management these bees are productive, and beekeepers in Brazil, now two generations removed from the bees' introduction, wouldn't do without them. More details on the management of these bees are covered in **Chapter 5**.

The place of beekeeping in the world

The very word "beekeeping" implies the existence of a bee that can be "kept." And the wonder of this fact should not be lost on the writers and readers of beekeeping books. Among the 20,000 or so bee species on Earth, only a handful tolerate some degree of human management. Standing above them all, *Apis mellifera* not only tolerates human management, but thrives under it, achieving colony populations and productivity far in excess of other species. It is the dual assets of manageability and productivity that have secured for *Apis mellifera* its special place in human hearts and imagination, history and economy.

Before Alexander the Great introduced cane sugar to the western world, honey constituted the chief sweetener for human societies within the native range of *Apis mellifera*. As such, bees were a symbol of industry and riches, and the world literature, mythologies and religious texts are full of references to bees and their products. Who can forget Icarus, his man-made wings, his reckless flight toward the sun, and his fatal fall when the heat loosed the beeswax that held his feathers? Who can forget Samson and his riddle: "Out of the eater, something to eat/Out of the strong, something sweet" and the answer: "What is sweeter than honey?/What is stronger than a lion?"

Beekeeping was practiced on a commercial scale in the ancient empires of Egypt and Rome and persisted as a cottage industry through the middle ages and Renaissance until the era of European expansion when the bees and craft were exported all over the world. During that time bees inspired artists and poets. Who is immune to the spell cast by Irish poet Yeats in *The Lake Isle of Inisfree*:

I will arise and go now, and go to Inisfree,
And a small cabin build there, of clay and wattles made;
Nine bean rows will I have there, a hive for the honey bee,
And live alone in the bee-loud glade.

And who cannot delight over Dickinson's

The pedigree of honey
Does not concern the bee;
A clover, any time, to him
Is aristocracy.

We cannot tarry over the poetry inspired by honey bees, except perhaps long enough to excuse Dickinson for her 19th century confusion over worker bee gender. But before moving on we must note that entire books are devoted to the historical and literary gold mine afforded by bees, and readers are encouraged to consult such works as Hilda Ransome's *The Sacred Bee* and Eva Crane's *The Archaeology of Beekeeping*.

Today, the western honey bee occurs on all continents except Antarctica. Its management is practiced by beekeepers at all levels, from garden hobbyists to commercial operators with tens of thousands of colonies. Honey retains its prestige as the most sublime of sweeteners, and like wine expresses a range of locally-derived characters distinctive enough to entertain the most sophisticated of palates. Beekeeping can be practiced anywhere gardening can be practiced, flowering plants occur, and a measure of isolation made possible from livestock, pets and human traffic – in isolated urban lots, margins between meadow and forest, margins of suburban lots, fence rows, and farms. A newcomer to beekeeping will be welcomed not only into the fascinating world of the honey bee, but into the fraternity of beekeepers that exists at national, state, and local levels. Numerous supply companies sell large volumes of standardized bee equipment, readily available by mail-order on the Internet or from local dealers. Books and videos on beginning beekeeping are available in catalogs and from vendors at beekeeping conventions. A few state agricultural universities have programs in honey bee research, teaching and continuing education. County extension agents and local bee clubs are sources of invaluable personal guidance. In short, a new beekeeper doesn't have to go it alone.

Besides honey, a bee hive produces a cornucopia of other products and benefits. Besides Icarus's wings, beeswax can be used to make candles, cosmetics, ornaments, soaps, and furniture polishes. Large quantities of beeswax are recycled into the beekeeping industry as *foundation* – the embossed sheets of wax used to help bees build their combs (see **Chapter 3**). Bee-collected pollen is in demand at health food stores as a human food supplement, as is *royal jelly*, the glandular product used to feed female larvae and trigger their conversion into queens. Long valued almost everywhere except North America, propolis has a reputation as a bacteriostatic wound dressing and active ingredient for cold remedies.

In spite of the fame and mystique of bee hive products, their contribution to human economies pales in comparison to the pervasive benefit of honey bee *pollination* – the transfer of pollen from the male parts of a flower to the female parts of the same or different flower. Bees do this automatically as they fly from flower to flower collecting pollen and nectar for their food. For many seed- and fruit-bearing plants this process enhances the quantity and quality of seeds and fruits. As the importance of this process became clear, in recent decades pollination has become a deliberate agricultural input, and hundreds of thousands of bee hives are rented annually in the US to ensure pollination of crops as diverse as almond, apple, blueberry, cantaloupe, cherry, clover, cranberry, cucumber, onion, pear, squash, and watermelon. For the intermediate- to large-size beekeeper, pollination has emerged as a significant source of revenue. For one thing, the agricultural ecology has changed in recent years to increase demand for pollination. The arrival of exotic honey bee parasites in the 1980s, most notably the varroa mite (see **Chapter 8**), caused a serious decline in wild honey bee colonies. This meant that there were fewer wild honey bees providing free background pollination. With fewer wild pollinators and an associated decrease in fruit yields, there was increased demand for supplemental pollination in the form of managed bee hives. It is true that bees of all sorts, including native bumble bees and solitary bees, are effective and important pollinators. But for the most part they cannot be managed as effectively as honey bees, so the preeminence of *Apis mellifera* as a commercial pollinator seems assured for the near future. At last count, their annual contribution to US food production was over $14 billion.

But let's face it. Most people get into beekeeping without the least interest in pollinating crops, making money, or helping the environment. They get into beekeeping because there's something fascinating about insects living together in a complex society inside a man-made box that I can keep in my backyard and open any time I want to. If they make me honey and pollinate my garden, so much the better. It is this contingent, the backyard hobbyist, that constitutes the largest fraction of beekeepers in the United States. It is this contingent, unfettered by large financial commitments, that turns to honey bees in their leisure hours, on the weekends, by choice and not necessity. It is this contingent that most accurately describes readers of this book. And if my experience is representative, it is this contingent that finds beekeeping an enriching divergence from their normal work week – a chance to dabble in wood-working, biology, agriculture, animal husbandry, food production, botany, marketing and business. The fact that many pass from backyard hobbyist to sideline or commercial levels is simply testimony to the economic legitimacy of beekeeping.

By now it has become apparent to the reader that honey bees are a portal upon the natural world as well as human world, past and present. Their grip on the imagination is well-earned. Just as they were for the ancient lore-masters, they remain today poignant symbols of industry and riches.

If we are more inclined in the 21st century to measure riches in terms of knowledge, understanding, personal fulfillment, and leisure, so be it. That's just further testimony to the timeless relevance of beekeeping. By reading this book and thinking about becoming a beekeeper, you are taking the first steps toward joining this ancient and noble stream of human enterprise.

Chapter 2

The Honey Bees' World

Go to the bee, and learn how diligent she is,
and what a noble work she produces,
whose labours kings and private men use for
their use, she is desired and honoured by all,
and though weak in strength she
values wisdom and prevails.

Proverbs 6:8 [Septuagint]

It is safe to say that the bees' agenda are not necessarily the beekeeper's. The one is interested in securing a large honey supply to ensure the colony's survival and ability to reproduce itself. The other is interested in securing a large honey crop to sell at the market. Both goals involve large honey supplies, but the beekeeper wants to accomplish this without permitting colony-level reproduction which, as you will learn in **Chapter 5**, is a road-block to maximum honey crops. A solid grounding in bee biology is necessary to be a successful beekeeper.

Social life

The agenda of a honey bee colony is this – to reproduce itself and survive next winter. A peculiarity of the honey bee and other social insects is that they have chosen a colonial life structure to help them do this.

Most people have an intuitive sense of what the term social insect means; there is something fundamentally different between a wasp colony in my carport and a cockroach family under my sink. By *social insect* entomologists mean a species that possesses all three of the following characteristics: (1) cooperative brood care, (2) reproductive division of labor, and (3) overlapping generations. By cooperative brood care we mean that females of the species share the burden of rearing the young, whether their own or others'. Reproductive division of labor means that some individuals in the society abandon their own efforts at reproduction in favor of helping their sisters reproduce. By overlapping generations we mean that some offspring remain at the nest to help their parents rear more siblings. All these criteria imply that the society is living together in a shared nest, and in fact the ability to "nest" or habitually return to a specific shelter would appear a prerequisite to social behavior. In nature it is possible to find species that exhibit only one or two of the three defining characteristics, but one that possesses all three simultaneously for at least part of the year is termed truly social, or *eusocial.* All species of honey bees are eusocial, as are all termites and ants. Bumble bees are considered primitively eusocial because they achieve a truly social state only after the solitary overwintering queen rears her first batch of brood in early spring. Wasps display a range of life histories from solitary to eusocial

All this means that when we discuss honey bee biology it must be discussed on two levels: the individual level and the colony level. Individuals reproduce, develop, interact with their environment in a way to optimize survival, senesce, and die. So do colonies. It just looks different.

The biology of individuals

There are three types of individuals in a honey bee colony: female workers, female queens, and males often called *drones* (Figures 1-3). The fact that there are two different types of female is an example of what is called a *caste* – a functionally different form of the same sex. One often reads that workers, queens, and drones constitute three honey bee castes. This is not true; they constitute two sexes, the females of which are divided into two castes.

Figures 1-3. (top left) A female worker honey bee; (top right) A female queen honey bee; (left) A male drone honey bee

Some things in common

The three types of bees share some fundamental characteristics. Bees, as members of *Class Insecta*, share with other insects a body plan comprised of three major regions: the *head*, *thorax*, and *abdomen*. The head houses a large share of the sensory organs, chief of which are the eyes and antennae, as well as the mouth parts comprised of sucking parts (together called the tongue) and chewing parts. The middle body region, the thorax, houses the locomotory appendages, the legs and wings, and the muscles for powering them. The abdomen is the chief repository for organs of digestion and reproduction.

Bees belong to that group of insects that engages in *complete metamorphosis* – that is, insects in which an individual passes through four developmental stages: egg, larva, pupa and adult. In the case of honey bees, the queen deposits an egg singly in the bottom of a beeswax cell (Fig. 4a). The *egg* is sausage-shaped, about 1/16-inch in length, and hatches after three days into the *larva*, or feeding stage. The larva is an undistinguished white grub and quite active, although this movement is undetectable to a casual observer (Figures 4-5). As worker bees place food in its cell, the larva moves forward to consume it; hence, the larva adopts a C-shaped posture during its feeding career. A few days later,

Figure 4a. Honey bee eggs and young, first-stage larvae. Eggs deposited by a normally functioning queen are laid each singly in the center of the cell. Each larva assumes a C-shape and swims in a bed of food.

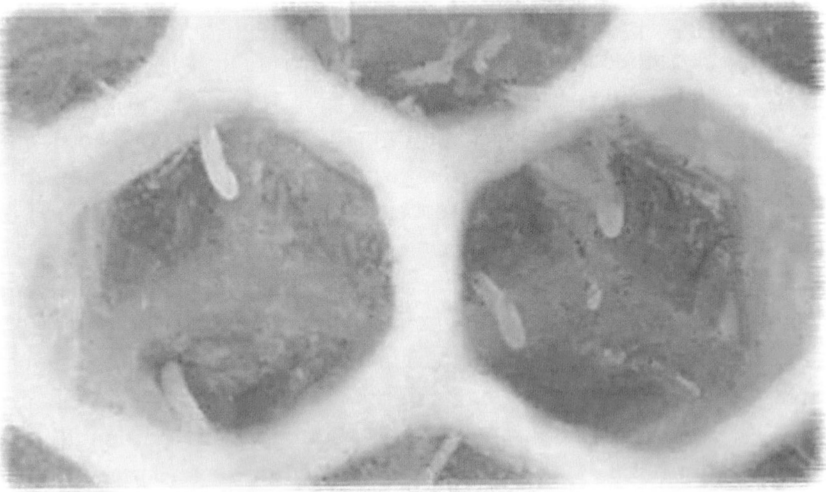

Figure 4b. Honey bee eggs deposited by laying workers. The eggs are laid multiply or singly in an irregular pattern inside the cell.

when the feeding phase is over, the larva enters an intermediate stage known as the *prepupa* (Fig. 6); the larva elongates to fill most of the cell, workers cap the cell with beeswax, and internal changes begin which result in the prepupa's transformation after a few hours into a quiescent white pupa (Fig. 6). The *pupa* looks superficially like an adult. The three major body regions become apparent for the first time, but there is no pigmentation, hair or wings, and the individual moves little or not at all. In the remaining days of development, the pupa darkens gradually and develops hair and wings and after a few days chews through its cell capping and emerges as an *adult* (Fig. 1). In general the number of days from egg to adult is 21 for the worker, 24 for the drone and 16 for the queen, but these numbers vary by race and location. Worker cells are by far the majority, tend to occupy the central regions of a comb face, and have uniformly flat cappings (Fig. 7). Drone cells are larger in diameter, the cappings more rounded or bullet-shaped (Fig. 8), and patches of drone brood tend to concentrate toward the bottom edges of combs. Queen cells are the least numerous, totaling at most around 20 per colony. They are the size and shape of a peanut and comprise the only brood cells oriented in a vertical posture relative to the comb face (Figs. 9a & b).

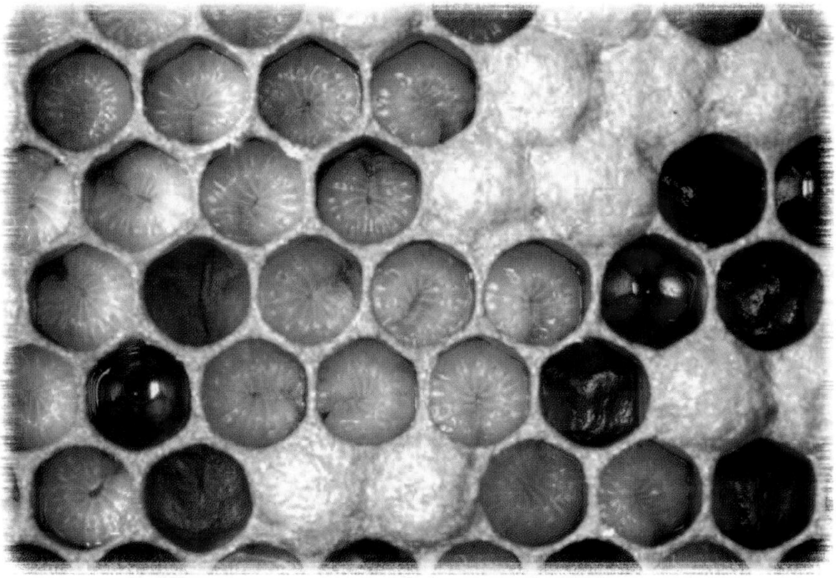

Figure 5. Mature honey bee larvae

Figure 6. A honey bee prepupa (11:00 position) and pupae (below)

Figure 7. Worker brood is uniformly flat and tan colored.

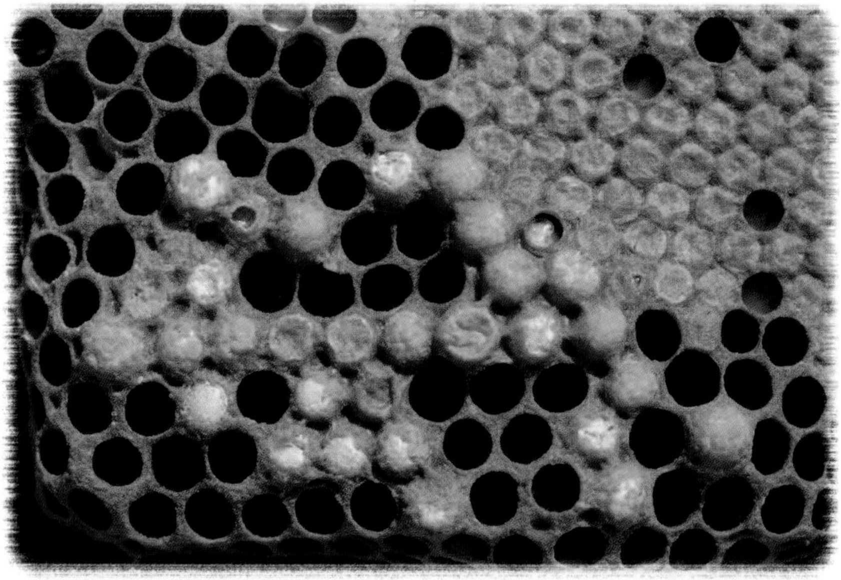

Figure 8. Drone brood is bullet-shaped and extends outward from the surface of the surrounding comb.

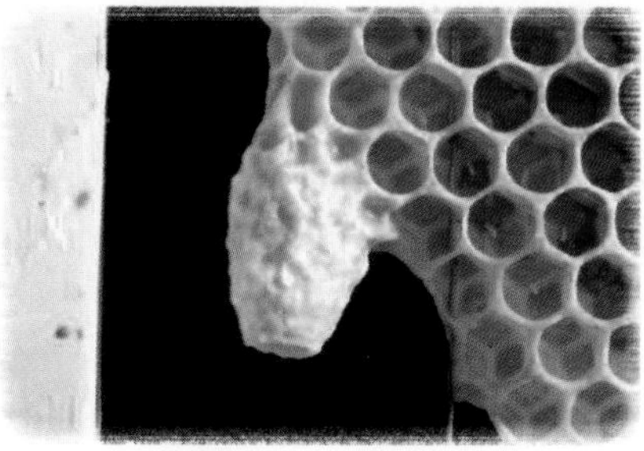

Figure 9a. A queen cell in its original state

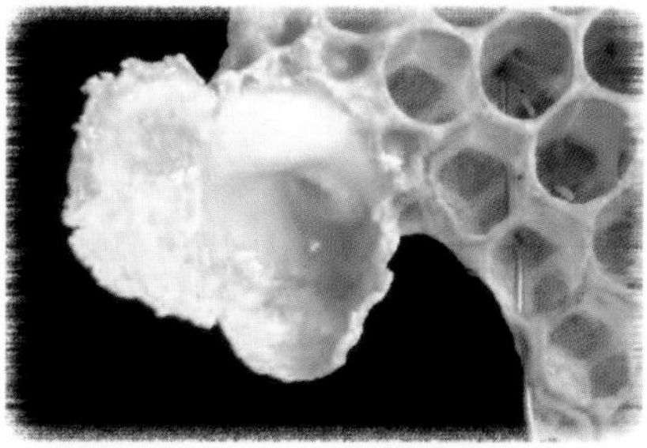

Figure 9b. Queen cell opened to show the larva within resting on a bed of royal jelly

The biology of workers

Of the three bee types, workers are the most numerous, behaviorally diverse and interesting. It is workers that care for the queen, feed the brood, clean and defend the nest, forage for food, recruit nestmates to food sources and make the kind of decisions popularly ascribed to the queen. For example it is workers, not the queen, who determine the types of resources – protein, carbohydrates, propolis or water – needed by the colony and communicate that fact to the workers engaged in foraging. Similarly, it is workers, not the queen, who decide if and when the colony reproduces – a complicated process called *swarming*.

Just as they are the most behaviorally complex, workers are the most anatomically complex. To carry liquid loads of nectar or water, workers suck up liquids into their *honey stomach* – the first chamber of a three-chambered stomach, and regurgitate their loads back at the nest. On their hind legs they have a complicated structure called the *pollen basket* in which they carry pollen loads. The most famous worker anatomical specialization is their persuasive sting assembly comprised of a *venom gland* and barbed *stinger*. Glands occur on other parts of the body for producing brood food, beeswax, and *pheromones* – external hormones that regulate the behavior of other bees. It should come as no surprise that workers, not the queen or drones, have the greatest cognitive powers, displaying remarkable ability to exchange information, learn, make decisions and navigate.

As one of the two female castes in the honey bee colony, workers have functional ovaries and are capable of producing eggs and progeny. However, workers are not capable of mating, and in the ants, wasps and bees this condition results in eggs that have half the normal number of chromosomes which, in turn, results in progeny that are exclusively male. In a normal colony with a queen (called *queenright*), this type of worker reproduction is limited by the interaction of queen pheromones and brood pheromones that collectively suppress activation of worker ovaries. But in *queenless* colonies there is no such pheromonal suppression, and a condition of laying workers results. Workers are notoriously poor egg-layers, and they deposit eggs either multiply or singly in an irregular pattern inside cells (Fig. 4b).

The biology of queens

In the beginning, any female egg has the potential to develop into either a queen or a worker. It all depends on the kind of diet the young larva receives after it hatches. If the colony wishes to rear queens, nurse bees choose one or more young female larvae and begin feeding them a special glandular secretion called *royal jelly* which triggers development of queen-like characters. This window of opportunity is brief. The larva must begin its royal jelly diet within a few hours of hatching and continue the diet uninterrupted its whole larval feeding career. There is a direct relationship between the duration of the royal jelly feeding regimen and quality of queen that results. A queen whose royal jelly diet is delayed or truncated will be sub-optimal in her queen-like morphology and performance. In controlled laboratory feeding conditions it is possible to rear bizarre *intercastes* – individuals with varying degrees of worker-like or queen-like traits simply by varying the days spent on royal jelly. In a normal situation, the female larva experiences accelerated growth, and the nurse bees accommodate this by enlarging the larva's cell into the typical vertical peanut shape. The royal jelly triggers development of queen-like characters such as full-sized ovaries, the ability to mate and store sperm, and glands for producing queen pheromones.

Within the first two weeks of life, a newly-emerged queen takes a succession of mating flights during which she mates with up to twenty drones on the wing. She is able to store their sperm in an organ called the *spermatheca* over which she has muscular control to release, or withhold sperm. As an egg passes down her median oviduct, the queen can fertilize it and produce a female, or withhold fertilization and produce a male. The egg-laying proficiency of queen bees is legendary, with numbers up to 1500 per day not uncommon (Fig. 10). The ability to fertilize eggs seems to de-

Figure 10. A queen inserts her abdomen into the cell to deposit an egg.

Figure 11. One of the signs of a failing queen is if she begins intermixing drone brood with worker. Drone cells are conspicuous because they stick out beyond the surface of the comb. See also figure 65.

teriorate in aged or failing queens, with the result being a disproportionately large amount of drone brood in the colony, intermixed in uncharacteristic fashion with worker brood (Fig. 11).

Almost equal in importance as her eggs are a queen's pheromones. I've already mentioned one function of queen pheromone, partial suppression of worker ovaries, but these chemicals are also responsible for stimulating foraging, prolonging worker life, and coordinating swarms during colony reproduction. Workers constantly lick and groom the queen, pick up her pheromones and pass them on to other workers. In this manner, queen pheromone is constantly circulating throughout the colony exerting its profound behavioral and physiological effects on the inmates. This stabilizing effect is easily demonstrated when a beekeeper removes a queen; the colony shows visible signs of agitation within 30 minutes.

The biology of drones

In explaining immature development and the mating behavior of queens I have almost by default exhausted the biology of drones. Yes, what you've heard is true. Drones are good for little besides mating with queens. Drones stay in their natal colony for the first couple weeks of life, living off the largesse of nest bees before reaching maturity at which point they begin participating in daily afternoon flights. These tend to be gregarious affairs in which large numbers of drones from numerous colonies pool together to fly in a comet-like mass around the neighborhood. The paths followed by these drone comets tend to be the same year after year and are associated with permanent landmarks such as prominent trees, hedgerows and the edges of forests. Some beekeepers have made a life hobby of monitoring drone congregation areas (Fig. 12). The persistence of drone congregation areas is especially distinctive when one considers that short-lived drones have no chance for inter-generational learning, as for example with salmon who are spawned in the same pool as their parents. Young queens on their mating flights seek out drone congregation areas and fly through them, inciting a frenzied chase during which she copulates with several drones. It is apparent that drone congregation areas are an effective strategy for both drones and queens to optimize mating success.

Figure 12. Mr. Karl Showler has made a life hobby of tracking drone congregation areas in Wales, UK using queen pheromone lures suspended by a cane fishing pole.

The biology of the colony

The grand objectives

I said earlier that the agenda of a honey bee colony is to reproduce and survive the next winter. This is essentially the same for a solitary insect, but in choosing a year-round colonial habit, honey bees are obligated to possess efficient behaviors in foraging, recruitment, food hoarding, and cold temperature survival. Moreover, the colony must reproduce as early as possible in the season to permit the new colony enough time to make a nest, forage, and store food for its winter needs. Some social species have solved the problem by rejecting colonial life over winter; in these species it is only the newly-mated queens that survive winter, entering a state of hibernation over the cold months and emerging the following spring to single-handedly forage and establish a new colony. Examples of these so-called *annual* colonies are found in the bumble bees and most social wasps.

Overwintering

With that background we can now examine the annual cycle of a colony of *Apis mellifera*, and I begin in the dead of winter. At this point, the bees are clustering in the center of their nest to conserve heat. Their precautions against winter chill actually began months or even years before when the colony chose its nest site. Cavities in old-growth trees, with high insulating properties, constitute the natural nest site for European *Apis mellifera*. Deep inside this nest, individual bees make the cluster contiguous in spite of the intervening combs by entering empty cells head-first; in this way the only distance separating bees is a thin comb mid-rib, not the entire comb. In the center of the cluster are the queen and a cadre of workers that are actively generating heat by consuming honey and shivering their thoracic flight muscles. The heat dissipates outward through the mantle bees that conserve the heat by clustering more or less tightly, depending on ambient temperature. Over-heating is also a risk, and the mantle bees regulate this by opening channels through which cool air can flow into the cluster. Thus, winter temperature maintenance is a dynamic process of heat generation, conservation, and compensatory cooling. It is also energetically costly, requiring continuous withdrawals from limited food stores. For this reason, the cluster is never far away from stored food, and in a typical winter nest the clustering bees cover and occupy open cells while immediately above them is an arc of stored pollen and above that an arc of stored honey. The cluster is capable of moving slowly (usually up or laterally, rarely down) to access fresh food stores.

Spring and the reproductive cycle

There is no brood the first half of winter, which means the cluster can tolerate relatively wide temperature swings at its core. But once the winter solstice is passed, usually when temperatures are coldest, the colony now does the unthinkable – begins building up for its reproductive phase. In the center of the cluster the queen begins laying eggs and immatures begin developing. Temperature swings can be tolerated no longer and this signals an increase in the rate of food consumption and heat generation. It is no surprise that the greatest risk of colony starvation and freeze death happens in mid- to late-winter. Moreover, it is no surprise to learn that many colonies fail at this high-stakes gamble. In a study in New York state in the 1970s, only 25% of new colonies were still alive after their first twelve months. It is sad but true, winter starvation is the norm not the exception for *Apis mellifera*.

But under a happier scenario, the colony is able to accommodate its reproductive rate with its food stores. And once the earliest nectar sources become available, the colony can supplement its precious stores with new provisions. At this point colony growth leaps forward rapidly: a growing number of newly-emerged workers are able to incubate an increasingly larger brood area.

This pattern of reckless growth continues for several weeks, limited only by the daily ebb and flow of food resources. It is aimed at one thing: colony-level reproduction which in honey bees happens by a process of colony fission, or splitting, called *swarming*. The process necessarily involves the production of queens, and a point is reached, usually around mid-spring, when the colony begins rearing queen cells. The process is fitful, and over the course of weeks a colony may tear down its *swarm cells* if foraging turns bad, only to start them again once fortunes improve. But if all goes well a day will come when the colony has several queen cells in various stages of construction, including some nearly ready to emerge. The actual event tarries until afternoon – nearly always a warm day with a good nectar flow in progress. Groups of workers begin a frenzied wave of running action around and around the interior of the nest. The old queen mother is bitten, jostled, and otherwise worried into a state of excitement. Then at once about half the colony's population, along with the queen mother, takes wing and pours out of the colony's entrance, forming a cloud of bees easily filling a space equal to a suburban back yard. The queen alights on some object, usually a tree branch, and her pheromones orient the cloud or *swarm* into an increasingly tighter radius, as bees discover the queen and begin alighting on the branch around her. Before long a conspicuous ball of bees forms on the branch (Fig. 13). This is a temporary staging situation and lasts only a few hours. From the cluster, scout bees confirm the location of a nest cavity and before long the swarm takes wing again and enters its new home. There is evidence that the nest scouting process begins days in advance of the actual swarm, so that the function of scouts on the day of swarming is more accurately described as reorientation relative to the new position of the swarm.

Once established in the new cavity, there is one over-riding objective: survive the next winter. The bees, engorged with honey from the parent nest, immediately begin secreting wax scales and forming them into the combs necessary for brood production and food storage. Comb building must continue even after the initial honey supplies are consumed and since the stimulation of wax glands requires continuing supplies of nectar, colony growth can be stalled if floral resources temporarily dry up. The queen begins egg laying as soon as combs are built – within hours. In the remaining weeks of spring and summer, combs are built, brood reared, a forager force produced, and food gathered.

Figure 13. A swarm in the intermediate clustering phase. After a few hours it will relocate to a permanent nest site.

But turning our attention back to the day of swarming, there is another drama playing out back at the parent colony – queen succession, by no means a neat and tidy affair. In the simplest scenario, the first of the emerging daughter queens engages in a campaign of fratricide, personally killing each of her rival sisters in their cells. It is easy to identify aborted queen cells because they are opened from the side. Cells opened at the tip indicate that a queen emerged from them normally (Fig. 14). Once her rivals are eliminated the new queen takes her mating flights and begins laying eggs, and the parent colony settles down to rebuilding its foraging force and storing up a winter food supply. Frequently the scenario isn't so simple. If a colony is especially populous it may swarm not once, but twice or even three times. Each swarm requires a queen, the old mother in the case of the first, and a daughter in the case of the later. The workers regulate this process by protecting, or not protecting, queen cells from rival sisters. But once the reproductive impulse is satisfied the workers cease protecting queen cells, the last surviving daughter assumes headship of the colony, and the colony spends the rest of the season preparing for winter.

Queen supersedure

It is important for a beekeeper to know the difference between queen cells made to replace a failing queen – called *supersedure* cells – and those made under the swarm impulse. Supersedure cells can occur any time in the active season when a queen is failing or is lost. Because they are made in response to a time-specific event – the loss of a queen – they tend to be uniform in age. They tend to occur on the comb face, not along the comb edge (Fig. 15). They also tend to result in comparatively poor queens because their construction is not necessarily associated with resource-rich times of year. Swarm cells, on the other hand, are more numerous, occur at various stages of maturity, and are associated with early spring nectar flows (Fig. 16).

Foraging regulation and recruitment

Over the course of twelve months a honey bee colony ranges in population from about 10,000 to 60,000 insects. This translates to an average biomass of ten pounds, the size of a small dog. This dog-sized entity needs at least 100 pounds of accumulated honey and pollen to survive winter. So far so good. But what makes these numbers impressive is the fact that honey bees have so few weeks of a 52-week year in which to harvest that

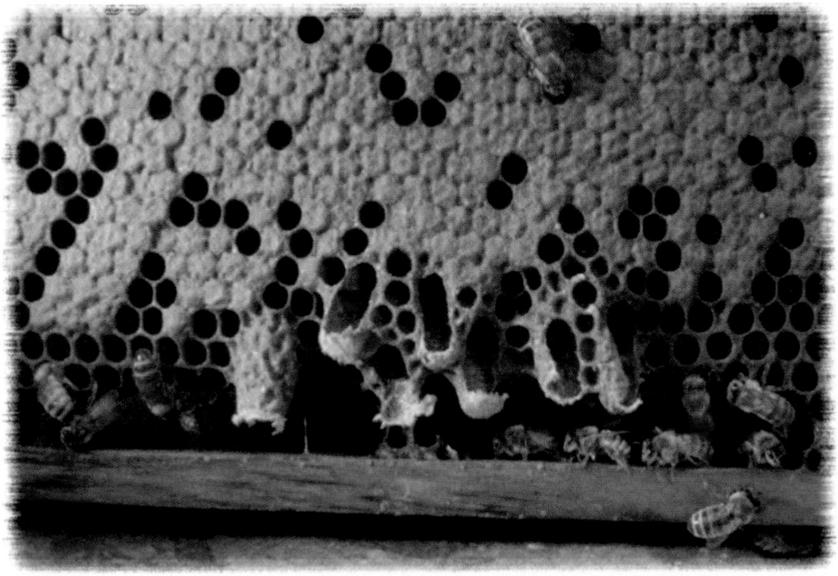

Figure 14. A series of swarm cells along the bottom margin of a comb. The queen from the cell at the far left emerged normally, as seen by the exit hole at the tip. Cells to the right were aborted, as seen by the exit holes in the sides.

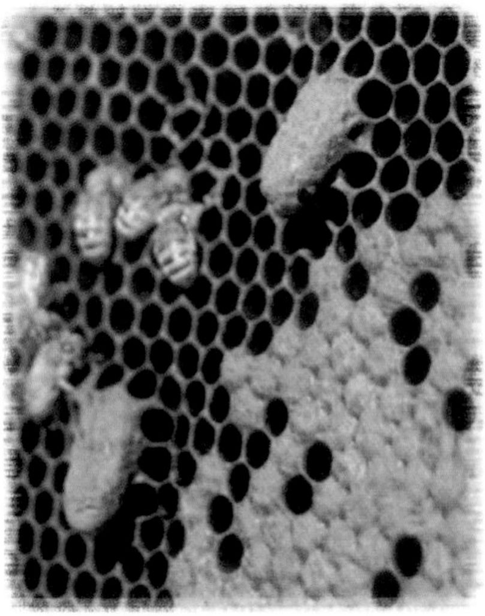

Figure 15. Supersedure queen cells tend to be uniform in age and occur on the comb face, rather than margins.

nutrient income. In most temperate regions the nectar season is brief, measured in weeks not months. Therefore, honey bees must be efficient foragers. Honey bees express this efficiency in at least two notable ways: foraging regulation and nestmate recruitment.

There is evidence that certain cohorts of bees in the nest are able to appraise the resource needs of the colony and communicate that need to foragers by way of a feedback loop. It works this way: If the colony's greatest need is energy (carbohydrates) then the "appraisers" relieve foragers of their nectar loads rapidly and eagerly. This enthusiastic reception encourages foragers to continue foraging for the same resource. But if, on the other hand, the greatest need is for water, then foragers with nectar are not relieved as quickly as those carrying water. A lackluster reception at the nest encourages foragers to switch to a different resource.

Foraging efficiency is also displayed in one of the most celebrated attributes of honey bees – nestmate recruitment. Honey bee foragers, upon

Figure 16. Young swarm cells tend to be numerous, variable in age, and associated with early-season nectar flows.

discovering a new resource, return to the nest and recruit nestmates by means of a dance language that communicates symbolically the distance of the resource from the nest and its location. Dancers communicate the relative richness of their resource by giving nectar taste samples to their sisters and varying the tempo of the dance: the faster the dance the richer, or nearer, the resource. Since any given colony has hundreds or even thousands of scouts and foragers dispatched at any time, there may be competing dances occurring on different parts of the comb. But foragers are able to assess the dances and concentrate on those communicating the richest resources. Because the network of recruiters is pervasive and responsive, spreading amoeba-like throughout the habitat, the colony is a model of rapid response. Once a rich resource is discovered a foraging force can be marshaled within minutes.

The sum effect of foraging regulation and nestmate recruitment is a high pitch of foraging efficiency at the colony level. Foraging efforts are focused on those resources most needed by the colony, and the recruitment network assures rapid exploitation of any resources available.

Chapter 3

The Bee Hive and its Accessories

First find your bees a settled sure abode...

Virgil, The Georgics, IV

To begin, let's get a couple terms straight. A "colony" of honey bees is the biological term for a nest of *Apis mellifera*, the entity discussed in the previous chapter. A "hive" is a man-made container designed to house a colony. The terms are often used interchangeably, but that usage is technically incorrect and does cause confusion at times.

That said, this book deals exclusively with the American version of the standard ten-frame Langstroth hive. With rare exception, hive designs pre-dating Langstroth's were exercises in fancy designed with little or no understanding of the biology of bees. A nagging problem was the inability to remove or interchange combs without damaging the nest. Lorenzo Lorraine Langstroth, a 19th century Congregational minister from Ohio, solved this problem, and it is no overstatement to say that the rapid expansion of beekeeping from a cottage industry to world-class enterprise is due to his genius.

Langstroth patented his moveable-frame hive in 1852. His inspiration was to recognize the fact that bees in a natural cavity preserve a certain minimum distance between combs. This *bee space*, 1/4- to 3/8-inch, is necessary to permit bee movement in the nest. When encountering a gap smaller than bee space, the bees fill it in with propolis; when encountering a gap greater, the bees build another comb. Applying this insight, Langstroth designed a box in which wood-reinforced combs could hang while maintaining bee space all around. This changed everything. For the first time, beekeepers could now insert, move, or remove combs without serious disruption to the colony. The simple box shape permitted equipment standardization and mechanized handling. In short, the intractable problem of practical bee management had been solved. Langstroth's revolutionary hive synergized a heady period of innovation in beekeeping technology, the brilliance and fertility of which was unprecedented and remains unmatched. In rapid succession followed the inventions of beeswax *foundation* – sheets of hexagon-imprinted beeswax used to guide bees in the construction of combs, the centrifugal *honey extractor* – a machine that non-destructively removes honey from combs, and the bee *smoker* – a portable device used to direct smoke into bee hives, a practice known since antiquity to calm bees. Today, the Langstroth hive and its variations are the standard the world over.

Hive parts in the US are standard in spite of the presence of numerous competing manufacturers. In the following sections I describe the parts and construction of a standard US Langstroth hive from the ground up. Unless you specify differently, hives will come to you pre-cut and unsassembled. In general, I recommend the use of wood glue and nails at all joints. Most manufacturers pre-drill nail holes at exterior joints; in the event this is not provided I recommend drilling pilot holes before nailing to minimize wood splitting. Exterior surfaces should be painted with a good quality exterior paint. It is not necessary, nor advisable, to paint interior surfaces. All parts mentioned here are standard and readily available in bee supply catalogs.

Bottom board

The *bottom board* is the floor of the colony. It consists of floor boards set into two side rails with a block of wood across the back. There is a gap at the front to provide an entrance for the colony. The grooves in the side rails that accommodate the floor boards are off-center. This provides two possible settings, one with a narrow entrance (Fig. 17), and one wider (Fig. 18). The narrow setting is generally limited to cold con-

Figure 17. The floor of the bottom board is offset to provide one of two positions; this one is the narrow setting.

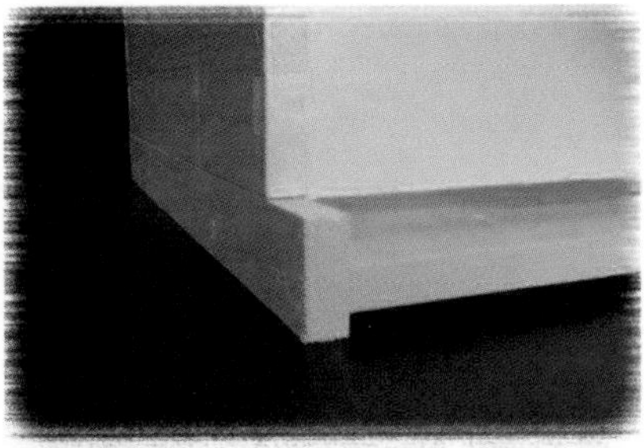

Figure 18. This bottom board is in the wide setting. This position is more common and has the advantage of accommodating a Boardman feeder.

ditions, but the wide setting is the most widely used and considered acceptable for all parts of the country. The bottom board should not be placed directly on the ground but rather on concrete blocks or similar water-proof material.

Since the late 1990s there has been increased interest in the use of bottom boards with screen floors instead of solid (Fig. 19). There is evidence that screen floors increase brood production and reduce the growth rate of parasitic varroa mites (see **Chapter 8**).

Figure 19a. Screened bottom board

Figure 19b. Screened bottom board in place below a hive body

Figure 20.
The standard super sizes, from the bottom up: a deep super or hive body, medium honey super, and shallow honey super.

Hive bodies

Directly on top of the bottom board go one or two *hive bodies*, sometimes called *deep supers*. At 9-½-inches, these boxes are the tallest in the bee hive inventory (Fig. 20). The deep size provides for broad, uninterrupted egg-laying space for the queen, and as such this space is sometimes called the *brood nest*. This is the heart of the colony. It is here that the queen produces brood and most of the management occurs that dictates success or failure for the beekeeper. The ambiguity concerning one or two hive bodies is traced to differences in geography, tradition and personal preference. One hive body provides enough space for a good queen to produce an optimal colony population of 50,000 to 60,000 workers. From a practical perspective, I like one hive body because it economizes equipment and simplifies certain labor-intensive practices such as hunting for the queen. However, two hive bodies is considered necessary by many beekeepers because it provides a large space for winter food stores and relieves brood nest congestion – a prime stimulant for swarming which, as we will see in **Chapter 5**, is a problem in honey production. In general, I recommend one of two basic hive configurations: (1) one hive body for brood production plus a queen excluder plus one honey super for food stores (Fig. 21) or (2) two hive bodies for both brood and food (Fig. 22). Configuration #1 is more common in warm regions and #2 in colder; but this is not mutually exclusive. I will allude to these two configurations throughout the book.

Figure 21. Base configuration #1: one hive body to house the queen and brood, a queen excluder, and one or more honey supers for food stores

Figure 22. Base configuration #2: two hive bodies for queen, brood, and food stores. Whether using configuration #1 or #2, this space is regarded as the domain of the bees. Honey is harvested from supers added above this base configuration.

Queen excluder

This device is a metal grid (Fig. 23) gauged such that the worker bees can freely pass through, but the larger queen cannot. It is placed between the brood nest and honey supers, and its purpose is to exclude the queen – and her eggs and brood – from the area of the hive dedicated to honey production. The utility of queen excluders is controversial; some beekeepers believe they limit the movement of worker bees and the size of honey crops. But I think they are useful, especially if one chooses to adopt the one-hive body configuration.

In order to defend this recommendation I must talk about the concept of *honey barrier*. In nature, a honey bee nest has a central core of brood with the honey stores above. Generally, a queen is reluctant to cross this honey barrier and deposit eggs above it. In a two-hive body configuration the honey barrier occurs naturally in the second hive body, but in a one-

Figure 23. A queen excluder goes between the brood nest and honey supers. The wires are gauged to keep the relatively large queen out of the honey supers.

hive body configuration it is likely to occur in the honey super. Since the purpose of this honey super is food storage, it is inefficient to permit the queen to use this space for brood production. By using a queen excluder in a one-hive body configuration, the beekeeper maximizes efficient use of equipment; brood is restricted to the brood nest and food stores to the food super. To summarize, queen excluders are useful in a one-hive body configuration, but not necessary with two.

Honey supers

The purpose of honey *supers* is to provide storage space for honey. Except for the food super in a one-hive body configuration, this represents the honey for the beekeeper's use. As the name implies, supers are above, or "superior" to the brood nest. Honey supers come in one of two sizes: a medium depth of 6-5/8 inches and a shallow depth of 5-3/8 inches (Fig. 20). A third size exists, at 4-3/4 inches, but it is exclusively for the production of comb honey, covered in **Chapter 6**. Honey supers are shorter than hive bodies simply because honey is heavy and the shallow size makes it easier to handle.

Foundation

Some type of *foundation* is necessary for every frame. Foundation is a sheet of beeswax or plastic imprinted with the shape of hexagonal cells. Bees use foundation literally as the "foundation" or mid-rib upon which they build their natural combs (Fig. 24). Without foundation, there is no assurance that bees would build their combs parallel to the frames, or even inside them. Most foundation is milled to worker-sized cells, but drone foundation is also available for queen breeders who wish to increase output of male bees.

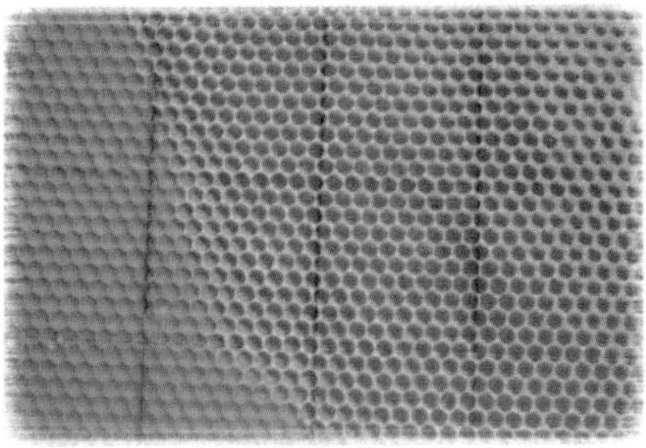

Figure 24. Bees use the hexagonal template provided by foundation to draw out their natural cells.

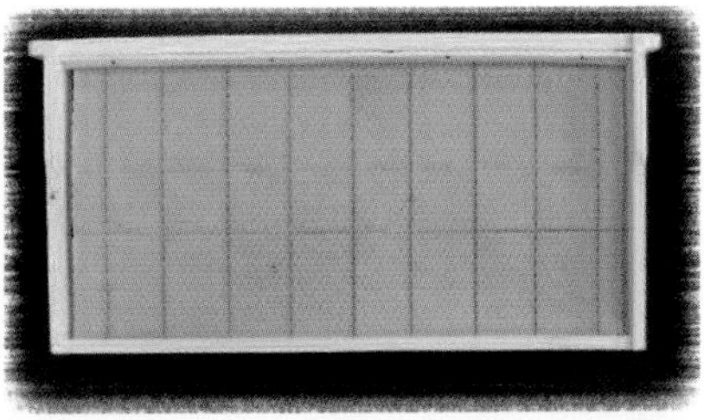

Figure 25. A deep frame displaying a sheet of 100% beeswax foundation. Vertical support wires are embedded in the foundation to add rigidity.

Foundation is size-specific to each frame type (deep, medium, shallow, or comb) and made of a variety of materials. The traditional is made of 100% beeswax and has reinforcing wires embedded in it vertically (Fig. 25). The vertical reinforcement is adequate for shallow or medium frames, but for deep frames the beekeeper needs to add additional horizontal reinforcement, discussed below under **Frames**. Foundation for comb honey is extra-thin 100% beeswax without wires; the extra-thin size is necessary to ensure palatability of the wax which is consumed along with the honey.

The problem of comb durability has long motivated beekeepers to consider plastic as a foundation material. The first practical plastic foundation, Duragilt™, is still marketed today and consists of a flexible plastic core coated on each side with beeswax (Fig. 26). Recent years have seen an upsurge in popularity of rigid plastic foundations, some of which are coated in a thin layer of beeswax (Fig. 27). The beeswax coating seems to improve acceptance by bees. Rigid plastic foundation has the added advantage of being easy to install. There is every indication that plastic foundations will command an increasing market share in the years ahead.

Frames

Standard hive bodies and supers are each made to accommodate ten frames. Naturally, the size of frames is specific to their respective super. As the name implies, each of these components "frames" a beeswax comb,

Figure 26. Duragilt™ foundation features a plastic core covered in beeswax with metal-reinforced edges.

Figure 27. Rigid plastic foundation is easy to install. Frames for this type of foundation come with grooved top bars and bottom bars. The foundation is simply snapped in place.

giving it rigidity and strength and uniform shape. Without a stiff reinforcing frame, a natural comb would bend and break with handling. The parts of a frame and methods for construction are universal. In the illustrations I show the construction steps for deep frames in hive bodies.

A frame is comprised of four parts: a top bar, two end bars, and a bottom bar (Fig. 28). The traditional top bar comes with a removable wedge – a piece made to break off and be re-nailed into position, holding the foun-

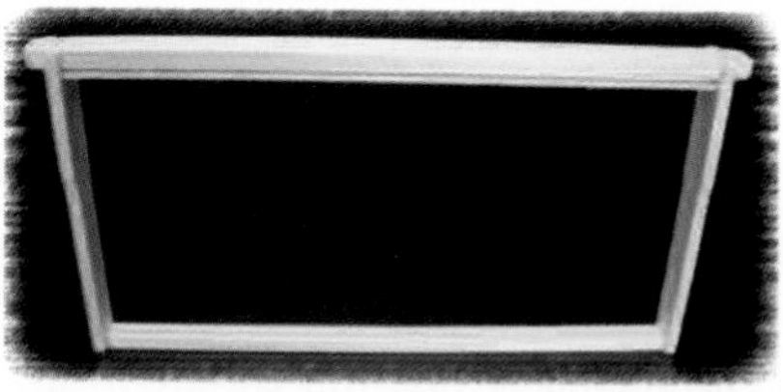

Figure 28. A frame consists of a top bar, 2 end bars, and one bottom bar. The top bar and bottom bars each have grooves that face each other inwardly.

Figure 29. Construction of a traditional wedge top-bar frame. The first step is to cut away the wedge.

dation in place. Take a knife and remove the wedge (Fig. 29). Next, use wood glue and nails and assemble the frame as shown in Figures 30-31. Note that a properly constructed frame has ten nails, including two going horizontally from the end bars into the top bar.

If you choose 100% beeswax foundation, you will need to provide reinforcement beyond that provided in the embedded vertical wires. One option is to put support pins in the two center holes of the end bars (Fig. 32), but a better option is to use horizontal frame wires. Insert brass grommets

Figure 30. Nail the bottom bar to the end bars so that the groove in the bottom bar faces inward.

Figure 31. When nailing top bars to the end bars, include a nail going horizontally from the end bar into the top bar.

Figure 32. Support pins are made to go through the holes in the end bar and into the foundation.

into the two center holes in each end bar (Fig. 33), and run a taught length of frame wire back and forth between them, secured with a nail (Fig. 34). The grommets are necessary to keep the wire from cutting into the soft wood. Next, insert the sheet of foundation so that it threads between the two center horizontal wires, with a wire on each side (Fig. 35); this step secures

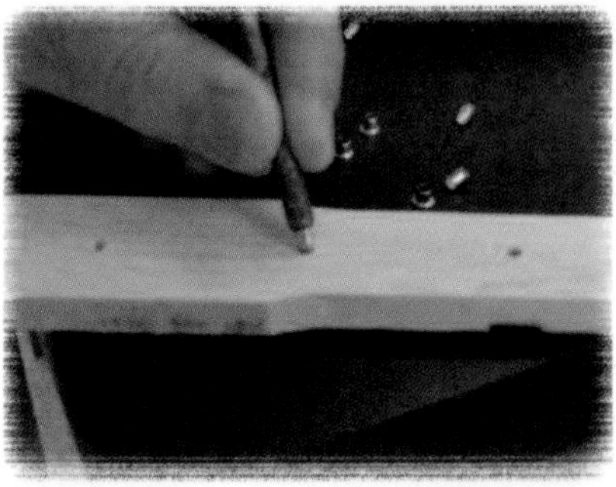

Figure 33a. A punch tool is handy for inserting grommets into the end bar holes.

Figure 33b. Grommet fully inserted

Figure 34. The grommets protect the soft wood from the cutting action of the horizontal support wires. Note the nail that secures the ends of the support wire. Two strands in the middle are sufficient.

Figure 35. Insert the beeswax foundation so that it threads between the horizontal support wires – with one wire on each side. This keeps the foundation from bowing in the middle.

the foundation so that it won't bow in the middle. At the same time you must insert the foundation sheet so that the hooks in the vertical wires lay against the top bar as shown in Figure 36 (the edge without hooks simply rests in the groove of the bottom bar). Return the wedge against the hooks, and nail it in place (Fig. 37). The final step is to sink the horizontal wires

Figure 36. The hooks from the vertical wires must rest in the top bar groove so that the wedge secures them when it is nailed back in place.

Figure 37. The wedge properly nailed in place, securing the wire hooks

Figure 38. Sink the horizontal wires into the foundation with a spur embedder; if you don't, bees may build the cells in a disorderly fashion along the wire.

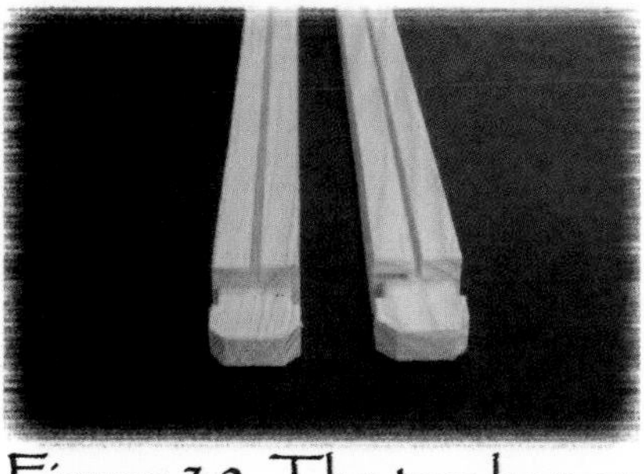

Figure 39. The top bar on the left is grooved to accommodate rigid plastic foundation. The top bar on the right is a traditional wedge top bar. You can see how the wedge is only lightly attached, making it easy to remove with a knife (see Fig. 29).

into the wax with a spur wire embedder (Fig. 38).

Things are a little different – and easier – with rigid plastic foundation. For one thing, the top bars have center grooves (Fig. 39) instead of wedges. After the frame is built, you simply flex the foundation and snap it into the grooves of the top and bottom bars. Neither support pins nor horizontal cross-wires is necessary.

Inner and outer covers

The best cover system for a hobbyist is the combined use of an inner and outer cover (Fig. 40). The inner cover fits on the top-most super, maintaining bee space and providing insulating dead-air space. The telescoping outer cover fits over the inner cover to provide weather protection.

Figure 40a.
The inner cover

Figure 40b.
Outer cover telescoping over the inner cover

Feeders

There are long intervals in the year when no nectar is available. This is the reason bees make and store honey – to sustain themselves during protracted dearth. The stakes are high and constitute nothing less than life or death. But mitigating such crises is part of the beekeeper's job, and he must be prepared to step in with supplemental feed as needed. There are numerous types of syrup feeders. I will cover only four.

To make your syrup, mix equal parts of granulated sugar and water in the spring. However, in the fall use a heavier 2 parts sugar to 1 part water mixture. To achieve this higher sugar concentration, you will need to mix the sugar with heated water. Let the syrup cool before feeding it to your bees.

Figure 41. A Boardman feeder

Boardman feeder

This consists of a wooden or plastic base that slides into the entrance of the hive and holds an inverted quart jar of syrup (Fig. 41). Bees walk into a chamber inside the base and access the syrup through a perforated lid. This is an easy way to feed bees, but it has three disadvantages. First, by being limited to quart increments it dupes the beekeeper into thinking in small volumes. Paraphrasing the late Richard Bonney, when feeding bees we should think in terms of gallons per colony, not quarts. Second, by being placed at the colony entrance it is several inches away from the bee cluster; in cold temperatures bees in a starving colony will not be able to leave the cluster and access the syrup. And finally, by placing feed near the entrance it makes the syrup perilously accessible to robber bees. A young colony with a Boardman feeder in the same neighborhood with strong colonies is in danger of being robbed to death. In contrast to these negative examples, a Boardman feeder is an excellent way to feed water during hot, dry spells.

Figure 42. A division board feeder. The wooden block keeps the walls from collapsing outward or inward, and the folded hardware cloth in the reservoir minimizes bee drowning.

Division board feeder

This is an in-hive feeder shaped roughly like a frame and made to hang alongside frames in the brood nest. It can be constructed of wood and composite board (water-proofed at the joints) or manufactured as a single-piece molded plastic unit. The advantage of division board feeders is that they can be placed directly next to the clustering bees, and once installed it is reasonably easy to re-fill them. But there are disadvantages. First, it is necessary to open hives to re-fill division board feeders; this can be stressful on bees during cold temperatures or during hot temperatures when neighboring colonies are likely to rob. Second, there is a persistent problem with bees drowning in the syrup reservoirs. It is possible to provide a foot-hold for bees and reduce drowning by installing folded hardware cloth in the reservoirs (Fig. 42).

Plastic food bags

Like the division board feeder, this is an in-hive method, but has the advantage of eliminating risk of bee drowning. This method takes advantage of ordinary 1-gallon plastic food storage bags available in grocery stores. Simply fill a bag with syrup, seal it, and place it directly on top of the clustering bees, enclosing the space with an empty shallow super (Fig. 43).

Make a 1-inch cut in the top of the bag with a razor knife so that a small amount of syrup can well up. Bees will quickly discover it and consume the bag's contents. This method of feeding is cheap, neat, and practical. It places food close to the clustering bees and eliminates the messy job of pouring syrup in the field.

Figure 43. Plastic food bag filled with syrup and placed on top of the brood combs. A nick in the top releases the syrup. The extra space is enclosed with an empty super.

Pails with perforated lids

This method is similar to plastic food bags and constitutes the only functional way to feed bees in an emergency starvation situation in winter. Clustering bees can move little or not at all in extreme low temperatures, and if a colony is starving in winter the food must be placed immediately on the cluster. Plastic pails especially for this purpose are available in supply catalogs, and most hold one gallon. Put a heavy syrup of 2 parts sugar to 1 part water in the feeder, expose the clustering bees, place the pail on the cluster with the perforated lid down, and enclose the space with an empty super and lid.

Smoker

Since ancient times beekeepers have recognized the calming effect of smoke and used it in their bee hive manipulations. The earliest smokers were simply torches, but when Moses Quinby invented his smoker in the 1870s, beekeepers for the first time had a practical means to direct smoke where needed. The modern variant of the Quinby smoker consists of a bellows attached to a fire chamber. Acceptable smoker fuels include pine straw, ground corn cobs, pelletized wood shavings, or dried cow manure. Instructions for lighting a smoker are given in **Chapter 4, Working a colony**.

Hive tool

Some kind of hive tool is necessary to pry apart bee hive parts which the bees invariably glue together with propolis. The prying ends are broad because a narrow prying surface (such as a screwdriver) would cut into and damage wooden parts. There are two popular versions of hive tool. The more traditional consists of a broad flat prying end with the opposite end shaped as a general scraper (Fig. 44). A newer version also has a broad prying end, but the opposite end is a lever designed for prying frames out of supers (Fig. 45).

Figure 44. Traditional hive tool

Figure 45. Newer style of hive tool designed as a lever to pry up frames

Veil

A veil is the minimum necessary protective clothing. The traditional veil is used in conjunction with a fiber or plastic helmet. The draw-strings are passed around the waist and tied in front (Fig. 46). Some newer styles are one-piece with a hat and can be laundered. A zip-on veil used in conjunc-

Figure 46.
A traditional
tie-on veil

Figure 47.
A zip-on veil
made to be worn
with a full bee suit

tion with a suit provides seamless protection (Fig. 47), but the fact is not all beekeepers, even hobbyists, find a full bee suit the most desirable garb for outdoor work in summer temperatures. Hence, tie-on veils remain the most popular because they can be used with or without bee suits.

Gloves

Most beginners begin their beekeeping adventures with the extra protection and assurance afforded by beekeepers' gloves (Fig. 48). But surprising as it may seem, gloves are not always good insurance against stings, and many beekeepers abandon them as they gain experience. The reason for this is traced to the simple fact that a beekeeper with gloves is more clumsy

Figure 48.
A complete bee suit

than one without. When you wear gloves, there is risk that you will work the bees more roughly, inadvertently crushing some and releasing alarm pheromone in the process, and excite a greater defensive response than you would without gloves. Experienced beekeepers find that they can avoid stings and work the hive with less trauma to themselves or the bees when they work with bare hands. I do wear gloves, but only for messy jobs like harvesting honey or those rare days when the bees are incorrigible. In summary, it's ok to buy a good set of gloves, but make their use the exception not the rule.

Bee suit

The most complete form of sting protection is a full bee suit, consisting of white coveralls, a zip-on veil, and gloves (Fig. 48). The biggest problems with bee suits are heat-stress to the beekeeper and the risk of rough-handling the bees. I do use a suit, but mostly for protection against sticky honey during harvest or at times when nectar is flowing and dripping from the combs. In summary, it is nice to have a bee suit for messy jobs or the rare event when bees are uncontrollably defensive. But the beekeeper's best defenses against stings will always be a smoker and good bee handling skills.

Chapter 4

Getting Started

"We are getting near," said Gandalf. "We are on the edge of his bee-pastures."

J.R.R. Tolkien, *The Hobbit*

Apiary locations

In choosing an apiary site the beekeeper must be mindful of his neighbors, his bees, and himself. It's a fact of life that most people are afraid of stinging insects, and for this reason it's a good idea to locate hives in out-of-the-way places that don't invite attention from neighbors, motorists, or pedestrians. Some beekeepers take this one step further and paint their hives in camouflaging greens and earth tones. It's a good idea to keep hives away from livestock or penned animals and to situate hives so that the bees' flight paths don't cross sidewalks, parking lots or playgrounds. One of the most common neighbor complaints is bees foraging for water at swimming pools or pet bowls. The easiest way to minimize this problem is to provide each hive with water in a Boardman entrance feeder (see **Chapter 3**, **Feeders**).

Next, you want to avoid low wet spots that accumulate humid cool air over winter. Bee colonies do best in direct sun which not only stimulates foraging but aids in the control of parasitic varroa mites (see **Chapter 8**). Some windbreak is necessary if you live in an area with severe winter winds. This can take the form of a tree line, bales of straw, or a solid fence. It is good to situate hives where there are abundant sources of flowering plants and natural water. In some parts of the country the beekeeper must fence his hives against ranging livestock or predatory bears.

Finally, you must consider your own convenience. There are endless advantages to an apiary site easily accessible by truck. Weed problems can be preempted if you place your hives on a gravel surface, concrete, or a large square of carpet. Some beekeepers make permanent all-weather stands of concrete blocks and rails in order to raise hives to a comfortable height and reduce back-bending.

Four ways to get started

There are four main ways to get started keeping bees: installing package bees, installing swarms, installing nucleus colonies, and buying established colonies. Installing packages, swarms, and nucleus colonies has the advantage of using new equipment built to your own standards; plus there's great pleasure in participating in the establishment and growth of your first new colonies. Buying established colonies has the advantage of owning

Figure 49. Ignite a handful of fuel; pinestraw is used in this example.

Figure 50. Puff the fuel to excite a brisk flame.

colonies that are fully mature and ready to make honey. The disadvantages of established colonies are the risk of disease and the acquisition of substandard or old equipment.

Working a colony

As I have mentioned before, a smoker is the most important tool for working a colony of bees. If you start with package bees or a swarm, you will not need a smoker until the second visit to the hive because it is only at the second visit and after that the bees will perceive the hive as their home and express defensive behavior. However, in every case of start-up you will need to employ a certain minimal skill in bee handling.

The most important principle to remember about lighting a smoker is to have the flame below the fuel, not above it. As one puffs the bellows, air enters below the flame, pushing the flame upwards into fresh fuel. Pine straw, chipped corn cobs, dried cow manure, and extruded sawdust pellets make good smoker fuel. To light a smoker, ignite a small handful of newspaper or pine straw and drop it in the smoker, puffing constantly to produce a brisk flame. Add another handful of fuel, puffing constantly to ignite the fresh fuel. Add another handful, then another, puffing as you go until the smoker is full of fuel at which point you can add the cap. The objective is a cool dense smoke (Figs. 49-51).

Figure 51. After the fuel is well-lit, pack the smoker tightly with more fuel, puffing as you go.

Once the smoker is reliably lit, don your protective clothing and puff the entrance of the hive. Pry open the lid and puff under it to alert the bees at the top. Use the hive tool to pry apart the lid, supers, and frames which will be glued together with propolis. Move frames carefully to avoid crushing bees against other hive parts. A few puffs of smoke at the beginning is usually sufficient to calm a small colony for the duration of the inspection. For bigger colonies it may be necessary to smoke the bees more often. Avoid laying propolized hive parts directly onto cut grass or leaves because propolis is sticky and will pick up loose debris.

A beekeeper must be concerned about robbing during periods when the bees are active but nectar scarce. At these times bees from a strong colony will not hesitate to rob honey from a weaker. The biggest stimulant to robbing is the odor of exposed honey. For this reason it is prudent to avoid opening colonies during periods of robbing, or if hive management is unavoidable then work as rapidly as possible to minimize the release of hive odors.

Installing package bees

Installation

Packages of bees, each with 2-3 pounds of workers and a mated queen, are available by shipment or pick-up in spring and early summer. The advantages of package bees are their relative economy and the fact that they can be shipped anywhere in the world as long as they are protected from temperature extremes. The disadvantage is the fact that package colonies grow slowly because of the 21-day delay between the first eggs and emergence of the first workers. Hundreds of thousands of packages are sold in this country every spring, constituting the most ready source of bees for beginners.

Demand exceeds supply, and this means you must place your order as early as possible, preferably with payment, to guarantee early spring delivery. You should also notify your local post office to expect package bees and to call you when the bees arrive so you can pick them up in person. Keep the package cool and shaded until you can install it.

On the day of installation, set up an empty hive at your apiary site. You will need a veil, hive tool, water sprayer, a syrup feeder full of 1:1 sugar syrup, and the package of bees (Fig. 52). Rest the hive on concrete blocks or similar water-proof base, and lean the hive forward so that rainwater can run out the entrance. Remove half of the frames and temporarily set them aside (Fig. 53); you will return them to the hive after 24 hours. Next turn your attention to the bees. Put on your veil, then spray the bees through the screen with clean water from the sprayer, gently rolling the package as you do so, to coat the bees with water and diminish their flight (Fig. 54). Use your hive tool to pry off the lid, exposing the can of sugar syrup provided by the shipper to feed the bees while in transit (Fig. 55). Use your hive tool to help you grip the

(left) Figure 52. The necessary ingredients for package installation: a complete one-story hive, veil, hive tool, a hand sprayer full of water, a syrup feeder (base inserted in bottom board) with jar of 1:1 sugar syrup (shown on lid), and the package of bees. (right) Figure 53. Temporarily remove and set aside half the frames.

can, then lift it out of the package. Immediately next to the can, usually suspended by a strip of soft metal, is the queen in her cage (Fig. 56). As you lift out the can, be sure to hold onto the queen cage so it doesn't fall into the package. Remove the queen cage, temporarily replace the lid on the package, shake off the bees adhering to the queen cage, and inspect the queen to be sure she is alive. It's a good idea, especially for beginners, to pay the extra charge for the shipper to mark your queen with a dot of paint on her thorax.

The standard *Benton* queen cage (Fig. 57) is a wooden block with holes drilled in both ends, each plugged with a cork. The cage has three circular chambers, two of which house the queen and one of which is filled with white *queen candy*, a soft sugar paste made by the shipper to sustain the queen in transit and provide a slow release mechanism for the queen. Remove the cork from the end with candy and use a nail to punch a hole through the candy, being careful to not injure the queen (Fig. 58). This hole provides an edge for workers to begin chewing through the candy to release the queen. Suspend the queen cage between the two center-most

(left) Figure 54. Spray the bees to minimize flight and make them easy to pour. (right) Figure 55. Use the hive tool to pry up the feeder can so you can get a grip on it. The queen cage is suspended alongside the can by a band of soft metal.

Figure 56. Bees will tightly cluster around the queen. Spray bees with water if they are flying too much.

Figure 57. A Benton queen cage

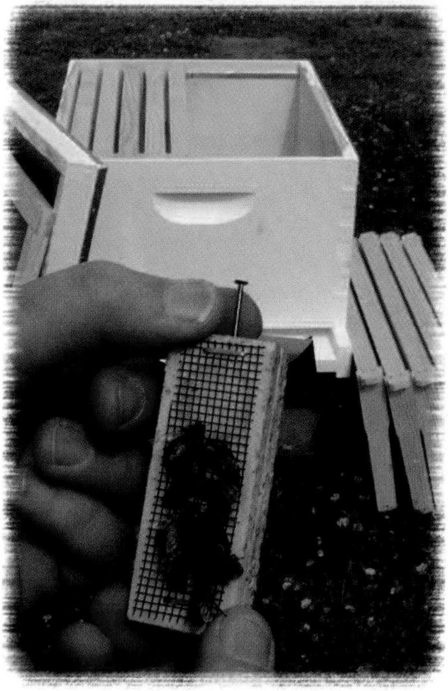

Figure 58.
Use a small nail to bore a hole through the queen candy; this helps the workers release the queen.

frames in the hive (Fig. 59). Next, spray the bees one more time with water, remove the lid, and shake a small cluster of workers directly on top of the queen cage. Put the package, bees and all, into the space you made in the hive when you removed half the frames, close up the hive, and provide a full feeder of syrup. Over the next few hours the workers will leave the package, take up residence on the combs surrounding the queen, begin chewing through the candy to release the queen, discover the syrup feeder, and begin drawing out comb on the foundation (Fig. 60).

After 24 hours, return to the hive and remove the package which by this

Figure 59. Suspend the queen cage between two center frames.

time will be mostly empty of live bees. You can lean it against the hive for another 24 hours to allow the remaining bees to enter the hive (Fig. 61). Even at this early stage you will see the construction of new comb, including perhaps some spurious irregular combs about the queen cage which should be removed (Fig. 62). Check to see if the queen is released from

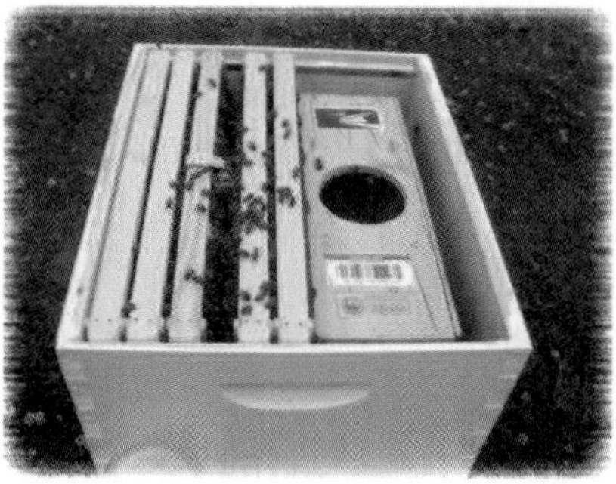

Figure 60. Put the opened package in the space you made when you removed half the frames.

Figure 61. After 24 hours remove the package and lean it against the hive so remaining bees can exit.

Figure 62. Within the first 24 hours bees make white new wax combs, including some irregular ones around the queen cage which should be removed.

her cage. If so, you may find her walking slowly about one of the center combs. If not, return the queen cage, return the frames you removed yesterday, and close up the hive. If after three days the bees have not released the queen, you should do it yourself. I do this by removing the queen cage, closing up the hive, removing the cork from the cage end without candy, and sliding the same end of the cage half-way into the front entrance. It's important to keep the cage hole closed with your finger until it's in place. In this manner the queen, who may be excited and prone to flight, will run directly into the hive instead of fly away (Fig. 63).

Wait at least 48 hours after the queen's release before you examine the colony again. By this time you should find more advanced comb construction and cells filling up with syrup, nectar, or pollen. Equally important, you will find hundreds of cells with eggs (Fig. 4a) which signals that the queen has been accepted by the workers and begun producing the next

Figure 63. The queen can be manually released by removing the cork from the non-candy end, closing the hive and sliding the same end of the cage half-way into the hive entrance. Be careful that the queen doesn't fly out before you insert the cage.

Figure 64. A good comb of sealed worker brood will be light brown in color, the cappings flat, and the pattern solid.

generation of workers. At this point there is nothing left to do except make sure that the syrup feeder is never empty. Bees will continue taking syrup until natural nectar flows begin, at which point you can suspend feeding.

If you do not find eggs, this indicates that the queen has died or failed. This is a serious problem and warrants immediate correction. Telephone your supplier and order a replacement queen without delay. Introduce her in the same manner described above.

Three-week check

Three weeks from the day the queen was released signals an important milestone in the life of a new package colony. If all goes well, this day should witness the emergence of the first workers which constitutes the first population increase after three weeks of decline. When you examine the colony, you should see several combs of sealed brood, having the appearance of brown cardboard (Fig. 64). You may see young bees emerging from their cells. If this is what you see, then close up the colony and continue feeding sugar syrup until natural nectar flows begin and bees lose interest in the syrup. If the brood quantity is small or irregular (Fig. 65), this indicates a bad queen that must be replaced. See **Chapter 5**, **Requeening**.

A good queen tends to lay eggs in the center of the center-most combs and radiate outward as she expands her activities. Thus, the oldest brood will be toward the center and it is here the young bees emerge first. After nurse bees clean out the cells, the queen returns and lays eggs in them again. We call this one "cycle" of brood, with the queen refilling empty cells with eggs as the previous occupants emerge.

With a good queen and good feeding and good nectar flows, colony growth will be rapid from this point on. Once bees occupy 6-7 combs it's time to give them more room. If you decide to use one hive body (see

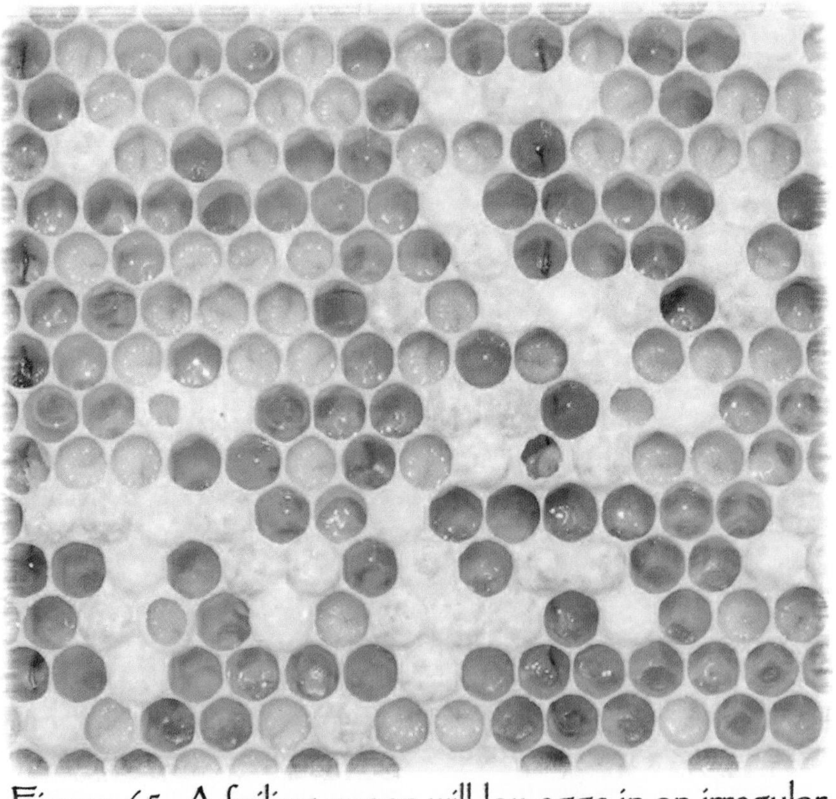

Figure 65. A failing queen will lay eggs in an irregular pattern so that the pattern is spotty, with brood of different ages next to each other or next to empty cells.

Chapter 3, Hive bodies), now is the time to add a queen excluder and a honey super. If you decide to use two hive bodies, now is the time to add the second hive body without a queen excluder.

Installing swarms

Package bees are really nothing more than artificial swarms. Thus, the practices for installing a natural bee swarm differ little from the methods I describe above for packages.

The primary difference lies in retrieving the natural swarm from its clustering site. Personal safety rules here. If the swarm is located so that it can be conveniently and safely reached, then it is a simple job (Fig. 13). But if the swarm is located in high or inaccessible places, the risk of personal injury eclipses the value of the bees.

If you determine that the swarm can be safely reached, then the required equipment is little more than protective clothing and a plastic 5-gallon bucket with tight-fitting screen lid. Depending on location, you may also need a ladder, water spray bottle, bee brush, and pruning shears.

The simplest retrieval is to engulf a hanging swarm inside a plastic bucket, then give the branch a sharp, decisive shake to dislodge bees into the bucket. Cover the bucket with screen and you're ready to go home. Sometimes the position of the swarm permits you to cut off the limb above the swarm, then use the limb like a handle to carry away the clustering bees (Fig. 66). The most difficult swarms are not hanging in a convenient ball, but rather spread across some surface like a wall. In these cases, misting the swarm with water and brushing bees into the bucket is an option.

In many cases it is possible to take an empty hive to the swarm. If you can position the hive entrance immediately next to or even touching the swarm, there is a good chance the bees will enter it on their own within minutes.

Once the bees are in a bucket it is a simple thing to install them. Set up an empty hive in advance, complete with full syrup feeders, and pour the bees onto the ground in front of the hive. What follows is one of the most fascinating sights in beekeeping: the immediate and determined stampede of thousands of bees into their new home, rivulets of bees climbing over the grass and pouring into the hive in response to the odor of comb and the orienting pheromones released by their sisters and queen (Fig. 66b). It is to be hoped that the queen is among that throng. It is not necessary nor possible

Figure 66a.
Sometimes the swarm can be carried to the hive on the branch on which it clustered.

Figure 66b. Simply shake the swarm in front of the hive and the bees enter.

in many cases to find her in this mayhem, but her presence is vital to the successful outcome of the project.

Two days after installation is time to check the new colony. The most important thing is to be sure the colony has a functioning queen. Look for large numbers of cells with eggs in the center of combs and stored honey and pollen around the edges. From this point on, management is the same as for a package colony.

One more thought is worth mentioning. If and when Africanized bees move into your area, the practice of hiving swarms may no longer be advisable. Frequent swarming is a hallmark of these bees and a chief mode of their dispersal. Africanized bees in the swarm phase tend to be gentle and indistinguishable from their more gentle European cousins, but they begin expressing their exaggerated defensive behaviors soon after the nest is established. Thus, a swarm that was gentle and pleasurable the day of installation may be vicious on your next visit.

Installing nucleus colonies

This is one of the best ways to get started. The name "nucleus," *nucs* for short, implies a young, incipient colony that will quickly grow to full size. The process involves the purchase from a beekeeper of whole combs complete with bees and brood. The buyer takes his empty hive to the seller's bee yard, and the seller puts the combs in the hive. Four or five combs is typical, with the rest of the space taken up with empty combs or frames of foundation (Fig. 67). A new caged queen (either purchased beforehand or provided by the seller) is inserted in the center of the combs, the new colony is closed, its entrance screened, and the buyer moves it to his own yard. Feed the colony and monitor the release of the new queen as described in this chapter, **Installing package bees**.

The greatest advantage of nucs is their rapid build-up. Because combs are sold with food and brood of all ages, there is little interruption to colony growth. With a good queen and good forage conditions it is not unusual for nucleus colonies to reach full production strength their first season. Selling nucs is advantageous to the seller because it knocks back the strength of rapidly growing colonies that may otherwise swarm (see **Chapter 5, Swarm management**). The disadvantages of nucs are their general inability to be shipped and risk of spreading pests and diseases.

Figure 67. Making nucs, or splits, is one of the most useful ways to increase colony numbers. Take 4-5 combs of bees and brood from a strong hive (R) and place them in an empty hive body with a new caged queen (L).

Buying established colonies

This represents the simplest and most direct way to get started. Autumn is the best time to find colonies for sale. Check for advertised listings in bee magazines and local beekeeping club newsletters.

Unless you know what you're doing, it's a good idea to have an experienced friend accompany you on your inspection visit. The visible condition of the equipment is a good indicator of the quality of attention the bees have received. The woodenware should be painted with few gaps or rotten joints. The hives should have a standardized appearance; there should be one or two hive bodies on the bottom board and possibly one or more honey supers above. Hives of varying height or with boxes randomly positioned – supers on the bottom, hive bodies on top – suggest management that was either careless or ignorant. If it is warm outside, there should be evidence of bee flight and activity at the entrance. It will be necessary to open the colony to appraise its health and strength. The colony should be populous. Bees should well up immediately and cover the top bars of frames (Fig. 68). There should be no sulfurous decay-like odors, but if you are inspecting in autumn be aware that normal fall hive odors can be spicy and pungent. If it is cold outside the cluster should be at least the diameter of a basketball (Fig. 69).

Figure 68a. Bees in a populous colony will immediately well up and cover the tops of frames.

Figure 68b. Bees in a weak colony well up very little and cover only a few frames.

Figure 69. A strong winter cluster. Note the tight, circular edges.

Colonies should be queenright, and unless it's late autumn or winter, there should be at least some evidence of brood production. Hives should be heavy with honey, pollen, or syrup. Seventy-five to 150 pounds is a normal range of weights for much of the country.

Cold weather is a good time to move hives because the bees will be cold and sluggish and there is little risk of suffocation and overheating in transit. Moving hives is a two-man job. Fasten each hive body and super to the bottom board or super below it with high-tension straps or hive staples. Secure the lids with straps or duct tape. Screen hive entrances with hardware cloth. It takes at least two people to safely lift a hive and gently set it in a truck bed or trailer. Strap hives down and move them to their new location. See this chapter, **Apiary locations**.

The biggest advantage of starting with established colonies is the immediate possession of production capacity. There is a risk, however, of acquiring disease contaminants and old or poorly-constructed equipment. And finally, this fast-track approach bypasses the personal involvement a beginner enjoys when he or she build their own equipment and install their own bees.

Chapter 5

Management for Honey Production and Pollination

Bee folk, settle here,
Do not go from this place,
I give thee house and place,
Thou must bring me honey and wax.

Bessler, Geschichte der Bienenzucht

The timing of tasks outlined in this chapter is distinctive to the particular region of the country in which you live. Consult with local beekeepers to learn when to expect the major nectar flows in your area and time your tasks accordingly.

Early season build-up

As I have mentioned before, late winter/early spring is the period of greatest risk of colony starvation. This is when the beekeeper needs to watch his or her colonies carefully and step in with supplemental carbohydrate (sugar syrup) and protein (pollen supplement) as needed. In general, if the hive is light weight (under 75 pounds) when you lift it from the back, it needs feeding. You can use any one of the traditional syrup feeders (see **Chapter 3**,

Feeders) to feed a syrup no leaner than 1 part sugar to 1 part water. Don't be frugal. If a colony needs feeding at all, it probably needs gallons, not quarts. Additionally, prepare any one of the commercially available pollen supplements. The dry mixture is mixed with sugar syrup into the consistency of dough, made into a hamburger-sized patty on wax paper, and placed on the top bars of hive body frames (Fig. 70).

Feed each colony until it achieves your target weight or else natural floral resources become available. You will know when nectar is coming in because bees lose interest in sugar syrup. A concerted feeding regimen will not only sustain a colony in its weakest hour, but stimulate population growth in anticipation of the honey production season.

Figure 70. Protein supplement patty.
This example includes natural bee-collected pollen.

Requeening

One thread running through this book is the value of strong colonies. Nowhere is this drilled home more fervently than in the next section, **Swarm management**, but here is a good place to talk about one of the most important tasks that contribute to this goal – the replacement of poor-performing queens.

To begin, a beekeeper should become comfortable with the notion of replacing a queen at the first sign of trouble. Her effects on the colony are so profound and immediate that a colony's fortune literally rises and falls with that of its queen. A good queen will not only carry good genetics but perform well as an egg-layer, producing comb after comb of brood in a solid, contiguous pattern (Fig. 64). The result will be a colony dense with bees; when you open a colony there should be so many bees that they well up immediately and blanket the tops of the combs (Fig. 68a). The colony should forage vigorously. It should show no sign of disease; indeed for many disorders the only practical solution is to requeen the colony (see **Chapter 8**). The colony should not be excessively defensive. Any deviation from these standards is justification for replacing a colony's queen. The method for replacing an established queen in an established colony is slightly different than that described in **Chapter 4** for package installation.

First you must acquire a new caged queen. Immediately before you are ready to install her, you must first take her inside an enclosed, well-lit place (a truck cab is perfect), remove the cork from the non-candy end of the cage and remove all the attendant bees. You can do this by blowing on the bees to make them move and covering the hole with your thumb to control which bees stay and which leave. Research has shown that foreign attendants reduce the likelihood of new queen acceptance. Return all corks, including the one covering the candy. Next, find and remove the old queen, insert the new caged queen between two combs in the center of the brood nest, and close up the colony. Return after 48 hours and examine the behavior of hive bees on the outside of the queen cage. You may see a moderate amount of "balling," which is an aggressive response in which bees cling tightly to the offending queen in a solid mass. In nature this usually results in the death of the queen, but a caged queen is reasonably protected. In our case, balling to a high or moderate degree (Fig. 71a) is a sign that the hive bees are not ready to accept the newcomer. Return the caged queen and close up the hive for another day or two. During these inspections you are doing a second important task to increase queen acceptance – systematically cutting out natural queen cells. Immediately after the old queen is removed, hive bees invariably begin constructing supersedure cells in various parts of the brood nest. It is important that the beekeeper remove these because supersedure cells decrease the chance of new queen acceptance. Hopefully, after

Figure 71a. Workers balling a caged queen will cluster tightly over the screen, biting it with their mandibles.

Figure 71b. A non-aggressive response by workers is apparent when they walk loosely over the queen cage without biting the wires.

3-4 days you will find that the balling response has dwindled to nothing (Fig. 71b). There is no reason to delay queen release any longer. At this point I remove the queen cage, close up the colony and remove the cork from the non-candy end, while keeping a finger over the hole to keep the queen from flying out. I release the queen into the colony by sliding the open end of the queen cage half-way into the hive entrance (Fig. 63). This maneuver ensures that the queen runs out of the cage and *into* the hive, instead of taking wing and flying away. It's an easy matter to return after a few minutes to check that the queen has left the cage and take it away. After queen release, wait 48 hours before you check to be sure the new queen is laying eggs.

The process of requeening is handicapped in colonies with laying workers (Fig. 4b) as workers in these conditions are prone to repeatedly reject introduced queens. The same introduction practices apply as described above, but in addition it's advisable to add one or two combs of emerging worker brood from another colony next to the caged queen. The rapid influx of young workers seems to help queen acceptance rate.

Swarm management

Before research proved otherwise, beekeepers thought that swarm-catching was the best way to increase colony numbers and the size of honey crops. After all, if one colony swarmed and you caught it, you now had two. Thus the old rhyme:

A swarm of bees in May is worth a ton of hay.
A swarm of bees in June is worth a silver spoon.
A swarm of bees in July ain't even worth a fly.

But now it is understood that swarming is the greatest insult to honey production short of colony disease or death. This insight was gained through research done by C.L. Farrar, a USDA scientist working in the 1940s who showed that colony foraging efficiency increases as bee population increases. This forms the basis for modern honey production management, which is fundamentally the pursuit of very large colonies. Since a prime swarm deprives a colony of about half its workforce (see **Chapter 2**, *Spring and the reproductive cycle*) and since swarm season occurs immediately before the heaviest nectar flows of the year, these two phenomena conspire to ruin a beekeeper's chance of making a decent honey crop from that colony.

Since avoiding swarms is so important, it is paramount that beekeepers understand and manage the conditions that lead to the actual swarm event. First of all, the swarm impulse is to be expected every spring as part of the natural cycle. But there are a few predisposing factors that a beekeeper can control and which constitute opportunities for minimizing swarms. Briefly, these are the presence of hive congestion and the presence of queen cells.

The most important of these factors is hive congestion. There is evidence that a high population of bees compacted within a limited hive space stimulates the production of queen cells and the beginning of the swarm cycle. Thus, one way of discouraging swarms is to relieve hive congestion. This can be accomplished by making nucs or splits, equalizing colonies, reversing hive bodies, and supering.

The production of nucs is described in **Chapter 4**, **Installing nucleus colonies**. The process results in young colonies that the beekeeper can either sell or use to build up her own colony numbers and restore winter losses. (In inexplicable beekeeping parlance, the word "nucs" is used when

Figure 72. A 4-frame nuc box (front) prepared to receive frames of brood and bees from the strong colony

the new colony is intended for sale or is housed in 4- or 5-frame boxes (Fig. 72). "Splits" or "divides" is more commonly used when the new colony is intended for one's own spring increase.)

Equalizing can take two forms: equalizing brood and equalizing adults. To equalize brood, simply take 1-3 frames of brood (shake off the bees first) from a strong colony and give them to a weaker. Replace the combs you take from the strong colony with empty combs, keeping the remaining brood frames together in the center of the brood nest. This procedure provides more egg-laying space for the queen and relieves congestion in the strong colony. It also provides a needed boost to the weaker colony. Be careful to not give a weak colony more brood than it can keep warm. Equalizing adults involves moving hives, so it is a two-man job. Wait until the middle of a warm spring afternoon when bees are flying vigorously and simply trade places between the strong hive and the weak, putting the strong hive at the site of the weak, and *vice versa*. Foraging bees return to the site of their original nest, oblivious to the fact that you switched them, and under conditions of good nectar flow there is little or no fighting between non-nestmates. In this manner, the weak colony gains population at

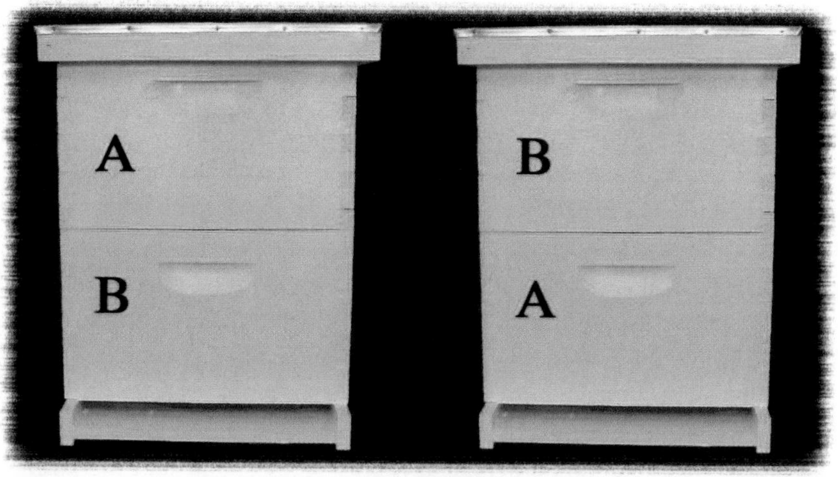

Figure 73. Reversing hive bodies once or twice in spring can help discourage swarming. If most of the bees are in the upper hive body (A at left), then place A on the bottom and B on top (right).

the expense of the stronger: the weaker is strengthened and the swarm impulse in the stronger diminished. Equalizing is not a one-time action, but rather an ongoing process during the weeks leading up to the major nectar flow of your area.

If you subscribe to the two-hive body configuration (see **Chapter 3, Hive bodies**), there is a procedure you can exploit which takes advantage of the fact that bees move upward in the brood nest during the course of the winter months. In these cases, by late winter/early spring the upper hive body is full of bees and brood, while the lower is mostly empty. Bees at this time of year are unwilling to move downward, so this constitutes a congested situation as bees are pressed against the hive lid. The beekeeper can relieve this perceived congestion, and reduce the swarm impulse, by simply "reversing hive bodies." Switch the hive bodies, putting the lower on top and the upper (with most of the bees and brood) on the bottom (Fig. 73). This immediately relieves congestion as bees perceive an abundance of space above them.

Another way to relieve hive congestion, whether in one hive body or two, is to provide honey supers. Simply add one or two honey supers early in the honey season when nectar is coming in the hive. You will know when this is happening by the presence of freshly-made white beeswax in the honey supers (Fig. 74). Additionally, when you gently shake combs at this time, thin raw nectar literally rains out of the open cells.

The second short-term factor that stimulates swarming is the presence of queen cells. Sometimes a beekeeper has equalized an apiary to its maximum potential and has no interest in increasing colony numbers through the production of splits. Besides adding supers, the only other recourse to discourage swarming is culling queen cells. This technique is effective but laborious. It amounts to systematically visiting every colony every ten days, examining every brood comb, and cutting out every queen cell. Care must be exercised to look carefully. Incipient queen cells can be inconspicuous and tucked away in odd corners, and it only takes one to start the swarm cycle.

By now it should be apparent that spring management is a delicate balancing act for the beekeeper. On the one hand, the beekeeper must stimulate growth to achieve maximum forager populations. But on the other hand, he or she must strategically diminish the strength of strong, congested colonies

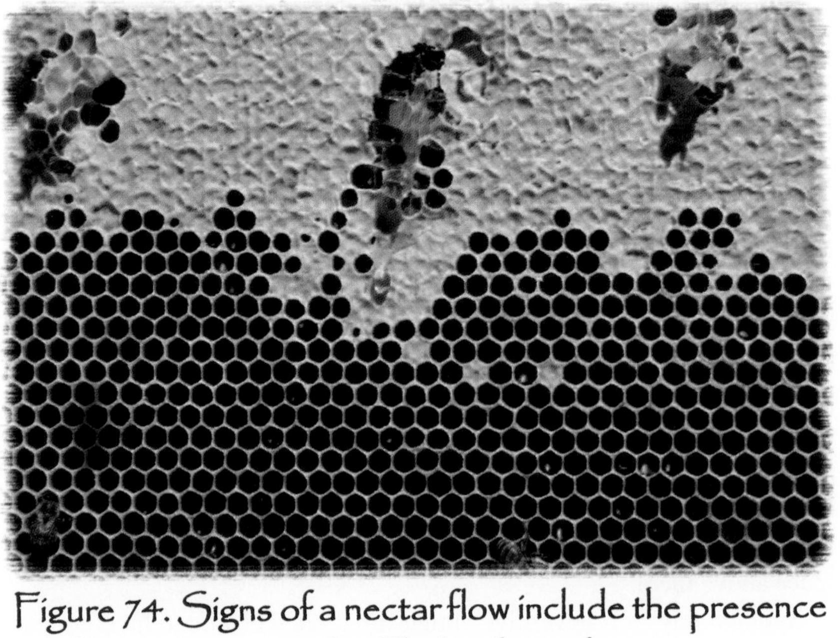

Figure 74. Signs of a nectar flow include the presence of white new wax combs filled with raw honey.

that would otherwise swarm. The difference between controlled diminishing and natural swarming is that a colony that swarms loses up to 60% of its forager force and sustains a protracted period of decline while a new daughter queen emerges, matures, mates, and begins egg-laying. Controlled equalizing by the beekeeper, on the other hand, results in far smaller population loss for the donor colony and sustains the original queen at a high egg-laying pitch. This balancing act is where science ends and art begins, and like any art it's not mastered overnight.

Supering for the nectar flow

There comes a time when nectar is pouring in and it is no longer practical to remove honey supers to reach the hive bodies and perform swarm prevention measures. This is the peak of honey production season, and its timing varies according to the floral cycle of any given region. At this point swarm prevention is abandoned in favor of supering up for the honey flow.

There are two principles that govern "supering," that is, the addition of supers for a honey crop: (1) the odor of empty comb stimulates honey foraging and (2) decreasing hive density diminishes hoarding efficiency. In practice, principle #1 is accommodated by adding lots of honey supers and principle #2 is accommodated by crowding bees. At first blush these principles appear antagonistic, but as we shall see, there is a way to exploit both.

The path to reconciliation is thus: the beekeeper should be liberal with supers early in the season and frugal with supers when it's late. Let's say it's early spring and many flowers are in bloom. When you open the hive cover and peer onto the combs, you see lots of bees between combs and perhaps a considerable bit of new, white wax. If this is the case, it's a good idea to add one or two empty honey supers to exploit the benefits of the stimulatory effect of empty comb. But let's say it's near the end of nectar season. At this time, it is advisable to crowd the bees. You should refrain from adding supers, and maybe even remove supers the bees haven't worked. This crowding forces bees to work the corners of combs, resulting in supers dense with harvestable honey. In practice, it is typical for most parts of the US to require 3-6 honey supers per hive during any given nectar flow, but I have used as many as nine in an extraordinarily good season.

Beekeepers debate the relative merits of *top supering* versus *bottom supering*. Top supering is simply adding the next honey super on top of existing ones. Bottom supering involves removing all previous honey supers, by now partially filled, placing the newest one immediately on the brood nest, and replacing the partial supers on top of the new one. The rationale for bottom supering is that it places empty combs near the hive entrance and thus encourages bees to more quickly fill them with honey. Although this method has merit in the case of comb honey production (see **Chapter 6**, *Comb honey*), research has shown that it does not significantly increase honey yield. I recommend that beekeepers save themselves the extra labor and simply use top supering.

Other considerations in honey production

The over-riding objective in spring and summer management is to procure large bee populations in time for the major nectar flows. Swarm management is paramount, but there are other actions that contribute to this goal.

As the beekeeper works his hives, he will encounter some that are stronger than others. It is always worth asking *why* a particular colony is weak. Is the queen sub-standard? If so, she should be replaced. Is there a

Figure 75. Commercial beekeepers place several hives to a pallet. This allows mechanized handling.

health disorder? If so, it should be addressed (see **Chapter 8**). Are the combs empty of honey or pollen? If so, the colony is starving and needs sugar syrup and pollen supplement. Is there an unexplained drop in the foraging population? If so, there may be insecticide application in the area. Are the brood combs black and heavy with age? If so, they should be replaced as research has shown that old combs decrease colony growth. Are the hives shaded or exposed to direct wind? If so, they should be placed in direct sun and provided a wind-break. Monitoring colony conditions, preventing swarms, maintaining bee health, solving problems, and supering appropriately are the jobs of the honey producer. This is the stuff beekeeping is made of.

Working with Africanized bees

This is a good place to talk about the differences in management techniques required when working Africanized bees. With these bees the beekeeper must be constantly ready for unpredictable and fierce defensive responses. Fortunately, Africanized bees can be reasonably well-mannered if the conditions are right and the beekeeper sufficiently skilled.

First and foremost is the importance of good apiary locations. All the conditions mentioned in **Chapter 4, Apiary locations** apply, with the added emphasis on apiary isolation. It is paramount that apiaries of Africanized bees be located well away from penned animals and human traffic.

Experience in Latin America has taught beekeepers the utility of using single hive stands. In contrast to this is the use of rails or pallets (Fig. 75) designed to house many hives. The problem with multiple hives on one platform is that with Africanized bees the vibration of working one hive excites all the others, thus compounding an apiary-wide defensive response. Single hive stands (Fig. 76) minimize this problem.

Adequate protective clothing is important. Beekeepers in Brazil use veils that are white-faced instead of black (Fig. 77). Under the worst defensive conditions it is possible for highly agitated bees to mass around the black field represented by the screen of a conventional veil, rendering it difficult for the beekeeper to see. The simple switch to a white screen eliminates this problem.

Smoke figures prominently in the handling of these bees – specifically, large quantities and applied often. A Brazilian-designed extra-large smoker

Figure 76. Single hive stands, like these in Honduras, minimize Africanized bee defense response when a beekeeper is working an apiary.

is now available in the US (Fig. 78). Upon approaching an Africanized apiary the first thing to do is smoke the entrance of every hive before you begin working any one. This deadens an incipient defense reaction. While working a colony, it may be necessary to smoke it incessantly. Cautious and gentle handling is also important. In spite of all these precautions, it is possible that a colony will achieve an uncontrollable state of defensiveness. At that point, there is nothing to do but close the colony, leave the apiary, and come back another day.

Africanized bees are not all bad news from a beekeeping point of view. They are comparatively disease- and pest-resistant. Because they do not tolerate handling to the extent of European bees, their management is necessarily simplified. Much of it boils down to stimulatory feeding in early-season, followed by generous supering. In good honey flow conditions their productivity can meet or exceed Europeans.

Figure 77. White-faced veils help reduce Africanized bee defense responses.

Figure 78. A Brazilian smoker (L) compared to conventional American model (R)

Honey plants

Because the link between bees and flowers is such a close one, it's natural for beekeepers to have more than casual interest in the honey-yielding plants available to their bees. The color, texture, flavor, and crystallizing properties of the honey your bees make are overwhelmingly the product of the floral potpourri unique to your neighborhood. The locality-specific nature of honey is one of its most alluring selling points.

Even though honey bees can and do make honey from a wide assort-

Figure 79. Dandelion

Figure 80. Red maple

Figure 81. Gallberry

Figure 82. Orange

ment of flowering plants, there are a handful that make up the most dependable nectar sources and the largest floral constituents of US honey. These major honey plants tend to be regional, and I will cover only a few of them here.

Some early nectar flows contribute little to the actual honey crop, but are valuable nevertheless for building up colonies after winter. These include the ubiquitous dandelion (Fig. 79) and in the South, red maple (Fig. 80). In the southeastern coastal plain from Texas to Virginia, gallberry, an understory shrub, is a major honey source (Fig. 81). Orange blossom honey is a regional favorite from Florida and parts of the Southwest (Fig. 82). The clovers – yellow sweet (Fig. 83), white sweet and Dutch (Fig. 84) – collectively represent the largest honey source in the United States. They grow throughout much of the northern latitudes of this country, but predominate in the upper Midwest, where they are the target of an annual influx of migratory honey producers who truck in bee hives by the thousands. Soybean (Fig. 85) is an important surplus flow, chiefly in the Midwest and central South. It curiously fails to produce surplus honey in the Southeast. An assortment of brambles, chiefly blackberry, make significant honey crops throughout much of the country (Fig. 86). Tulip poplar makes a flavorful dark honey throughout much of the East (Fig. 87). Fireweed is a regional

Figure 83. Yellow sweet clover

Figure 84. Dutch clover

Figure 85. Soybean

Figure 86. Blackberry

specialty from the Pacific Northwest and Alaska (Fig. 88), and sourwood has regional distinction in the southern Appalachians (Fig. 89). Closing out this brief list is goldenrod (Fig. 90), well-known as a dark, strong fall honey that rarely makes its way to the table, but is important for winter food stores.

In perusing this list one sees that America's honey derives from a cornucopia of plants wild and cultivated. Depending on your unique local flora, your honey may be mono- or multi-floral. This depends on the

Figure 87. Tulip poplar

Figure 88. Fireweed

comparative richness of any given nectar source. Because honey bees are efficient at concentrating on the best energy sources within their foraging range, they will concentrate almost exclusively on one plant species if its rewards are sufficiently rich. If this superior nectar flow is permanent, *i.e.*, feral or repeatedly sown, the resulting monofloral honey will have a high degree of consistency in color and flavor year after year. In contrast, if numerous more-or-less equally attractive nectar flows are available in your neighborhood, the resulting honey will be multi-floral and prone to sensory variation between years.

The practice of migratory honey production hinges on the fact that different honey plants bloom at different times. If a beekeeper is willing, it's possible to move bees, prolong the honey production season, and enlarge

Figure 89. Sourwood

Figure 90. Goldenrod

one's crop. In my state of Georgia, for instance, a beekeeper can move bees to Florida in March for orange, to south Georgia in April for gallberry, to north Georgia in June for sourwood, and back to south Georgia in July for cotton. This is, granted, a lot of work and not too easy on the bees either, but it does represent a strategy for revenue-optimization.

A final word is worth mentioning about deliberate plantings for bees. Unless you have large acreage at your disposal, it probably won't make any difference in the size of your honey crop. The foraging range of one colony is measurable in square miles, and within that area the bees will seek out and forage on the richest available nectar sources. For an average-sized land holding of a few acres, it is difficult to plant enough of anything that would significantly increase honey yields. Nevertheless, many people enjoy planting bee forages near their house so they can watch bees work. Some ornamentals that fit the bill include crape myrtle, purple coneflower, various sages and sunflower. There are numerous websites that list plants for bee gardens.

Pollination

Much of the management covered in this chapter about strengthening colonies for honey production applies as well to colonies used for crop pollination. It is important that pollination colonies be queenright and meet a certain minimum standard of population strength. The goal is a large forager force motivated to visit plants for pollen. A general standard of six frames of brood with bees to cover applies to most crops. Research has shown that protein (*i.e.*, pollen) foragers do a better job at transferring pollen from flower to flower. Thus, the key factors boil down to the presence of brood and a vigorously laying queen. The two are, of course, causally connected, but there are synergistic effects in which the two combine to maximize pollen foraging. First of all, the queen produces the brood that matures into foragers, and her own pheromones have a stimulatory effect on worker foraging. Secondly, the brood create a protein demand as nurse bees require protein to produce brood food. And finally, research has shown that brood itself produces pheromones that have a stimulatory effect on pollen foragers.

What this means for a pollinating beekeeper is that there is less incentive to have colonies with maximum populations as with honey production. It is preferable that pollination colonies be in a growth mode with a high ratio of brood per bee. This also has a practical convenience for the beekeeper because crop pollination necessarily entails moving hives, and single-brood chamber hives (or at most singles plus one food super) are far easier to move than colonies supered up for a honey flow.

A target density for most crops is one hive per acre; however for reasons given in Chapter 1, **The place of beekeeping in the world**, this density is woefully obsolete and should be adjusted upwards. The grower must keep in mind that the foraging range of any given bee colony is large – up to several square miles – and steps must be taken to increase the likelihood that bees will forage on one's crop instead of the weeds one mile distant. One way to do this is to simply increase the density of hives per acre. When colonies are in a state of competition, they are forced to forage more thoroughly within their flight range to procure the pollen they need. A second strategy is to delay moving hives to the crop until the crop has achieved about 10% bloom. When the bees discover the new floral source close to their hives, they fixate on it, at least for a day or two, until and if scout bees discover better sources in the neighborhood. For some early-setting crops such as apple, a few good days of bee visitation is all it takes to set a commercial crop.

It is advisable that the beekeeper study the pollination market in his area to arrive at pricing that is fair yet sustainable. The frequent moving associated with pollination invariably means that pollinating hives suffer both in condition and in their potential for making a honey crop. These costs must be considered when setting pollination fees. And finally, it is strongly urged that beekeepers and crop growers enter pollination agreements under the mutual protection of a legally-binding contract. Model contracts are available from state and provincial extension services.

Chapter 6

Products of the Bee Hive

Of air-born honey, gift of heaven, I now
Take up the tale.

Virgil, *The Georgics*, IV

The bee hive is a bonanza of products used for food, crafts, cosmetics, art, and folk remedies. It makes an exciting inventory for people with a savvy for marketing and a knack for capitalizing on consumer demand for natural products. Add to this a widespread appeal for locality-specific products, and a beekeeper/entrepreneur has all the ingredients necessary to build a successful home-based business. For those less business-inclined, beekeeping is a handy way to make gifts for friends and family. Just imagine the Christmas possibilities with one-pound jars of honey and one bee hive producing 100 pounds per year.

Processing honey

Honey moisture

Honey is the premier product of the bee hive, whether in its liquid extracted form or in the comb. One of the chief and universal concerns with honey is avoiding fermentation which is caused when honey is harvested before it is "ripe," that is, before bees have removed enough water from the nectar to prevent yeast growth and spoilage. Honey is considered safe from fermentation once it has been dehydrated to a water content of 18.6% or lower. In the field, this is thought to correspond roughly to the degree to which bees have capped the honey cells with beeswax, with a two-thirds capping rate being the minimum threshold. But this is not reliable. Dry regions may fail to reach the two thirds threshold simply because the honey season ended early and bees had no nectar with which to secrete more beeswax. Alternatively, humid conditions can result in fermented honey even in cells that are fully capped. Beekeepers in your area can help you appraise your risk of fermentation. Nowadays it is possible to purchase relatively inexpensive pocket refractometers to measure honey moisture in the field and remove all doubt. Finally, borderline moisture levels can be remedied with post-harvest dehydration, described below.

Harvesting honey

Before honey supers can be brought indoors for processing, they must be emptied of bees. The method I prefer is the combined use of a fume board and chemical bee repellent (Fig. 91a). A fume board looks like a hive lid but on the inside surface has absorbent material designed to soak up the repellent. Wait until a warm sunny day and remove the hive lid to expose the first super you want to harvest. Sprinkle about one tablespoon of repellent uniformly over the inside surface of the fume board, then immediately place it on top of the exposed super (Fig. 91b). Performance is enhanced if the sun is beating down directly on the fume board. Within 3-4 minutes the super will be nearly empty of bees as the insects retreat downward in response to the repellent. In this manner you can proceed downward, harvesting one super at a time. Once removed from the hives, the empty supers must be covered carefully with lids top and bottom to prevent entry by robber bees. Fume boards are a practical and efficient harvesting method even for large beekeepers. Four or five fume boards running at the same time can keep one person fully occupied.

Post-harvest dehydration

There are occasions when the beekeeper wants to remove excess water from honey directly rather than leave the job to the bees. The extreme example of this happens in commercial operations in the prairies of Canada where the honey flow is intense but brief. The bees' time is more efficiently

Figure 91a. The combined use of bee repellent and a fume board is a fast and efficient way to remove honey. Repellent is sprinkled on the cloth interior of the fume board.

Figure 91b. The fume board is then placed on the top-most super. If the sun is shining brightly, only about 3-4 minutes is required to clear the super of bees.

spent gathering nectar rather than secreting wax and capping cells, so the beekeeper removes supers of un-ripe honey and dehydrates them in buildings equipped with forced air and dehumidifiers. The process differs in scale but not in principle for the hobbyist whose honey is on the borderline of 18.6% water. It must be done after supers are harvested, but before honey is extracted. To remove excess moisture from honey supers, first place supers in an enclosed room and stack them criss-cross fashion so that the ends of each super are exposed. Run a space heater, fan, and dehumidifier in the room constantly, being careful to not overload electrical circuits. The time required to remove water in this manner is variable, but will probably take at least 1-2 days. Check the honey with a refractometer until your target moisture level is achieved. If you extract supers immediately following this process, it has the added value of warming and thinning the honey, a step that improves extracting efficiency.

Extracting honey

There is a minimum amount of specialized equipment you must acquire before you can produce liquid honey "extracted" from the comb. This is detailed in Figures 92-96. After you have brought the supers into the processing room, turn on your uncapping knife so it can be heating up. Remove a frame of honey and set its end bar on the nail point that sticks up from the uncapping tub. The nail point permits you to easily swivel the frame from one side to the other. The uncapping tub is designed to receive wet cappings on a mesh floor which permits honey to drip through and out a spigot. Use the uncapping knife to slice off the cappings from each side of the comb, using a gentle sawing motion to cut the wax instead of tearing it (Fig. 92). Begin at the top and work downward; it is dangerous to work from the bot-

Figure 92. Use a heated uncapping knife to remove cappings in a gentle sawing motion from the top down.

Figure 93. A capping scratcher is handy for removing cappings in low spots the uncapping knife can't reach.

Figure 94. Uncapped combs are ready to go in the extractor. This setup shows a 20-frame radial extractor suitable for mid-sized operators.

tom up because you may slip and cut or burn your face. Invariably there will be low spots that are difficult for your knife to reach. It's easiest to open these low spots with a cappings scratcher (Fig. 93). It's tempting to use the scratcher for all your uncapping needs, but the problem is that it fills the honey with small wax particles that plug filters downstream in the process.

After it is uncapped, each frame is loaded into the extractor (Fig. 94). Most hobbyist-scale extractors hold two or four frames, and their weight must be balanced equitably to prevent the extractor from walking across the floor as you spin it. Once loaded, begin spinning the frames slowly, then gradually faster. Centrifugal force flings the honey out of the empty cells onto the walls of the extractor, where it then drips to the bottom and out a spigot (Fig. 95). A *radial* extractor is to be preferred because the frames fit inside like spokes in a wheel and honey spins out of both sides at once. An older design of extractor, still manufactured, is the so-called *reversible* extractor which extracts only one side of frames at a time. If you are using this type of extractor, begin spinning the first side, but on the first round don't go too fast or you risk breaking the combs as the weight of honey on the inner side presses out. When the first side is about half done, reverse the combs and begin spinning the other side. You can go faster this time because there's not as much weight pressing outward. Finally, reverse the frames again, and this time spin to completion the original sides.

Honey requires straining after the extractor to remove bits of wax, dead bees and other debris. On a hobbyist scale, paint strainers placed above 5-gallon buckets will work nicely (Fig. 95). It's convenient if you can fit each

(left) Figure 95. Liquid honey, extracted from the comb, empties out the spigot at the bottom of the extractor. A paint strainer above a 5-gallon bucket makes a suitable strainer system. (right) Figure 96. Honey is ready to bottle after it has settled 24 hours.

bucket with a honey valve at the bottom for bottling. Let the honey settle at least 24 hours and keep it covered to prevent entry of dust and dirt. During this time the suspended air bubbles will rise to the top, forming a foam on the surface. By bottling from the valve at the bottom, the honey in your jars will be crystal-clear and foam-free (Fig. 96).

Figure 97. Be sure to comply with your state's food labeling laws.

Honey should be bottled in standard honey containers. The most popular sizes are the one-pound jar and 12-ounce plastic honey bear. A variety of containers and adhesive labels is available from any of the major bee supply companies. State departments of agriculture regulate minimum standards of design for food labels (Fig. 97), but these specifications are highly uniform across the country and usually met by default when you order labels from a well-known supplier.

Some honey is prone to granulate, that is, turn into a semi-solid phase with large visible crystals of precipitated sugars. Granulated honey is still perfectly edible; some people prefer it, but others consider it unsightly. In general, granulation is viewed negatively by honey consumers and is to be avoided. Heating and straining honey during the extracting process delays onset of granulation, as does keeping honey covered to prevent airborne dust from settling in it. Any kind of particulate matter – dust, pollen clumps, or wax particles – can stimulate the formation of crystals and escalate the granulation process. Fortunately, it is easy to return granulated honey to its liquid state by re-heating it. Loosen the lid and set the jar of honey in a pot of boiling water until the honey is re-liquified. Another way to deal with granulating honey is to make it into creamed honey. Creamed honey is essentially granulated honey, the difference being that the crystallization process is controlled to result in tiny crystals instead of large, unsightly, chunky ones. The end product is smooth and spreadable, and commands a premium price. There are several websites that give step by step directions for making creamed honey.

This is a good place to note that states also have minimum licensing requirements for facilities that process food for sale. I have found these requirements to be common-sense and reasonable. Moreover, I have found state inspectors to be more interested in helping parties reach compliance than levying fines. In short, if you intend to produce honey for sale, be sure to study and comply with your state's food handling requirements.

Comb honey

The production of comb honey is especially satisfying to the traditionalist because it represents honey in its most basic and ancient form. Until the invention of the honey extractor in the 19th century, all honey was comb honey.

The most popular form of comb honey is actually a combination of comb honey and extracted honey – the so-called *chunk* honey which is packed in pint or one-pound increments. The basic presentation consists of a rectangle of comb honey inserted into a pint or one-pound jar, with the surrounding space filled with extracted honey. We have already talked about extracted honey, so let me focus now on the comb honey component.

The goal of comb honey production is to produce perfect, fully-filled, and fully-capped combs of honey. A bite of comb honey should almost burst in one's mouth, with individual beeswax cells delicately breaking and releasing their sweet contents as one chews. When the honey is gone there should be only a small bite of beeswax remaining because, being virgin comb, the cells are delicate and thin. Appearance is everything: the cappings must be white, clean, and uniform. Comb honey requires the use of special extra-thin 100% beeswax foundation. Comb honey foundation lacks embedded support wires because the foundation is ultimately eaten along with the rest of the comb. It is extra-thin to further enhance the delicate palatability of the final product. The foundation is inserted in shallow honey super frames. It is not even necessary to insert a whole sheet; I use only a 1- to 2-inch strip across the top (Fig. 98). The advantage of this method is two-fold: first, it is simply economical and second, it maximizes the likelihood for all-natural, extra-thin combs.

Figure 98a. Foundation for cut comb honey is extra-thin 100% beeswax. All that's required is a narrow starter strip.

Figure 98b. The starter strip is inserted in the frame top bar. Bees draw out the remainder of the comb in extra-delicate, first-year wax. Thin, delicate, and clean wax is of paramount importance in comb honey production.

The production of comb honey differs little from that for extracted honey. Since appearance is so important, this may be the only valid occasion for bottom supering (see **Chapter 5**, **Supering for the nectar flow**)

Figure 99. Cut out the comb from the wooden frame.

Figure 100. Cut away all natural edges.

Figure 101. Fill the remaining volume of the jar with extracted honey.

as the lower position of comb honey supers may minimize bee travel stain on cappings and encourage bees to fill out the corners more thoroughly. Another management step is to crowd the colonies a little more than one would ordinarily for extracted honey. This again encourages bees to fill out the combs more thoroughly.

In the honey house use an ordinary sharp kitchen knife to cut away the comb from the frame (Fig. 99). Cut away natural edges and sections of comb that are uncapped (Fig. 100). Next, cut individual sections of comb, so that they closely accommodate the available space in the jar; wide-mouth jars are necessary for chunk honey to make it easy to insert the comb section. Finally, fill the remaining space with extracted honey – preferably of the same floral variety as in the comb (Fig. 101).

Beeswax

The uncapping procedure means that beeswax is an automatic by-product of extracted honey. Moreover, cappings wax is the very best beeswax because it is virgin wax from that season and relatively free of accumulated debris and contaminants. When rendered, premium beeswax has a pleasing aroma and lemon-yellow color.

Cappings are ready for processing as soon as most of the honey has dripped from them in the uncapping tub. Wash them in water to remove remaining honey and let them dry. You want to avoid direct heat when melting beeswax and instead use an indirect method such as a double boiler. Beeswax is flammable, so exercise all prudent caution. After the beeswax is melted, pour it through a clean nylon filter into some type of

Figure 102. Clean, rendered cappings wax ready for use

Figure 103. The beauty and sales appeal of beeswax candles and ornaments are self-evident.

mold. Clean, rendered beeswax blocks are ready for any number of art or craft applications (Fig. 102). The beekeeper should consider supplementing his revenues with beeswax ornaments and candles (Fig. 103), although details for their making are beyond the scope of this book.

Pollen

The collection of pollen requires a pollen trap installed at your hive entrance and its operation for a few days during the most intense pollen season. Because pollen is necessary to colony health and productivity, you must exercise caution and not over-exploit colonies.

Figure 104. A pollen trap from New Zealand. All designs are some variation of a screen through which returning pollen foragers must pass. The screen combs the pollen pellets off the foragers' legs.

It is advisable to limit trapping for any given colony to no longer than one afternoon on alternate days. This is especially true during the buildup season leading up to the major nectar flows when colonies are at their highest growth rate.

There are numerous styles of traps, the fundamental design of each being a screen or grid through which returning foragers must pass before they can enter the hive. The screen combs off their legs the pollen pellets which then fall into a drawer which the beekeeper can open daily to remove that day's catch (Fig. 104). The pollen should be cleaned of visible debris and dried to the point that individual pellets will not stick when you press them together. Pollen cleaned and dried in this manner can be packaged and labeled in standard honey containers. Health food stores are ready markets for this bee hive specialty.

Chapter 7
Off-Season Management

But long ere Virgo weaves the robe of sleet,
Or binds the hoar-frost sandals round her feet,
Close seal'd and sacred, leave your toil-worn hosts,
The last kind dole their waning season boasts . . .

Evans, in Bevan, *The Honeybee*

This is a good time to remind the reader of the over-riding objective of the honey producer, which is to achieve maximum colony populations in time for the major nectar flows. This is a year-round consideration. A colony that comes through winter with a large bee population has a good start toward that spring and summer goal. But the challenge is formidable. Winter is the longest food dearth of the year combined with cold temperature extremes, and many natural colonies fail in this high-stakes game. It is the beekeeper's job to improve the odds for his colonies through deliberate fall preparations.

Optimum colony configuration

I said in Chapter 2 that in a typical winter nest the clustering bees cover and occupy open cells, while immediately above them is stored pollen and honey. Achieving this base configuration is crucially important for the win-

Weather protection

The ability of colonial honey bees to survive winter is a marvel of biology. One of the ways they do this in nature is choose nest cavities that have good insulating properties and small entrances. Unfortunately, the ¾-inch stock lumber used in today's bee hives has less insulating power than a hollow tree, and cracks between supers can afford entry to chilling drafts. Again, it's the beekeeper's job to compensate for these deficiencies.

Having said that, it is normal for colonies in Langstroth hives to overwinter in North America without special insulation. The only exceptions are in the northernmost prairie states and prairie provinces of Canada where beekeepers pack their hives in insulating materials (Fig. 106) or else move them into specially-designed overwintering buildings. For the rest of the continent, less drastic measures will suffice.

Severe wind exposure can be more damaging than extreme low tem-

Figure 106. Beekeepers in cold climates, like these in Nova Scotia, adopt special measures to improve bee winter survival. This pack contains twelve single-body hives, wrapped in insulation material and sharing a common lid.

Figure 107. A block of wood between the inner and outer covers helps vent warm, moist air outside the hive.

peratures. If you live in an area with high winds, you should provide your hives a windbreak. For all but the warmest parts of the country it is advisable to reduce hive entrances to an inch or two. Make sure hives are located in high, sunny locations with good drainage so that they don't sit in cool, damp air. Make sure hive entrances lean forward so rain water can drain out. Provide some sort of upper ventilation in your hives so that warm, most air from the cluster can vent out; I use a block of wood between my inner and outer covers (Fig. 107). If you use screen hive bottoms for varroa mite control (see **Chapter 8**), it is advisable to close them over winter unless you live in a warm area with brood production more or less year-round. Manufacturers provide a corrugated plastic floor that can slide in place for this purpose.

Warm winter days

During warm days in winter you will see bees flying. Bees defecate and forage for water during these so-called cleansing flights. You may see them collecting grain dusts and other unusual sources of vegetable protein. It is also normal to see a sprinkling of dead bees on the ground or snow in front

Figure 108. Checking to see if an overwintering colony is still alive

of hives. If there is a hive from which no bees are flying on such a day, it is worth an extra look. You can find out if a colony is alive by pressing your ear flat against the wall of the hive and giving it a sharp thump with your hand (Fig. 108). You will immediately hear a buzz from within which quickly subsides. The absence of sound indicates that the colony is dead. Open it up, brush out the dead bees, and store the equipment for use next spring.

Warm days are also a good opportunity to heft each hive from the back to appraise its comparative weight. Light colonies should be fed immediately with a heavy 2:1 syrup. It's important to remember that clustering bees are relatively immobile and any syrup you feed must be placed immediately on top of the cluster. For this reason, the method of choice is plastic pails with perforated lids as described in **Chapter 3**, **Feeders**.

Chapter 8
Honey Bee Disorders, Parasites, and Nest Invaders

I do believe, induced by potent circumstances,
that thou art mine enemy . . .

William Shakespeare, *King Henry VIII*

The honey bee nest represents a rich trove of resources, not only to the beekeeper who is content with a sustainable harvest from his tenants, but also to a number of pathogens, parasites, and nest scavengers who have no such benevolent restraints. Honey bee health maintenance is a big component of beekeeping, and it's safe to say the job hasn't gotten easier. There is an old list of familiar bee diseases, and that list has grown in recent years due to the increase in man-assisted global movement of organisms of all kinds. Nowadays, one cannot be a successful beekeeper without knowledge of the major honey bee disorders and the methods for their environmentally responsible management.

Integrated pest management

The regular use of synthetic chemicals inside bee hives began in America shortly after the 1940s with the introduction of Terramycin antibiotic to prevent bacterial brood diseases. This limited pharmacopeia expanded in the latter part of that century after the successive introductions of tracheal mites in 1984, varroa mites in 1987, and small hive beetles in 1998. Scientists and regulatory agencies responded quickly to test and approve a small arsenal of in-hive pesticides targeting these pests, and today it is standard practice to employ any number of these chemicals inside hives of living honey bees. The efficacy of these chemicals is generally good, and it is no question that they have saved the lives of countless bee colonies.

It is equally true that the early 21st century is a time of heightened awareness of the risks of acutely toxic pesticides. In the case of beekeeping, there are studies showing that in-hive chemicals used to control hive invaders are themselves harmful to the honey bees they are designed to protect. The specter of chemical-resistance in pest populations, long known in other sectors of agriculture, has appeared in beekeeping in the form of antibiotic-resistant bacteria and pesticide-resistant parasites. As a final consideration, one must be mindful of chemical residues in the environment and agricultural products. Pesticide use in beekeeping is especially unsavory given honey's reputation as a wholesome, natural food. This reputation in the marketplace is both priceless and fragile.

In short, a growing body of evidence biologic, ecologic, economic, social, and ethical demonstrates that it makes good sense to employ pest management practices that reduce our reliance on acute toxins. In this chapter I emphasize pest control practices that minimize chemical inputs. I also acknowledge that pesticides can be efficacious and their risks minimal when they are used lawfully, according to manufacturers' recommendations. Nevertheless, pesticides should always be thought of as a last recourse after a string of prior measures.

That last statement implies that we can know when the time for the last recourse has arrived; in other words, what level of pest infestation warrants a rescue pesticide application? This question brings us to the pest control philosophy and practice called *integrated pest management* (IPM), and that crucial pest level is called variously the *economic* threshold, *treatment* threshold, or *action* threshold. For a given pest or crop system the treatment threshold is a specific number – a pest number, density, or level of damage – derived by research. As long as pest levels stay below the treatment threshold, it is not necessary to use an acutely toxic pesticide. Rather than treating at the first sign of a problem, the objective now becomes keeping pest levels below the treatment threshold, and this is done by a variety of means including genetic host resistance against the pest, cultural practices that resist the pest, and beneficial organisms that parasitize or prey upon the pest. The most mature IPM programs integrate more than one component because research has shown that pest populations are best controlled when they are attacked at more than one point in their life cycle. For those disorders for which treatment thresholds and confirmed non-chemical practices are known, a beekeeper is equipped to control pests and diseases with little or no inputs of acutely toxic pesticides.

Diseases of brood

American foulbrood

This is historically the most damaging disease of honey bees. It is a disorder restricted to brood, but adult bees play an important role in the disease cycle by spreading the highly-durable and long-lived spores. The causative agent is a bacterium, *Paenibacillus larvae larvae*. Owing to its ease of spread and high infectivity, American foulbrood (AFB) management centers around prevention and the destructive elimination of positive colonies. AFB was the motivation behind the formation of state bee inspection programs in the early 20th century and remains a chief concern for regulators of interstate and international bee movement.

The disease cycle begins when a larva ingests spores in contaminated food. Inside the larva's gut the bacterial spores germinate into an active vegetative stage which multiplies rapidly, penetrates the gut wall, and invades body tissues. The immature bee dies after it is capped, usually as an elongated prepupa, but sometimes as a pupa. Dead brood have a characteristic chocolate-brown color. If the immature died as a pupa, its tongue will be sticking upward toward the cell roof (Fig.109). There is a sulfurous odor of decay, reminiscent of a chicken house. The most decisive field symptom is the so-called "ropy test." If you find a suspicious cell of brood, take a small stick and twirl it around inside the brood cell. When you withdraw it, the brood is stringy and ropes out an inch or more (Fig. 110).

If a colony does not remove the brood while it is freshly dead, the dead immature continues drying and the vegetative bacteria are gradually re-

Figure 109. Brood that dies from AFB in the pupal stage will have its tongue extending toward the cell roof.

placed by the long-lived spores. Eventually, the brood dries down to a hard brittle scale that adheres tightly to the cell floor, each of which houses billions of spores (Fig.111). These scales are difficult for bees to remove, and they persist in the colony as potent reservoirs of disease. Spores are spread by adult bees to all surfaces of the hive. They are also spread between colonies by the robbing activity of adults and careless handling by the beekeeper. Once a colony is at the scale stage, there is little hope of recovery for the present inmates, and the equipment is a hazard to future occupants.

The virulence and persistence of AFB are the reasons most states require destruction of infected hives by burning. In other words, there is no recognized treatment threshold; instead, there is a zero tolerance policy. If you find a colony with AFB, the most conservative course of action is destructive burning. Close the entrance and staple together all supers. Place the hive, bees and all, in a shallow pit, burn the hive completely in a brisk fire, covering the ashes with dirt. By burning the colony in a pit you contain the spreading honey and melting beeswax that would otherwise attract robber bees and spread the disease. It is sometimes possible to salvage supers and

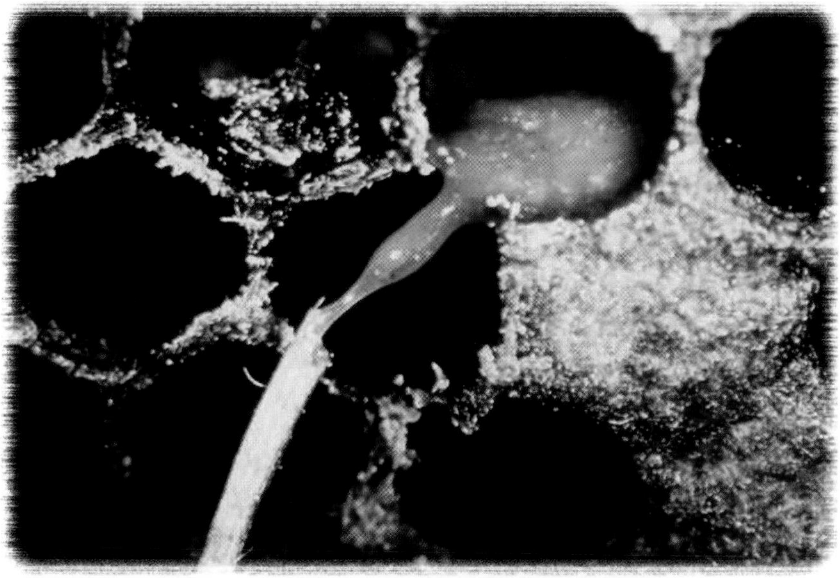

Figure 110. The ropy test is the definitive field test of AFB.

Figure 111. AFB scales are seen in many of these cells. The comb is turned upside down to permit sunlight to strike the floor.

other large hive parts by scorching their interiors with a propane torch; however, the contaminated frames are not salvageable and must be burned.

There are two antibiotics registered for use in the United States for preventing AFB - Terramycin® and Tylosin®. Each is mixed and delivered to the bee colony according to manufacturer's directions (Fig. 120). It is an off-season treatment, limited to early season at least four weeks before the first marketable nectar flow or to fall after the last marketable honey flow. These timing restrictions are designed to prevent antibiotic residues in honey. It is important to stress that these drugs are for preventing disease, not treating disease. Their killing activity is limited to vegetative bacteria; thus, they can intercept early-stage infections, prevent spore formation and disrupt an incipient disease cycle, but they cannot kill spores. If, therefore, a hive has a history of even one successful disease cycle that means there are potentially billions of spores on any hive surface. The continuation of the disease cycle and expression of symptoms are held in check by the repeated application of antibiotic. This is a non-sustainable situation that leads predictably to antibiotic-resistant bacteria and drug residues in honey.

There is a better way to control AFB. In fact, sustainable AFB management is one of the biggest success stories of IPM, specifically IPM components employing cultural control and genetic host resistance.

Since the spread of the causative bacterium, *Paenibacillus larvae larvae*, depends exclusively on mechanical transport, the chief management tactic is simple common-sense sanitation. A zero-tolerance approach is economical in the long term. If you see a brood comb with AFB, it should be burned immediately. It's a good habit to heat-sterilize your hive tool between colonies. It's a good idea to avoid feeding your colonies pollen or honey from unknown sources. Be cautious when buying used equipment that you don't introduce combs with AFB scales into your operation.

The second critical component of sustainable AFB management is the use of so-called *hygienic* queens. Bee stocks genetically selected for hygienic behavior are capable of detecting abnormal cells of brood, uncapping them, and removing their compromised contents. The beauty of this trait is that it is generic, that is, effective against a number of brood disorders including AFB, European foulbrood, chalkbrood, varroa mites, and small hive beetles. Numerous queen suppliers in the US advertise hygienic stock. Needless to say, we will be discussing hygienic queens again in the pages to follow. But for now it is sufficient to say that an IPM program centered on hygienic queens and sanitary hive handling practices will reduce your incidents of American foulbrood to near zero.

European foulbrood

European foulbrood (EFB) is a brood disease caused by the bacterium *Melissococcus plutonius*. The symptoms are superficially similar to AFB, but the inherent virulence less; therefore it is important that beekeepers be able to distinguish the two.

The disease cycle begins when young larvae eat food contaminated with *M. plutonius*. The bacteria multiply in the gut, eventually achieving densities sufficient to compete with the larva for nutrients. The infected larvae respond with increased appetites. In a normal colony the nurse bees respond by ejecting larvae with abnormally high appetites and thereby keep the disease in check. But in situations where the ratio of nurse bees to brood is high (ie., just prior to foraging season) it is possible that infected larvae will be accommodated. In these conditions the infected larvae may persist in the colony without expressing symptoms visible to the beekeeper. This dynamic explains why the disease can spontaneously appear after the onset of foraging season: nurse bees switch to foraging duties and the infected larvae receive less in-

Figure 112. Larvae dead from EFB

dividual attention, express symptoms, and die. Thus, EFB in a strong colony can be self-limiting. The bacterium does not form long-lived spores like the AFB bacterium, but it can persist in the feces of infected larvae.

Larvae dead from EFB look superficially like larvae dead from AFB. However, there are important differences, summarized in the table. Larvae that die from EFB die before the quiescent prepupal stage; this means that they die young while they are still mobile in their cells and therefore appear in a variety of twisted postures (Fig. 112). Their color can range from off-white, to grey, to black. If they are black, it is often possible to see the white respiratory tubes through the translucent skin.

EFB can be prevented with the same antibiotic regimen indicated for AFB. It can also be prevented with the same IPM regimen of sanitary hive handling practices and hygienic queens. There is evidence that donated brood and supplemental feeding help a colony overcome the disease. The addition of young brood (open cells) provides young larvae that compete with infected larvae

A comparison of field symptoms of American foulbrood and European foulbrood

Character	American foulbrood	European foulbrood
Brood stage at death	After capped	Before capped
Brood posture	Uniformly flat on cell floor; tongue extended upward in pupae	Variable, a twisted appearance
Color	Chocolate brown to black	Off-white, yellow, grey, to black; white respiratory tubes often visible
Ropy?	Very ropy, up to one inch	Little or none
Odor?	Sulfurous, like a chicken house	Sour or none
Scales?	Hard, brittle, tightly adhered to cell floor	Rubbery, easy to remove
Appearance of cappings	Sunken, often perforated	Not applicable as brood are dead before capping

for attention from nurse bees so that sick larvae die sooner and are eliminated. Likewise, the addition of supplemental syrup stimulates brood production and the competitive elimination of infected larvae.

Chalkbrood

This is the third brood disease on our list, and this one is caused by a pathogenic fungus, *Ascosphaera apis*. The disease cycle begins when a larva encounters the fungal spores, either by direct contact or ingestion. If the larva is subsequently cooled, the fungal spores germinate

Figure 113. Larvae dead from chalkbrood at first swell and turn white, superficially resembling a piece of chalk.

and the fungus aggressively invades its gut and competes with the larva for nutrients. If the larva dies, the fungus invades its body and eventually forms sporulating bodies that propagate the pathogen. A larva dead from chalkbrood turns dull white, hardens, and swells to accommodate the entire cell, taking on the namesake appearance of a piece of chalk (Fig. 113). Fungal sporulating bodies form a black/grey patina on the surface of the dead brood (Fig. 114). These chalkbrood mummies are loose in their cells and easily removed by bees; hence, the first sign for a beekeeper may be piles of mummies on the bottom board or hive entrance (Fig. 115).

There are no chemical controls registered for chalkbrood, so IPM carries the day by default. Fortunately, the disease is not highly infective or virulent, and damaging outbreaks rare.

Chalkbrood disease can be prevented through good management and the use of hygienic queens. First, bearing in mind that fungi of all types thrive best in cool, damp conditions, it makes sense to maintain hives in conditions that are not cool or damp. This hearkens back to recommendations I made in **Chapter 4**, **Apiary locations**, specifically, to place hives in spots

Figure 114. As the chalkbrood disease progresses, larvae take on a grey or black patina of fungal fruiting bodies.

Figure 115. Chalkbrood mummies are easily removed from the cells and bees will dump them at the hive entrance.

that are protected from wind and avoid spots that are low and accumulate heavy, damp air. It's a good idea to provide upper hive ventilation (Fig. 107). It's also a good idea to replace brood combs systematically; every five years is a general consensus. Culling old brood combs removes accumulated toxins and pathogens and contributes to disease control and optimal brood production. There are also management mistakes that contribute to chalkbrood disease, the most common being any manipulation that results in more brood than the nurse bees can cover and keep warm. This can happen in spring when the beekeeper is making nucs or splits to replace winter losses. If the beekeeper gives too much brood to a small colony, the brood on the nest periphery may get chilled at night and contract chalkbrood disease.

Superimposed on all these recommendations is the use of hygienic queens. Chalkbrood is one of the many disorders that hygienic bees can detect and remove. An apiary-wide use of hygienic queens combined with good management will keep chalkbrood on the beekeeper's list of minor problems.

Sacbrood

This is a relatively minor and rare disease of brood. It is caused by a virus, and like with all viruses there are no remedial medications. Visible symptoms are limited to brood in the elongated prepupal phase. The dead larvae are flaccid and watery, curved in a shape resembling a Chinese slipper, and have darkened heads (Fig. 116).

Hygienic queens and regular brood comb culling can be expected to keep sacbrood a negligible problem. If the disease occurs, it's a good idea to replace the queen with another hygienic queen in the event the original queen had poor resistance to this disease.

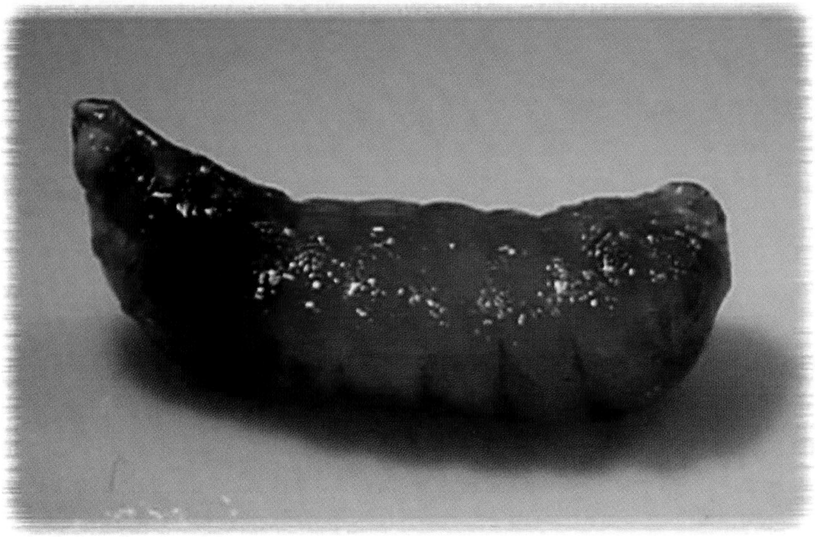

Figure 116. Prepupa dead from sacbrood disease

Diseases of adults

Nosema

This is historically considered the most serious disease of adult bees. It is caused by a single-celled protozoan *Nosema apis* which exists in two stages – a moderately long-lived spore and a replicating vegetative stage. If an adult ingests spores, they germinate into the vegetative stage which penetrates the cells lining the bee's gut. Nosema rarely kills a bee outright, but instead triggers a host of associated morbidities, including reduced lifespan, reduced output of brood food and, in the case of queens, increased supersedure rates. The collective result is colonies with low populations and sluggish spring buildup. The disease is generally regarded as more damaging in cold climates or under conditions that promote a protracted period of confinement in the hive.

A second species, *Nosema ceranae*, a natural associate of the eastern honey bee *Apis cerana*, has emerged in recent years as a problem in Europe where it is suspected of causing large-scale colony dwindling. *N. ceranae* is known to occur in the US as well where it probably contributes to similar occurrences of colony morbidity. Being a non-natural parasite on *A. mellifera*, there is concern that *N. ceranae* may have elevated virulence toward the western honey bee – a pattern typical with many non-natural parasite relationships.

There are no IPM approaches specifically targeted against Nosema disease, and its management centers on the maintenance of robust colonies and biennial application of the antibiotic Fumagilin® B. The medication is mixed in sugar syrup, according to manufacturer's recommendations, and fed to bees in spring and fall. As with any medication, it is applied in the off-season when there is no chance it will contaminate marketable honey.

Viruses

Interest in bee viruses has increased in recent years in association with the worldwide spread of parasitic varroa mites. Evidence mounts that a significant fraction of the bee morbidity associated with varroa is in fact due to viruses that the mites vector or activate.

Three of the most visibly discernible adult bee viruses are chronic bee paralysis, Kashmir bee virus, and deformed wing virus. Field symptoms for the first two are generally indistinguishable: the bees lose body hair, taking on a black shiny appearance, and their movement is disorganized and trembling. Bees expressing the third virus have wings wrinkled longitudinally (Fig. 117).

As I mentioned above for sacbrood, there are no remedial chemicals available for bee viruses, so their management centers on brood comb culling and the requeening of colonies that express symptoms. It is also apparent that management of varroa mites constitutes indirect management of bee viruses.

Figure 117. A bee expressing symptoms of deformed wing virus

Parasitic mites

Tracheal mites

The mite *Acarapis woodi* has a long and perplexing history in the annals of beekeeping. It is the suspected culprit of the infamous Isle of Wight bee epidemic in England in the early 20th century. It was in response to this epidemic that the US Congress passed the Honeybee Act of 1922 which closed our borders to bee imports for the next 83 years. The perplexity of this mite's history involves its variable effects on bees and inconclusive evidence for its direct involvement in the Isle of Wight epidemic. What is not controversial is its clear association with large-scale bee deaths in North America after its arrival here in 1984. The late 1990s and early 21st century saw a general decline in bee morbidity from this mite, and today tracheal mites are considered a moderate to severe problem in cold climates and moderate to minor problem in warm climates.

A. woodi is a microscopic mite that lives and reproduces in the breathing tubes, or tracheae, of adult bees. Bee-to-bee transfer occurs in the nest when the mite climbs the hairs of its present host and jumps onto another. Young bees are preferred. The mite makes its way to the tracheal opening,

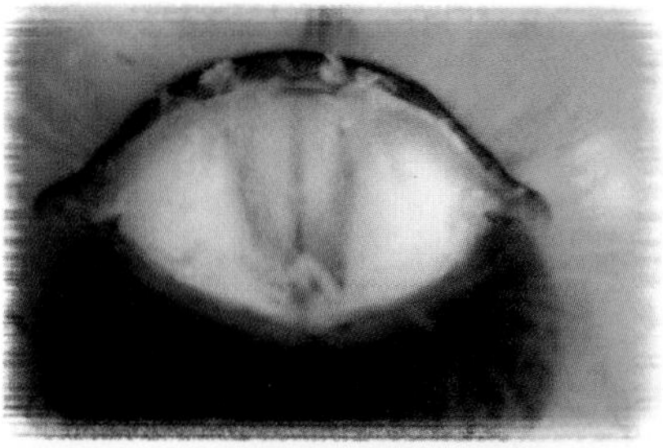

Figure 118a. The thoracic tracheal trunks of a bee negative for *Acarapis woodi*

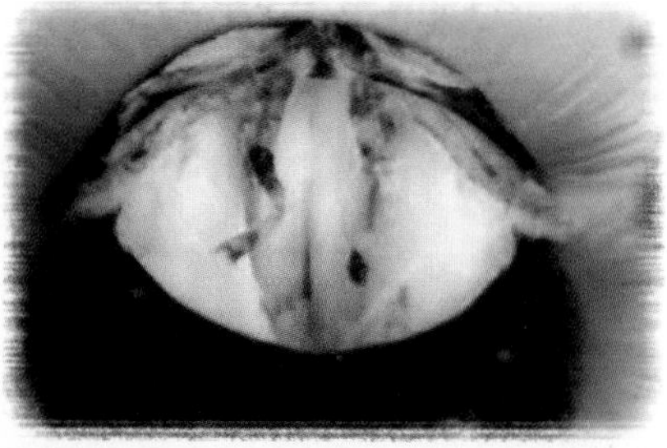

Figure 118b. In this positive specimen, the tracheal trunks are clearly blotched with dark scar tissue.

or *spiracle*, on the bee's thorax. It enters the tracheal tube, pierces the wall of the trachea to feed on the host's blood, and produces a clutch of eggs and brood. The immature mites develop in the protected environment of the tracheal tube; females mate and exit the trachea to resume the cycle. The tracheae of infested bees can be mechanically blocked with the mites and the tracheal walls pierced and discolored with scar tissue (Fig. 118).

Field symptoms of tracheal mites tend to occur in late winter/early spring and range from non-detectable to catastrophic, depending on the percentage of bees infested and the average parasite load per bee. A bee infestation rate of 25% (percent of bees positive) in fall is considered damaging; hence control efforts should aim to stay far below this level. At its worst, tracheal mite-infested bees are incapable of forming contiguous winter clusters, and disjointed clumps of them appear on different areas of the combs. The bees will crawl in the grass around the hive entrance, incapable of flying (Fig. 119). Once a colony is expressing symptoms like this, it is unlikely that it will survive much longer. Because of the crawling and wandering behavior of terminally-infected individuals, the most common symptom of a colony killed by tracheal mites is simply an empty hive.

There are two pesticides registered for control of tracheal mites. One is pelletized menthol crystals sold in pre-measured packets designed to fit on the top bars of brood combs. Evaporative action releases the menthol fumes which kill and desiccate the mites. A second pesticide is Mite-Away II® – an absorbent pad impregnated with formic acid. As with all pesticide

Figure 119. In the terminal phase of tracheal mite infestation, bees are seen crawling in the grass in front of hives.

formulations, menthol and formic acid must be used exactly after manufacturer's recommendations. An effective, low-toxic option is the so-called "extender patty" – a simple mixture of vegetable oil and powdered sugar. The ingredients are mixed together to the consistency of cake icing and delivered to the top bars of brood combs on wax paper (Fig. 120). As bees try to reach the sugar, they become covered with the oil, which serves as a behavioral disruptant to mites in the host-seeking phase. Extender patties are effective at reducing tracheal mite densities and have the added benefit of

Figure 120. This beekeeper uses an ice cream scoop to deliver extender patty material to his colonies. The white powder is confectioner's sugar mixed with Terramycin® antibiotic for preventing bacterial brood diseases.

being harmless to the environment and the honey bee hosts. They can be applied in spring and fall.

There are cultural practices that help keep tracheal mites below the 25% damage level. Although host-seeking mites prefer young bees, it is the older bees that host larger numbers of mites and serve as parasite reservoirs in the colony. Any hive manipulation that reduces the ratio of old to young bees can be expected to reduce the number of mites in the colony. Young vigorous queens that produce a high output of young bees will accomplish this. So does making splits in spring, especially when the splits are made in mid-day when older bees are out foraging and the new splits moved immediately to a new site to avoid returning foragers.

Varroa mites

The varroa mite, *Varroa destructor*, is recognized as the most damaging pest of the western honey bee *Apis mellifera* in the world today. Its story is one of the negative ecologic consequences that can happen when organisms are moved outside their native ranges. *V. destructor* is a natural parasite of the eastern honey bee, *Apis cerana*, on which its damage is limited to drone brood and its overall impact on the colony negligible. Man-assisted movement of the western honey bee into eastern Asia provided varroa the chance to move onto a new host. On the western honey bee, varroa parasitizes worker brood as well as drone, and this bee has little behavioral or physiological resistance to this alien parasite. The presence of varroa on *Apis mellifera* became alarmingly obvious in Europe in the 1960s, and today it is found everywhere honey bees are kept except Australia and a smattering of oceanic islands. Throughout much of that range, an infestation by varroa has meant a death sentence for a colony of western honey bees unless a beekeeper intervenes with treatment, but in recent years there is evidence that a degree of genetic resistance in *Apis mellifera* is emerging.

Varroa has been the focus of a huge research effort world-wide for almost

Figure 121. The mite *Varroa destructor* attacks both adult bees (two on bee in foreground) and larvae (background).

Figure 122. Varroa are monitored with a piece of sticky paper placed below an 8-mesh screen. The whole assembly is slid into the hive entrance. After 1-3 days the screen is removed and number of mites retrieved in 24 hours calculated.

40 years. Consequently, there are several well thought-out IPM approaches to its management. Sadly, the spread of varroa mites has also been the occasion for much chemical abuse in the beekeeping industry. Beekeepers who are either careless or ignorant or irresponsible have used any number of chemicals – lawful or not – in misadvised attempts to control the mite.

V. destructor is a relatively large mite, visible to the unaided eye. It parasitizes both adult bees and brood (Fig. 121). The life cycle begins when a gravid female enters an open cell of brood. After the larva is capped and transforms to the prepupal phase, the female mite moves onto the abdomen of the prepupa, chews a wound in its integument, and lays eggs near the feeding site. One son and several daughter mites emerge, mature, and mate. The foundress mite keeps the wound in the abdomen open to provide a feeding site for her young. If the bee survives this trauma, it emerges from its cell and the mated daughter mites emerge with it to disperse and renew the cycle. The bee's health is inevitably compromised. The individual suffers from mechanical injury, reduced blood volume, reduced blood protein and any number of viruses and bacteria. The net result is reduced individual longevity which, when compounded across the colony, spells a general waning and collapse. Mite depredation is most severe in late season when brood area is naturally declining. In these situations a large number of mites are competing for a shrinking pool of brood. It is not uncommon at this stage for multiple foundress mites to invade and parasitize one brood cell. At this point the colony begins an exponential and irrevocable decline. As with tracheal mites, the most common symptom of a mite-killed colony is simply an empty hive. The biggest difference is that colony death with varroa is typically in late-season, not early.

There are two research-derived treatment thresholds for varroa in the US, one for the Southeast and one for the Northwest. Each is based on a mite sampling technique called the "sticky sheet," the parts of which are available in numerous bee supply catalogs. It is a sheet of sticky paper placed below a screen of 8-mesh hardware cloth. The whole assembly is slid into the hive on the bottom board (Fig. 122). Mites that fall onto the floor are trapped on the adhesive. The hardware cloth protects bees from entanglement. After 1-3 days the sticky sheet is withdrawn and the number of mites counted and adjusted to yield mites caught per 24 hours.

Armed with a treatment threshold, the objective now becomes keeping varroa mites below the treatment threshold. This can be done with a variety of chemical-free IPM practices; again, the more simultaneously employed the better. As I mentioned in **Chapter 3**, **Bottom board**, screen hive floors are known to reduce colony mite levels, as well as increase brood production (Fig. 19). Genetic host resistance exists in bees in numerous forms – hygienic behavior, self- or nestmate-grooming, accelerated development time, and likely other physiological or behavioral characters so far unknown. Hygienic lines and Russian lines have shown special promise for their measurable varroa mite resistance. Drone brood trapping is a useful way to remove a large fraction of the mite population, taking advantage of the fact that varroa mites prefer drone brood. Foundation milled to drone size is available for this purpose. A comb of open drone cells is inserted in the brood nest, and once the drone brood is capped, it is removed and frozen to kill mites (and unavoidably the brood). The brood is returned to the bees, who will remove and eat the brood, thereby recovering a part

Treatment threshold for varroa mites derived for the Southeast US and Northwest. Values are mites caught per 24 hours on sticky sheets. Pick the value closest to your geography and climate conditions. Mite levels below these numbers do not warrant treatment with an acutely toxic pesticide.		
	Early season	Late season
Southeastern US	1-12 (February)	60-190 (August)
Northwest US	12 (April)	23 (August)

of their nutrient investment. This method is helpful as long as drone-rearing season is under way. Another proven method of mite IPM is dusting with powdered sugar. The method is laborious, but effective. The operator removes every comb in the brood nest, dusting the bees on each side with powdered sugar. This triggers a frenzied grooming response by the bees which dislodges large numbers of mites. It is presumed most effective if the operation is conducted over screen floors, so that dislodged mites fall out and away from the bees.

It's a good idea to sample hives with sticky sheets every four weeks or so during the active season, especially in the late summer weeks preceding fall. Ideally, IPM measures such as those described above will keep varroa mites below treatment thresholds indefinitely. But, if mites do achieve treatment threshold, then it is warranted to use an acutely toxic mite pesticide according to manufacturer's recommendations. There have been numerous changes in recent years in the availability of registered varroa pesticides. They generally fall into three camps: synthetic nerve poisons such as Apistan® (fluvalinate) and Check-Mite® (coumaphos), concentrated botanical oils such as Api-Life VAR® and Apiguard®, or other organic active ingredients such as Sucrocide® (sucrose octanoate esters) and formic acid. In general, natural compounds rather than synthetic have reduced likelihood of causing pesticide resistance in pests.

After the lawful application of a varroa pesticide, it's back to IPM business as usual. It is to be hoped that with unwavering application of IPM practices, in combination with increasing genetic host resistance in our bees, the use of acute toxins will decrease steadily in the years ahead.

Nest scavengers

Wax moths

The greater wax moth, *Galleria mellonella*, is an Old World associate of the western honey bee that simply moved with its host to North America. In the natural scheme of things, *G. mellonella* is a beneficial member of the honey bee's community. It is a nest scavenger, a consumer of old combs and the organic detritus therein. It cleans out abandoned nest cavities, including any associated disease spores, and renders them clean and ready for the next occupants. The trouble happens when wax moths expand their activity into beekeepers' hives. At its worst, unchecked wax moth activity can destroy entire supers of combs and frames, rendering them into a mass of webbing and moth feces (Fig. 123).

The life cycle of wax moths begin when mated female moths gain entry into the bee nest, usually at night. If the nest is occupied by live inmates, the moths may or may not be challenged. Once inside, the moth deposits eggs in any crack or crevice small enough to exclude the policing activity of bees. The tiny larva emerges and immediately begins foraging on the protein litter in the bee nest, expanding through several stages to a mature larva about one inch long (Fig. 124). The larva seeks a protected spot,

Figure 123. Combs ruined by wax moths and moth cocoons on the end bars of frames

Figure 124. Mature wax moth larva

chewing a cavity into wood if necessary, and spins a tough silken cocoon and pupates. As long as the bee colony is strong, it can sustain a moderate number of these more-or-less cryptic larvae on the nest periphery. It is only when a colony is terminally weakened that moth larvae increase dramatically and forage at will in the center of the brood nest.

There are two arenas of concern with wax moths: moth activity in living colonies and moth activity in stored equipment. The activity in living colonies is quickly dispensed with. In short – wax moths are a secondary problem, not a primary problem. Encountering a colony rife with wax moths, a beekeeper's first question should be: Why was this colony so weak in the first place? It can usually be traced to a warm-season problem such as queenlessness or varroa mites. At this stage, there is nothing to do but shake out any remaining bees into other colonies and try to salvage the equipment.

Stored combs are at risk because there are no bees present to do the policing. At this juncture, there are two sub-arenas in wax moth management: moth management in honey combs and moth management in brood combs. It is chiefly combs with a history of brood production that are at risk. Honey combs can be satisfactorily protected non-chemically by par-

Figure 125. An open-sided shed with supers stored criss-cross fashion to permit air and daylight to penetrate combs

tially exposing them to air and daylight (Fig. 125). One year I visited the apiary of the Warsaw Agricultural University in Poland. The apiary managers have a shed dedicated to comb storage. The shed is well-roofed and the walls screened to permit entry of air and daylight. Inside are racks made specially to hold combs – without the super boxes – and expose them to the elements. Moth damage is nil, especially with combs used exclusively for honey production. Depending on the thoroughness of exposure to air and daylight, even brood combs can be stored this way.

Beekeepers can also use a chemical fumigant to kill moths in stacked supers. The product is paradichlorobenzene, an aromatic compound akin to – but not the same as – traditional moth balls. The supers must be stacked tightly and covered. Fumigant crystals are introduced to the top and throughout the stack, according to manufacturer's recommendations. After fumigation, as long as supers remain protected from re-entry of moths, the combs should be safe throughout the storage period. Supers must be aired thoroughly before they are returned to living colonies.

Small hive beetles

The small hive beetle (SHB), *Aethina tumida*, is one of the most recent additions to the list of North American pests of beekeeping. Like wax moths, it is classified as a nest scavenger, and like wax moths, it is kept at bay in colonies that are strong. It departs from wax moths, however, in the fact that it is capable of destroying colonies that are simply *relatively* weak, not just *terminally* weak. In other words, the smallest colony in your apiary, even if it is otherwise healthy and robust, is at risk of SHB, as long as the other colonies in the apiary are much stronger. In the Southeast, small hive beetles have proven themselves a major pest in colonies that are managed to be small, ie., observation hives or nucleus colonies used by commercial queen producers to house queens on their mating flights (Fig. 126).

The life cycle begins when adults (which are vigorous flyers) enter a colony. The beetles are about ¼-inch long, dark brown, oval, slick and hard (Fig. 127), and they easily resist the defensive advances of the bees. At first, beetle activity is limited to the nest periphery. Females deposit eggs in protected crevices, and the larvae emerge to eat honey, brood, and protein litter and grow through a succession of stages. The larvae must exit the hive to complete their life cycle as pupae in the soil. The larvae superficially resemble wax moth larvae, but beetle larvae are smaller, tougher,

Figure 126. Small hive beetles are especially a problem in unnaturally small colonies such as baby nucs used to commercially produce queens.

Figure 127. Small hive beetle adult (photo: J.D. Ellis)

don't spin webs, and forage openly in daylight (Fig. 128).

As long as the bee colony remains strong, it is possible for it to sustain indefinitely a modest population of SHB at its periphery. Treatment threshold is about 300 adult beetles per colony; beyond this point a colony begins showing measurable declines in bee population and foraging rates. However, the decline becomes terminal once the health of the colony is compromised in any way. At this point beetles begin expanding their activity toward the center of the brood nest. Female beetles deposit eggs directly into brood cells, and the carnivorous larvae grow rapidly on this rich protein diet. The larvae forage freely over the honey combs, and their feeding activity triggers formation of a slime that covers the combs and renders the honey unfit for consumption by man or bee alike (Fig. 129).

An IPM approach to SHB centers around keeping colonies strong, using genetically resistant bees, and trapping beetle adults and larvae. There is evidence that colonies are at special risk whose queens produce brood in a spotty pattern (Fig. 65). Bearing in mind that SHB females deposit eggs

Figure 128. Small hive beetle larvae are not repelled by daylight. Wax moth larvae, in contrast (see Fig. 124), quickly retreat if exposed to light.

Figure 129. Honey covered in slime from SHB activity

inside the walls of brood cells, as well as under the cappings, a spotty brood pattern affords more egg-laying sites. Additionally, a spotty queen will not produce the strong bee populations necessary to ward off SHB depredations. And finally, there is evidence that hygienic bee stocks can detect and remove brood cells with SHB eggs.

There are at least two SHB traps on the market. The "Hood" trap (Fig. 130) targets SHB adults and is comprised of a plastic reservoir attached to the bottom bar of a brood comb. The reservoir is filled with vinegar and vegetable oil; the vinegar has a modest attractant property and the oil makes it difficult for beetles to escape. The entrance to the Hood trap, although not strictly one-way, nevertheless impedes beetle exit, especially if beetles are made slick with oil. The "West" SHB trap (Fig. 131) is designed to intercept SHB larvae as they move to the hive floor in their exodus to the soil outside the hive. The trap integrates into the design of the bottom board and consists of a reservoir to receive vegetable oil. A plastic grid superimposed over the reservoir protects bees from drowning.

Small hive beetle IPM contributes the only example in beekeeping of the IPM tenet of "beneficial organisms." This category constitutes organ-

Figure 130. The in-hive Hood trap for adult SHB. It fastens onto the bottom bar of a frame.

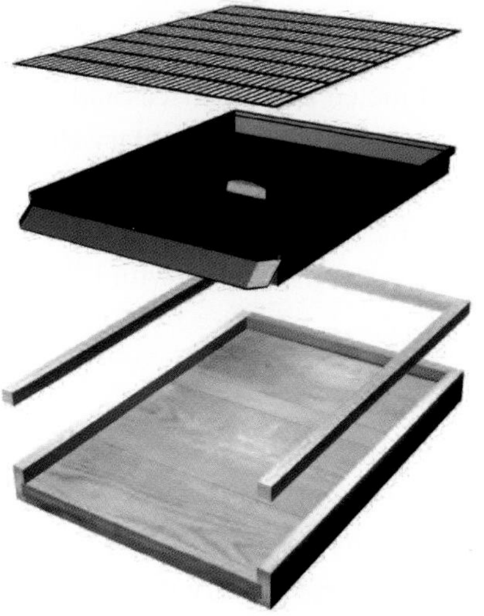

Figure 131. The West SHB trap chiefly targets SHB larvae.

isms deliberately introduced into the system for their predatory or parasitic action on the pest. In the case of SHB, there is a good research track record for the use of carnivorous nematodes that prey upon SHB larvae as they move into soil for pupation. Beneficial nematodes are available from organic gardening supply companies where they are marketed for control of a number of soil-dwelling insect pests.

Chemical control of SHB has had a mixed track record. In some states the same Check-Mite® strip (coumaphos) used to control varroa mites is registered for use against SHB. A strip is cut in half and stapled to the bot-

Figure 132. Check-Mite® (coumaphos) strip used for SHB control

tom of a piece of corrugated cardboard or plastic (Fig. 132). The assembly is placed on the bottom board; beetles are attracted to the crevices and enter them, receiving a toxic exposure to the chemical. A complementary chemical treatment is the use of Gard Star® (40% permethrin) in soil in front of the hives to target SHB larvae. In my opinion, the efficacy of these treatments is doubtful and a beekeeper could do as well or better with IPM.

Non-infectious disorders

Queenlessness

After having written more pages about diseases and parasites than anything else, it may come as a surprise when I say that all of them pale in comparison to the lost productivity represented by queenlessness. I say this because queenlessness is common – you can expect it every year – and its impacts as damaging as any other disorder.

Moreover, it is a growing problem. I mentioned earlier that studies have shown that remedial hive chemicals are themselves harmful to the bees they are intended to protect. Nowhere is this more evident than in the negative effects of chemicals like fluvalinate and coumaphos on queen longevity and performance. Most long-term beekeepers agree that the rise in chemical use has corresponded to a general decline in queen performance approaching almost pandemic proportions. It is not uncommon for a queen to live no more than six months, whereas older beekeeping literature typically cites two years. When queens fail, their colonies respond with the construction of supersedure queens, and given that the process from start to finish is complicated and fraught with peril, it is no surprise that many colonies end up terminally queenless. It is the beekeeper's job to note failing queens, the presence of laying workers (Fig. 4b), the presence of spotty brood (Fig. 65), excess drone cells (Fig. 8), under-sized brood areas, or the absence of brood altogether. As long as a viable worker population persists, it is time to requeen the colony as described in **Chapter 5**, **Requeening**. If the worker population is no longer viable, then it is time to cut your losses and retire the colony as described in **Chapter 7**, **Achieving optimum colony configuration**.

Robbing

In one sense, the most efficient predator of a honey bee colony is a honey bee colony. Any time a weaker colony is in close proximity to a stronger, there is risk that foragers from the stronger will overwhelm the defenders of the weaker and deplete the weaker of its honey stores. This makes a strong argument for maintaining all colonies in an apiary at a uniform strength, which involves equalizing colonies, solving problems, and all the other management imperatives covered in the previous chapters.

In the early stages of robbing, the foragers from a strong colony will be attracted to the odor of honey emanating from a weak colony, attempt to enter the hive, and if successful, boldly fill their crops with honey from the combs and return to their own hive with the stolen booty. At this stage, robbers can be distinguished by their nervous zig-zag flight pattern, lack of pollen loads, and attraction to any crack or crevice of the hive exuding the odor of honey – not necessarily the hive entrance (Fig. 133). This is a sign for the beekeeper to take immediate corrective action – by closing excess cracks with tape, moving the weak colony to another location, and ultimately solving the underlying problems that made the colony weak in the first place.

There are other common-sense ways to minimize robbing. Most importantly, one must be careful to not spill syrup, expose honey, or unnecessar-

Figure 133. A colony being robbed. Notice how bees are attracted to any crack exuding the odor of honey, not necessarily the hive entrance. Robbers have a nervous zig-zag flight pattern.

ily open colonies during periods of the year when nectar is scarce. The odor of exposed combs is a potent stimulus to robbing during a dearth. Secondly, robbing seems to be aggravated in apiaries in which hive density is "too" high. It is hard to assign an optimum hive density per apiary because it depends on the richness of any local habitat. But, whenever colonies are competing with one another for limited floral resources there is a risk of predatory robbing. In the Southeast it is generally understood that any particular apiary should not exceed 25 colonies.

Visible mutations

One day when I was a youngster I was shocked to discover in one of my apiaries drones *with green eyes* (Fig. 134). It was years later that I

Figure 134. A drone expressing the visible mutation chartreuse

learned that the visible mutation *chartreuse* is just one of many visible honey bee mutations, including ivory eyes, tan eyes, red eyes and cordovan body color. Because drones carry only one set of chromosomes, any recessive genes they carry are expressed because there are no dominant forms to mask them. Hence, visible recessive mutations show up first in drones. Visible mutations are not associated with any economically important traits. For the scientist they are useful in a variety of experiments; for the beekeeper they are interesting and fun to have around.

Predators, vertebrate or otherwise

There is a rather short list of significant honey bee predators, each of which tends to be location-specific. The most important of these is bears.

In certain parts of the country, beekeepers must take precaution against the destructive predatory action of these large mammals. Bears visit apiaries at night, sometimes over a succession of nights, and overturn hives and disassemble them to eat the brood and honey. The scene after a bear raid is chaos – strewn hive parts everywhere. The best precaution against bears is an electric fence (Fig. 135) powered with 12-volt car or solar batteries. Fences are also good precaution if you must place your apiary in pastures with cows or other livestock.

Beekeepers in most parts of the country have intermittent problems with smaller vertebrate predators, chiefly skunks. These nocturnal visitors will scratch the hive entrance in a deliberate ploy to excite the bees (Fig. 136). When the hive defenders rush out to investigate, the skunks eat them with relish, apparently unaffected by the large numbers of stings received in the mouth and throat. Beekeepers report good success at repelling skunks by placing boards in front of hive entrances with nails sticking up out of them, but this is an obvious safety hazard to the beekeeper. I have successfully used individualized hive fences made with stout stakes and chicken wire.

Figure 135. A bear fence in north Georgia electrified with a solar powered battery

Figure 136. The scratchings in the ground at the hive entrance are tell-tale signs of nocturnal visits by a skunk.

The chief insect predator of honey bees is hornets, or "bee wolves" as they are called in Europe (Fig. 137). These artful predators will swoop down on the entrance of a colony, seize a forager in mid-air and take it away to feed its brood. Although their behavior can be conspicuous in an apiary, it is doubtful that hornets exact a large drain on bee populations.

The final insect predator I will mention is ants. Fortunately for us in North America, ants fall into the category of nuisance more than pest. There are a number of ant species that nest in the peripheral parts of hives, such as the space between the inner and outer covers. Even though they are conspicuous, they rarely prey upon live honey bees or their brood. If you have a problem with ants, you can fashion a hive stand that creates a moat of water or oil to create an impassable ant barrier (Fig. 138).

Figure 137. Predatory hornets are a serious problem for this beekeeper in Albania.

Figure 138. This concrete hive stand from Belize is designed to trap rain water to serve as an ant moat.

Pesticides

Earlier in this chapter I discussed the intentional use of pesticides in beekeeping. These compounds are targeted at bee pests that are themselves arthropods – near cousins to insects such as bees. It is no stretch, therefore, to understand that the use of pesticides in hives is risky to the very bees the pesticides are intended to protect. But in this section I concentrate on unintentional pesticide exposure. As bees forage widely in their habitats, it is not uncommon for them to encounter insecticides and other toxins in crops, home gardens, or ornamental plants. Bees are susceptible to most insecticides. The good news is, bee kills from insecticides are generally on the decline thanks to the increasing use of IPM in agriculture, newer "softer" chemicals with lower impact on non-target organisms, and improving public awareness of the value of honey bees and other pollinators. The bad news is, bee kills still happen and a beekeeper must know how to deal with them.

From a beekeeper's perspective there are two kinds of pesticide kills: acute and chronic. The acute kind, although more dramatic and catastrophic, are easier to diagnose. There is no question what happened: the beekeeper returns to his apiary and finds masses of bees dead between the combs, on the hive floors, and on the ground in front of hives (Fig. 139). These kinds of kills indicate a delivery of acute toxin onto hives, usually indirect and unintentional, but regrettably sometimes direct and malicious.

Chronic bee kill is more difficult to diagnose. In some cases the toxin acts immediately upon foragers in the field; the insect dies and simply never returns to the nest. In other cases, an intoxicated forager becomes disoriented in the field and cannot find her way back to the nest. In yet another scenario the forager survives long enough to deliver contaminated pollen or nectar to the nest; a low level of toxin makes its way into the food supply and exerts a damaging effect on brood and adults for weeks afterward. The net result of these scenarios is a "dwindling" of the colony or otherwise inexplicable decline in bee population.

The solution to avoiding pesticide bee kills is the placement of apiaries outside of high-risk areas. It's inadvisable to place an apiary next to a crop or orchard where one can expect regular pesticide inputs – cotton, pecan, or sweet corn, for example. It's similarly inadvisable to place bee hives alongside urban streets that are regularly fogged for mosquitoes.

If one experiences a pesticide bee kill, it may be possible to rehabilitate damaged colonies. The most important thing is to relocate the apiary away

Figure 139. Signs of an acute bee kill are masses of dead bees on the hive floors, between combs, and on the ground in front of hives.

from the source of exposure. The next thing is to appraise whether the queen is still functioning normally and replace her if the answer is no. Cull old combs from the brood nest that may contain contaminated stores and feed syrup and pollen substitute to stimulate production of new comb and brood. Provide combs of emerging brood from other colonies to speed population rebound.

Good neighbor relations is another key to avoiding pesticide kills. By far, the majority of people understand the value of bees and wish no harm upon their beekeeping neighbors. A farmer may apply insecticide to his crop with no regard to his beekeeping neighbor simply because he has never been in the habit of thinking about bees. A jar of free honey, delivered once a year with a smile and a request for prior notification of sprays is good policy. It is possible to temporarily move an apiary to avoid a scheduled spray – or even restrict bee flight for a day by enclosing a hive under bee netting and shade. But these measures are cumbersome and in the end it's best to permanently site apiaries away from high-risk areas.

There are situations in which it is impossible to avoid exposure risk. At these times it's useful to know that not all pesticides are equally damaging to bees. State and provincial extension services publish lists of pesticides and rank them according to acute bee toxicity. Whenever possible, choose a pesticide with comparatively low bee risk. Second, it's useful to know that the formulation of an active ingredient can have tremendous effects on its toxicity. A granular formulation of an active ingredient is almost always safer for bees than the same chemical in a dust or spray. And finally, the timing of application is important. Most active ingredients today have faster degradation times than chemicals of a few decades ago. This means that a spray applied at night or early evening can be expected to control the resident pest population, but be degraded to non-damaging levels by morning when bees resume foraging. In general, daytime sprays on flowering crops are disastrous to honey bees, other pollinators, and other non-target organisms and are quite simply environmentally irresponsible. Knowledge of the basic toxicology covered in this section, along with good neighbor relations will help you avoid most pesticide bee kills.

Epilogue

The strain in her voice was palpable over the telephone. "Ants," she said, "they're *all over* the inner cover, a whole nest of them. Eggs and all. What can I do?" I hesitated a beat, knowing my answer would leave her skeptical and my stock diminished. "Well you know," I said, "Ants don't really cause that much damage. They're just trying to stay warm and that inner cover is nice and toasty." Now it was her turn to pause. "Really?" she said. The contrast between the evidence of her own eyes and my appraisal was hard for her to reconcile.

Fortunately, for this beekeeper the answer really was yes because ants as a rule aren't a problem in Georgia. It's at times like this that I'm reminded that a large part of the learning process with beekeeping – and with anything for that matter – is learning to discriminate what's important from what's not. In these concluding pages I want to distill and present what I consider to be the important things. Remember these principles and apply these principles, and you won't go wrong.

The driving objective of a honey bee colony is to reproduce itself and survive the next winter. This is accomplished by early season swarming, a process which results in two compromised colonies – a weak incipient swarm and a severely depleted mother nest. Both must forage efficiently over the remaining weeks of bloom to procure a winter food supply.

The driving objective of a honey producer is to achieve colonies that are at maximum population on the eve of the major nectar flows. This necessarily pits a beekeeper's interests against the reproductive interests of the colony. Early-season management is essentially the artificial stimulation of colony growth coupled with repression of swarming.

Good queens are central to success. Queens should be replaced at the first sign of failing performance or loss. Beekeepers should adopt queen lines with proven performance and disease- and pest-resistance.

Numerous pests, scavengers, and parasites make a living at the expense of a colony's health. It is the beekeeper's job to monitor pests and intervene with corrective action to keep pests at non-damaging levels. Most bee disorders can be managed effectively without the use of antibiotics or acutely toxic pesticides.

A good neighbor policy pays good dividends. Keep hives away from human and animal traffic and work them in a manner to minimize bee activity that alarms non-beekeeping neighbors.

The quality and perceived wholesomeness of honey is a valuable and fragile market asset. Beekeepers should do everything possible to protect this image, both in perception and reality.

Finally, the theory and practice of beekeeping is dynamic, not static. Our knowledge of bee biology and management grows exponentially with the passing of years. Read, attend bee meetings, share your knowledge, and strive to be a good citizen in the fraternity of beekeepers.

Home at fall of eve the bees come winging;
Happy is their flight and happier their singing.
As the night draws closer and the light grows faint,
Darker still their air-lines 'cross the skies they paint.
Peace is all about them; a calm and healing peace
Fills the heart and fills the mind and brings the soul release.
Nothing now can trouble, nothing can distress,
Here, where bees are humming songs of happiness.

Josephine Morse

Glossary

Abdomen — Posterior major body segment of insects specialized for organs of digestion and reproduction

Acarapis woodi — See *tracheal mite*

Adult — Final developmental stage in insect metamorphosis, characterized by fully-formed wings and ability to reproduce

Aethina tumida — See *small hive beetle*

Africanized bee — An African race of honey bee imported to the New World in the 1950s, well known for its exaggerated defense behavior

American foulbrood — Most serious bacterial disease of brood, highly contagious

Annual colonies — Social insect colonies in which new females overwinter and singly start new colonies every spring (see *perennial colonies*)

Antenna — Sensory organ on insect head for detecting odor and numerous other chemical cues

Apiary — A site of one or more managed bee hives

Apiguard — Miticide used for controlling varroa mites

Api-Life VAR — Miticide used for controlling varroa mites

Apis cerana — Latin name of Eastern honey bee

Apis mellifera — Latin name of Western honey bee

Apistan — A miticide used for controlling varroa mites

Ascosphaera apis — Causative fungus of chalkbrood disease

Balling — Describes an aggressive response by workers toward a queen, usually in association with requeening

Bee brush — A soft brush used for swiping bees off a surface

Bee space — An average distance bees maintain around and between combs and nest surfaces, usually about 3/8 inch

Beeswax — A natural glandular excretion of honey bees, a true wax, malleable, and used by the bees to construct cells and combs

Benton cage — Traditional wooden, 3-compartment mailing cage for queens

Boardman feeder — A design of syrup feeder incorporating a quart or pint jar of syrup inverted into a base at the hive entrance

Bottom bar — The lower horizontal member of a frame

Bottom board — Floor of a bee hive

Bottom supering — The addition of new honey supers beneath previous ones, but above the brood nest, see *Top supering*

Brood — Describes all immature phases of the bee: egg, larvae, prepupae, or pupae

Brood food — Describes exudates produced by nurse bees to feed immatures; includes worker jelly and royal jelly

Brood nest — That part of the bee hive housing the queen and producing brood, the heart of the colony, usually 1-2 9-½-inch *Deep supers*, but sometimes 3 or more 6-5/8-inch *Medium supers*

Cappings — Beeswax coverings of cells; can cover either brood or honey

Cappings scratcher — A tool used in honey processing to remove cappings from low spots on a comb not easily reached by an uncapping knife

Carniolan bee — Honey bee race from east central Europe, widely used in North America

Caste — Describes in social insect colonies the presence of two or more forms within the same sex that differ morphologically or reproductively

Caucasian bee — Honey bee race from Caucasus Mountain region, known for gentleness

Cell — Individual hexagonal unit in a comb; can hold immatures, honey, or pollen

Chalkbrood — A fungal disease of honey bee brood

Chartreuse — One of several visible honey bee mutations, specifically, light green-colored eyes

Check-Mite — A pesticide used for controlling varroa mites and small hive beetles

Chunk honey — A food product consisting of comb honey packaged in a jar surrounded by extracted honey

Cleansing flight — Describes bee flights on warm winter days for the purpose of defecating after protracted periods of confinement

Cluster (*n.*), clustering — An overwintering behavior in which bees move together densely in the center of the nest to generate and conserve heat

Colony — A group of related individuals of a social species inhabiting the same nest

Comb — Fundamental architectural unit of a honey bee nest, each consisting of a panel of repeating and contiguous hexagonal beeswax cells

Comb honey — A food product consisting of whole honey comb

Complete metamorphosis — The developmental progression in insects characterized by egg, larva, pupa, and adult phases

Cooperative brood care — Occurs when females of the same nest cooperatively care for the brood cells of one another

Cordovan — One of several visible honey bee mutations, specifically, light red-colored body and hair

Creamed honey — A food consisting of honey in which the granulation process has been controlled to result in small crystals and a smooth, spreadable product

Dance language — A symbolic language performed by bees by dance, sharing food samples, and vibrating comb that communicates to nestmates the location of new colony resources

Dearth — A period of resource scarcity

Deep super — One of the three standard box sizes comprising a bee hive, 9-½-inches tall and most commonly reserved for housing the queen and producing brood, see *Brood nest*

Dickinson — American poet 19th C., author of *The Pedigree of Honey*

Divides — See *Nucleus colonies*

Division board feeder — A design of syrup feeder shaped roughly like a frame, made of plastic or wood, and holding about 3 quarts of syrup, can be placed anywhere inside a hive body

Drone — A male bee

Drone congretation area — A persistent and highly localized area in which drones are known to aggregate on the wing in wait for queens on their mating flights

Duragilt — Brand name of a plastic-core, beeswax-coated foundation

Economic threshold, *syn.* action threshold, treatment threshold — Size of a pest population shown to result in economic loss unless grower intervenes with an acute control measure

Egg — First developmental stage in insect metamorphosis; reproductive germ cell of female possessing half the species's genetic complement

End bar — One of two vertical members of a frame

Equalizing — Process by which colonies in an apiary are made uniformly strong with bees and brood

Extracted honey — Liquid honey removed from the combs by a honey extractor

Extractor — A device designed to remove honey from uncapped combs with the aid of centrifugal force

Exudate — Compounds released by glands for activity either inside or outside the organism; examples: pheromones, hormones, brood food

Extender patty — A patty of sugar and vegetable oil, mixed to a doughy consistency and used as-is for tracheal mite control or with antibiotics for foulbrood prevention

European foulbrood — Bacterial disease of brood, non-spore forming and generally considered less dangerous than American foulbrood

Eusocial — Describes a species exhibiting (1) cooperative brood care, (2) reproductive division of labor, and (3) overlapping generations

Farrar, C.L. — Scientist who discovered the principle that populous colonies are most efficient at hoarding honey

Fermented honey — Honey, generally >18.6% water content, in which spoilage yeasts have produced alcohols

Food super — Describes one or more supers of honey or syrup, usually medium or shallow, left on top of the brood nest to provide food reserves for the colony

Formic acid — A miticide used for control of tracheal and varroa mites

Foundation — Sheets of beeswax, plastic, or both, imprinted with hexagonal shapes of cells and used to encourage bees to build standardized combs

Fumagilin — Antibiotic used to control Nosema disease

Frame — A wooden structure integral to the Langstroth hive, designed to delimit and support a comb of beeswax and hang suspended from a super

Fume board — A temporary hive lid used in conjunction with bee repellent chemicals to remove bees from supers during harvest

Galleria mellonella — See *wax moth*

Gard Star — Pesticide used for controlling small hive beetle larvae

Genetic resistance — Generally used in context with honey bee characters that are heritable, confer resistance to pests, and respond to artificial selection

Glands — Tissues in an organism specialized for the production of exudates – hormones, pheromones, or nutrient compounds

German black bee — Original honey bee race introduced to North America from northern Europe

Granulation — The process by which liquid honey turns to a semi-solid state of large sugar crystals

Hive — A man-made structure designed to house a honey bee colony

Hive body — See *Deep super*

Hive tool — Tool designed to pry apart hive parts without damaging wood

Honey — The product resulting from bees dehydrating and enzymatically altering plant nectar; a fermentation-resistant form of stored carbohydrate

Honey flow — Describes a seasonal and local period during which plants are yielding surplus nectar

Honey bound — Describes a brood nest in which cells are filled with honey to the extent that bees cannot rear brood or enter empty cells to form a contiguous winter cluster

Honey barrier — A rim of honey that occurs naturally above brood and over which queens are reluctant to cross to deposit eggs in higher cells

Honey valve, *syn.* honey gate — A valve at the bottom of storage tanks from which honey can be released for bottling

Honey stomach — The most anterior section of the bee's three-chambered stomach, modified to enable the forager to carry and regurgitate liquid loads

Honey super — One of two box sizes, 5-3/8- or 6-5/8-inches tall, generally reserved for honey production, see *Medium super* or *Shallow super*

Honeybee act of 1922 — Act of US Congress that virtually closed the country to legal bee imports for most of the 20th century

Hood trap — An in-hive trap designed to catch adult small hive beetles

Horizontal wires — Wires tightly stretched between end bars of a frame and embedded by the builder into 100% beeswax foundation

Hygienic — Describes bees expressing the heritable ability to detect and remove unhealthy cells of brood

Icarus — Character in Greek mythology who made wings of feathers and beeswax

Incomplete metamorphosis — The developmental progression in insects characterized by a series of nymphal stages, each superficially resembling the adult and successively larger than the previous

Inner cover — Part of two-component system (see *Outer cover*) for weather-proofing a bee hive; inner cover maintains bee space and prevents propolizing shut the outer cover

Integrated pest management — A pest control approach characterized by the use of non-chemical means to keep pests below damaging levels

Intercaste — An individual bee possessing both worker-like and queen-like characters; usually the product of experimentation or other conditions that alter normal immature diet and development

Italian bee — Historically the most popular honey bee in North America; introduced from the Italian peninsula

Isle of Wight disease — Name of a bee epidemic in Great Britain in the early 20th century, widely believed caused by tracheal mites

Langstroth, L.L. — Inventor of a moveable-frame hive, bearing his name, that incorporates the concept of bee space

Langstroth hive — Moveable-frame hive incorporating bee space around all interior parts and consisting of wood-reinforced frames that delimit, support, and suspend combs from supers

Larva — Immature insect phase dedicated to feeding and rapid growth; in bees, a non-descript white grub

Laying worker — Describes a condition in which some of a colony's workers, when deprived of a queen, develop ovaries and lay male eggs

Mating flight — Describes one or more flights a young queen takes in which she mates with up to 20 drones

Medium super, *syn.* Illinois super — One of the three standard box sizes comprising a bee hive, 6-5/8-inches tall and used for either the *Brood nest* or for honey production

Menthol — Crystalline botanical extract used to control tracheal mites

Melissococcus plutonius — Causative bacterium of European foulbrood disease

Metamorphosis — The developmental progression in insects from immatures to adult; in bees: egg, larva, pupa, adult

Miticide — A pesticide specialized for killing pestiferous mites, in the case of honey bees, tracheal and varroa mites

Nosema — A protozoan disease of adult honey bees, occurring in two forms: *Nosema apis* and *N. ceranae*

Nectar — Sugary liquid secreted by flowering plants to attract pollinators; collected by bees as a source of carbohydrate

Nematode — Microscopic, soil-dwelling worms predatory on small hive beetle larvae

Nucleus colonies, *syn.* Nucs — 1. Small colonies used to house extra queens, 2. Small colonies used to house queens during their mating period, 3. A start-up method whereby 2-5 combs of bees and brood are purchased and installed in the buyer's supers; done similarly to make one's own colony increase

Nurse bees — An age-specific category of workers specialized for excreting brood food and caring for immatures

Outer cover — Part of two-component system (see *Inner cover*) for weather-proofing a bee hive; outer cover is sturdy and partially telescopes over the top-most super

Ovary — Female organ that produces eggs, highly developed in queen, rudimentary in worker

Overlapping generations — Occurs in a social insect colony when offspring remain at the nest to help their mother produce more siblings

Package bees — Parcels of 2-3 pounds of bees plus a queen, commonly used to start new colonies

Paenibacillus larvae larvae — Causative bacterium of American foulbrood disease

Paradichlorobenzene — Pesticide used to protect stored equipment against wax moth

Perennial colonies — Social insect colonies in which the colony persists as a social unit year-round (see *annual colonies*)

Pesticide — A substance used to control pest organisms, includes miticides, insecticides, herbicides, and fungicides

Pheromone — Air- or contact-borne chemical excreted by insects to regulate the behavior or physiology of other individuals; conceptually similar to "external hormones"

Pollen — 1. Granular bodies produced by flowering plants containing male germ cells for plant reproduction; collected by bees as a nutrient source of protein, 2. A food product consisting of pellets of bee-collected pollen

Pollen basket — Colloquial name for *corbiculum*, the apparatus on a bee's hind leg adapted to hold the forager's pollen loads

Pollen substitute — A commercially formulated protein feed, mixed with honey or syrup, and fed to bees to supplement stores of natural pollen

Pollen trap — Device placed at hive entrance and used to harvest bee-collected pollen

Pollination — The transfer of pollen from the male parts of a flower to the female parts of the same or different flower

Prepupa — Intermediary stage in immature development between larva and pupa

Propolis — "Bee glue" collected by bees from plant resins and used to seal nest cracks and discourage invaders

Pupa — Immature insect phase in which larval tissues and morphology are reorganized into those of an adult

Queen — One of two female castes in the bee colony, fully functional reproductively

Queen cage — Cage, either plastic or wood, designed to hold one queen and her attendant workers while in transit

Queen candy — Thick, dry, and pasty sugar candy used in queen cages to delay release of queen

Queen cell — A brood cell of an immature queen, elongated and peanut-shaped

Queen excluder — A metal device usually placed between the brood nest and honey supers designed to prevent passage of the queen out of the brood nest

Queenless — Describes a colony lacking a queen

Queenright — Describes a colony with a normally functioning queen

Quinby, Moses — Inventor of a practical, portable, bellows-driven device made to deliver smoke to calm bees

Race, ***syn.*** **subspecies** — Regionally distinctive reproducing population of a species

Radial extractor — Type of honey extractor in which frames fit inside like spokes in a wheel; both sides of frame are extracted at once

Refractometer — Instrument used to measure percentage water content in honey

Reproductive division of labor — Occurs when some individuals in a social insect colony abandon self reproduction in favor of helping their mother reproduce

Requeening — Process whereby a failing queen is replaced with a new queen by the bees or beekeeper

Reversible extractor — Version of honey extractor in which honey is removed from one side of frames at a time; frames must be reversed

Reversing hive bodies — Process by which the placement of deep supers (in a 2-hive body configuration) is exchanged once or more in early spring to discourage swarming

Robbing — Predatory foraging by a stronger colony on the honey stores of a weaker

Ropy test — Field test used to confirm American foulbrood disease

Royal jelly — A glandular exudate fed by nurse bees to female larvae to trigger expression of queen-like characters

Russian bee — Honey bee imported into the US for its comparative Varroa mite resistance; probably a biotype of the Carniolan bee

Sacbrood — Viral disease of prepupae

Samson — Biblical character known for making riddle about honey comb in a lion's carcass

Scale — Dried remains of a diseased brood cell, most commonly in reference to American foulbrood, but also European foulbrood

Scout — A worker bee specialized for discovering new colony resources – nest sites or food sources

Shallow super — One of the three standard box sizes comprising a bee hive, 5-3/8 inches tall and used for honey production

Small hive beetle — *Aethina tumida,* a scavenging beetle species that feeds on bee colony honey, pollen, and brood

Smoker — Device used to puff smoke onto bees during handling to calm them, consists of a fire container and bellows

Sperm — Reproductive germ cell of male possessing half the species's genetic complement

Spore — Inter-generational stage of certain microbial pathogens, used in reference to American foulbrood, chalkbrood and Nosema diseases

Spermatheca — Organ in queen bee in which sperm is stored from her mating flights

Spiracle — Opening of tracheae to exterior of bee or other insects

Splits — See *Nucleus colonies*

Sporulating bodies — Fungal structures on surface of brood infected with chalkbrood disease, responsible for releasing spores

Sticky sheet — Adhesive sheet placed on bottom board and used to catch varroa mites and monitor mite population levels

Sting — Morphological structure possessed by bees and other stinging Hymenopterans for delivering defensive venom

Sucrocide — Miticide used for controlling varroa mites

Super — General term for boxes (9-1/2-, 6-5/8- or 5-3/8-inches tall) comprising a bee hive; term is more appropriately reserved for honey production boxes placed above the brood nest, see *Deep super*, *Honey super*

Supersedure — The process by which a failing queen is replaced by her workers

Support pins — An easy-to-install substitute for horizontal wires

Swarm (*n.*), swarming — Colony-level reproduction in which the colony rears a new queen and up to 60% of the workers fly away with the queen to found a new colony

Swarm cells — Describes queen cells constructed under the impulse of colony reproduction

Terramycin — An antibiotic used for the prevention of bacterial brood diseases

Thorax — Middle major body segment of insects, specialized for muscles and appendages of locomotion

Top supering — The addition of new honey supers directly on top of previous ones, see *Bottom supering*

Top bar — The upper horizontal member of a frame

Tracheae — Breathing tubes of honey bees and other insects

Tracheal mite — *Acarapis woodi*, microscopic parasitic mite that lives in breathing tubes of adult bees

Tylosin — An antibiotic used for the prevention of bacterial brood diseases

Uncapping knife — Tool used in honey processing to remove beeswax cappings from sealed combs of honey in preparation for the extractor

Varroa mite — *Varroa destructor*, parasitic, blood-feeding mite of immature and adult honey bees

Venom gland — Tissue in bees near the sting specialized for releasing alarm pheromone which acts to incite nestmates to defensive behavior

Vertical wires — Support wires embedded by the manufacturer into 100% beeswax foundation

Wax glands — Specialized tissue cells on the ventral side of bee for excreting beeswax

Wax moth — *Galleria mellonella*, a scavenging moth species that eats abandoned comb and its contents

West trap — An in-hive trap designed to catch small hive beetle larvae

Worker — One of two female castes in the bee colony, reproductively functional only intermittently and responsible for nest maintenance tasks

Worker jelly — A glandular exudate fed by nurse bees to female larvae to trigger expression of worker-like characters

Yeats, W.B. — Irish poet, b. 1865, author of *The Lake Isle of Inisfree*

INDEX